PUBLIC POLICY PRAXIS

THEORY AND PRAGMATISM:
A CASE APPROACH

Randall S. Clemons
Mercyhurst College

Mark K. McBeth
Idaho State University

Prentice
Hall

UPPER SADDLE RIVER, NEW JERSEY 07458

Library of Congress Cataloging-in-Publication Data

Clemons, Randall S.
    Public policy praxis—theory and pragmatism: a case approach/Randall S. Clemons,
    Mark K. McBeth.
        p. cm.
    Includes bibliographical references and index.
    ISBN 0-13-025882-2
        1. Policy sciences.   2. Policy sciences—Case studies.   I. McBeth, Mark K.   II. Title.

H97.C56 2000
320.6—dc21   00-055080

VP, Editorial director: Laura Pearson
Director of marketing: Beth Gillett Mejia
Editorial assistant: Beth Murtha
Editorial/production supervision: Kari Callaghan Mazzola
Prepress and manufacturing buyer: Ben Smith
Electronic page makeup: Kari Callaghan Mazzola and John P. Mazzola
Interior design: John P. Mazzola
Cover director: Jayne Conte
Cover design: Bruce Kenselaar
Cover art: William Huber/IMA USA, Inc.

This book was set in 10/12 Times by Big Sky Composition
and was printed and bound by Courier Companies, Inc.
The cover was printed by Phoenix Color Corp.

© 2001 by Prentice-Hall, Inc.
A Division of Pearson Education
Upper Saddle River, New Jersey 07458

Printed in the United States of America
10   9   8   7   6   5   4   3   2   1

ISBN 0-13-025882-2

PRENTICE-HALL INTERNATIONAL (UK) LIMITED, *London*
PRENTICE-HALL OF AUSTRALIA PTY. LIMITED, *Sydney*
PRENTICE-HALL CANADA INC., *Toronto*
PRENTICE-HALL HISPANOAMERICANA, S.A., *Mexico*
PRENTICE-HALL OF INDIA PRIVATE LIMITED, *New Delhi*
PRENTICE-HALL OF JAPAN, INC., *Tokyo*
PEARSON EDUCATION ASIA PTE. LTD., *Singapore*
EDITORA PRENTICE-HALL DO BRASIL, LTDA., *Rio de Janeiro*

Contents

PREFACE

When we wrote *Public Policy Praxis* we were guided by several underlying principles. We believed that the book must be all of the following:

- practical as well as theoretical
- useful as well as cutting edge
- fun as well as thorough
- focused on the great issues and big themes as well as on specific techniques
- about the politics of the policy process as well as how to do policy analysis
- both readable and teachable

Although our book targets future and current professional policy analysts, anyone who wants to understand and affect public policy (e.g., elected officials, citizen activists, interest group leaders, public administrators) must be a policy analyst.

The genesis of this book was a discussion we had about policy cases. Although both of us believe in and utilize case studies, they are often too technical and fail to capture the essence of politics. They seldom require the application of the techniques the chapters introduce, or make clear the relationship of the concepts and theories covered in the chapters to what the students are to do with the cases. We complained that we had increasingly found ourselves writing our own cases. Moreover, the policy analysis texts available gave short shrift to politics, democracy, and how policy is made. We both believe that knowledge is as important as skills. So we were supplementing our cases with reserve readings, and writing lectures concerning politics, power, democracy, and the social construction of problems as well as policies.

So we decided to write a case book with self-contained cases—that is, each case would be preceded by a discussion of a major topic. Students would complete the case—using the information, learning the material, and recognizing the importance of theory by doing. As it turned out, the self-contained case write-ups became full-scale chapters. The result is a public policy analysis book that we hope helps move the teaching of policy analysis in a direction that is more democratic—but ultimately practical. Our book is, essentially, a postpositivist view of social construction. Gone is the hegemonic, sometimes almost exclusive, emphasis on rational decision-making models. Instead the balance is tipped toward discussions of value conflict, power, political systems, democracy, subjectivity, and ambiguity. We think of policy analysis as requiring a combination of knowledge and skills. As in our classrooms, we teach "how to" but also teach the limitations, practical political problems, and ethical implications of different techniques and methodologies.

Policy analysis is larger than, and often encompasses, program evaluation or productivity measurement. Our definition of policy analysis includes the initiation of policy as well as the review of or implementation of policy. Whatever the level of analysis, ultimately the goal usually is to establish a bottom line that facilitates decision making. This often leads to a focus on technical efficiency, cost-benefit analysis (CBA), and other efforts such as output measures, per unit cost estimates, client satisfaction surveys, statistical testing, and decision trees.

Originally, policy analysis was seen as a way to assist democratic decision making. Somehow, along the way, policy analysis became part of elite and expert decision making. The theory and knowledge of politics, power structures, and the subjective human construction of public problem definitions was lost in a forest of rational decision models, complicated mathematical and analytical tools, microeconomics, and other scientific techniques. Yet good policy analysis requires investigation into the major actors and their roles, the political context (including economic conditions, social conditions, dominant values and beliefs), and the goals or purposes of the policy (which takes us to the crucial ideas of problem definition, values, interests, and power). We recognize that policy analysts are going to work in bureaucracies and that the imperatives of the bureaucratic culture push analysts toward work that is quantifiable, rational, and thus accountable. But our job, as scholars and authors, is not just to accept the fact that bureaucracy tends to value efficiency over democracy, but rather to promote more democratic ways of doing realistic analysis. We don't accept the idea that "that's simply the way the world is." The world is socially constructed, and we can change it.

Far from being a facilitator of democracy or an astute political analyst, the policy analyst has become the central point of the decision process. Sometimes analysts are used by powerful actors, but frequently they become a power center themselves, guiding the policy choices of elected officials. Emulating a neutral and value-free approach, policy analysis has based much of its work on analytical techniques used in private business analysis and on assumptions about human behavior from economic models that assume absolute self-interested rationality, complete knowledge, and free competition. Of course, the techniques have never been value-free or neutral, government and business are not the same, and neither the surrounding conditions nor the behavior of the actors in the civic arena match the assumptions of the economic model.

The rational models vary, but they tend to postulate rational individuals choosing what is in their own best interests, and to suggest that analysis treads the following general path: A problem is recognized; a procedure is determined; goals are agreed upon; alternatives are formulated; alternatives are evaluated; a decision is made; the policy is implemented; the policy is reviewed, evaluated, and possibly modified or terminated.

The postpositivist critiques are too numerous and varied to characterize as neatly as one can characterize the positivist approach, but one of the key insights relates to the very subjective element of problem definition and the role that compelling and competing stories play in the policy process. Postmodernism's contribution to this understanding is perhaps best captured by a brief quote that sets up Arundhai Roy's 1997 novel, *The God of Small Things*: "Never again will a single story be told as though it's the only one" (John Berger).

Another motivation for our writing this book was the seemingly contradictory yet twin beliefs that (1) policy analysis has not kept pace with changes in the social sciences, and (2) the powerful critiques of the dominant approach are not being put into practice. While policy analysts are being taught that their approach should be "scientific," the scientific method of policy analysis comes out of the 1950s and 1960s. With a heavy emphasis on positivism, the teaching of policy analysis, especially as an applied field, has largely ignored innovative theoretical and methodological advances in the social (and physical) sciences. Recently these theories and methods (e.g., postmodernism, postpositivism, narrative analysis) have found a place in the academic literature, but they have not successfully filtered down to the classroom in the form of practical *and* readable textbooks.

We are not unaware of the practicality of the positivist method. As practicing analysts (extensively in the past and continuing into the present) we are well aware of the pragmatic needs that drive practice. This involves usable, understandable, teachable, and efficient methods. We understand the reasons behind rational analysis. We applaud efforts to make policymaking more careful, more reasoned, and less haphazard and sloppy. However, along with the other critics of positivism, we also recognize the policy process as inherently political; messy, not meticulous; subjective, not scientific. Yet, somewhat ironically, the criticism of the postpositivists, that positivism is neither realistic nor useful, seems equally applicable to its critics. Being relevant is at least as important as being right. Nor is it adequate for positivists to nod their heads toward the extensive criticisms, to admit that policy analysis is a process not a product, and to continue unabated. What is needed is synthesis; what is needed is praxis.

In response to these needs, Part I focuses more on theory than on practice, and presents the debate between the rational and nonrational models as well as providing a method to evaluate models. Readers are challenged to rethink their beliefs and to decide which approach is most accurate and meets their needs and values. We sought balance in our presentation, but do not claim to be neutral. Readers also learn about democracy, the policy process, stakeholder mapping, political I.O.U.s, the strategic use of words and numbers, and the role that the analyst's values play in policy analysis.

Part II moves us into greater emphasis on practice than on theory. In Part II the text builds carefully on Part I and offers a five-step methodology for policy analysis that is informed by postpositivism and inspired by postmodernism, and that blends a nonrational political approach with a rational method. In Chapter 5 readers learn more about problem definition, criteria establishment (to evaluate alternatives), generating policy alternatives, evaluating and selecting policies, and evaluation research. Chapter 6 focuses on the power of language and problem definition. Chapter 7 focuses on democracy as the key ethical issue in policy analysis, and on civic engagement (or, how to "do" democracy). Although flaws and problems are explained, the reader learns how to do content analysis and narrative analysis, and how to conduct focus groups, futuring sessions, and meetings designed to resolve conflict and build consensus. Professors who adopt this text are also invited (in Chapter 8) to reach into the Positivist Toolbox and pick which positivist tools to teach from among the following seven choices: sampling and mail surveys, extrapolation and forecasting, measures of central tendency, discounting, deflating money, per capita analysis, and cost-benefit analysis. Once again, both the advantages and disadvantages are highlighted.

Part III consists of one short chapter that presents no new material. Throughout the text we have encouraged an integrated understanding of the component parts. In Part III we present a case that takes the readers back to the first chapter, so they can demonstrate knowledge of policy analysis as a coherent whole and utilize all of the separate elements they have learned about.

Let us state our biases up front: We do want to change our readers' understanding of the policy process. Politics is at the heart of policy and administration. Policymaking is rooted in storytelling; it is not "about" objective material facts, but about battles between ideas, about socially constructed categories of shared meaning (e.g., about what men and women are, about what is deviant or criminal or normal, and about who is undeserving or deserving). Policymaking is choosing. The selection of tools and procedures is a value-laden choice that can determine the outcome and the winner or the loser. Similarly, the structure of the organizations involved reflects and affects value choices and whose interests are best tended to. The policy process is complex, messy, and indeterminate, and centers on value conflict. One must learn the ideas behind the process, as well as the process.

We also want to affect the practice of policy analysis. Democracy is both the key ethical issue facing analysts and one of the most ambiguous terms in the policy arena. Public policy analysis is fundamentally not about technical questions, and neutral experts on white horses are not coming to the rescue. Policy analysis is culture-bound and value laden, and yes, the values of the analyst have an affect on policy analysis. Individuals make a difference in the policy arena and individual analysts can make a difference. *Public* policy analysis is, in the end, about people.

We believe in synthesis. To be complete, policy analysis must consider the political, but analysts must also know the rational methods and technical tools—and their limitations, biases, and potential for manipulation. (The cases readers confront integrate both.) Alone, the positivist methodology leaves you empty and leaves democracy stranded; alone the postmodern critiques leave you without a map. Good politics is an essential element of a good analysis. Technical skills and a strategic approach are both needed. You must be savvy and have street smarts, but it is also important that you have tangible skills and a careful, rigorous methodology.

The crucial first three words of the title of this book are Public Policy Praxis. We haven't yet directly addressed the idea of praxis. Let us pause to define (more or less) our term: A simple definition is that praxis is about the application of a field or branch of learning. Earlier we spoke of synthesis; in one sense, praxis represents synthesis. The dialectical idea of synthesis is the idea that thesis begets antithesis which begets (hopefully or inevitably) a higher truth, a synthesis. In the field of policy analysis we begin with a dominant method (positivism), and seek praxis for the insightful but often irrelevant critiques of positivism from postmodern and postpositivist scholars. In a very real sense we also wrote this book seeking synthesis between theory and pragmatism—theory must inform practice and practice must inform theory. Public policy praxis requires analysts to recognize the connections between theory and practice. Indeed, that is another definition of praxis—theory guided practice.

Public policy studies continue to be one of the fastest growing subfields in political science, at both the graduate and undergraduate levels. Policy analysis is a crucial skill in Public Administration, Social Work, Environmental Politics, and Criminal Justice. The National Association of Schools of Public Affairs and Administration (NASPAA) created a Committee on Undergraduate Education that spent three years studying undergraduate policy education and came to the emphatic conclusion that colleges and universities should offer professionally oriented undergraduate degree programs with concentrations in public affairs and administrations. (More than 150 universities already do.) Cleveland State University has an innovative program focusing on public service careers at the baccalaureate level.

Our primary target audience is Masters-level graduate students and upper-division undergraduates in Public Policy Analysis courses. All portions of this book have been class-tested in graduate courses; indeed, graduate students at three different colleges have used various case studies from our text. However, both of us teach both undergraduate and graduate students, sometimes in the same class, and we believe that undergraduates and students with limited backgrounds in politics and the policy process are capable of handling very sophisticated material if it is presented in a way that makes it accessible. Thus, professors can teach students who come in with stronger backgrounds and still reach those who don't. Our first two reviewers thought the book appropriate not only for graduate courses, but also for 300-level courses in Social Welfare Policy, Public Policy Analysis, and Public Administration. Professors teaching at four-year colleges and universities, as well as some at the more than one thousand community colleges, might be interested to know that one of us very successfully utilized the first chapter of the book while teaching a 100-level public administration course.

While refusing to "dumb down" our writing, we wanted this to be readable, not a scholarly dissertation. It is written to the student and in a nearly conversational style. We sought to fill a void in the policy literature by clearly linking important conceptual ideas and theories with relevant well-constructed case studies. Our unique case studies are designed to breath life into the terminology, to be interesting, and to augment the material. Graduate criminal justice students in a class taught by one of us admitted doubting the relevance of working on a policy case involving bison, but ended up believing it was the most useful part of the course.

The intentionally varied case settings (county, city, federal, urban, and rural) and topics (expansion of human services in the Pittsburgh area, building a health care clinic in a small town, environmental protection and economic development in the West, an inner-city drug program, and the Vietnam war) capture the diversity of public policy and the intergovernmental nature of politics. Devolution has made it even more true that, for the practicing analyst, exposure to a wide variety of issues and skills is better in the long run than a narrower, more specialized focus. Some of our cases are set in fictional settings, others in real places. There are advantages to both, depending on the lessons being taught and the issues being explored. Similarly, some cases are very short and others much more involved.

The chapters are supplemented with stories and feature boxes that discuss diverse and current topics that back up and supplement the material. These topics range from AIDS and needle-exchange programs to timber sales, from conflict between candymakers and sugar beet growers to conflict over a prison siting, from George Orwell's *Animal Farm* to an atomic powered airplane, from drug abuse to the Holocaust, and from debunking the idea of black letter law to trying to secure federal funds for the homeless.

We provide questions designed to provoke thought and discussion, and at the end of each chapter we offer "Concluding Thoughts" designed to be helpful in summarizing but not to serve as substitutes for reading the chapter. Also at the end of each chapter we list "Key Concepts for Review." We use boldface in the text to identify glossary terms. "Glossary Terms" are listed at the end of each chapter and defined in the end-of-book glossary. Full end-of-chapter "References" are also provided for anyone wanting to follow up on a topic we have introduced. The end-of-book "Glossary" is not extensive because most key terms and concepts are carefully explained and defined within the text. The glossary is designed more to make sure that we aren't taking for granted knowledge of certain terms that—while not the focal point of our discussion—will help readers grasp our point.

It is traditional at this point in the Preface to take responsibility for problems with the book. We have decided to encourage you to blame all errors on Mark, and any omissions on Randy. Any other problems (and all major problems) we encourage you to blame on the Y2K deadline that fell in the middle of the publishing process.

Finally, we want a word with the students. Please consider the following invitation: We sincerely want to hear from you. Feedback from your professor would be great, but feedback from you would be even better. As you will see, although the Preface is generally aimed at your professor, the book is written directly to you. We see our readers, like the students in our classrooms, as unique. We know that the world and our book, as seen through your eyes and worldview, is different for each of you. At the end of the book there is an appendix on using the internet for research. In it we provide you with our e-mail addresses and a few questions to prompt your response. Learning is a loop, and over the years our students have taught us much; we hope you will continue that tradition.

Acknowledgments

Mark McBeth wishes to make the following acknowledgments: Thank you to my colleagues in the Department of Political Science at Idaho State University for their continued support throughout the years. Particular thanks go to Cheryl Hardy for her expert and good-natured assistance. Thanks also to the many undergraduate and graduate students at Idaho State University whose insights into, and interests in, the field of policy analysis have greatly challenged me and have been a tremendous source of inspiration. Students in the Spring 1998 Public Policy Analysis course were especially instrumental in helping develop ideas about the relationships between postpositivist analysis and practice. The work of this class on the Yellowstone bison controversy remains a career highlight. There are so many students who have greatly impacted my life and teaching that I dare not list any in deference to length constraints and out of fear of leaving some deserving soul out in the cold. As always I thank my family and friends. Lastly, I thank Randy for first bringing me into the world of postpositivist policy analysis, for knowing when to let me experiment with ideas and for telling me when I went astray, and for his patience in editing my ramblings.

Randy Clemons wishes to make the following acknowledgments: The list of those to whom one owes intellectual debts is too long to list comprehensively, and trying to compose a list of just the most significant contributors would guarantee that many who deserve to be mentioned would not receive their due. However, for their steady support I must thank my colleagues in the Social Science Division at Mercyhurst College. I also want to thank Dr. Garvey and Mercyhurst College for my sabbatical, Maggie Closson for her editorial suggestions on three of our chapters, Richele Rohrer for her expert assistance on key figures and tables, and the graduate students and political science majors and minors of Mercyhurst from whom I have received so much and of whom I expect so much. Also, thanks must go to my children, Jack and Kate, and the small group of family and friends whose well of support I have particularly drawn from (you know who you are). And I owe much to Mark for his encouragement throughout, but mostly for his role in a process that was intellectually reinvigorating and rewarding, never rancorous, and frequently filled with serious insights and laughter. His commitment to teaching is balanced by his passion for learning.

This book is truly co-authored. No matter who originally wrote what, nothing is mine and nothing is his, and we believe it is a better book because of that. Also, we both want to thank the reviewers of our book: Raymond J. Rushboldt, SUNY Fredonia; James H. Lare, Occidental College; and, especially, Morton Coleman, University of Pittsburgh. We also want to thank Beth Gillett Mejia, at Prentice Hall, for believing in our book, and Kari Callaghan Mazzola and John P. Mazzola of Big Sky Composition.

Finally, we wish to dedicate our book to our students (past, present, and future), who allow us to help them learn; to Rick, and others, who have taught us how to help; to our families and friends, who always support us; and to Laura and Lisa, who both tolerate and inspire us.

Randall S. Clemons
Mark K. McBeth

PART I: THEORY AND PRACTICE

CHAPTER 1

PUBLIC POLICY, POWER, THE PEOPLE, PLURALISM, AND YOU

<u>Mini-Case</u>
"Drug Abuse and Waterville"

<u>Case Study</u>
"Nightcrawlers and Cappuccino: The Old West versus the New West"

According to Proverbs 1:7–9, fear is the beginning of knowledge, fools despise wisdom and instruction, and you should listen and heed teaching for it will gain you honors and rewards. We tend to agree and would rather scare you than bore you. So, we begin this chapter and the book by throwing you right into the political firestorm of doing public policy analysis. Good luck!

Drug Abuse and Waterville

This case is typical of cases administered, as part of the application process, during competitions for public management jobs and internships. Such cases are designed to evaluate how much prospective public managers know about public policy analysis. You would be given directions similar to the following:

1. Read the information carefully.
2. Respond to the one-page case study in any format you feel is appropriate.
3. All necessary information to analyze this situation is provided in the background section.
4. Your response should be no more than three pages long.
5. Please note that calculations and research are not necessary for your response.

Background

The community of Waterville, Pennsylvania (population 6,543), once mostly known for its historic hotel where both George Washington and the French General Lafayette slept, has recently taken note of what many community residents term "a major teenage drug problem." The recent busts by the state police of five "meth houses" in the space of one month and the arrests of several well-known Waterville High School athletes who are allegedly involved in the community drug trade have led to calls from community leaders to combat the drug problem.

Waterville is a community with a per capita personal income of $23,500. This compares to a state average of $28,000. The story of local businesses closing has been a frequent one in recent years and the one major industry in Waterville left town last summer when the corporate bosses in Houston, Texas, decided to relocate the plant to Mexico. This left slightly over four hundred people, who had been earning above-average wages, unemployed. It will also cost Waterville a significant portion of city and school tax monies.

Divorces and births to unmarried teens have been steadily increasing in the past decade and have soared beyond the state and national averages. There is also a great deal of racial tension in the town, where 25 percent of the population is Hispanic. There have been significant conflicts between city officials and leaders within the Hispanic community. Conflict has centered on issues such as use of the city parks; zoning; dances; and police practices, hiring policies, and priorities.

Several members of the city council are concerned that the drug problem is an "epidemic" and are calling for a "war on drugs." Mayor Joyce Allen told the local paper that without some type of action from the city government this problem will destroy the community and drive out more businesses. A local priest told his congregation that the very soul of the town and its children were on the line.

The city manager has asked you to conduct a public policy analysis to identify the potential problems, issues, and policy alternatives, and to prepare and present a recommendation to the city council. What do you do?

Unless you have conducted a public policy analysis in the past (and possibly even if you did), you undoubtedly have several questions. You may be asking: (1) How do I best present the information; (2) what do I include in the analysis and what do I leave out; (3) how do I separate my own feelings from what should, or should not, be done; and (4) how do I write three pages on this subject based on only one page of information?

Don't panic or doubt yourself. This exercise is partially designed to demonstrate to you that your policy analysis skills leave something to be desired, thus encouraging you to continue reading this book. Throughout the book you will be learning and applying lessons, skills, and a public policy analysis methodology, all of which would help you tremendously with this task. At the end of the book you will be offered the opportunity to redo this case. In the meantime, give it your best shot and tackle this before reading on.

Introduction

Thanks for completing the case. Now you need to think about, and be prepared to discuss, the following questions: How would you describe the process you used to respond to your task? Did you try to be objective? Did you recognize your values coming into play? Do you believe that it is appropriate for an analyst's personal values to affect policy recommendations? Who in Waterville would you be trying to please? Who do you work for?

The case and the discussion questions above were successful in preparing you for the rest of the book if they made you think about issues that you normally do not think about. Policy analysis is complex and requires a method, tools, and political knowledge. It is also affected by the analyst's values—especially his or her understanding of democracy and view of the appropriate role of government.

In this chapter we will examine the theory of "value conflict" as first elaborated by sociologists Fuller and Myers, and then consider how value conflict relates to what political science tells us about political systems. The chapter also looks at power structures in general and at power structures in rural communities in particular. Democracy, representative democracy, pluralism, and elitism are discussed, and insights provided into how knowledge of power and one's normative view of power affects a public policy analysis. We explain how to conduct a stakeholder analysis, and conclude with a case study that will allow you to apply what you learn and to learn by applying.

The case helps to illustrate the process of policymaking and demonstrates how "value conflict" and views of "power structures" fit into the analysis. In completing the case, you—the student policy analyst—must confront, consider, and decide your role in democratic governance. Ultimately, how analysts analyze is tied directly to how they believe policy problems are created and to their view of the proper role and location of political power. A discussion of these two concepts follows.

Value Conflict

What is a public problem? This is a question that every policy analyst must confront. Deciding what is or is not a problem is a highly subjective process. For example, a medium-size community is experiencing population growth at a rate of 3.5 percent per year.[1] A native of the community who has a stable job might define the growth as "urban sprawl." To her, growth means increased traffic and pollution; it means that her favorite fishing hole will become congested and polluted, her taxes will increase to pay for new community infrastructure, and the culture of her community will change. This individual wants her local government to enact policies to stop or control this growth. These might include strict land-use zoning that would prohibit subdivision development and commercial development or increasing fees on utility hook-ups to discourage commercial, industrial, and residential in-migration.

---

[1] Three and one-half percent might sound insignificant, but the Rule of Seventy tells us that this rate of growth would double the population in twenty years. To calculate the time for doubling, simply divide the rate of growth into 70.

However, not everyone in the community will share this view of the situation. Another individual, perhaps a local real estate agent, will see the growth not as a problem but rather as an opportunity. He will see the growth as contributing to more business for him, better education for his children, better health care, better shopping, and more cultural opportunities. He will not want the city government to discourage growth but instead to implement policies that will increase growth, including actively recruiting new businesses, lowering utility fees, and having a pro-growth zoning policy that will accommodate developers.

What does a policy analyst do in such a situation, when some in the community subjectively view the "objective fact" of growth as a problem and others perceive progress? Does this community have a "problem," and, if so, what policies should be implemented? Who decides if an objective fact is a problem and requires government policy? What if the community is evenly split between those who want growth and those who want to stop it? What policies, if any, should be recommended? The answers to these questions are not simple or clear and are determined by the analyst's view of democracy, power, and government.

As a rule, politicians and interest groups strategically portray issues in a dualistic manner. In this example, a **Hobson's Choice** would likely be offered by each of the competing sides. The pro-growth proponents would argue that "the community must either grow or die."[2] This statement is designed for concerned citizens who, of course, do not want their community to die and would therefore want to continue growth policies. Similarly, the antigrowth coalitions would posit that "we must stop the growth or live in a cesspool of filth, crime, and drugs." Again, this hyperbolic statement is aimed at the typical citizen who is unlikely to want to live in a community such as the one described by the antigrowth coalition as the consequence of further growth.

The analyst, however, must recognize these predictions of dire consequences as political posturing.[3] It is important to realize that such stark, zero-sum, and dualistic choices do not often correspond closely with reality. Competing interests can often find compromises, shared values, and, most important, shared interests that can be used to create a **win-win policy**. Perhaps after reading this book you will decide that an appropriate role for an analyst in a democracy is to facilitate a consensus-building

---

[2]Inspired by the metaphor of living organisms, the German apologist General Karl Haushofer used Rudolf Kjellen's idea of "living space," or Lebensraum, to justify Nazi imperialism, arguing that Germany had to either expand or die. It did both.

[3]Often the people making political statements are consciously trying to tell a persuasive story that they themselves may not fully believe, but frequently they do believe exactly what they are saying. This can still be called political posturing though, because (as we will discuss in some detail in the next two chapters) proponents of different policies clearly try to frame the issue in politically astute ways. When President Clinton signed the Family and Medical Leave Act into law in early 1993, it was against the backdrop of more than five years of hard lobbying against it by corporations and the groups that represent them (e.g., the U.S. Chamber of Commerce and the National Association of Manufacturers). The dire warnings they issued were that giving employees twelve weeks of unpaid leave for serious medical problems or family emergencies would lead to reduced competition in the global market, reduce productivity, and (according to the National Federation of Small Businesses and others) cost jobs. Somehow, the economy has managed record expansion anyway.

process, or at least a process that widely seeks input and that provides the opportunity for increased collective understanding of problems and policies with greater collective acceptance.

In their classic study of social problems, Fuller and Myers (1941) identify such differing definitions of the "social facts" as illustrative of what they term "value conflict." Value conflict theory centers on objective and subjective conditions. The objective condition is an empirical fact (e.g., the community *is* growing in population). The subjective condition is the perceptions of the objective condition by individuals or groups with different values or interests (i.e., one person sees the growth as bad and another sees the growth as good).

Fuller and Myers argue that social problems (public problems) go through a natural history of (1) awareness, (2) policy determination, and (3) what they labeled "reform" (implementation of policy). Importantly, the values and interests of individuals and groups will conflict at each stage.

Stage I: Awareness

In the first stage, some individuals and groups will see the objective condition as threatening their values and interests. For example, the AIDS virus was well-known in the U.S. medical community by 1982, when 300 Americans had already died of the disease. But it was viewed by many in the medical profession, and by the vast majority of the American public who knew about it, as a "gay disease" that did not threaten the values and interests of society. By 1983, 664 Americans had died and over 2,000 were dead by 1984. Still, there was no federal funding forthcoming to combat the disease.

The death of actor Rock Hudson in June 1985 was a **triggering event** that brought the AIDS epidemic to the attention of the American people. However, the problem was viewed primarily as one affecting gays and intravenous drug users. By the mid-1980s, AIDS groups had successfully organized into a political force and were putting pressure on the federal government for funding and action. Finally, in 1987, President Reagan gave a speech in which he formally recognized AIDS as a major problem needing federal policy action. The disease had officially become a problem that required policy action.[4]

Why did it take so long for this deadly disease to become a public problem? Other far less deadly diseases such as "legionnaire's disease" received federal attention and policy almost immediately. The principles of value conflict explain why the problem definition was so slow.

Problem definition occurs in a highly political environment. For a problem to receive swift government attention it must threaten the values and interests of the most powerful in the society, or a significantly large number of citizens, or seem a serious threat to a small but favorably perceived group or to a group that has traditionally received protection from the government.

---

[4]For an excellent case study of the politics of AIDS\problem definition see Shilts (1987).

In the case of AIDS, the disease threat initially seemed aimed at some of the least powerful and most stigmatized people in society (drug users, gays, and blacks—especially Haitians). It was not perceived as a threat to the majority of citizens or to wealthier Americans who have tremendous influence over policymaking in American government.

Problem definition occurs in the context of values, interests, and political power, but not necessarily in the context of public interests. There are, however, methods for disenfranchised groups to gain power and have problems that threaten their interests defined as policy problems. The "means of politics" include trading, compromising, rewarding, and coercion. Through aggressive political organizing, AIDS groups were able to use the legitimacy of their cause and their growing political strength to bring the problem to the attention of the federal government. Additionally, actor Rock Hudson's collapse and tragic appearance was laid on the AIDS doorstep. The number of victims grew to epidemic proportions and soon AIDS became recognized not just as a "gay disease" but rather as a disease that affected "innocent" victims like Ryan White, Elizabeth Glaser, and hemophiliacs. These victims personalized the threat via blood transfusions, making everyone potentially vulnerable.

These things, in addition to political organizing, increased public and eventually government concern. A crucial role was played by U.S. Surgeon General Dr. C. Everett Koop.[5] Koop met with and listened to dozens of groups and issued a starkly clear report that portrayed AIDS not as a gay disease but as a serious public health issue.[6] In his role as an advocate, his prominence, credibility, and official role gave his problem definition immediate legitimacy and led to an increased sense of urgency in terms of a public policy response to this tragedy.

Stage II: Policy Determination

Just defining an objective condition as a social or public problem does not automatically lead to successful policy adoption. Instead, the values and interests of individuals and groups will continue to clash. In the case of AIDS, the policies that were proposed by various key groups were ideas such as increased sex education in public schools; education about, and free distribution of, condoms among young people; and the distribution of free, sterilized needles to IV drug users. These policy suggestions caused great conflict since the behaviors they recognize conflicted strongly with views of acceptable behavior held by powerful groups in the country, such as the religious right. In addition, there was worry among other more organized and politically powerful health political action committees that funding for AIDS would diminish funding for other important health issues.

---

[5]Still active in public health advocacy, Dr. Koop has partial ownership in a healthcare-information website on the internet that began selling shares on the Nasdaq Stock Market in June 1999. <DrKoop.com> is the site address.

[6]David Schuman's concise discussion (*A Preface to Politics*, 5th ed., with Dick W. Olufs, III, pp. 78–83, 1991) of the unfolding AIDS epidemic and of Koop's role in this story, was also a helpful source for our portrayal of this issue.

Stage III: Policy Implementation

Even after policies are adopted, value conflict continues in the implementation process, as well as affecting changes in awareness and continued battles over problem definition and what, if anything, to do about it. Fuller and Myers stress that value conflict is a never-ending process. One such conflict in the AIDS policy arena is over whether private drug companies should benefit from publicly subsidized research. Various AIDS drugs have shown success in alleviating the symptoms of the disease and slowing its progress. Drug manufacturers will make billions of dollars from these and future drugs that will combat the disease, yet significant percentages of these drugs originated from federally funded research. It seems unfair to many that drug companies will profit so greatly when they did not invest their own money in the research.

In addition, value conflict over educational policies and condom and needle distribution continue. Groups continue to organize politically at the national, state, and local levels to resist AIDS education, in the fear that such education will lead to sexual promiscuity among the young or to an acceptance of the gay lifestyle. If these groups gain in political power, they may ultimately undo many AIDS policies. Ironically, the success of many of these policies can lead to reduced concern about the problem and undercut support for such controversial policies.

1-1. Needle Exchanges Needle Governor Whitman

Common in many countries, states, and communities, government programs exchanging clean needles for used ones have consistently been deemed a valuable way to prevent the spread of H.I.V. infection. New Jersey—a state with more than 9,000 orphans who lost their mothers to AIDS, 26,000 people with AIDS, the nation's third highest rate of intravenous H.I.V. infection, and the nation's highest rate of infection among women and children—not only won't pay for needles, it used undercover police and arrests of those distributing clean needles to prevent AIDS activists from violating the state ban on distributing syringes. Governor Christine Todd Whitman (R) is adamantly opposed to needle giveaways, claiming they send the wrong message to children about drug use.

The U.S. Surgeon General, the Centers for Disease Control and Prevention, and most public health experts support such exchanges, citing studies that show they reduce the spread of H.I.V. significantly and that providing syringes does not increase drug use or addiction. David W. Troast (a personal acquaintance of Whitman and a prominent businessman) was appointed by the governor to lead New Jersey's Advisory Commission on AIDS. Like Koop, he studied the problem, talked to experts, read the studies, and came to believe that a needle exchange was necessary. The commission believes new H.I.V. infections in New Jersey could be cut in half by a needle exchange program. Across the border in New York and in Pennsylvania, fellow Republican governors of large states support needle exchange programs as cost effective for taxpayers (treating AIDS victims often tops $20,000 per year) as well as saving lives.

The governor is not alone, though. Although President Clinton will admit that the spread of H.I.V. can be decreased—with no increase in drug use—he gave in to pressure from the "drug Czar" General Barry R. McCaffrey and the Republican majority in Congress, and agreed to prohibit federal monies from being used to pay for needles.

Her opposition is so strong she finally wrote the New Jersey commission and told them to move on to other proposals because she would not change her mind. She says common sense, her experience as a mother, and her experience holding children born with problems stemming from their mother's drug use have led to her being convinced that the conventional wisdom is obviously wrong. She has called the studies that deny it leads to increased drug use "dubious, at best." Needle exchange proponents are largely resigned to waiting until her term expires in the year 2001.

Source: David Kocieniewski, "New Jersey's Hard Line on Needle Exchanges." *New York Times*, February 2, 1999, A-20.

In the equally political realm of implementation, value conflict also plays out. For example, implementation is never uniform because (1) the American political system is not unified and policy is almost always fragmented and uneven, and (2) state and local elected officials, administrators, and even low-level bureaucrats have considerable discretion in how policies are implemented. Accordingly, in some states and local communities education has been used extensively, whereas in other communities it has rarely been used. In some areas education is done well and implemented wholeheartedly, in other areas education is poorly done and grudgingly and haltingly implemented. The box on needle exchange programs (above) also demonstrates how different states and different governors could decide to ignore or enforce laws. Implementation, discretion, and fragmentation are crucial political issues that will be discussed further in Chapter 3.

A Political System

The process described over fifty years ago by Fuller and Myers is better understood in the context of a political systems model.[7] The political system model is composed of six separate but highly interrelated parts: system parameters, government, linkage mechanisms, political demands and political supports, public policy, and a feedback loop. (See Figure 1-1.) Like most models, ours is a simplified representation that tries to capture the key aspects, not all aspects.

The term *politics*, as used in the field of political science, differs from how the typical American uses the term. To most Americans, politics means "campaigning for office," or it may have a more negative connotation whereby politics is "something

[7]Like all discussions of political systems, we owe a debt to David Easton (1965). Our model is an adaptation of his systems model.

FIGURE 1-1   A SIMPLIFIED MODEL OF A POLITICAL SYSTEM

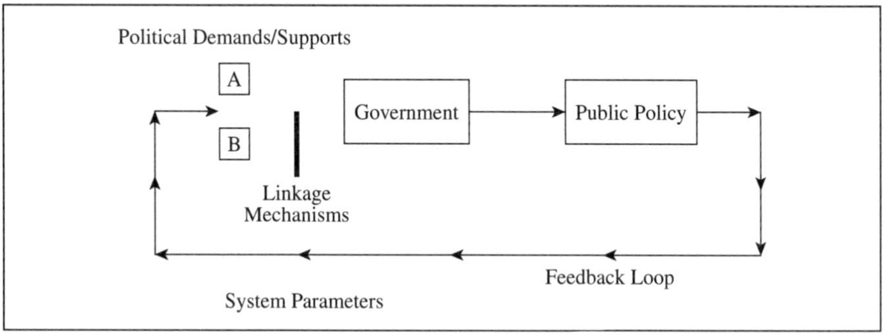

Political Demands/Supports

A

B

Linkage
Mechanisms

Government ──→ Public Policy

Feedback Loop

System Parameters

Political Demands (A–B): Value conflict over an issue.

Political Supports (A–B): Activities that support stability of the system and preservation of the parameters.

Linkage Mechanisms: How political demands get on the government's policy agenda.

Government: Authoritatively allocates values.

Public Policy: What government does or does not do.

Feedback Loop: Public policy changes the political demands and political supports, and sometimes can even affect the system parameters.

Parameters: The rules and culture of the system.

that politicians use to get their way." Sometimes it is equated with the sort of politics found in families and the workplace, as well as in the public arena, where favoritism defeats merit. Sometimes people use the word politics to describe the value conflict inherent in a political system. In political science, politics has a very definite meaning and one that is somewhat different from typical usage. Harold Lasswell (1958) supplied us with the classic definition when he described politics as being about "who gets what, when and how."

In a political system there are political demands. Individuals have different values (wants and desires) and only government can authoritatively allocate these demands.[8] There are also inputs into the system other than demands. Inputs can also take the form of supports for the government and its policies. These supports may be as simple as obeying the law, voting, telling a pollster you favor an existing policy, or checking off the box on your federal income tax return to provide money to presidential candidates who agree to abide by certain campaign spending limits. There is one more topic, crucial to the operation of the political system, that needs a thorough explanation. That topic is linkage mechanisms, and it is discussed next.

---

[8]Another pertinent and equally famous definition of politics was penned when David Easton (1965) defined politics as the "authoritative allocation of values."

1-2. Backward Loops in the Political System

Traditionally, we think of linkage mechanisms as linking the demands of citizens to the government's policy agenda—that is, there is a one-way loop first linking citizens to the linkage mechanism and then a second loop that connects the linkage mechanism to the government. However, this unidirectional view is too limited. Linkage mechanisms (e.g., political parties, interest groups, the media, and elites) do not merely represent citizen interests; they actively and purposely shape citizen values and interests.

Citizens can also use the media as an instrument to get political causes on the government's agenda. For example, citizens upset by the failure of the government to respond to a particular issue may call in the media to expand the issue to a wider public, thus putting political pressure on the government to act.

This happened recently in one community. Local citizens were concerned about high school student drug use and were frustrated by a lack of action by the city government. Students were smoking pot in a park across the street from the high school. When the city police refused to act, concerned citizens invited the television media to secretly videotape (with faces blurred) the high school students engaging in the use of this illegal drug. The video outraged the community and subsequently the mayor and police chief received hundreds of angry phone calls and letters demanding police clean up the problem. Prompted by the citizen response, the police began patrolling the park across the street from the high school.

The use of the media in this manner is how we traditionally understand the workings of the political systems model. Citizens used the media to expand their views to a wider public and this led to government policy. But the media, like any linkage mechanism, also shapes citizen inputs and values without any prompting from citizens.

In another city, a local television station has shown almost nightly coverage of "meth busts" (methamphetamine), which in turn has led many citizens to conclude that the drug is a major community problem deserving further government action. Without the media's nightly report on methamphetamine, most citizens would have no idea that a problem even exists. The media thus plays a constituting role by what it decides to cover and not cover. The media is a powerful political force that can work either to maintain or to undo the status quo.

Undoubtedly the television station that covers meth busts could also have nightly news coverage of spousal abuse, arrests for driving while intoxicated (DWI)/driving under the influence (DUI), or even focusing on "excessive binge drinking" by community leaders. Imagine that the media did decide to conduct a nightly investigative report on well-known community business persons and other elites who frequent drinking establishments and frequently drive home intoxicated. The television station could have undercover reporters in the bar counting the drinks consumed by these community influentials. Then a television crew could show the influential tipplers (with blurred faces and license plates) driving away.

Nightly or even weekly television reports (Thursday night specials, like dollar import night, would probably be one good scheduling clue) could bring to the attention of citizens the idea that perhaps DWI enforcement in the community is uneven and unfair. A study of the DWI lists might show that only working class citizens and college students are charged with DWI.

Imagine an informant reporting that a college professor stopped at a DWI road-block was allowed to sit in his car and sober up before being officially tested and sent home, the same night that several fraternity brothers were arrested at the same road-block. Perhaps the media's investigation would discover that the police have "profiles" of cars that are likely to have intoxicated drivers. These cars tend to be older, smaller, or are "jacked-up" pick-ups or low-rider cars. Thus, the police single out certain vehicles and ignore more expensive automobiles, sport-utility vehicles, and newer four-wheel-drive pick-ups. Such a media investigation would likely prompt citizen demand for more equal and consistent DWI enforcement.*

The major point is that the linkage mechanisms exist independently of citizen demands and, in acting, they shape citizen values and interests. We have seen how the media can "create" problems while ignoring other issues. Likewise, interest groups link citizen values to government, but interest groups also actively seek to shape citizens' values. Interest groups (most often using the media) produce messages that support their political values. Environmental interest groups may produce television commercials and documentaries showing the negative impact of timber clear-cutting or the violence of government-sanctioned bison killing. Timber interest groups may produce commercials and documentaries showing the positive uses of the forest, describing forests as a renewable resource, and portraying themselves as stewards managing resources wisely. Ranching interest groups may produce messages showing that ranchers take care of the land, telling how hard ranchers work to bring quality beef to the American consumer, and claiming that government policy is hurting their traditional way of life.

Political parties and elites also actively seek to shape and influence public opinion. Therefore, when looking at the political systems model, we must remember that there are also "backward loops" from the government to the linkage mechanisms to the citizens. Figure 1-2 (on page 12) compares the traditional and the backward loop models.

---

*In other than a major media market, the elite drinking binge story would most likely never be covered (despite the real bias of the media—toward sensationalism, scandal, and hype). Since media management is typically part of the community's elite network, and the media rarely devours its own, don't hold your breath waiting for this story.

Public Policy and Linkage Mechanisms

Public policy is defined by Thomas Dye (1987, 3) as "what governments choose to do or not to do." If government decides to cut taxes, then this is a public policy; if government decides not to cut taxes then this too is a public policy. Government action, or inaction, is still a value choice. These choices, or, in other words, public policy, are determined by "political means." As we discussed earlier, the means of politics include: bargaining, compromise, reward, and coercion. Politics is the driving force of what American government does. It is the grease of the political system.

How do citizens influence government? You can, of course, write your senator and tell him or her that you support or do not support free trade. Legislative staff certainly do count up letters, e-mails, phone calls, and telegrams from supporters and opponents of prospective legislation. You can also set up a meeting with your congressional representative (or their staff) to discuss the pros and cons of free trade. In your letter, e-mail,

FIGURE 1-2   THE BACKWARDS LOOP VARIATION

The Traditional Political Systems Model

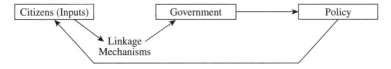

The Backward Loop Model

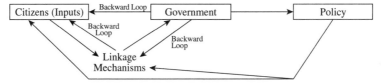

Traditional Political Systems Model (top): Linkage mechanisms link political values (inputs) to the government policy agenda. Everything in the system starts with the citizens, who are sovereign. Backward Loop Model (bottom): The citizens are not sovereign; they are strongly influenced by political parties, interest groups, the media, elites, and the symbolism of the government.

or personal meeting you could try to use political means to influence your senator. "Vote for free trade or I will not vote for you in the next election" (coercion). Perhaps you could say, "Vote for free trade and I will strongly support you for reelection in the next election" (a reward). If you are an average citizen, it is doubtful that the senator would take your advice too seriously. The senator may listen to you and even respect your views, but the average citizen, speaking as an isolated individual, does not sway the congressperson's vote.

In American democracy, the average individual citizen does not have a great deal of influence. As a result, individual citizens do not typically engage in the means of politics.[9] Rather, they influence government by voting, by joining political parties, and by joining **interest groups**. It is these "linkage mechanisms" that link citizens with the government and it is at this level that political means are used.

For instance, let us return to our free trade example. Your individual view may not influence your senator, but if you joined an interest group and this group represented a hundred thousand individuals in your state, coercion and rewarding may work. Thousands of e-mails merit more attention than one does. You could also join a political party that agrees with your position on free trade and the political party could work to elect a senator who agrees with all of your views on trade. Elections are a method whereby individuals collectively influence government by voting for candidates that represent their points of view. The following is a list of linkage mechanisms:

1. *Interest groups* lobby elected officials for specific policies using political means.

---

[9]Throughout the text the term "citizen" will be used to refer to nonelite individuals as differentiated from interest group leaders and other elites. While we clearly recognize that such elites are citizens, we prefer to use the term to denote the common person.

2. *Political parties* bring together broad groups of citizens who nominate candidates who represent the views of the people who belong to the party.

3. *Public opinion*: Elected officials often follow aggregated individual opinions in deciding policies.

4. *Voting/Elections*: People vote for candidates who represent their points of view.

5. *The media* plays an important role in influencing public opinion and in setting the policy agenda.

There are other ways that individual citizens collectively influence government. Public opinion showing strong support or opposition for an issue can persuade an elected official to vote for the public's choice. The media, of course, can play a significant role in shaping public opinion. Newspapers columnists, television commentators, and radio talk-show hosts are consistently given credit or blame for influencing the public's opinion. The media, just like interest groups and political parties, helps set policy agendas. In contemporary America, the media plays an increasingly large role in influencing government policy.

In essence, those who use political means (trading, rewarding, bargaining, coercing) most effectively get their values and interests turned into public policy. These groups or individuals hold the power in government policymaking. One of the best examples of citizens organizing and then using the means of politics to collectively influence public policy is the powerful American Association of Retired Persons (AARP). The AARP is widely and appropriately considered one of the most effective political players in domestic politics. Whether the issue is regulations relating to nursing homes, Medicare coverage and fees, or Social Security benefits, this group effectively works to protect its understanding of the interests of senior citizens.

For example, in the early 1980s the Reagan administration generated a proposal that would have reduced Social Security benefits for eligible recipients. AARP got its members to bombard members of Congress with messages of protest. At town hall meetings, in telephone calls and telegrams, and in letters, the politically mobilized AARP members made their displeasure known and promised that there would be political hell to pay if the proposed changes went through. With at least 50,000 members in every congressional district in the United States, incurring the wrath of AARP is not something to be done lightly.

The linkage mechanisms certainly do not perfectly reflect what an ideal democracy might produce but, like a universal joint in an automobile, they connect demands and the system together in a way that transmits energy into movement. They are also protected by the First Amendment's guarantees of freedom of speech and press, the right "to peaceably assemble," and "to petition the Government for a redress of grievances." The fictional story on pages 14–15 provides you with a realistic example of the political system at work.[10]

---

[10]This story, originally written in 1991 and inspired by a history of protection for the sugar beet industry by the late Senator Frank Church (D-ID), was imitated by real life several years later when corporate sugar users (including the Hershey Food Corporation) tried to get Congress to eliminate the sugar price supports but were defeated by lobbying from a coalition nearly identical to the one described in our story. See Keith Bradsher's *New York Times* story, "Budget Ax Misses in Swing at Sugar-Crop Aid," September 29, 1995: A-1, A-26.

1-3. Sugar Beets versus Candy

An example may give you a better understanding of how demands are authoritatively allocated and of how a political system works. In our story, the U.S. government is considering a new public policy alternative. The policy, if passed into law, would allow the importation of sugar from Caribbean countries (which is forbidden under an earlier bill passed long ago). Why is this policy being considered? The answer lies in the workings of the political system. Certain citizens and business interests desire an authoritative allocation.

In our story the interested party is the candy industry. Their value is to increase profits. One way for them to increase profit is to cut the price of their raw inputs. In this case, the most important raw good is sugar. So, in our story, members of the candy industry band together and form an interest group and a political action committee (PAC). The interest group then lobbies members of Congress (ideally those on the appropriate committees) to pass a law that would allow for the importation of sugar from the Caribbean. This importation would increase the supply of sugar, thus lowering the price and subsequently lowering the cost of production. The end result of this would be increased profits.

Which members of Congress are going to be interested in the demands of the candy industry? Well, those members who come from districts and states that are home to candy companies are going to listen to their demands with a relatively sympathetic ear. Perhaps the representative from the 17th District in Pennsylvania would be interested in helping the candy industry since Hershey, Pennsylvania (home of a main street called Chocolate Avenue and lampposts topped with ceramic Hershey's Kisses), is in their district and the candy company is a very large employer.

The candy industry's interest group will use the means of politics to entice members of Congress to introduce a bill that would allow for sugar importation. One means of politics would be to promise a "reward." For example, the industry could promise that if the law is passed the candy industry would strongly support the reelection bid of that member. The flip side of reward is "punishment," which means that if the representative does not actively support such legislation then the interest group will work to have the member defeated in the next election.

The actions of the candy lobby are only part of the story. Having asserted that politics is about value conflict, we recognize that other individuals and groups would not favor passage of a Caribbean sugar import bill. Idaho sugar beet farmers might logically be against this policy change, seeing it as a threat to their economic viability, perhaps even as a threat to their way of life. Idaho sugar beet farmers would also use a linkage mechanism (the Idaho Sugar Beet Association) to fight the legalization of the importation of Caribbean sugar. Sugar beet lobbyists would use political means to persuade congresspersons who represent areas where sugar beets are grown. Lobbyists might also appeal to the public by portraying sugar beet farmers as potential victims of an international cartel. They might try to frame the issue as one of protecting either family farms or "greedy, cavity-causing corporations."

Interestingly, if you look carefully at this example you can see that in reality this issue will significantly affect only a very small group of citizens. How many cities or states have a strong candy industry? How many states grow significant amounts of sugar beets? Remember that for a bill to pass Congress it must receive a majority vote in both houses of our legislative body. Yet, most members of Congress would seem to be indifferent toward this bill. To understand the fate of this proposed bill, we must turn again to politics, which occurs at all levels of the political system. So far we have only focused on the fact that interest groups, operating at the linkage mechanism level, would be busily utilizing various means to try to influence members of Congress.

If congressional members decide to act, they too must engage in the means of politics. They must reward, coerce, bargain, trade, and compromise. In this story, let's assume that the members of the House of Representatives from districts in the eight key sugar beet-producing states (Colorado, Idaho, Michigan, Minnesota, Montana, Nebraska, North Dakota, and Wyoming) want to put together a coalition with enough votes to defeat the sugar importation bill. How can they achieve their goal when the majority of members are indifferent to, and some are in favor of, this new legislation?

A first step would be to identify other allies. Although traditionally competitors,* representatives from districts in the sugar cane-growing states (Florida, Hawaii, Louisiana, and Texas) would also have constituencies hurt by this legislation. Legislators from the Midwest (e.g., Kansas) might also be opposed since the profitable corporate production of corn sweeteners (e.g., by Archer Daniels Midland Company) could also be endangered. Still, this coalition will not produce the necessary majority—and remember that the corporate sugar users (Hershey's, Wrigley's, Pepsi, and Coca-Cola) will be lobbying to try to gain a majority as well.

The best political means would likely be a trade. Assuming some sympathy from members from other agricultural districts, the sugar beet states' representatives could approach members of Congress from urban areas (without powerful candy interests) and offer a trade along the lines of: "You vote against the sugar bill and we will support you on that urban renewal bill that you want passed." Political scientists term this vote trading "logrolling."**

In the end, whether the sugar importation bill passes or not is determined largely by which side plays the best politics, not by whether or not this is "best for our country," "a sound policy," or some other supposedly objective standard. Often there are solutions generated from the political process that benefit both sides. Politics often involves compromise. To conclude our story and reflect this last observation, let's imagine a roaring domestic economy, fierce international competition, and a windfall of tax revenues generating a budget surplus. One option, given all these other pieces of the puzzle, would be to disallow these new imports, but provide tax breaks for the candy industry that will lower their costs and increase their profits.

---

*It is both a cliche and a truism that politics creates strange bedfellows.

**Remember that this story is a simplified version of reality designed to clearly convey some key concepts, not the full richness of politics nor all possible factors or outcomes.

Power and Policymaking

"Power" is often defined as the "ability to influence others more than they influence you." This definition is useful when we think about "value conflict" or "political demands" as discussed earlier. The citizen, the interest group, or the party that has their political demands or values turned into public policy has the power in government. They are influencing government through the development of policies that reflect their values rather than allowing others to influence public policy in ways that they do not want it to be influenced.

The policy analyst must understand how power structures really work (description) and should possess a value judgment about how they believe they should work in a democracy (prescription). The key questions, then, are: "Who has the power over government" (a descriptive question), and "Who should have the power over government?" (a **normative** question).

If the citizens influence government more than elites, interest groups, or the media, then we term this government a "democracy" (literally, rule by the people). If interest groups control government, we call this a "pluralist democracy" (rule by interest groups). Finally, if elites have the power over what government does and does not do, the government is an elite democracy, a bit of a contradiction in terms, where elites rule in the interests of the people, or it is an oligarchy where a few rule for the benefit of the few. If only one person has the power over policy, this is called an autocracy or dictatorship (rule by one).

An Ideal (Direct) Democracy

Before we can explore power in American democracy, we must look at the characteristics of an "ideal democracy." An ideal democracy provides us with a measuring rod to examine American government. Is the United States a genuine democracy? The following are some key elements of an ideal democracy.[11]

Preference Expression

Equality in voting and effective participation are the two key elements of preference expression. The voting booth is where the quintessential expression of preference happens. The essence of the idea of equality in voting is often captured in the simple phrase, "one person, one vote." Each person would have an equal say in public policy formation.

American democracy is based on the fact that each of us as adult American citizens can vote. The right to vote is called suffrage. If everyone had the right to vote it would be called universal suffrage. Many of us do not regularly exercise this privilege. Typically, in the United States, less than 50 percent of eligible voters turn out in

---

[11]This discussion leans heavily on one of the most noted theorists of democracy, Robert Dahl, in particular, on his text *Democracy in the United States: Promise and Performance* (1972, 39) and *Dilemmas of Pluralist Democracy* (1983, 6).

presidential election years. Twenty-five percent or less turn out in midterm elections. Typically, less than ten percent of eligible voters cast ballots in local mayoral, city council, and other local elections. We all may have one vote, but many of us choose not to cast it.

So we can say that the United States is an ideal democracy with virtual universal suffrage, in that today each person over eighteen years of age (who has not lost the right to vote through being convicted of a felony or legally judged insane) has the right to vote. Apathy, however, as we shall see, does not speak well for democracy. Many citizens question whether voting really makes any difference at all.

The second element of preference expression is effective participation. Access to the voting booth is not enough. Space for other forms of expression, such as petitioning the legislature, interest group activities, and public demonstrations must also be provided and utilized. Broad and representative participation in the political system is required.

This means that if democracy is "rule by the people," then our elected officials and top nonelected policymakers should be representative of the people. Several questions and their answers bring this aspect of American democracy into doubt.

Allow us to pose several questions about participation and the composition of our institutions: (1) How many citizens attend public hearings? (2) How many citizens run for elected office? (3) How many women are in the U.S. House, the U.S. Senate, state legislatures, and city councils? (4) How many minorities are in these elected bodies? (5) How many women and minorities hold positions of influence in bureaucracies? (6) From what social classes do elected officials generally come?

The answers to these questions tell us something about the nature of American democracy. The short answer is that elites are not typical of the masses. American political institutions are dominated by older, white males, primarily from the upper-middle classes to upper classes. These types of individuals are also the most likely to participate in the political process. The vast majority of elected officials at the federal level are attorneys who attended prestigious universities. Store clerks and machinists are seldom our elected officials. In general, the typical citizen probably hasn't thought much about participating in politics.

Does this matter? Some would say that men can make policies for the benefit of women as well as men, or that people from the upper socioeconomic classes can make policies that benefit all of us, not just the upper classes. Whether this is true is a source of considerable debate. While this is not the place for a detailed discussion, thinking through your views on this issue and understanding your own views of democracy and public policy is very important.

Unimpaired Opportunity to Develop Political Preferences

The goal is "enlightened understanding" and that depends on the following:

- a formal education process
- unimpeded access to alternative sources of information
- a media system and an electoral system that both present clear alternatives
- the opportunity to engage in real debates about the issues

Democracy has often been said to be a marketplace of ideas. An ideal democracy rests on an informed public willing to debate ideas and search for truth.

Unfortunately, political discussions are mostly divided into camps of "us" versus "them." The media contributes to this with television shows like CNN's *Crossfire* where conservatives and liberals battle it out without seeking common ground. In addition, tabloid journalism now influences even mainstream sources. Reporters, editors, and the media corporations concerned with ratings and sales, believe citizens are more interested in peering into the bedrooms of elected officials than in finding out about the latest budget or health care bill.

Even our elected leaders are practicing such a mean-spirited, scorched-earth politics that getting together to get things done has become more difficult. Combined with the negative advertising so prevalent today, many citizens tune out either from boredom or disgust, and the others are encouraged to see the opposition as evil, venal, and corrupt.

Democracy relies on consensus and compromise, as well as on free speech and freedom of the press. Inclusion of all who want to be citizens, knowledge of how to effectively participate, and broad participation are also necessary. Together, all of this implies that each of us must put in our two-cents worth and somehow blend the cacophony of our individual voices and values into an American chorus singing out a clear vision—if we are to be a genuine democracy.

However, Americans' knowledge of politics is also low. Confusion about how a bill becomes a law, the two houses of Congress, state legislatures, and other basics are well-documented. Ignorance, even about one's own senators and representatives, is rampant. One survey discovered that many more Americans could name all three of the Three Stooges than could name three of the Supreme Court justices.[12] One reason may be the point that the media is often more interested in sensationalism than it is in informing citizens. It is perhaps worth keeping in mind that the media is a business whose bottom line is profit, not public service.

The media is also accused of being manipulated by government. During the Gulf War, the media and the public had to rely largely on Pentagon briefings for information. Only reporters from a limited "pool" could go out into the battlefield, and only with American military escorts. Access to U.S. troops was limited. Moreover, the press agreed not to file any reports without first allowing the military to censor their stories. The American public's right to know was clearly thrown aside for political purposes. The media went along with this systematic control of information with hardly a whimper, and the public was very supportive of surrendering their First Amendment right.[13]

---

[12]A widely cited poll conducted for the *Washington Post* (October 12, 1995) showed 59 percent of the public able to name all three of the Three Stooges, but only 17 percent able to correctly identify three of the nine Supreme Court justices.

[13]*Taken by Storm: The Media, Public Opinion, and U.S. Foreign Policy in the Gulf War*, W. Lance Bennett and David L. Paletz, eds., is an excellent source for information on the media and the Gulf War.

Expressed Preferences Must Affect Governmental Conduct

Citizen's views, collectively speaking, must weigh in to government debate, conduct, and personnel. Simply put, citizens would control the policy agenda. In an ideal democracy citizens have the final say over what issues government deems important and ultimately over what government does or does not do. An important question you should ask as a student, an analyst, and a citizen, is who really controls policy agendas? Is it elites, PACs and special interest groups, the media, or citizens?

The answer to this question is complex. Interest groups claim to represent citizen interests and therefore their influence on government would seem to simulate rule by the people. Interest group leaders, however, are often accused of separating from the interests of their groups. Rule by interest group leaders is not democratic rule. Similarly, we know that elites often have unequal access to government. Money does not always directly buy favorable public policy outcomes. But money almost always does buy access. People with access, in turn, are more likely to have their views heard by government and ultimately have their views turned into public policy.

An "ideal" democracy generally means a direct democracy, in which the people get together to make laws. In the United States, with over 270 million people, a direct democracy, of course, is impractical. Ross Perot, during his 1992 and 1996 presidential campaigns, however, suggested that the United States could be a direct democracy. Perot argued that, through technology, Americans could vote on issues as they came up before Congress. In addition to impracticality, a direct democracy is also problematic due to the aforementioned problems of apathy and ignorance.

Genuine democracy also means that if elected officials' preferences and policies are different from those of the citizenry, the officials must be at risk of losing their positions. Joseph Schumpeter (1950) once defined democracy in terms of a competitive struggle for people's votes.

Representative Democracy

In reality, the United States has never been a direct democracy except perhaps at the local level with New England townships. Nor was the Founders' intention to create a direct democracy. Instead, the U.S. government was created to be a representative democracy in which elites could dampen the dangers presumed to flow from direct democracy.

In a representative democracy, people choose agents who act on their behalf (and sometimes these agents choose other agents who act on the people's behalf—e.g., Supreme Court justices, who are even more protected from the buffeting winds of democracy and elections). Citizens choose these agents through elections. Power still remains with citizens because everyone has an equal voice in the selection of leaders (one person, one vote) and elections make leaders accountable to public preferences.

There are several problems with representative democracy. First, for representative democracy to work, elected officials must act in accordance with the preferences of the citizens. This is not an easy task since it assumes that citizens have clear policy preferences. We know from survey data that citizens often hold contradictory positions on major policy issues. The American public may want improved education but may resist increased taxation necessary to pay for improving that education. The public may desire clean rivers but staunchly oppose the environmental regulation necessary to achieve this goal. A related issue is that contemporary politics is dominated by divisive wedge issues, symbols, and sound bites, and not by serious discussions of policy options. Elected officials are most often elected because they support family values, oppose gun control, or are pro-choice. Citizens elect candidates based on the emotional impressions that they have of the individual, not necessarily on some well-thought-out decision about policy preferences.

A second problem is simply whether or not elected officials should follow the demands of the people in the first place. Polls have consistently demonstrated that the public is less supportive of civil liberties (e.g., freedom of speech—even for unpopular ideas, protection against unreasonable search and seizure, and the suffrage rights of unpopular minority groups) than are elected officials. Many times elected officials may be better informed than the public and may indeed make better decisions. This view of representative democracy asserts that elected officials are still held accountable through elections.

A third problem with representative democracy is that, for this type of democracy to work, the system must produce highly qualified candidates. The pool of American citizens who run for elected office is quite small. As previously discussed, attorneys and other professionals are vastly overrepresented. Working-class citizens are virtually eliminated from running for federal office. Candidates for office are figuratively and literally put under the microscope by a media that believes an individual's personal as well as public life is fair game for investigation. General Colin Powell's decision not to run in the 1996 Republican presidential primaries was apparently based significantly on his unwillingness to allow his personal life to be open to media investigation. The incredible cost of running a credible campaign today has also deterred many candidates and given an advantage to the Perots, Forbeses, and Huffingtons in our society. As a result of these problems, the system may not produce the best candidates.

Interest Group Democracy (Pluralism)

Two major questions confronted early political scientists studying power in American government: One, if neither direct democracy nor representative democracy adequately describes the American political system, then how are matters resolved? Two, who holds the power in American society? These questions continue to be relevant today.

Beginning in the 1950s a group of American political scientists decided that representative democracy did not adequately describe or explain the American political system. A political scientist by the name of Robert Dahl (1961) introduced the concept of *pluralism*. The root word of pluralism is *plural* (many). Pluralists believe that American democracy (rule by the people) is achieved through rule by many competing interest groups. Interest groups, as their name denotes, represent private interests. Interest groups become the intermediary between the citizen and the government, but the citizen ultimately rules. Pluralism holds that democracy is alive and well, with interest groups representing citizen desires.

Further, pluralism believes that power in American society is widely scattered and that power comes through resources. Every interest group (and hence every citizen) has access to these political resources. Anyone can join, or even organize, an interest group. In fact, as mentioned earlier, the right of association is protected by the First Amendment. Unlike those who believe elites run the government, pluralism believes that money is only one type of political resource and that other political skills can overcome money. The following list elaborates on pluralism's view of power:

1. Power is widely scattered (this is the essential point).
2. Power comes through resources.
3. Everyone has at least some resources.
4. Resources are not limited to money. Other resources include things like access, sheer numbers, wide geographic distribution, a cause, effective leadership, and a reputation for winning.
5. Potential power exceeds actual power.
6. No one is all powerful (functional areas).

The following is a list of the characteristics of pluralism:

1. American government is influenced by a multiplicity of competing small groups.
2. The system is open.
3. Group strength is derived from the masses.
4. Politics is based on compromise.

Pluralism, as we have already stated, argues that American government is influenced by a multitude of groups. Pluralism further states: (1) Interest groups can enter and leave the political system at any time; (2) interest group strength is derived from the masses; and (3) because power is scattered, the competition provides a check on power, and politics becomes the art of compromise. As a political theory of government, pluralism is by nature abstract and very conceptual.

The principles of pluralism are among the concepts the case studies in this text will help to illustrate and make more concrete by studying them in a real political setting. In the end, you may decide that elitism, the theory we will explain next, is a better description of how policy is produced—or you may think they both identify important pieces of the policy puzzle—but either way you need to understand this dominant model of American politics.

Elitism

Many political scientists believe that pluralism does not adequately describe the American political system or that its description is limited. Elitism has a long history in the social sciences.[14] As we shall see, however, elite theorists are severely divided on what

---

[14]An early elaboration of elitism is in Gaetano Mosca (1939).

the term means for democracy and government. The most fundamental expression of elite theory is the idea that in any large organization (including governments) there will always be a small ruling minority (the elite) and a large group (the masses) largely without power.

Not surprisingly then, elite theory's critique of pluralism is based on the "Iron Law of Oligarchy" (Michels 1949). The iron law of oligarchy attacks the theory of interest group representation directly. The iron law of oligarchy asserts that two classes will always appear, the few with power and the many without. Even if the elites are chosen from the masses, their interests, resource base, and functional value diverges from the majority.

1-4. Another Look at Orwell's *Animal Farm*

George Orwell (also the author of *1984*) wrote this classic story during the Second World War. Boxer, Benjamin, Old Major, Napoleon, the guard dogs, the birds, and all the other animals who establish "Animal Farm" are obviously symbols. Trade with the outside world, the easily changed rules painted on the barn wall, Farmer Jones, and the windmill are also symbols. While it is generally agreed that the best analogy to what happened at Animal Farm was the former Soviet Union, his point can be seen in a much broader context.

Is there an iron law of oligarchy? For all societies, all organizations, and all revolutions? Are revolutions ultimately just a change in personnel? Once in power, elites inevitably increase the amount of information they control, their expertise increases, and as typical "humans" they are subject to human temptations (i.e., power corrupts—that's why "checks and balances" are more important than efficiency when designing a government). We witness the use of oratory, propaganda, and fear by an educated and articulate elite to control the inattentive, trusting, and hard-working masses. A moment of crisis becomes a chance to manipulate. Like Benjamin (the jackass), Orwell suggests we often see the glue truck coming too late.

But what if Boxer, the representative of the working class, had been more politically astute? What if Benjamin had not been a jackass. What if Old Major—and his commitment to equality—had not died when he did? Are all elites really pigs? And, could Jones have avoided the whole revolution by allowing limited social mobility, perhaps co-opting the pigs, or even by simply being more fair and efficient?

Maybe Orwell's classic tale still speaks to us today, even here in the good old U.S. of A.

Source: George Orwell, *Animal Farm*. San Diego, CA: Harcourt Brace Jovanovich, 1990/1946.

Elite theory does not necessarily dispute pluralism's emphasis on the role of interest groups in the political system. Elite theorists, however, dispute the notion that interest groups represent the views of the public. Instead, elite theorists contend that pluralism is really "rule by interest group leaders." Interest group leaders are likely of a high socioeconomic status and their decisions will ultimately benefit themselves rather than the group they represent. Many citizens are not represented by interest groups, and those from the lower socioeconomic strata are less likely to belong to interest groups.

Elitism argues that interest group leaders are elites. Elites are derived from the same social class (the upper class), go to the same type of universities, serve on the same boards, and have similar interests. Therefore, they also see more cooperation and less competition than does pluralism. Citizens are apathetic, ill-informed, disorganized, and allow interest group leaders and elected officials (who according to elite theorists are controlled by elites) to develop policy.[15]

Elite theorists suggest that the reason citizens are apathetic is because elites socialize citizens into complacency by delivering a steady diet of television and by providing the illusion that "consumerism" is a sign of personal wealth and happiness. Or, perhaps apathy stems from what has been termed "rational ignorance." Since involvement takes time and energy, and can have monetary costs, and since the chances of making a difference seem so small, it is rational to focus on feeding one's family, on school, on the church, on sports, and such—rather than on politics.[16]

Elite theorists believe that money is power. Political skill cannot overcome the power that money delivers. Money may not buy votes or policies but money buys access and access in turn often leads to policies favorable to those who have access. While he was in office, former Texas Senator Lloyd Bentsen created what the media called the "Bentsen Breakfast Club." Bentsen would allow individuals to have breakfast with him once a week for a $1,000 contribution to his election coffers. Individuals who ate breakfast with Bentsen could discuss a variety of issues with him. Again, politicians, like all of us, are likely to take action on issues that are brought to their attention.

Elite theorists believe that the public may be involved in some small decisions, and interest groups may be involved in slightly larger decisions, but large and important decisions are made by the few. According to these political scientists, policy decisions are analogous to a tree. There are twig decisions, branch decisions, and trunk decisions.[17]

Twigs are part of the tree but are not a very important part. Twig decisions are made by citizens and grass-roots interest group efforts. Twig decisions are minor decisions that change little. Branches are a more important part of a tree but are not the most important part. Branch decisions are important but do not explain the entire political process. Interest groups, elected officials, and occasionally citizens make branch

---

[15]Note that pluralism would view apathy as a good sign of democracy. Citizens are satisfied with the system and do not want changes. Ironically, as you will see shortly, some elite theorists also believe apathy is good, but for a very different reason.

[16]Critics sometimes point out that we are rarely taught about organizing and policy victories by the weak. Si Kahn's classic text on organizing (1991), Howard Zinn's *A People's History* (1980), and David F. Schuman (1991) all provide examples and serve as counterweights to this problem.

[17]The tree metaphor is a useful teaching method found in Reynolds and Vogler (1991). The tree metaphor will also surface later in our discussion of decision trees and is used in a somewhat different manner in Charles E. Lindblom's classic works on policy formulation (including "The Science of 'Muddling Through'" [1959]; and in *A Strategy of Decision* [1970], coauthored by David Braybrooke.)

decisions. The most important part of a tree is the trunk, which supports the whole tree. Without a trunk you do not have a tree. Trunk decisions, according to elite theorists, are made by elites.

Elite Democracy: The Irony of Democracy

Going back to the time of Socrates, elite theorists have been divided on whether elitism is good or bad for democracy. Plato writes of elites as guardians of democracy whereas Thrasymachus, a friend of Socrates, exclaims (18):

> In every case the laws are made by the ruling party in their own interest.... By making these laws they define as right for their subjects whatever is for their own interest, and they call anyone who breaks them a wrongdoer and punish him accordingly.

More recently, a generation of introductory political science students have been exposed to this major debate. Thomas R. Dye and Harmon Zeigler contend that elitism in the United States has been good for democracy, whereas Michael Parenti argues that elitism is exploitative of the masses. The debate has also surfaced in the popular press with the publication of William Henry's *In Defense of Elitism* (1994)—a book that argues that the United States has suffered from too much democracy and not enough elite decision making; and the counter argument—that democracy is not threatened by the masses but by today's elites—is made by Christopher Lasch in his (1995) national bestseller *The Revolt of the Elites: And the Betrayal of Democracy.*[18]

Dye and Zeigler (1996) believe that throughout American history, elites have always been more democratic than the masses. They array a wealth of polling data to support their claim. The masses are seen as too passionate, too emotional, too swayed by clever sound-bites, and not strongly committed to basic democratic principles. Elites are more tolerant on issues such as freedom of speech, homosexual rights, and religious tolerance. The irony is, therefore, that for our democratic rights to survive the elites must continue to govern and govern wisely.

In short, Dye and Zeigler take a **paternalistic** approach to American government. Elites, who understand issues better than ordinary citizens, control government but generally have done so for the benefit of all.[19] A contrary view is offered by Michael Parenti. In *Democracy for the Few* (1995), he argues that elites rule for the benefit of elites (which is an oligarchy). He puts it quite plainly in his 1994 text, *Land of Idols*, on the first page of Chapter 1: "Government in the hands of the privileged and powerful will advance the interests of the privileged and powerful..."(3).

Parenti and others follow a Marxist interpretation of American government. Karl Marx (1848) believed that interests are driven by economic concerns and that history

---

[18]We note that the discussion that follows draws heavily on introductory American Government textbooks. We purposely chose these works because they provide an appropriately general overview to the debate over elite interpretation that is desirable for applied policy analysis.

[19]However, Dye and Zeigler do worry that, increasingly, American elites have been making policy more often for their own short-term benefit.

is a struggle of class interests (people with different economic interests). The capitalists (who own the means of production) create laws and institutions that benefit their class at the expense of the proletariat (the working class). American democracy, according to Marxist elite theorists, is a fraud.

Dye and Zeigler make a similar, but slightly less harsh, appraisal. Elections are seen as a ritual perpetuating the myth of control by the people, yet voters are merely picking personnel, not policy. Like most elite theorists they do admit the masses influence elites and that elections create some accountability.

According to Dye and Zeigler, for elections to mean what pluralists say they do (that they allow voters to determine policy), all four of the following conditions would have to be met. That is, they are all necessary but only sufficient as a complete package. The four conditions are as follows:

1. Competing parties and candidates would have to offer clear policy alternatives rather than obscuring and obfuscating as they seek votes.
2. Voters would have to be concerned with policy questions (well-informed and voting on the basis of policy concerns not personality or image).
3. Election results would have to be interpretable in a way that would clarify majority preferences on these questions (but what if one prefers and votes for Candidate X although disagreeing with their position on the death penalty).
4. Even if we pretend that the first three conditions are regularly met in the United States, unless elected officials are bound by their campaign positions (which might not be a good idea) the pledges of our politicians are not necessarily the policies we receive (1996, 191–93).

The following list lays out the rudimentary principles of elite theory. It is important to remember that fundamentally, elite theory and pluralism are competing, but not totally dissimilar, descriptions of how we "do" politics. You can accept either as a description without endorsing it as a prescription.

1. American government, like all large organizations, is dominated by elites (the few), not the masses (the many).
2. Financial and social class background, and control of large institutions, are the most important political resources. While skilled and knowledgeable nonelites can rise to power, the norm is elites from society's upper strata.
3. Elites are more democratic than the masses (Dye and Zeigler).
4. Elites primarily benefit themselves, not citizens (Parenti).
5. Democracy and pluralism are, to a degree, a sham. While masses have some influence, elections are ritualistic.

Effect of Power Structures on the Policy Analyst

Power structures directly affect the work of the policy analyst. The analyst's view of how government really operates (a descriptive view) and how government should operate (a normative view) is key to conducting a policy analysis. We know from our discussion of "value conflict" that different groups and individuals will have different perceptions of what are policy problems and what are acceptable solutions to these problems. The analyst's view of power will determine the depth and breadth of stakeholders in any given policy area. This, in turn, will determine what evaluative criteria are used and not used, what policies are suggested and not suggested, and ultimately what policies are chosen and how they are implemented.

An analyst may believe that the system is controlled by elites but should be controlled by citizens. The analyst might make the decision to attempt to gather citizen views but ultimately give in to the political reality that they perceive, namely that elites make policy choices. If an analyst believes in the "irony of democracy" the analyst would be convinced that the stakeholders should be elites because their policy ideas will ultimately benefit the masses.

Conversely, an analyst might believe that the system is controlled by interest groups (pluralism) and therefore stakeholders would include only major interest groups involved in the policy area. While the analyst may want to include citizens, she would believe that their interests are represented by interest groups. Also, while she may worry that some interests are not represented by groups, she is comforted that since the system is open new interest groups can easily form for nonrepresented interests.

Another analyst may decide that he represents elected officials and they in turn represent citizens (representative democracy). This analyst would typically listen to the views of elected officials when making policy analysis choices.

Finally, an analyst might decide that the system is controlled by elites and interest groups, but that citizens should really rule. This analyst may go out of her way to include citizens outside the major power structures in the political process. She may suggest policies that favor these citizens over more powerful elites and interest groups. This analyst may risk political repercussions and may have her job threatened or even eliminated by the influence of elites and interest groups.

Table 1-1 demonstrates the choices facing the policy analyst and the implications of those choices. The center column in Table 1-1 focuses on stakeholders. In an informal way, we have already discussed the issue of stakeholder analysis. This is a critical factor for policy analysts, especially crucial for the view of policy analysis that this text endorses, and essential as you engage the case studies to follow. Thus, it is now time for a fairly thorough and formal discussion of stakeholders.

Stakeholder Analysis

Stakeholder analysis, or mapping, is in one sense a recognition that the policy process is political. It is a recognition that there are actors whose cooperation, or at least willingness not to obstruct, is necessary for policy success. It is a recognition that differences in values, roles, perceptions, and interests, are probable. Consider for a moment the idea known as the stand/sit principle (sometimes called Miles Law). The essence of the stand/sit principle is the old cliche, "where you stand (on an issue) depends on where you sit." The key idea is empathy. It is important to try to see things from others' vantage points—not just to be nice, but to strategize. It is also a recognition of power differences. The reality is that there are key players, political heavy-hitters, and (especially in a federal system like ours) the need to put together coalitions and to gain the cooperation of other key organizations and agencies.

TABLE 1-1   The Role of Policy Analysts and Their Normative View of Power

Analysts' View of Power	Stakeholders' Decision	Democratic Outcomes/Problems
Ideal Democracy	Includes all citizens and groups as stakeholders.	This is excellent for democracy in theory but is unworkable in practice. In addition, citizens are uninformed about most issues and would most likely prefer choices that are not in the public interest.
Representative Democracy	Analysts include stakeholders who are politically important to the elected bodies that the analyst serves.	This is how democracy is supposed to work. The elected official is accountable to the public through elections. The problem is that representatives do not really represent the public in demographic or substantive ways. Many people do not vote and elections are probably not that important to them.
Pluralism	Analysts include all interest groups in a policy issue area.	Democracy is effectuated since any citizen can join an interest group. The problem is that most interest groups are tied to powerful economic interests. Many citizens are not represented by interest groups. And, it is questionable whether interest group leaders represent the interests of their group.
Elitism	The analyst only includes important and influential individuals as stakeholders.	Since citizens are uninformed, elites and expert analysts make policy decisions. The irony of democracy suggests that this form of policymaking has saved democracy from the emotional desires of the masses. The criticism here is that elites control the sources of information and knowledge and this is why the masses are uninformed. In addition, the interests of elites and the interests of the masses are not always the same.

One of your authors grew up in several very small towns. One of the things he learned is the idea of the Rule of Five (or four or six). The point is that in a small town, and in any policy arena, there is a small group of people with the power to kill or sustain almost any project. Sometimes their veto power is formal, other times it is not. Without their support you are usually wasting your time. With their support you are golden.

In its simplest terms, performing a stakeholder analysis is a process used to inventory, rank, and assess the positions of the individuals, groups, and organizations (internal and external to your "organization") affected by or interested in the organization, issue, program, or policy being considered. It is the act of determining the "who," detailing what they value and want and how salient this issue is to them, evaluating the resources they can bring to bear effectively on both the adoption and implementation of policy, and strategizing about how to get them on board.

Table 1-2 (on page 29) is a Stakeholder Map that captures the essential steps of the stakeholder analysis process. The most crucial aspect of performing a stakeholder analysis centers on correctly identifying who the stakeholders are, so before moving on, here are a few hints. First, very often the most important stakeholder will be the political executive (e.g., president, governor, mayor, county executive, etc.). Second, if you look around carefully, the key power brokers from the community, the essential representatives of the various populations and groups affected (e.g., union leaders), the key program managers and agency heads, and the most important elected officials (e.g., perhaps the head of a legislative committee who will have to authorize funding) are often rather obvious. Third, there are questions that can help you identify the stakeholders most likely to be consequential. Questions to ask include the following:

- Are there actors whose support in implementation is vital?
- Which actors control the resources (personnel, legal authority, funding, clients, etc.) that are indispensable?
- Who has traditionally been consulted or given the right to influence or control this matter?
- Do any of the actors have superior competence or reputations as eminent authorities in this area?
- Are there any leaders of concerned groups of significant size or groups with intense interest in this issue?
- Is there a leader whose support would be enough to grant legitimacy or at least compel serious consideration?

As you can imagine, doing a thorough stakeholder analysis can take quite a bit of time and effort. Consequently, a formal mapping should be reserved for important issues and projects. However, the analyst is always choosing, always determining who the "real" stakeholders are, and deciding who to include in the process and who to exclude.

TABLE 1-2 STAKEHOLDER MAP

STAKEHOLDERS	STAKEHOLDERS' ATTITUDE			STAKEHOLDERS' POWER		
INTERNAL AND/OR EXTERNAL	COOPERATION (+) OR OPPOSITION (−)	VALUES AND OBJECTIVES SHAPING THEIR ATTITUDES TOWARD THIS MATTER	SALIENCE OF THIS ISSUE HIGH/MED./LOW	ADOPTION POWER YES (Y) NO (N)	IMPLEMENTATION POWER YES (Y) NO (N)	WHO THEY INFLUENCE / WHO INFLUENCES THEM

Note: Trying to rank stakeholders exactly is probably not worth the trouble, and the key players are probably self-evident after completing the map, however, it may be useful to use an asterisk to note those most essential to success. (Rule of Five)

Concluding Thoughts

Analysts must make a philosophical choice of who their stakeholders are and ultimately who their clients are. The choice is not necessarily one of being an elitist and defining your stakeholders narrowly, or being more democratic and defining them broadly. The preferred choice may well be what Danziger (1995, 445) suggests:

> Once they have recognized the political power wielded by technological analysis, policy analysts must acknowledge their responsibility to communicate directly to the public—most likely through the popular press—to ensure that interested citizens have the intellectual ammunition to defend themselves in the midst of policy battles that affect them. This requirement means that students need to learn the rhetorical skills that will enable them to translate for the lay public the results of, for example, their complex regression analyses. Equally important, they must accept the task of educating citizens to question those quantitative results, perhaps by ensuring that the relevant counter-data are made available for public consumption as well.

This view expressed by Danziger sees the analyst as a potential neutral party in that they can reveal the hidden assumptions, ideologies, and values in data collection, problem definition, criteria establishment, and consequently in policies considered and not considered. In this view then, being neutral does not mean being uninvolved. We will state explicitly what Danziger states implicitly: Policy experts (including front-line public servants) have knowledge and expertise that they are morally bound to share. Education has often been termed a privilege and privileges create responsibilities. Indeed, if you are not committed to making a difference, you should reconsider your choice to be a public administrator, social worker, policy analyst, probation officer, or the like.

Within this framework then, the most important goal for the analyst is to gather input from as many stakeholders as possible, given limited time frames. Realize that policy decisions will frequently favor some groups and individuals over others and that policymaking is always based, consciously or not, on some theory of power and government. The analyst should provide their policy decisions to elected officials honestly and perhaps should use persuasion to convince the elected officials to adopt policies that favor a wide cross-section of the society. Ultimately, policy adoption is the job of the elected official, but the policy analyst can play a crucial role in framing the debate.

The case study that concludes this chapter—"Nightcrawlers and Cappuccino," pages 32–42—will draw you into the world of the policy analyst, force you to review and employ the major concepts covered in the chapter, and encourage you to honestly consider the philosophical base from which you operate.

Key Concepts

backward loops (p. 10)

elitism (p. 21)

ideal democracy (p. 16)

Iron Law of Oligarchy (p. 22)

irony of democracy (p. 24)

linkage mechanisms (p. 11)

means of politics (p. 11)

pluralism (p. 20)

political inputs (p. 9)

political system (p. 8)

politics (p. 8)

power (p. 16)

power structures' effect (p. 25)

public policy (p. 11)

representative democracy (p. 19)

social problem/stages of development (p. 5)

stakeholder analysis (p. 26)

value conflict/problem definition (p. 3)

Glossary Terms

Hobson's Choice (p. 4)

interest group (p. 12)

normative (p. 16)

paternalistic (p. 24)

triggering event (p. 5)

win-win policy (p. 4)

References

Bennett, Lance W., and David L. Paletz, eds. 1994. *Taken by Storm: The Media, Public Opinion, and U.S. Foreign Policy in the Gulf War.* Chicago, IL: University of Chicago Press.

Bradsher, Keith. 1995. "Budget Ax Misses Swing at Sugar Crop Aid." *New York Times*, September 29, A-1, A-26.

Braybrooke, David, and Charles E. Lindblom. 1970. *A Strategy of Decision: Policy Evaluation as a Social Process.* New York: Free Press.

Dahl, Robert. 1961. *Who Governs.* New Haven, CT: Yale University Press.

———. 1972. *Democracy in the United States: Promise and Performance.* Chicago, IL: Rand McNally.

———. 1983. *Dilemmas of Pluralist Democracy.* New Haven, CT: Yale University Press.

Danziger, Marie. 1995. "Policy Analysis Postmodernized: Some Political and Pedagogical Ramifications." *Policy Studies Journal* 23, no. 3.

Dye, Thomas R. 1987. *Understanding Public Policy.* Englewood Cliffs, NJ: Prentice Hall.

Dye, Thomas, and Harmon Zeigler. 1996. *The Irony of Democracy*, 10th ed. Belmont, CA: Wadsworth.

Easton, David. 1965. *Framework for Political Analysis.* Englewood Cliffs, NJ: Prentice Hall.

Fuller, Richard C., and Richard R. Myers. 1941. "The Conflict of Values and the Stages of a Social Problem." Reprinted in Ch. 4 of *The Study of Social Problems*, 4th ed. Edited by Earl Rubington and Martin S. Weinberg. New York/Oxford: Oxford University Press, 1989.

Henry, William A., III. 1994. *In Defense of Elitism.* New York: Anchor Books Doubleday.

Kahn, Si. 1991. *Organizing: A Guide for Grassroots Leaders.* Washington, D.C.: NASW Press.

Kocieniewski, David. 1999. "New Jersey's Hard Line on Needle Exchanges." *New York Times*, February 2, A-20.

Lasch, Christopher. 1995. *The Revolt of the Elites: And the Betrayal of Democracy.* New York: W. W. Norton & Company.

Lasswell, Harold D. 1958. *Politics: Who Gets What, When, How.* New York: Meridian Books.

Lindblom, Charles E. 1959. "The Science of 'Muddling Through.'" Reprinted as art. 25 of *Classics of Public Administration.* Edited by Jay M. Shafritz and Albert C. Hyde. Pacific Grove, CA: Brooks/Cole, 1992.

Michels, Robert. 1949. *Political Power.* Glencoe, IL: Free Press.

Mosca, Gaetano. 1939. *The Ruling Class.* New York: McGraw Hill.

Parenti, Michael. 1995. *Democracy for the Few.* New York: St. Martin's Press.

———. 1994. *Land of Idols: Political Mythology in America.* New York: St. Martin's Press.

Plato. 1945. *The Republic of Plato.* Translated by F. M. Cornford. New York: Oxford University Press.

Reynolds, H. T., and David Vogler. 1991. *Governing America.* New York: Harper Collins.

Schuman, David F., with Dick W. Olufs, III. 1991. *A Preface to Politics.* Itasca, IL: F. E. Peacock Publishers, Inc.

Schumpeter, Joseph. 1950. *Capitalism, Socialism and Democracy*, 3rd ed. New York: Harper and Row.

Shilts, Randy. 1987. *And the Band Played On: Politics, People and the AIDS Epidemic*. New York: St. Martins Press.

Zinn, Howard. 1980. *A People's History of the United States*. New York: Harper & Row Publishers.

Nightcrawlers and Cappuccino: The Old West versus the New West

A Policy Case of Rural Economic Development and Environmental Protection in the Columbia River Basin

Nightcrawlers and Cappuccino
—posted on a grocery store sign in rural Montana

The Case

Major economic, social, cultural, and political change is happening in the rural west of the United States. Large-scale immigration, depressed natural resource markets, increases in service sector employment, and growing concern over the preservation of the environment have led many policymakers to reevaluate economic development policy in the region.

Historically, the region has relied almost exclusively on natural resources for their economic survival. This resource use includes mining, timber cutting, the use of public lands for cattle grazing, and farming. A culture has emerged around this way of life that celebrates individualism and vilifies governmental regulation. For decades, this culture, known as the "old west," has dominated rural politics.

But in recent years the rural west has seen dramatic changes as urban immigration and increased reliance on service sector and nonresource-related employment has grown. With these changes a new culture has developed. It is a culture that emphasizes the preservation rather than the use of natural resources. Slowly, this "new west" culture has made some political inroads. However, the old west retains strong political control even if their economic superiority may have passed into history.

Economic development policy seemingly must make the transition from merely promoting the use of natural resources to finding economic development strategies that contribute to economic prosperity but that also preserve the environment. This type of development is called "sustainable development."

The Assignment

Each of you is a policy analyst working for the hypothetical "National Rural Development Council" (NRDC). Your agency is part of the nonhypothetical U.S. Department of Agriculture (USDA). The NRDC was founded in 1998 and has the following mission statement: "The National Rural Development Council shall assist in the coordinating of rural development activities at the federal, state, and local levels."[1]

The NRDC is charged with helping rural communities in the Columbia River Basin (CRB) make the transition from resource dependent communities to communities that practice "sustainable development" strategies. In fact, the federal government will eventually set aside over $50 million dollars annually for rural communities in the region. These communities will be allowed to apply for individual grants (up to $1,000,000 each) for the creation and implementation of sustainable development policies. However, before a community can become eligible for such funds they must create a sustainable development economic plan showing how their new development strategies will both create economic prosperity and protect natural resources.

Your assignment is to provide an initial policy report to the NRDC director. Based on your understanding of Chapter 1, and after reading the rest of the case, complete the key task assigned below and then answer the three questions that follow it.

Key Task: The director of the NRDC told you that your job depends upon your completing a strong stakeholder analysis. Use the stakeholder process described in the chapter so that you do well.

1. Who has interests at stake in this potentially major change in economic development policy? What groups or individuals would promote this new policy initiative? What kind of political maneuvering would you expect? What type of linkage mechanisms would various opponents and supporters likely use?

2. What model(s) of democracy did you follow in creating your stakeholder analysis? What type of insight into power and democracy would you want to provide to the director?

3. Does value conflict theory come into play in this case? If so, how?

So You Want to Be a Rural Policy Analyst?

It was a beautiful October in the rural western United States. The leaves were a bright yellow, the sky a dark blue, and bull elk bugled in the mountains above a small mining community. On this day, a rural development analyst from a local university (150 miles away) had arrived to give a presentation to a group of citizens. The university was sponsoring a $300,000 revitalization program for rural communities and some in this small mining community wanted assistance. The university rural development program assisted communities in finding alternative economic development policies that were to end decades of reliance on natural resources.

This mining community was at the time severely depressed. A downturn in the mining market had left the community with dozens of empty homes and businesses. Mining communities follow what are called "boom and bust" cycles. When mining prices

---

[1]It might seem unusual to have a USDA agency work on sustainable development strategies. In reality, the USDA has spent considerable money and resources in the last decade helping rural communities find methods to become less reliant on natural resources. Much of this effort has come through the U.S. Forest Service (the Forest Service is part of the USDA). The Forest Service has provided millions of dollars to timber-dependent communities in the form of "action grants" designed to help those communities become less reliant on timber cutting.

are good, the community will prosper and grow, with many well-paying jobs. During these times, new homes will be built and new businesses will open. When mining prices collapse, jobs disappear, homes are abandoned, and businesses close.

The rural development analyst arrived early for the 1:00 P.M. meeting. He walked around town admiring the mountains and talking with local residents. As the meeting time moved closer, he walked to the meeting place and began to set up flip charts and prepare handouts. After a short time, two women arrived and began to nervously pace outside the small meeting room. Next, the head of the community's development efforts arrived. The analyst had met with her a month ago and they had talked several times on the phone in recent weeks. The contact person pulled the analyst into an adjoining room and informed him, "Those two women out there are here to sabotage the meeting; they very much want you and the university to stay out of here." The analyst reassured her, "There is always conflict with these types of things [but] I can handle it."

The analyst moved to the meeting room where the two women had been joined by some eight other citizens, introduced himself, and began to explain the university's development programs. He began what was called a "community puzzle," which was a simple method designed to identify different segments of the community and then compare these segments with the people who were attending the meeting. At this point, the two women who were apparently there to sabotage the meeting both proclaimed, "We will tell you who we are; we are taxpayers and our goal is to stop you outsiders from spending our tax dollars and then telling us how to live our lives." The verbal attack was unprovoked and even though the analyst had been invited into the town, nobody in attendance countered the views of the two women. One woman, it turned out, was a state elected official and the second woman was a former community city council member.

Pressing on, the analyst explained that the university program concentrated on leadership development, organization development, grant writing, and research. He also discussed various small technical assistance monies that were available and that such a grant would help fund a part-time local coordinator for development efforts. At this point, the two women became enraged and one (the state elected official) asked, "What type of tax-dollar-wasting program is this?" The analyst explained that the grant dollars funding the university program came from a nonprofit corporation and were not taxpayer dollars.

The second woman then stated, "Sure, we will take your money but then there will be strings attached; you will tell us what to do with the money." The analyst reassured the audience that the university believed very much in local planning and that any reporting requirements would be only to ensure that the money was spent for development purposes. The analyst stated, "We have to be accountable to the granting agency. We must document that the community spent the money on development-related activities and not for a new car for each of the committee members."

This sent the state official into a verbal sparring match with the analyst. Some of the exchanges (recorded for history by a local newspaper writer) were quite humorous. Here are a few examples:

State official: "How can a urban person like you know anything about rural issues?"
Analyst: "I grew up in a town of 4,000."

State official: "Why aren't you at the university teaching instead of out here telling us what to do?"

Analyst: "The university is charged by the state board of education, as you probably know, with providing outreach to communities in the region. As you probably also know, this has been a priority of the state legislature."

State official: "We don't need leadership training here, we have good leaders, look at the mayor here."

(Incredibly, the mayor had dozed off and had to be nudged in order to wake him up.)

After some forty-five minutes of this, the meeting broke up. Following the meeting, about six citizens apologized to the analyst and thanked him for his time. None of these individuals had said a word during the meeting. In fact, the two women were the only people to say anything. The analyst jumped into his university car and made the two and one-half hour trip back to the university in about two hours.

Later in the week, the two women circulated a petition in town that asked the city council to vote "no" on the university development project. The petition stated:

> We the people of _____ and surrounding area, strongly disapprove of the use of city and state tax money for the purposes of establishing a bureaucratic position of community encourager.... _____ people have always done whatever had to be done without a paid Big Brother to harass them. We hereby ask the city council to not approve any funds for this project.

In front of the council, the state elected official stated:

> The university says they need community support, all they really want is a resolution of support from a governing body. They won't care if there are only two people in town that support this stupid little project if they can get the council to sponsor. As far as I am concerned, the university people don't need to be coming to rural _____ and telling us how to do anything.

City council members all voted to reject support for the program. The university withdrew its offer the following week.

You may be wondering, "Who were these two women?" The answer is that one (the state elected official) had a direct financial interest in the mine that supported the town. The analyst later learned that she had threatened to lead boycotts against any business that supported the university development program. The second woman was her best friend and had the reputation of helping the first woman in her political activities.

Economic diversification is a real threat to a resource elite. In this case, these women enjoyed real power and influence in a depressed and isolated community and any attempt to diversify the economy was a real threat to their personal interests. Although a trained political scientist, the analyst was not fully ready for the blunt reality of power politics. Hopefully, his lesson will help future analysts think about the interests and politics of any policy initiative, no matter how small.[2]

---

[2]The analyst survived this episode and has vowed never to return to the mining town. He now finds shelter in the much friendlier confines of a college classroom.

The Area of Study

The Columbia River Basin (CRB) stretches from the crest of the Cascade Mountains in Oregon and Washington to the rugged peaks of the northern Rocky Mountains in Idaho, Montana, Wyoming, Utah, and Nevada. It is very large, including 100 counties in parts of seven states. It also includes 476 places (towns, villages, cities, and census-designated places) whose population is tracked by the U.S. Census. The CRB is the heart of what was, in the early 1800s, the Oregon Country. Native people have occupied the Columbia Basin for about 12,000 years. It is believed the Basin's original inhabitants arrived from northern Asia across the Bering Straits land bridge, finding abundant natural resources.

These harvestable resources of the Columbia basin were also the principal attraction for early European settlers. In addition to fur trappers, early adventurers arrived in the Oregon Country in the 1830s to establish trading posts between the United States and China and/or to attempt commercial development of salmon. In the 1830s and 1840s, missionaries—who wanted to encourage additional migration—demonstrated that family farming was feasible in the region. Taken together, the missions, fur trade, establishment of trading posts, and early attempts at commercial development of salmon resulted in about a thousand settlers from the United States being present in the Oregon Country by the mid-1840s.

Massive migration to the Oregon Country did not begin until the discovery of gold in the northern Rocky Mountains in 1859. The development of "local" economies resulting from mining led to the formation of new territories (Idaho in 1863 and Montana in 1864). Fires that repeatedly razed San Francisco, leading to repeated rebuilding, fueled a boom in timber production in the Northwest. Likewise, the growth of California cities created a market for food that could be produced in the Pacific Northwest and shipped south along the coast. In the late 1800s, canneries packed as many 630,000 cases of salmon per year (at 48 pounds of salmon per case).

Similarly, the arrival of the railroads in the late 1800s made it possible for ranchers to ship cattle and sheep to the major cities of the midwestern and eastern United States. This access to markets, coupled with the ability to acquire, through the Homestead Act, limited areas of meadowland and the better watering places (Penny and Clawson 1962) as a means of controlling the surrounding range lands, led to rapid growth in livestock operations. The land grants given to railroads spurred development in other ways. All of this led, in turn, to demands for water for agricultural, commercial and urban use. Dams on the Columbia, and later the Snake, Rivers were seen as a means to provide flood control and water for agriculture as well as to improve navigation. By the time construction of dams began in the 1930s, the pump-priming effects that they would have for an economy still struggling with the depression were also seen as beneficial.[3]

Contemporary Politics

The rural western United States is viewed by politicians, the public, and the media as an area dominated by ranchers, farmers, miners, and loggers. The idea that the western United States is somehow fundamentally different from the rest of the country

---

[3]"The area of study" description for this case study was written by, and is included courtesy of, Keith Bennett. Mr. Bennett is a retired economic geographer for both the U.S. Department of Interior and the U.S. Forest Service.

remains entrenched in the minds of the public. It is the myth of the frontier, the myth of rugged individualism, and the myth of western independence.[4] In policy terms, at the federal, state, and local levels of government, the myth lives. Politicians, administrators, interest groups, and others view the rural west in terms of the symbols previously described. As a result, public policy is based not on the facts of the rural west but rather on the "myths of the rural west."

In no policy area is this more apparent than in the formulation and implementation of environmental policy and economic development policy. There has been much discussion of the "old west" and the "new west." The old west refers to an economic and political structure tied to natural resources (mining, logging, ranching). The new west refers to an economic structure that is much more diverse (manufacturing, services, retail). The new west has failed to make significant political inroads into much of the rural west. Western senators are overwhelmingly antienvironmental in their voting records. The table below presents the average "League of Conservation" (LCV) voting ratings for senators in the Columbia River Basin (CRB) compared to the rest of the nation. The CRB senators, all of whom come from states that are considered rural, have an average LCV rating that is 17 points lower than the rest of the Senate, on a 100-point scale.

LCV RATINGS

CRB	SENATORS	ALL OTHER SENATORS
Mean	29.50	46.30
S.D.	38.02	39.93
N	14	86

Note. CRB states include Idaho, Montana, Nevada, Oregon, Utah, Washington, and Wyoming.

Note. Senate average for all 100 senators was 45 percent. The higher the score, the stronger the voting record on environmental bills. A score of 0 percent means that a senator never voted with the LCV position. A score of 100 percent means a senator always voted with the LCV position.

Note. The average score for senators from Idaho, Montana, Utah, and Wyoming (i.e., excluding Nevada, Oregon, and Washington) is 9.25 percent

Source: *1998 National Environmental Scorecard.* League of Conservation Voters. http://www.scorecard.lcv.org/senate.cfm

Rural Economic Development and Power Structures

Rural areas experienced depopulation in the first thirty to forty years following World War II. As a result, rural development became a significant policy concern at the federal, state, and local level. Despite the idealistic notion that rural areas, because of their small population bases, are more democratic than urban areas, empirical studies of rural areas suggest that rural communities have monolithic, not pluralistic, power

---

[4]Myths are the influential traditional stories, true or false, that a culture tells about itself and its world. An excellent discussion of the "myth of the west" is found in Foster (1991). Foster demonstrates how the western United States has always been dependent and subsidized by the eastern United States, despite the rhetoric of western independence.

structures. Madison, in *Federalist 10*, actually suggested such a consequence, arguing for an enlarged body politic that would be more difficult for any one faction to
dominate.

Indeed, urban areas often have pluralistic power structures where growth-machine
elements (chamber of commerce, real estate, banking groups) battle for policies that
would enhance the growth of the community. Rural areas, conversely, are often controlled either by progrowth elites or antigrowth elites. The progrowth elites would benefit from increased markets (more houses to sell, more money to be deposited in the
bank, more cars to sell, etc.). There are several case studies that illustrate how rural
communities dominated by such groups grow into larger communities.

Conversely, some rural communities are dominated by antigrowth elites (typically manufacturers) who do not want increased growth because such growth would increase competition for labor and increase wages. In traditionally resource-dependent
communities, the economy is dominated by one business (the timber mill, the mine,
etc.). Typically, resource elites desire economic growth built only around their industry. Timber companies want expanded cutting of the forest, ranchers want expanded use
of public lands for grazing, mining companies want further exploration of lands for mining purposes. These elites generally resist development efforts that are based on services (retail trade, tourism, etc.). This is partly to protect their political power in the
community. (See pages 33–35, "So You Want to Be a Rural Policy Analyst?")

Currently, rural communities in the western United States are experiencing a reversal
in population and economic development groups have sprung up in nearly every rural
community. These development groups typically are dominated by retail, banking, and
real estate interests. They desire economic development strategies that would fundamentally change the economic and political (power) structure of rural communities. As
such, resource-based elites typically oppose such development efforts. Rural development groups are not necessarily promoting development that is compatible with the environment. Tourism development and industrial recruitment can result in economies
that are as detrimental to the environment as timber cutting, mining, and ranching.

Sustainable Development

In recent years, several rural policy experts have promoted the notion of "sustainable
development." This idea is one of the dominant themes in the areas of both global and
domestic environmental politics. Sustainable development is development that carefully
considers the impact of economic activity on the environment. Sustainable development
would not oppose timber cutting in public forests. Instead, the philosophy would argue
that there are limits to growth and that timber cutting must proceed at a pace at which
the forest can regenerate itself. This is good for the forest and in the long run is good
for the economy.

An example of unsustainable development is found in the Island Park area of
Idaho. Beginning in the late 1980s, much of the Targhee Forest was devastated by a bee-
tle infestation. With much of the forest dead, local timber interests were able to cut
trees literally at will. With timber supply at a maximum, the timber mills in St. Anthony
were at maximum employment. The economic impact was enormous as money flowed
through the local economy. Trees, however, are a finite resource (yes, they regrow, but
after clear-cutting it takes many decades for trees to grow large enough for timber). After

about five years, the dead, beetle-infested trees were all cut down. Timber production dropped some 80 percent and jobs were eliminated by the hundreds. The towns of St. Anthony and Ashton became part of what is known as "boom and bust" economies.

Boom and bust economies are part of an unsustainable development philosophy. Sustainable development would have cut the trees down over a long period of twenty to twenty-five years. Employment increases and economic growth would have been smaller but the economy would have been sustainable for a number of years. After twenty to twenty-five years, growth in the forest would have allowed for more sustainable cutting, but since the local economy engaged in unsustainable development, there is now conflict between timber interests and others in the community who see the forest as a resource to be protected.

In recent years, rural researchers have noted changes in the basic economic structure of rural communities. The leading theory espoused by Thomas Michael Power of the University of Montana is that the traditional "economic base" theory of rural communities no longer applies. Economic base theory suggests that every community has natural resources that create an economic base. The economic base then creates a labor demand; hence a community grows or declines with the success of the resource economy. Professor Power rejects this base approach in rural communities. Instead, he (and others) argue that there is evidence that the environment is what attracts individuals into the rural west. Citizens and businesses relocate to Montana and Idaho because they are attracted by the clean air, clean water, and open spaces. Empirical studies of rural Idaho have verified Power's theoretical assertions. Citizens live in rural communities because of its clean environment.

Citizens, however, do not control policymaking in rural areas. Development groups, as previously stated, are generally promoting strategies that are potentially destructive to the environment (one Idaho community vigorously went after a medical incinerator that would have imported medical waste from Utah). Furthermore, resource interests continue to promote unsustainable development of natural resources.

There is conflict between the development groups and resource elites (remember the resource elites do not want growth because of fears of loss of political control). In the meantime, the views of citizens who want a clean environment and a solid economy are ignored. If Power's thesis is correct, current economic development strategies will probably result in harming the environment, which in turn will harm the economy.

The Ambiguity of Economic Composition

There is controversy over the "true" economic composition of the region. Different methods of measuring economic composition lead to different results. For example, looking only at Idaho CRB regions and using the standards of the USDA, the rural Idaho economy is still dominated by natural resources. The USDA Economic Research Service (ERS) uses the straight ratio approach to classify rural counties into six economic types, depending on the percent of total labor and proprietor income derived from a given industry. The types are farming dependent (20 percent or more of total income), mining dependent (15 percent or more of total income), manufacturing dependent (30 percent or more of total income), government dependent (25 percent or more of total income), service dependent (50 percent or more of total income), and nonspecialized (counties not falling into one of the five previous types). The table below presents this economic composition data for Idaho. This approach states that 68 percent of Idaho's counties in the CRB are natural resource dependent.

Economic Composition of 41 Idaho Counties in CRB-USDA Measure

Economic Type	N	Percent
Forest Dependent	9	22%
Mining Dependent	3	7
Government Dependent	4	10
Agriculture Dependent	16	39
Diversified	9	22
Total Resource Dependent	28	68
Total Government Dependent	4	10
Total Diversified	9	22

Bennett and McBeth (1998) use a more sophisticated Ogive Measure (see the Case Appendix on page 41) and classify fifty-five Idaho rural communities instead of counties. Under this approach only 48 percent of Idaho's CRB region is resource dependent (as opposed to 68 percent). The table below presents these results.

Economic Composition of Idaho CRB Using the Ogive Measure and 55 Rural Communities

Economic Type	N	Percent
Somewhat Resource Dependent	6	11%
Moderately Resource Dependent	5	10
Extremely Resource Dependent	15	27
Balanced (Diversified)	13	24
Post-industrial	14	25
Traditional (Government)	2	4
Total Resource Dependent	26	48
Balanced/Post-industrial	27	49
Total Traditional	2	4

The argument over the economic composition of the CRB has important consequences. Resource elites (mining corporations, ranchers, timber corporations) are likely to argue that rural areas are still resource dependent. This dependency is a source of power since, as we have already discussed, most rural politicians still tend to vote for laws that benefit resource industries over environmental concerns. These resource use advocates contend that, despite large-scale urban immigration, environmental regulation, and depressed markets, resources are still the most important economic asset of the region and any attempt to move from resource dependent jobs to service or manufacturing jobs will have devastating economic consequences.[5]

---

[5]For example, a person working in a timber mill may make nearly $20.00 per hour. If that same person lost their timber job and took a service sector job, their hourly wage would drop to around $8.00 an hour.

Conversely, more environmentally inclined advocates use the Ogive Measure because it shows that resource-based economic power is severely declining and not as crucial as it once was. Thus, the lower percentage of communities dependent on resources becomes a political argument for policies that favor different economic strategies and more environmental preservation.

The Ambiguity of Sustainable Development

There is great controversy over what sustainable development is and is not. Once again, in its simplest form the terms refer to carefully considering the long-term environmental impact of economic development activities. It means selectively cutting only parts of the forest instead of clear-cutting. It means restricting grazing rights if these rights might have detrimental environmental consequences like river damage.[6] But in reality, the battle to define "sustainable development" is a political battle.

In recent years there have been several conferences in the rural west that have attempted to build consensus definitions of sustainable development. Instead of consensus, these forums have demonstrated how various interest groups and elites attempt to define sustainable development in a method consistent with their own interests and values. For example, in one conference, a major state commerce official defined sustainable development as "providing a job for every high school graduate in the state each year." This official contended, "Our state graduates 18,000 students each year, so to be sustainable, we must produce 18,000 jobs." Nowhere in this definition is there any mention of the environment.

Many communities have tried to jump on the sustainable development bandwagon. Beginning in the mid-1990s, granting agencies began funding sustainable development activities. Communities throughout the rural west began to "spin" their economic development activities as "sustainable." One such grant proposal included building a multimillion dollar shopping and hotel complex on a historic lava bed. This community called their strategy "sustainable tourism." Unfortunately, they had no plans for how their development strategy would benefit the environment other than claiming that "increased tourism would lessen dependence on ranching and farming and thus would save the environment."

Case Appendix: Methodology of Economic Composition

The methodology used for economic typing is very important. The simplest measure of dependency is industry dominance—the percentage of employment concentrated in the largest sector. According to Power (1994), industry dominance is generally determined using the following equation:

Relative Economic Importance of Industry = Contribution of Industry/Size of the Total Economy

This equation is the one used by the USDA in its characterization of economic dependency.

---

[6]Grazing cattle can severely erode river banks and the silt damages rivers, particularly fish populations. Another major river problem in rural areas is water run-off contaminated by fertilizer and pesticides.

The formula used to determine a community's economic structure with the Ogive Measure is $D = [PELES*(PTC-PPC)]/N^2$ where PELES is the percent of the local economy's employment (or income) concentrated in the most dominant single component; PTC is the proportion of the local economy that comprises all traditional components; PPC is the share of the local economy that comprises all postindustrial components; and N is the number of sectors whose share of jobs is equal to or less than 10 percent of total employment. In that formula, dependence is directly and proportionally related to the degree that the economy is dominated by a single component and inversely related to the number of components present.

Suggested Readings

Alm, Leslie R., and Stephanie L. Witt. 1995. "Environmental Policy in the Intermountain West: The Rural-Urban Linkage." *State and Local Government Review* 27: 17–25.

Bennett, Keith, and Mark K. McBeth. 1998. "Contemporary Western Rural USA Economic Composition: Implications for Environmental Policy and Research." *Environmental Management* 22, no. 3: 371–81.

Chambers, Robert E., and Mark K. McBeth. 1992. "Community Encouragement: Returning to the Basis of Community Development." *Journal of the Community Development Society* 22, no. 1: 20–38.

Flora, Cornelia Butler, Jan L. Flora, Jacqueline D. Spears, Louis E. Swanson, with Mark B. Lapping and Mark L. Weinberg. 1992. "Power in Communities." *Rural Communities: Legacy and Change*. Boulder, CO: Westview Press.

Foster, Richard H. 1991. "The Federal Government and the West." Pp. 77–102 in *Politics and Public Policy in the Contemporary American West*. Edited by Clive Thomas. Albuquerque, NM: University of New Mexico Press.

McBeth, Mark K. 1996. "The Environment v. the Economy: Attitudes of State Rural Development Officials." *Spectrum: The Journal of State Government* 69, no. 1 (winter): 17–25.

McBeth, Mark K. 1995. "Environmental and Economic Development Attitudes: An Empirical Analysis." *Economic Development Quarterly* 9, no. 1: 39–49.

McBeth, Mark K., and Richard H. Foster. 1994. "Rural Environmental Attitudes." *Environmental Management* 18, no. 3: 401–12.

Power, Thomas Michael. 1988. *The Economic Pursuit of Quality*. Armonk, NY: M. E. Sharpe Publishers.

Pulver, Glen C. 1988. "The Changing Economic Scene in Rural America." *The Journal of State Government* 61, no. 1: 3–8.

Templet, Paul H. 1995. "The Positive Relationship between Jobs, the Environment, and the Economy: An Empirical Analysis and Review." *Spectrum: The Journal of State Government* 68, no. 2: 37–49.

Tremblay, Kenneth R., and Riley E. Dunlap. 1978. "Rural Residence and Concern with Environmental Quality: A Replication and Extension." *Rural Sociology* 43, no. 3: 474–91.

Chapter 2

The Rational Public Policy Method

Mini-Cases
"McNamara's Retrospective: Rational Decision Making?"
"The Small Town Health Clinic"

To understand and evaluate the rational model of policy analysis, you need to understand its genesis, history, and evolution, including the critical reaction it spurred. After providing you with that base we explain the rational model and one case (Vietnam) where it is traditionally blamed, perhaps erroneously, for producing poor policy. Next we offer another case that demonstrates how the rational model can help policy analysis and we discuss its relevance in practice. We then provide you with the tools necessary to evaluate this and other models before concluding Chapter 2.

Genesis of the Rational Model

The debates over the U.S. Constitution revolved around notions of decentralization versus centralization and participation versus hierarchy. Alexander Hamilton, who favored a strong executive and decision making by experts, argued that democratic decision making could not be made by emotional citizens. Instead, Hamilton envisioned a democracy where an enlightened few made policy in the best interests of the masses.

Others such as Thomas Jefferson, although he was not in Philadelphia for the Convention, expressed the belief that democracy must be about decentralization and empowerment of the people. In theory, the Constitution created a republican (representative) system of checks and balances and separation of powers that would allow for calm deliberation. In practice, however, the initial reality was that Jefferson's view predominated.

For at least the first hundred years, the United States was a country with a relatively small federal government.[1] The political philosophy of the country was one of **laissez-faire** economics, and the primary role of the government was to protect property and control interstate commerce, and to control and protect U.S. interests in the realm of international trade. The states had the power to maintain the safety, health, welfare, and morals of the people under the Constitution.

Unfortunately, or perhaps inevitably, Jefferson's view of a decentralized government educating citizens in the principles of civic virtue was not realized either. Instead, state and local governments were plagued by patronage, corruption, and generally sloppy decision-making practices.

At the federal level, government had been transformed by the mid-1800s from a **Government by Gentlemen** to a system of patronage and frequent corruption. At the same time, after the Civil War, American society changed fundamentally from an insular agrarian country to an international and urbanized country. For the first time in its history, the country had to deal on a large scale with problems like crime, poverty, pollution, monopolization of industry, economic trade issues, and the growth of technology. These new problems generated the need for complex policy and competent civil servants.

The assassination of President Garfield in July 1881 at Union Station in Washington, D.C., by a disgruntled job seeker named Charles Julius Guiteau, helped spur Congress into creating a merit-based Civil Service by passing the Pendleton Act in 1883. This represented the first attempt to rationalize the bureaucracy and hence to rationalize government decision making. In accordance with Max Weber's dictum of the ideal bureaucracy, the federal bureaucracy was staffed (ideally) by neutral experts who would make decisions not under the influence of the irrationalities of politics but rather through rational, competent, business-like and scientific methods of analysis.[2]

Woodrow Wilson published *The Study of Administration* (1887), making a complex argument that politics and administration should be separated, largely to protect the administrative sphere from partisanship, exploitation, and corruption. The separation of politics and administration is known as the politics/administration dichotomy. Others followed Wilson's path. Goodnow (1900), more focused on this issue than Wilson, attempted to make clear the distinction between politics (legislation that follows the public will) and administration (the execution of that legislation by experts). Gulick (1937) argued that, over time, the decisions of government would become so complex that only expert bureaucracies could make informed and sound public policies.

---

[1]The Constitution was ratified in 1789. Fifty-two years later, in 1841, the total number of civilians working for the federal government was barely over 18,000. Fifty years later, in 1891, the total was still less than 160,000—but four years earlier (1887), Congress had created the Interstate Commerce Commission (ICC), the first regulatory agency. By 1990 the total number of civilian federal employees had peaked at over 3.5 million. Today there are under 3 million. Of course, it is also true that less than one-fifth of all government employees work for the federal government. The largest percentage, by far, work at the local level.

[2]It is generally acknowledged that Max Weber, a German sociologist, developed the classic exposition of bureaucracies. Weber referred to his model as "ideal" but was not implying that it was ideal in the sense of being perfect. Rather, he was merely laying forth the hypothetically pure, or archetypal, form. Clemons thoroughly explains bureaucracy as a principle of organization, considers the power of bureaucracies, and discusses the relevance of bureaucracy to democracy in an essay in Freeman (1997, 175–90).

The theories of "scientific management"—an idea most closely associated with the work of Frederick Winslow Taylor (1911)—also influenced the interpretation of what the relationship should be between politics and administration. Taylor, who pioneered time and motion studies, suggested that there was one best way to organize and accomplish tasks. The scientific practice of administration seemed clearly at odds with the idea of politics.[3]

In 1945 Herbert Simon introduced his classic work *Administrative Behavior*, which sought to overthrow what he termed the *proverbs* of classic public administration theory found in the work of Gulick, Goodnow, and Wilson. Simon wrote that ultimately public administration is about decision making, and that decision making involves some variant of three steps: scanning the environment, developing alternatives, and choosing alternatives.

Despite his emphasis on science instead of proverbs, his ideas actually reinforced the politics/administration dichotomy. Denhardt (1993, 85) writes, "Actually, Simon's conclusions were far less a departure from the mainstream of work in the field than his harsh language implied." Simon replaced the politics/administration dichotomy with the fact/value dichotomy and focused the study of public administration away from ends and on means. Denhardt concludes that Simon's major contribution was his emphasis on logical positivism, which separates facts and values, and his implicit endorsement of "generic" administration which, according to Denhardt, led to a situation where "more and more concern would be focused on means rather than ends, on administrative techniques rather than political principles." In short, Simon argued that decision making as well as decision administration can follow the scientific method.

Simon's rational model of decision making led to a host of rational models that all aimed at eliminating sloppy, uninformed, and "off the top of your head" decision making. Simon believed that we could and should separate "facts" from "values." Simon believed that decisions could be made scientifically using, among other things, computer modeling and mathematical models.[4]

The social sciences have long envied the more prestigious hard sciences—supposedly objective and free from the pollution of politics and culture, data based, and cloaked in the power of numbers. It is clear that the rational model was an attempt to move human decision making away from the emotional and sometimes corrupt world of politics to what was perceived as the calculated, dispassionate, impartial, and honest world of science. In general, this school of thought is called *logical positivism*.

Logical positivism is a scientific system that recognizes only nonmetaphysical and observable phenomena. The impact of this philosophy in many areas, including public policy analysis, has been extensive. It suggests training analysts to be value neutral,

---

[3]Scientific management, or Taylorism as it is sometimes called, is a theory of management closely akin to the idea of the assembly line. The task of management was to determine the most efficient step by step approach to task completion. The worker's task was then to implement that method. Scientific management was a major influence on public organizational and management theory especially as public administration sought to emulate the business approach, in which Taylor's views on efficiency, management, and subordinates was a guiding precept.

[4]In Chapter 3, we will discuss Professor Simon's *satisficing* concept, which recognized very real limits to just how scientifically we make decisions.

to objectively observe facts, and to let these empirical realities tell their own stories. Positivism has dominated policy analysis.

Within this still dominant worldview, the job of the analyst is to specify procedures to gather facts about the world as it is, to present those facts without error or prejudice, to formulate rational policy alternatives, and then to allow the politicians to make purposeful policy that will help solve the policy problem. An ice-cold, impartial review and evaluation of the policy should follow. All of this fits nicely with Gulick's call for informed and sound policy decisions by an expert bureaucracy. Box 2-1 suggests the positivist paradigm is still going strong.

2-1. APSA Newsletter as Evidence

We randomly picked a 1998 APSA Personnel Service Newsletter and examined the front and back of one page in the section where universities were trying to hire public policy professors. (APSA is an abbreviation for American Political Science Association, the national organization for political scientists.)

Among the universities hiring, those that described the approach they wanted provided strong support for our claim that positivism has dominated policy analysis. Consider the following descriptions from seven different universities:

1. The Department is looking for someone to teach courses in the following areas: Quantitative methods, micro-economics, policy evaluation, and analysis....
2. Candidates with interest and ability in quantitative methodologies are especially encouraged to apply.
3. (The same university offering a second position.) Candidates with interest and ability in quantitative methodologies are especially encouraged.
4. We seek candidates with strong methodological skills, who are able to teach policy analysis and policy evaluation. Research interests in ethnic- and minority-related policies are a plus, as are skills in microeconomics.
5. We seek promising scholars committed to policy-oriented research.... Candidates who have strong teaching and research interests in statistics and econometrics, macroeconomics, and public management are especially encouraged to apply.
6. The department seeks demonstrated strength in broad policy-analytic techniques, including quantitative and qualitative methodologies.... A political economy background is of particular interest.
7. (A position overseas.) Especially desirable is a perspective on public policy analysis that balances the traditional economic model of public policy with a more sociological (and qualitative) approach.

The qualitative approach is making some inroads, but it certainly appears the rational model is still the king of the hill. Positivism is still quite at home on the policy analysis range. The seldom heard, discouraging word (for post positivists anyway, who make an argument you will become familiar with in Chapter 6), is that hiring professors with a strong positivist bent will tend to perpetuate itself, and analysts like you will arrive on the scene unprepared for the day-to-day challenges of politics on the job, and for the democratic and ethical challenges you will face in your job.

A Critical Reaction

There were many, most notably Robert Dahl, who were severely critical of the separation of facts from values. This debate is not new; it dates back at least to the time of ancient Greece when Plato suggested rule by philosopher kings who would make rational decisions. This argument disgusted the **Sophists**. The Sophists believed that facts are simply what we are persuaded of (Danziger 1995). In the modern era, some critics argue that the rational model is impossible to achieve. On the other side of the coin, some critics argue against its use on the grounds that, when utilized, it produces poor policy.[5] (We will address the critiques of the rational model much more thoroughly in the next chapter.) A commonly cited, but not necessarily correct, example of the rational model producing poor policy can be found in the history of U.S. involvement in the conflict we call the Vietnam War.

Secretary of Defense Robert S. McNamara served both Presidents Kennedy and Johnson during the Vietnam War. Vietnam was, in fact, often called McNamara's war. Prior to his arrival at the Pentagon, McNamara had been the president of Ford Motor Company. He and his whiz-kid staff tried to bring with them an approach widely known as systems analysis. This management approach to organization and budgeting was based on statistics, defining clear objectives, examining long-term cost and benefit ratios, and systematically monitoring and evaluating progress.[6]

McNamara and the Pentagon were routinely attacked for an over-reliance on quantification—including the infamous use of body counts to prove that our side was winning. Jerome Agel (1972, 76), in an essay indirectly aimed at systems analysis, once took a slap at the legendary Public Broadcasting System show Sesame Street, arguing that "kids are razzle-dazzled with four following three—which is exactly what the guys who gave us Vietnam and pollution know."

The general critique was that, while carefully counting the trees, the managers of our war effort completely missed the forest. It is not too much to claim that the close association of the rational model with the carrying out and defense of U.S. policy in Vietnam was enough to largely discredit this model in the minds of a great many people.

For example, in their history of U.S. foreign policy from 1939 to the mid-1990s, *America Ascendant*, Thomas G. Paterson and J. Garry Clifford (1995) state:

> "Management" became one of the catchwords of the time. They had an inordinate faith in data. When a White House assistant attempted to persuade Secretary of Defense Robert McNamara, the "whiz kid" from Ford Motor, that the Vietnam venture would fail, McNamara shot back: "Where is your data? Give me something I can put in the computer. Don't give me your poetry." Danger lurked in a heavy reliance on quantified information. (151)

---

[5]Note that the idea of separating facts from values is still an often-cited goal of analysts, researchers, and decision makers prior to decision making and is offered as justification for the decision after the fact.

[6]The management technique known as "systems analysis" is not to be confused with the idea of political systems introduced in Chapter 1.

Stanley Karnow (1991), author of the premier text on the Vietnam War writes the following:

> McNamara ... looked at the figures and concluded optimistically after only forty-eight hours in the country that "every quantitative measurement ... shows that we are winning the war." No conflict in history was studied in such detail as it was being waged.... But the statistics somehow failed to convey an accurate picture of the problem, much less offer solutions. For the missing element in the "quantitative measurement" that guided McNamara and other U.S. policymakers was the qualitative dimension that could not easily be recorded.... (271) Approaching the Vietnam challenge like industrial managers.... Washington strategists reckoned that larger investments of men, money and materiel would logically yield larger results. (284)

And Loren Baritz (1985), author of *Backfire* (arguing that American exceptionalism and culture, our technology and our bureaucracy, led inexorably to the disaster of Vietnam) almost got it right when discussing the noise, political, and bureaucratic problems that affected the analysts and blocked rational analysis. But, in the end, he too resorts to the familiar critique, citing a critic who characterized systems analysis as a model that "discourages the study of one's opponents, his language, politics, culture, tactics, and leadership." He sums this up with the observation that "By now, this is a familiar point. Systems analysis reinforced the traditional American assumption that the enemy, or anyone else, is just like us" (241).

Yet we believe that even a shallow reading of McNamara's (1996) own riveting and moving history of the Vietnam war, *In Retrospect*, makes clear that the problem could not have been the following of the rational model, because it was not used.[7] To help you decide whether it was used or not, we will briefly delineate the rational model. We will then present the mini-case "McNamara's Retrospective: Rational Decision Making?"

The Rational Model

The rational model suggests the determination, clarification, weighting, and specification of goals/objectives/values (in other words, of the ends). Next, all plausible, available alternative means should be listed and their likelihood of achieving the ends be carefully scrutinized. All relevant consequences and reactions (including **side-effects**, **spillovers**, and **externalities**) would be forecast. Then methods are to be ranked, and the most appropriate method and implementing agent(s) chosen, to achieve the most desirable outcome. Decisions should then be made about how to measure success, gather feedback, and evaluate the policy. Review would happen as the policy environment is scanned, changes noted, and adjustments (or even policy termination) occur.

All of this is to happen with analysts operating with stony neutrality, robot-like

---

[7]One clearly can though, criticize the attempt to use it, the resources devoted to trying to use it, the tactical policy consequences of the attempt, and its power as an argument justifying a policy that was arguably not rational.

FIGURE 2-1   THE DECISIONAL TEETER-TOTTER: A GRAPHIC PRESENTATION OF THE RATIONAL MODEL

efficiency, and no politics to taint the expert's choices. In essence, the rational model is about the following:

- Gathering sufficient data and expert analysis
- Understanding the problem (including its seriousness, scope, and sociopolitical history)
- Discerning and **operationalizing** goals with clarity and precision so as to make them achievable and prioritized
- Intense and thorough thinking so that the ends drive the selection of the means
- Reasoned choice based on calculation, comparison, and cost-benefit ratios[8] so as to maximize the probability of the effective and efficient attainment of the determined objectives

Figure 2-1 (above) shows a policy decision that hinges on rational analysis. Presumably, an objective expert would have studied the problem and gathered facts to analyze. Goals would have been carefully thought through, articulated, and operationalized, so that the costs and benefits of the alternative means evaluated are relevant to the desired ends. In this example, only two alternatives policies are being weighed, but in the rational model all possible alternatives are considered. If all of this happens accordingly, theoretically the decisional teeter-totter will tilt toward the policy most likely to produce the optimal outcome. Of course, later policy evaluation will review how the policy is working and begin the process all over again.

The mini-case study below quotes exclusively and extensively from McNamara's tale. This verbal, and roughly chronological, quote collage will allow you to decide for yourself if the U.S. pursuit of the Vietnam War was hurt by, or perhaps would have been helped by, use of the rational model.

McNamara's Retrospective: Rational Decision Making?

T he following is excerpted from McNamara's *In Retrospect: The Tragedy and Lessons of Vietnam.*

… the Kennedy and Johnson administrations failed to take an orderly, rational approach to the basic questions underlying Vietnam…. (xxi)

Would Eisenhower ultimately have gone to war in Vietnam as we did? I do not know. What I do know is that we received no thoughtful analysis of the problem and

---

[8]Chapter 8, "The Positivist Toolbox," has a thorough discussion of cost-benefit analysis (CBA).

no pros and cons regarding alternative ways to deal with it. We were left only with the ominous prediction that if Laos were lost, all of Southeast Asia would fall. (37)

Looking back at the record of those meetings, it is clear our analysis was nowhere near adequate. We failed to ask the five most basic questions.... It seems beyond understanding, incredible, that we did not force ourselves to confront such issues head-on. (39)

But it shocks and saddens me today to realize that action which eventually led to the overthrow and murder of Diem began while U.S. officials in both Washington and Saigon remained deeply divided over the wisdom of his removal; no careful examination and evaluation of alternatives to Diem had ever been made by me or others.... Moreover, we allowed the controversy concerning the status of Diem to overshadow de Gaulle's proposal. We never did give it the consideration it deserved. Neutralization.... We discussed the issue only in a cursory way. (55)

Ironically, amid all the debate, we still failed to analyze the pros and cons of withdrawal. (63)

Moreover, Johnson was left with a national security team that, although it remained intact, was deeply split over Vietnam. Its senior members had failed to face up to the basic questions that had confronted first Eisenhower and then Kennedy: Would the loss of South Vietnam pose a threat to U.S. security serious enough to warrant extreme action to prevent it? If so, what kind of action should we take? Should it include the introduction of U.S. air and ground forces? Launching attacks against North Vietnam? Risking war with China? What would be the ultimate cost of such a program in economic, military, political, and human terms? Could it succeed? If the chances were low and the costs were high, were there other courses—such as neutralization or withdrawal—that deserved careful study and debate?

Lyndon Johnson inherited these questions (although they were not presented clearly to him), and he inherited them without answers. They remained unanswered throughout his presidency, and a good many years thereafter. (101)

I have quoted extensively from my memo for two reasons: to show how limited and shallow our analysis and discussion of the alternatives to our existing policy in Vietnam—i.e., neutralization or withdrawal—had been; ... we never carefully debated what U.S. force would ultimately be required, what our chances of success would be, or what the political, military, financial, and human costs would be if we provided it. Indeed, these basic questions went unexamined. (107)

The risk of Chinese escalation and the possibility that air attacks would neither break the will nor decisively reduce the ability of the North to continue supporting the insurgency in the South were recognized. But, because no better alternative appeared to exist, the majority of the group meeting in Saigon favored such attacks! This was the sort of desperate energy that would drive much of our Vietnam policy in the years ahead. Data and analysis showed that air attacks would not work.... (114)

I have reported the Honolulu discussion in some detail for two reasons: (1) we came close to the brink of a major escalation—without adequately examining its consequences or alternatives—but at the last moment drew back.... (122)

The Joint Chiefs agreed we should prepare plans for U.S. air strikes against North Vietnamese targets and the Ho Chi Minh Trail.... Neither then nor later did the chiefs fully assess the probability of achieving these objectives, how long it might take, or what it would cost in lives lost, resources expended, and risks incurred. (152)

In retrospect, it is clear that our presentation to the president was full of holes. We failed to confront several basic questions. (162)

All of us should have anticipated the need for U.S. ground forces when the first combat aircraft went to South Vietnam—but we did not. (175)

Senior army officers and field commanders proved far more realistic about the potential of airpower in Vietnam than did senior air commanders. For their part, senior air force generals and navy admirals were probably equally realistic about the limitations of ground operations. Each could see clearly the weaknesses of the other but was unable to realize their own limitations ... but I did not sense—nor was I made aware of—the important and revealing divisions among them. These divisions were therefore never fully debated at the highest level. They should have been. (176)

Meanwhile, the Joint Chiefs, CINCPAC, Westy, and I all continued to react on a day-to-day basis to the gathering force of events when we—and especially I, as secretary—should have been far more forceful in developing a military strategy and a long-term plan for the force structure to carry it out. (182)

Decisions were deferred as we groped for the least bad road to follow. (191)

Looking back, I clearly erred by not forcing—then or later, in Saigon or Washington—a knock-down, drag-out debate over the loose assumptions, unasked questions, and thin analyses underlying our military strategy in Vietnam. I had spent twenty years as a manager identifying problems and forcing organizations—often against their will—to think deeply and realistically about alternative courses of action and their consequences. I doubt I will ever fully understand why I did not do so here. (203)

The first option I presented—standing pat militarily and accepting a compromise political solution—received no serious attention. Others did not address it, and I did not force the issue. I should have. (223)

Walt Rostow succeeded Mac as national security adviser.... Walt viewed our Vietnam involvement, the conduct of our operations, and the prospects for achieving our political and military objectives there very uncritically. Optimistic by nature, he tended to be skeptical of any report that failed to indicate we were making progress. (235)

Looking back, I deeply regret that I did not force a probing debate about whether it would ever be possible to forge a winning military effort on a foundation of political quicksand. (261)

The differences between me and the chiefs were not hidden, yet they also were not addressed. Why? Most people wish to avoid confrontation.... I speculate that LBJ ... wanted to avoid an open split among his key subordinates, especially during wartime. So he swept our divergence of opinion under the rug. It was a very human reaction. But I regret that he, Dean, and I failed to confront these differences among us and with the chiefs directly and debate them candidly and thoroughly. (264)

We all agreed, but we stood poorly prepared to present proposals that would bring Hanoi to the table. The inadequacy of our thinking on this issue had come through clearly in a conversation I had two weeks before with Averell Harriman ... sadly, neither of us forced a debate within the administration on that fundamental issue, and no such proposal was presented to Hanoi. (300)

Johnson was asking the right questions. But in his poker-playing fashion, he had held back crucial knowledge the Wise Men needed to give fully informed answers ... they had received no written materials ... they did not receive Rear Admiral La

Rocque's devastating report that a military victory in Vietnam was highly unlikely. Nor did they see Dick Helms's analysis that the risk of U.S. engagement were limited and controllable. And, to my disappointment, the president did not disclose to them a memorandum I had given him the day before. (306)

A major cause of the debacle there lay in our failure to establish an organization of top civilian and military officials capable of directing the task. Over and over again, as my story of the decision-making process makes shockingly clear, we failed to address fundamental issues; our failure to identify them was not recognized; and deepseated disagreements among the president's advisers about how to proceed were neither surfaced nor resolved.

As I have suggested, this resulted in part from our failure to organize properly. No senior person in Washington dealt solely with Vietnam. With the president, the secretaries of state and defense, the national security adviser, the chairman of the Joint Chiefs, and their associates dividing their attention over a host of complex and demanding issues, some of our shortcomings—in particular, our failure to debate systematically the most fundamental issues—could have been predicted. (332)

Rationality or Something Else?

We repeat our questions. Was the U.S. pursuit of the Vietnam War hurt by, or would it perhaps have been helped by, the use of the rational model? Is it accurate to characterize decision making at the highest levels of government during the Vietnam War as following the rational model, or is it more accurate to claim that it was not used?

The story of decision making told by Robert McNamara reminds us not of the rational model, but of the model of decision making described in Richard Neustadt and Ernest May's 1986 book, *Thinking in Time*. Neustadt and May argue that policymaking is predominantly marked by the following characteristics, which are antithetical to the rational model:

1. Actors plunging toward action
2. Decision making heavily based upon "fuzzy analogies"
3. The issue's past given inadequate attention
4. Key presumptions not reexamined, or (sometimes) even examined
5. People and organizations seen through the lenses of "stereotyped suppositions"
6. "Little or no effort" made to consider choices in the light of an "historical sequence" (pp. 31–33)

This sort of decision making, what one might call the all-too-human model, not the rational model, is what was exemplified by McNamara's history lesson. The common critique is flawed. There is plenty to fault with the decision-making process during the Vietnam era, but upon examination we do not believe it can credibly be used to discredit the results derived from using the rational model.

But the questions raised by the critics remain. Can rational decision making occur and if it can would it help? Does the rational model offer any help in deciding public problems? The mini-case that follows illustrates the potential usefulness of the rational model in practice.

The Small Town Health Clinic

The community of Portersville (a fictional name) is located in a rural area in an underpopulated state and has a population of 500. The nearest community (population 3,500) is located 60 miles away. Portersville had a small health care clinic that was located in a decaying old drug store on the community's only paved street. In the fall of 1993, the city's building inspector closed the clinic after several bricks fell off the building's facade and onto the sidewalk. In addition, the building's roof was in disrepair and near collapse.

The health care clinic provided primary care to the citizens of Portersville, and without it citizens would have to travel sixty miles for basic immunizations, ankle sprains, flu symptoms, etc. The City decided to pursue the building of a new health care clinic. The decision-making process illustrated the usefulness of the rational model.

The community had received a grant for $10,000 to hire an urban architect to design a building for the clinic. The architect, unaware of rural realities, designed a spacious 4,100-square-foot building complete with the latest medical technology and a helicopter pad. The design stirred interest among the community's health care specialists and among some citizens. The problem was that the architectural design was made without any analysis.

Word of the multi-million-dollar design quickly spread throughout the community. The word around town was that the city leaders were trying to get the community to support a multi-million-dollar clinic that neither the community's tax base nor patient base could support.

City leaders feared the project was doomed. An outside university planner then entered the picture and took the community through a rational planning process. First, a mail survey was sent to all residents asking if they would support a new clinic, and, if so, under what circumstances. Second, focus groups were conducted at a town meeting one month after the survey mailing. From these two events, a problem was neatly defined.

Portersville citizens overwhelmingly wanted a primary (basic) health care clinic but only one that their small community could support without any large increases in taxes. From the survey and focus groups it was determined that the major evaluation criteria was simply cost and effectiveness (would the clinic meet the needs of the citizens?).

From this information, the community leaders brainstormed several alternative structures. Using local building contractors, cost estimates were conducted and the pros and cons of each design discussed. A medical planning expert was brought in and took the community through a "health care utilization" planning process. This process used the community's age profile from census data to show demand for basic medical services.

This formula predicts the annual number of primary care patients based on a community's demographic profile of age and gender. The formula was based on an empirical analysis of primary health utilization by age groups. For Portersville the predicted number of primary care patients per year was 1,339. Using this number, the health care planner then was able to use another formula to subdivide the categories of likely utilization. For example, a certain percentage of the primary care visits would be vaccinations, a certain percentage for flu, and a certain percentage for broken bones, etc. The data calculated here was then multiplied by the fees charged for each type of medical procedure, producing an estimated annual revenue flow for the proposed clinic.

With this revenue data in hand, and knowing what the county could afford to subsidize in the form of taxes, the planner decided that a much less expensive and elaborate structure should be built. It was clear that the proposed 4,100 square foot, $750,000 structure was well beyond the needs and resources of Portersville. This rational and empirical analysis helped the community understand both what Portersville would support financially and the correlated likely demand for services.

The leadership group then engaged in some brainstorming and quickly determined that a simple 2,500-square-foot customized house could easily serve the community's health care needs. So, the two options now on the table were as follows:

Option #1: A 4,100 square foot building at a cost of $750,000

Option #2: A customized house converted into a health clinic at around $100,000 in costs

Health care experts and community physicians all agreed that the customized house would make an effective health clinic. The costs were easily absorbed by the community and by the county's existing tax base.

The case above is a good example of the usefulness of the rational model. The $750,000 building first proposed by the architect could easily have destroyed the community's chances of getting a health care clinic. In retrospect, it is easy to see that the three-quarters of a million dollar building was not going to work in such a small community. But community leaders were excited about the elaborate design and the prospect of having such a facility in their town. Without rational analysis, the attempt to sell this structure to the community would have failed miserably, and if the building had been built it would have been under-utilized—a white elephant sitting mostly unused. The surveys, focus groups, and outside experts helped the community leaders focus on the problem and on a politically acceptable solution. Evaluation criteria were discovered, solutions generated, pros and cons discussed, and eventually a successful decision was generated.

The decision made in the Portersville case resulted in a policy in which problem definition was agreed upon and the policy change was small (the community already had a small clinic). The decision rested in Quadrant One of the 2 x 2 matrix represented in Figure 2-2 (adapted from Braybrooke and Lindblom 1970, 78).

Some scholars suggest that it is only on the rare and relatively less important issues like the Portersville Health Clinic, and unlike Vietnam, where the rational model makes

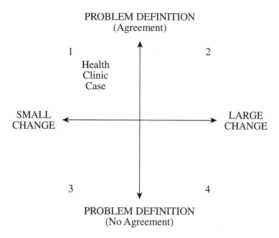

FIGURE 2-2   DECISIONAL TYPES

PROBLEM DEFINITION
(Agreement)

1   2

Health
Clinic
Case

SMALL   LARGE
CHANGE   CHANGE

3   4

PROBLEM DEFINITION
(No Agreement)

sense. (Deciding what to do in Vietnam, especially with all the value conflict over problem definition, places it squarely in Quadrant Four.) For example, Braybrooke and Lindblom (78–79), referring to a rational model of policymaking as synoptic methods, write that "Synoptic methods … are limited to … those happy if limited circumstances in which decisions effect sufficiently small change to make synoptic understanding possible." Braybrooke and Lindblom (39) also quote Herbert Simon stating: "Rational choice will be feasible to the extent that the limited set of factors upon which decision is based corresponds, in nature, to a closed system of variables."

In sum, the charge has been levied that the rational model is of little relevance or value to the policy analyst. Is this true? How does one evaluate models? An explanation of model evaluation follows.

Model Evaluation

The rational model, like almost all models, can best be judged by three criteria. The first criteria is the ability to *accurately describe*. The fancy word scholars use for this is verisimilitude. Verisimilitude translates to the two familiar words it sounds like—very similar. In other words, models are usually expected to describe accurately. A model of a B-52 bomber should look enough like the real thing that you can identify it or at least distinguish it from the model of the space shuttle (even assuming you know no more about airplanes than the authors of this text).

The second criteria is what has been called the ah-hah factor. That is, models should *explain* the world to us, they should help us make sense of what it is they purport to represent.

The idea that geography influences politics is sometimes called geopolitics. In essence, it is a model that claims to help explain why countries behave as they do. If we judge geopolitics by the first two criteria then, its description of how countries behave should match up with the behavior of countries that we have observed historically and in the present; and that explanation, of why they behave this way or that way, should help us understand that behavior, perhaps even prompting us to say "ah-hah, now I get it."

The third criteria is the most difficult one. This criteria states that if models are sound, they ought to be able to *predict*. The model must, like a crystal ball, predict the future as well as the past: 20/20 hindsight is not enough. Imagine a model formed by observing someone tossing a dime fifty times with the dime landing face down each time (in other words producing the result we call tails). The observer suggests that the protruding head image of President Eisenhower creates wind currents that steer the coin so that his face ends up pointed downward, thus producing the constant result of landing with likable Ike upside down.

If this was the first time you had watched such coin tossing involving a dime, it would, in fact, seem to be a model that accurately described; certainly the results you witnessed would not contradict the observer's theory. Moreover, it might seem a reasonable explanation for such an unexpected result. Thus, you might nod your head up and down, saying something profound like uh-huh or yep. However, if you continue to flip the dime, the odds are that within a very short time you would have significant evidence that this particular model—while great at "predicting" the past—was not such a hot prognosticator of the future. Moreover, at this point the verisimilitude of the model would start to fade and you would recognize that, as an explanation, it was not very satisfactory.

Concluding Thoughts

The problem with the rational model is not just that it cannot consistently predict the future, nor that it often fails to describe in a way that matches our observations, nor that it often seems unable to produce the desired ah-hah. Part of the problem is that there are many other (nonrational) models that seem to describe, explain, and predict policy and the policy process as well as or better than the rational model, especially when we are operating outside of Quadrant One.[9]

Chapter 8 is in some ways an appendix to the chapter you just finished. We call Chapter 8 "The Positivist Toolbox." Everyone who opens the toolbox will have access to seven key positivist tools of analysis: sampling and mail surveys, extrapolation and forecasting, measures of central tendency, discounting, deflating money, per-capita analysis, and cost-benefit analysis. The positivist tools are powerful. As befits power tools, these each come with basic operating instructions as well as warnings about misuse.

In Chapter 3 we offer a brief introduction to nonrational models and critique the rational model extensively. Before reading on, however, make sure you understand the rational model because, whatever else one says about the rational model, it can and does play a significant role in policy analysis. Remember to use the criteria for model evaluation as you learn more about the rational approach by studying alternatives to, and critiques of, this important approach.

Key Concepts

decisional teeter-totter (p. 49)

ideal bureaucracy (p. 44)

logical positivism (p. 45)

model evaluation (p. 55)

politics/administration dichotomy (p. 44)

Quadrant One (p. 55)

rational model (p. 48)

scientific management (p. 45)

Glossary Terms

externalities (p. 48)

Government by Gentlemen (p. 44)

laissez-faire (p. 44)

operationalizing (p. 49)

side effects (p. 48)

Sophists (p. 47)

spillovers (p. 48)

References

Agel, Jerome. 1972. *Is Today Tomorrow?* New York: Ballantine Books.

Baritz, Loren. 1985. *Backfire: Vietnam—The Myths That Made Us Fight, the Illusions That Helped Us Lose, the Legacy That Haunts Us Today.* New York: Ballantine Books.

Braybrooke, David, and Charles E. Lindblom. 1970. *A Strategy of Decision.* New York: Free Press.

Clemons, Randy S. 1997. "Bureaucracy." Essay 14 in *Political Concepts: An Introduction,* 2nd ed. Edited by David A. Freeman. Dubuque, IA: Kendall-Hunt Publishing Company.

Danziger, Marie. 1995. "Policy Analysis Postmodernized: Some Political and Pedagogical Ramifications." *Policy Studies Journal* 23, no. 3: 435–50.

Denhardt, Robert B. 1993. *Theories of Public Organization.* Belmont, CA: Wadsworth Publishing.

Goodnow, Frank. 1900. *Policy and Administration.* New York: Macmillan Publishing.

Gulick, Luther. 1937. "Notes on the Theory of Organization." Pp. 1–46 in *Papers on the Science of Administration.* Edited by Luther Gulick and L. Urwick. New York: Institute of Public Administration.

Karnow, Stanley. 1991. *Vietnam: A History.* Revised and updated. New York: Viking Penguin.

McNamara, Robert S., with Brian VanDeMark. 1996. *In Retrospect: The Tragedy and Lessons of Vietnam.* Vintage ed. New York: Vintage Books.

Neustadt, Richard, and Ernest May. 1986. *Thinking in Time.* New York: Free Press.

Paterson, Thomas G., and J. Garry Clifford. 1995. *America Ascendant: U.S. Foreign Relations since 1939.* Lexington, MA: D.C. Heath and Company.

Simon, Herbert A. 1945/1976. *Administrative Behavior: A Study of Decision-Making Processes in Administrative Organization,* 3rd ed. New York: Free Press.

Taylor, Frederick Winslow. 1911. *The Principles of Scientific Management.* New York: W. W. Norton Company. First reprinted 1967 in the Norton Library by arrangement with Harper & Row (original publishers).

Wilson, Woodrow. 1887. "The Study of Administration." *Political Science Quarterly* 2 (June): 197–222.

CHAPTER 3

CRITIQUES OF THE RATIONAL APPROACH

Mini-Case

"Policy Analysis, Ethics, and Role"

It might be comforting to imagine a world where public policy was the result of pure rationality, although for some that thought might also be quite frightening. Further, for policy analysts and public servants, trying to utilize the strengths of a rational process might be a really good idea. In Chapter 5, we will come back to exactly this issue.

Certainly most of us *try* to make our decisions rationally. The fundamental problem with the rational-comprehensive model of decision making is that, as a model, it is flawed in theory and in practice. Although the dominant model in terms of prestige, publishing, and the classroom, the rational model is subject to withering attacks both as a description and as an explanation of the policy process and the resulting policies. Worse, it sets up both unattainable and politically naive guidelines for the public analyst or public manager. In the end, this wonderful-sounding approach is simply not very satisfying to the scholar or the practitioner.

We begin with three models and an axiom from political science that will serve as brief introductory examples of the explanatory power of nonrationality. Following that introduction, the rather extensive arguments that have been marshaled against the rational model will be provided. In general, these arguments fall into three broad categories: intellectual/analytical, political/institutional, and ideological/philosophical.

Examples of the Power of Nonrational Explanations

Do you remember our discussion of pluralism? If you do, then the idea of group theory should sound familiar. Group theory is a model that argues that public policy is the result not of rationality but of the competition between groups that struggle with each other to shape public policy. The size and composition of the "members" of the group, the group's monetary wealth and access to policymakers, and its organizational health are all factors that influence the strength of these groups. For example, groups that are better organized and vote more (like senior citizens) tend to get better policy results than groups that are poorly organized and fail to vote in significant proportions (like college students).

Other models focus on how decisions are made. One of the most common suggests that incrementalism is more common than rationality. Incrementalism, a model first given a thorough defense in 1959 by Charles E. Lindblom's aptly entitled "The Science of Muddling Through", points out that rarely, if ever, are decisions made as if starting from scratch. Rather, decisions are made from the starting base of the current situation and small changes are much more likely results than dramatic or revolutionary changes. An agency with a budget of $1,000,000 is more likely to end up with a budget of $1,100,000 or of $950,000 than it is a budget of $0 or of $10,000,000. This model suggests a conservative bent to decision making that favors the status quo over dramatic, significant, and radical change, no matter which is more rational.

Another model that challenges the idea of rationality is known as elite theory. As explained in Chapter 1, elite theory suggests, at its most basic level, that the few with power in any society or organization (the elites) make decisions. Those decisions may not be rational—for example, they could make decisions that few would call rational, that favor their narrow interests in the short run rather than what is best for the long run (for themselves or for the many).

An axiom of political science—it cannot be called a model—is that attempts to produce a certain policy result will often produce unintended results. Unexpected consequences, even completely opposite the hoped-for result, are not uncommon. Whether due to our limited wisdom, or the free and often stubborn and contradictory will of human beings, producing the policy results we desire is not as easy as the rational model suggests.

A recent example was the attempt to improve the television viewing diet of youth in the United States through the use of ratings that warn parents about sexual or violent material. One reported consequence of this attempt to reduce the amount of "adult" content viewed by youth was an increase in the amount of "adult" content they viewed, as young children and teenagers could now more efficiently find the shows society sought to secure from them. No doubt the appeal of these television programs was increased by the very fact that they were labeled forbidden fruit.

It may be unnecessary, but it seems appropriate nonetheless, to clarify and reiterate the fact that the opposite of the rational model is not necessarily irrationality. Thus, we use the word nonrational quite intentionally. Additionally, we wish to foreshadow several important future topics by defining the term *positivism* (a task we began in the second chapter) and then defining two related, but importantly different, critical reactions to positivism—postpositivism and postmodernism. These approaches will be dealt with extensively in Chapter 6.

3-1. Positivism, Postmodernism, and Postpositivism

Positivism is a body of thought that recognizes only nonmetaphysical facts and ob-servable phenomena. In the social sciences this is illustrated in the work of social researchers that believe there is an objective reality outside of our own experience. Researchers, according to positivism, can come to objective conclusions that are "out-side" of their own minds; conclusions that are fair and neutral. That is, only empirical phenomenon explored with social scientific methods can yield knowledge. This typi-cally means that social scientists should follow a natural science approach to research, including **deductive theory construction** and hypothesis building and testing through the use of statistical techniques. The rational comprehensive model reflects a positivist orientation.

Postmodernism is a body of thought that emerged in the late 1960s, primarily in France. The postmodern movement denies universalism and the metanarratives (grand stories) that shape our self-meaning. Truth and meaning are found only in particular communities of belief or desire. On most issues every individual, operating outside of a metanarrative, has his or her own beliefs, interpretations, and desires. Interpre-tation is the product of a world view constructed through conversation, and thus be-liefs, interpretations, and desires are shared by small discursive communities. According to postmodernism, language plays an important role in metanarratives and thus in constructing our realities. Through the deconstruction of language we can find contradictions and assumptions. However, in its pure form, postmodernism denies the reconstruction of grand narratives and instead believes that human freedom is found only in individual-particularism. In a very real sense, postmodernism is a pe-culiar form of postpositivism.

Postpositivism is a body of thought that began to counter positivism in the social sciences in the 1950s and 1960s. There are several strands of postpositivism including **critical theory**, **symbolic interactionism**, and **phenomenology**. The overarching crit-icism that postpositivism makes of positivism is the latter's reification of the social world as an objective process. Postpositivism tends to use qualitative research method-ologies that include focus groups, field research, and content analysis. Postpositivism still retains some belief in generalization. That is, social scientists can come to gener-al conclusions about how individuals create their world.

Critiques of the Rational Model

I. Intellectual/Analytical

The core critiques offered under this umbrella all relate to the idea that there are signif-icant barriers, many of which are beyond overcoming, that make obtaining the rational-comprehensive ideal unrealistic. These obstacles have to do with the limited intellectual resources that individuals can bring to bear on analysis and with the analytical prob-lems that stem from both the nature of the problems and the nature of the task. The in-tellectual limits and analytical problems are separate but interrelated, and they exacerbate each other.

The Human Problem The intellectual limits can be characterized as "the human problem." In short, humans are neither omnipotent, nor totally rational, nor blessed with unlimited intellectual capabilities. Rather, there are inherent limits on our ability to comprehend, calculate, evaluate, and forecast.

We narrow, simplify, analogize, and separate problems into specialized, solvable chunks—losing valuable information and ignoring interrelatedness. We utilize models, metaphors, analogies, taxonomies, hierarchies, and categories to impose structure on the world, to provide a frame of reference, and to reduce the number of considerations and alternatives we face. Yet, situations are different, the creation of categories is a very subjective process, and we often reify—forgetting that just because we have given something a name or placed it in a certain group doesn't make the abstract real.

Stephen Jay Gould's classic text *The Mismeasure of Man* (1996) makes clear, for example, that the idea "that intelligence can be meaningfully abstracted as a single number capable of ranking all people on a linear scale of intrinsic and unalterable mental worth" (20) is fallacious, dangerous, and an all too common mistake.[1]

Further, humans frequently flee from the freedom of too many choices. Too many choices can overwhelm and paralyze us. We turn to routines and succumb to habits. We reduce that bothersome psychological discomfort called cognitive dissonance by rejecting facts that do not fit our preconceived world-view.

The Mismeasure of Man (Gould) is rich with examples of contorted logic, number finagling, and biased decisions about including and/or excluding evidence rather than changing our presupposed views. For example, Frenchman Paul Broca, who believed that brain size correlated with intelligence, made all sorts of adjustments to explain away evidence that Germans had bigger brains than did the French (including the very real factor of brain size relating strongly to body size). Yet when "miss-measuring" women he felt no need to correct for such factors (not even for body size), stating that since we *know* that women are, on average, not as intelligent as men, then we can conclude that part of the brain size difference is due to body size and part to "her intellectual inferiority" (121–37). Interestingly, while Gould discusses some fraud by researchers, mostly he discovered inadvertent and unconscious bias.

We surrender to wishful thinking and **hubris**, and reject results too catastrophic to swallow as improbable. We stay the course due not to rationality, but to sunk costs and the self-deception that historian Barbara Tuchman called "wooden-headedness". Wooden-headedness "consists in assessing a situation in terms of preconceived fixed notions while ignoring or rejecting any contrary signs. It is acting according to wish while not allowing oneself to be deflected by the facts" (1984, 7).

Some believe that as humans we, like other animals, respond instinctively (not rationally) to perceived territorial threats. Clearly, as humans, there are rationality problems based on physical limitations. People react intuitively, emotionally, and irrationally. Our memories falter, we tire, our intelligence is not unbounded, and we are sometimes aggressive and sometimes docile, but never purely rational.

One of the most famous and powerful critiques of the rational-comprehensive

---

[1] Gould's book is also an excellent refutation of the book *The Bell Curve*.

model came from Herbert Simon, discussed in the previous chapter. Simon stated that this view of humans attributed to them "a preposterously omniscient rationality" with "little discernible relation to the actual or possible behavior of flesh-and-blood human beings" (1976, xxvii).

In other words, although he sought to rationalize decision making, Simon argued that we practice bounded rationality. That is, we do not consider every possible alternative and all attendant consequences, but rather latch on to the first satisfactory solution we come to. He calls this *satisficing*. Humans "*satisfice* because they have not the wits to maximize" (xxviii—emphasis in the original).

He notes that "our perceptions capture only a drastically simplified model of the buzzing, blooming confusion that constitutes the real world" (xxix) and that we ignore "the inter relatedness of all things (so stupefying to thought and action)" and instead rely on "relatively simple rules of thumb that do not make impossible demands upon" our intellectual capacity (xxx).

Analytical Problems   As you can see, the analytical problem of complexity contributes to the human factor problem. Complexity, problems with prediction, problems that relate to the precious commodity of time, and problems that relate to data, represent the key analytical problems.

Today, complexity is widely recognized as a central problem of analysis. Hans Morgenthau, the premier realist scholar who explained how to understand foreign policy, argued that "The first lesson the student of international politics must learn and never forget" is complexity (1993, 22). Problem situations are interdependent and changing rapidly. The problems tackled are often vaguely defined, immense and extremely difficult problems; like poverty, racism, global warming, or teenage pregnancy.

Explaining why they believe that the incremental approach, not the rational approach, dominates in the real world, Braybrooke and Lindblom help characterize complexity. They note that we face "a cluster of interlocked problems with interdependent solutions" (1970, 54) and point out that the problems are often not clear; instead there is just a sense that "something needs to be done" (57). Lofty, vacuous, conflicting, and nondelineated goals, often too broad to operationalize, can leave policy analysts and decision makers without a guiding star. (What is the public interest? How do we define literate? What is safe and affordable housing? How do we measure education?)

The gist of the complexity argument is that the problems we face are so difficult, so undefined, so complicated, and so interrelated that they defy the utopian rational-comprehensive approach. Moreover, the specialization, simplification, and cognitive structures we apply to make the problems fit our intellectual scale, can be liabilities as we try to solve complex problems. The great uncertainty that the chaotic world represents; the vast and tumultuous imaginable potential outcomes, occasionally carrying life and death consequences; the unknowable factors; and the imperfect anticipation of unintended consequences; are all part and parcel of the analytical limitations on prediction and rationality.

Rationality would require that future results be foreseen (i.e., be known accurately). Yet, clearly that is not possible no matter how deeply we peer into our crystal balls.

Indeed, humans often spend inordinate amounts of time and money gathering "facts" in the deluded belief that the decision will make itself if we only can accumulate enough facts, when, in fact, the limits on what is gatherable and comprehensible are severe and the reality is that value questions will still need to be resolved.

The next analytical problem is time. It is common for critics of the rational-comprehensive model to note that time is a very limited and expensive commodity, and this factor is made worse because decisions in the world of the practitioner are usually made in a reactive mode, not a proactive mode. There are also situational, political, and economic time-pressures to make a decision. One major contributor to the time shortage relates back to the "blooming, buzzing confusion" the policymaker faces—namely the problem known as crowding out.

Crowding out relates to the fact that not only is analysis costly in terms of money, but more importantly in terms of time. Faced with an extremely full plate, the decision maker does not have the luxury of devoting all of their, or their organization's, attention to a single problem for the amount of time necessary to conduct a genuinely comprehensive analysis.

Robert L. Hutchings, author of an impressive insider's tale of how the Bush administration handled the end of the Cold War, discusses the way certain decisions were given inadequate attention due to preoccupation with other matters. An example of why this happens is provided below, when he describes the week of the historic first visit to the White House by a Bulgarian president, and how it was "overshadowed by a cavalcade of other events."

> It is worth digressing for a paragraph to enumerate the events of the week of Zhelev's visit, as they illustrate the enormity of President Bush's agenda during the period. After addressing the World Bank/IMF annual meeting and holding a signing ceremony for the transmittal to the Senate of the treaty on German unification, the president departed for New York, where he addressed the World Summit for Children (attended by more than seventy presidents and prime ministers, the largest summit meeting ever held). Later he spoke before thirty-five foreign ministers at a CSCE ministerial (the first ever held on U.S. soil), addressed the UN General Assembly, and held no fewer than 27 separate bilateral meetings with foreign leaders in his suite at the Waldorf Astoria. He ended his New York stay to return to Washington for an historic (and, as it turned out, politically disastrous) 'budget summit' in which he and congressional leaders agreed on 'revenue enhancement' (read: tax increase) measures. Upon returning to Washington, he hosted a Rose Garden reception on October 2 to celebrate German unity and taped a televised message to the German people. Small wonder that Bulgaria got neglected in the shuffle. (1997, 256)

A final time problem (there is not time to go into more) is known as the temporal problem. In short, this is a recognition that policies that work well in the short-term could cause major problems in the long-term. A closely related aspect of this is that it is usually easier to forecast the short-run results than to prognosticate the long-run implications.

The final analytical issue involves data. Data problems can begin with the co-equal dangers of having too little information and its opposite, having too much information. People who have to make decisions often feel as if they simply do not have all the information they need. Incomplete information is a frequent complaint. On the other hand, sorting through mountains of information requires time that is usually not available and the knowledge, familiarity, and wisdom to decide what is most relevant.

Geographical distance from data can make it difficult to evaluate; old data can be incredibly wrong; fudged or manipulated facts can mislead; information can be contrary to other knowledge you hold true; and the data can indicate contradictory trends. There is also the huge difficulty in gathering data and in reliable and valid measurement.

Jeff Leen, *Washington Post* staff writer, recently summarized how little we know about drug use in the United States. In one year a "statistical imputation" problem, according to the GAO, resulted in a report that the "number of habitual cocaine users in the United States had jumped an astounding 29 percent." He tells of a report by "a 79-year-old female respondent whose avowed heroin usage in one survey resulted in a projection of 142,000 heroin users, 20 percent of the national total." In other words, based upon a single response they (extrapolated) assumed that a certain percentage of all senior citizens would also be heroin users. Further, as Leen and others have made clear, there are initial problems in locating, questioning, getting responses from, and getting honest answers from hard-core drug users.

As an example of the problems with data, consider that one of the leading indicators of drug use in the United States comes from the Drug Use Forecasting (DUF) program conducted by the Justice Department. "The DUF program collects voluntary urine samples from 30,000 jail inmates in 23 cities across the country to test for cocaine and other drugs." This information was used by the Senate Judiciary Committee, in 1990, when Chairman Joseph Biden (D-Delaware) extrapolated these results to the general public (Leen 1998, 32–33).

The barriers, obstacles, and limits posed by human factors and analytical problems explain not only why rational analysis is so rarely, if ever, rational; but also why informal, intuitive, and fly-by-the-seat decision making, without extensive analysis or gathering of facts, is so common. Table 3-1 provides a brief summary of the intellectual and analytical critiques of the rational model.

TABLE 3-1   SUMMARY OF THE INTELLECTUAL/ANALYTICAL CRITIQUE

THE HUMAN PROBLEM	There are limits to the human capacity to comprehend, calculate, evaluate, and forecast.
	We utilize models, metaphors, and other techniques to impose structure on the world, to provide a frame of reference, and to reduce considerations.
	We use stories to explain the world, but also exclude other stories.
THE ANALYTICAL PROBLEM	Problems are complex.
	Time is never unlimited.
	We tend to emphasize the short-term at the expense of the long-term
	We have too much data; the data tells us little; we have too little data.

II. Political/Institutional

The word *politics* implies that choices are being made in a conflictual environment involving players with varying levels of power, and often involving the government. The critiques of the rational model central to the political/institutional category can be subsumed under two subcategories: the nature of the political system in the United States, and the nature of organizations and their impact on decision making and policy analysis.

Once again these categories are interrelated and influence each other. The factors discussed as falling under the intellectual/analytical umbrella also interact with these factors, and indeed both are intertwined with the ideological/philosophical factors to be discussed subsequently.

Political System   While there is no political system that could guarantee or deliver rationality, the political system that exists in the United States—for all its strengths—can be cited as proof of, and a contributor to, the nonrationality of the policy process and policy outcomes.[2]

The most commonly proclaimed essential characteristics of the polity known as the United States of America are political pluralism, federalism, fragmentation, legalism, checks and balances, incrementalism, and an element of democracy. These characteristics are also the key parameters of the political system. This is not the place for a discussion of these aspects, but rather for examining the impact these characteristics have for policy.

Policymaking in the United States generally requires consensus building to put majorities together. It is easier to stop policy development than to change or create it. Dramatic and radical change is rare. As Braybrooke and Lindblom explain, "Nonincremental alternatives usually do not lie within the range of choice possible in the society or body politic." (The) "nonincremental (is) often politically irrelevant ... we always begin somewhere, not ad nihilo" (73, 89, 83).

Clear mandates are extremely rare and for any given issue there are multiple stakeholders, with legitimate and conflicting claims (both individuals and groups) who can affect, and are affected by, policy decisions.

As the earlier discussions of group and elite theory suggested, not all players, or policies, are created equal. Nondecisions are common. Nondecisions occur when issues are taken off, or never placed onto, the table. The policy process offers many opportunities for contestants to get into the game, and it should be thought of as a never-ending, ongoing process in which the outcomes of earlier battles are relevant to, but not determinant of, today's policy outcomes.

The result is a messy process where, as John Kingdon (1984/1995) suggests: Policy tends to occur more than be made, and policies that can gain the necessary level of political support, not necessarily the most rational policies, are the ones that win out.

Writing about the making of environmental policy, Dean Mann (1986) powerfully captured the relationship between policy and the political system of the United States

---

[2]This discussion builds on, and makes more specific to the United States, the earlier explanation of political systems in Chapter 1.

that produces it. He described the pattern of policymaking as being marked by "a process of dramatic advances, incomplete movement in the 'right' direction, frequent and partial retrogression, sometimes illogical and contradictory combinations of policies, and often excessive cost...." He concluded this discussion with the observation that this "... should come as no surprise to students of American politics" (4). The political system is based on value conflict, politics, self-interest, the public interest, and coalition building; it is fragmented and tied to political culture, and as a result the making of policy is far from rational.

While a perfect following of the rational model seems impossible, a famous example of a rather rational and comprehensive policy is the energy policy that President Jimmy Carter, a nuclear engineer and policy wonk, devised. However, his political strategy was not nearly as well-developed as his policy plan. While Carter knew the details and substance of the issue, he did not understand the need for stroking egos, striking fear in opponents, or swapping political favors. The Carter White House failed to generate and garner the political support necessary for his policy. It failed to become law not because of its substance, but because of poor politics.[3]

In another political system the head of government might have been able to simply impose his or her policy on their society. Instead, the nature of the political system of the United States has produced an energy policy that much more closely fits the portrait painted of the making of environmental policy by Dean Mann. To the extent that the United States has an energy policy, (and not having a public policy is a policy) it was created through bursts of partial progress and steps backward, and features legislation and goals that contradict other legislation and goals.

The Nature of Organizations   The ideas that we have bundled under the rubric of "the nature of organizations" offer little comfort to anyone wishing to believe in the rational model. As descriptions of large organizations though, they ring true to astute observers and participants.

Organizations and their leaders designate authority and divide work. They train employees and establish organizational objectives. They limit access to information and standardize and fragment the information sought and recorded through, for example, the use of standardized forms. They limit the amount of time, money, and personnel available to work on any given problem. They institute rigid routines and standard operating procedures (SOPs). As Alexander George and others have demonstrated, the way decision makers and organizations are organized to process information is also important (1980). Permanent, professional policy shops and temporary ad hoc committees thrown together to quickly address a crisis are quite likely to produce different advice.

The effect of all the above is to create agency cultures, behavioral patterns, and decisional premises that guide decision makers. So, while in one very real sense individuals decide, in another equally real sense, organizations, or subunits within organizations decide.

---

[3]This paragraph draws upon Charles O. Jones' policy classic, *An Introduction to the Study of Public Policy*, 3rd ed. (1984), 107–8.

A related idea is role theory, and the contention of Miles Law—discussed in Chapter 1—that one's position on any given issue is determined by one's position (where you stand depends on where you sit). This may be stated too deterministically, but it is a crucial insight into decision making and the impact that the particular organization, or branch of an organization, involved in the decision can have. Units and subunits tend to view policies that are good for them and their particular clients as sacred cows; while issues that do not affect them may be ignored or marginalized. All things being equal, the top Air Force brass is undoubtedly less likely than the top Army brass to doubt the efficacy of aerial bombing. As McNamara detailed, this was indeed the case. The effect of role on policy analysis is not an easy one to deal with even for an ethical analyst. Consider briefly the mini-case below.

Policy Analysis, Ethics, and Role

Read the following scenarios and decide what you would do as an analyst. These scenarios raise several important issues, including the following:

- Who does the analyst really work for?
- Can the analyst really be a neutral party?
- Does organizational welfare outweigh honesty?
- Depending on how the analyst handles each case, who are the potential winners and losers? Would you really evaluate yourself out of a job?

Scenario #1: Metroville Urban Renewal

Henry is a policy analyst for the Metroville City Planning Department. His current assignment is to study the effects of ten years of urban development projects sponsored by the department. A significant amount (over two-thirds) of the project has been funded by federal grant funds. Federal guidelines accompanying these funds stipulate that "urban renewal must significantly assist disadvantaged populations." While conducting a stakeholders analysis he discovers that there is wide-scale citizen opposition to the continuation of the renewal work. Foremost, critics contend that the development policy in Metroville has uprooted poor families and small businesses and advantaged upper-middle class families and corporate interests.

The director of the planning department (who is Henry's boss) recently won a national award for his work in Metroville's urban renewal. If Henry reports the citizen's complaints, he might well trigger a federal investigation and Metroville might lose future funding and even face fines for misuse of past grant funds. Henry's position is funded by federal monies and the department has several exciting new urban renewal projects on the front burner. How does Henry handle the information from Metroville's citizen stakeholders?

Scenario #2: The Inner City Drug Program

Malinda is a policy analyst working for a state welfare agency. For the past five years the agency has sponsored antidrug programs in local school districts with inner-city high schools, including East High, which is right across the street from the house where Malinda lived when growing up. The program has been a tremendous political asset for the agency since it allows agency personnel to have considerable interaction with local school districts, parents, and others. Through hard work the agency's programs have increasingly reflected its commitment to a philosophy of community outreach. Malinda is very committed to the program, played a significant role in its planning and implementation, and believes in her heart of hearts that "this program really helps these inner city kids."

She has been charged with conducting an evaluation of the program. Her extensive evaluation has been unable to document any successes in reducing drug use among urban high school students. In fact, her data demonstrates that drug use in the schools in the program has actually increased over the last five years. Despite the data, she still believes in the program and in her work in implementing it. Many in the state legislature would like to see the program cut because they believe the welfare agency—in becoming involved in community outreach—has overstepped its mission. However, the director of the welfare agency recently wrote a report in which she stated, "The inner-city antidrug program is a model of how the agency can positively affect local communities." How does Malinda handle this evaluation task?

Scenario #3: Commercial Fishing in Lakeside

Joe is an analyst for a state commercial fishing agency. The job of the agency is to regulate commercial fishing in the state. Lakeside is a fishing community that has relied extensively on commercial fish catches from a huge lake. Recently the fish population has declined dramatically and fish catches have dropped precipitously to almost nothing. There are certainly not enough fish now to support commercial fishing. Three years ago, against heavy political pressure from environmental groups, Joe's agency implemented new regulations allowing for much larger catches of fish. In addition, the agency at that time allowed (for the first time) commercial and residential development along the shores of the waterfront. Joe's task is to determine the cause of the fish population decline and to write a report on his conclusions.

The governor of the state, the mayor of Lakeside, and the director of the fishing agency have all publicly stated that the cause is simply "mother nature" (increases in water temperature, disease, poor food years, etc.) The director of the agency (who hired him) told Joe directly that "This is a natural problem, but a lot of environmental groups will try to blame our new regulations. Your job is to show that our regulations had nothing to do with the problem." After much serious study, based on a wealth of scientific studies funded by his agency and the state university, Joe concludes that the decline in the fish population is due almost solely to a combination of over-fishing and pollution directly linked to the increased development on the shores of the lake. If he reports this information, his agency will face a major shakeup and the director will almost certainly be fired. The press and the environmental groups will have a field day with this and both the mayor and the governor will suffer politically. What should Joe do?

As you can see in the mini-case on pages 67–68, role tends to complicate things. Imagine a proposal to completely ban alcohol on a campus, including fraternity and sorority houses. Would the attitudes toward such a proposal likely be different, whether you drink or not, if you were one of the following?

1. A student living in an expensive on-campus apartment?
2. An officer in a fraternity?
3. A faculty member?
4. A vendor?
5. An employee of campus security?
6. A member of the administration?
7. An admissions counselor?
8. The college's attorney?

The point is that "policy decisions are made not by abstract people, but by people in particular roles and settings, using particular procedures, and addressing particular audiences" (Stone 1988, 20).

One of the classical bureaucratic pathologies often cited as a natural outcome of large organizations is over-quantification. Over-quantification is an example of confusing the ends and the means.[4] In a similar vein, the expansion, protection, and survival of the organization sometimes become the informal mission of the organization. Just as individuals within organizations occasionally make risky choices for purposes of self-interest, the parochial interests of the organization or subunit may dominate decision making.

In fact, one reality of decision making in the policy realm is the rarity of decisions being made solely by an individual. Accordingly, it is significant that the values of the group can sway independent reason, that the capabilities of decision-making groups vary, and that group think (subordinates fearing to dissent, exclusion of dissenters, pressure to reach consensus and preserve congeniality and cohesion, being impervious to information discordant with the desired outcome) is an ever-present danger in small working groups (Janis 1982).

Thus, the nature of the political system (and the messy, multiple entry, never-ending, incremental policy process it creates), and the nature of organizations and their impact on decision making and policy analysis (represented by ideas like role theory, parochial interests, and group think) do not suggest the rational model as a good description of, or explanation of, the world it models. Yehezkel Dror (cited in Crew 1992, 73–74) characterizes organizational decision making as political, not rational, in the sense that it is marked by the following:

- Bargaining and coalition formulation, in which exchanges of favors, power calculations, personal relations, and similar variables are often the most important factors

---

[4]Body counts during the Vietnam war, an off-shoot of McNamara's systems analysis, are often cited as an example of both over-quantification and confusing ends and means (it was not measuring strategic success, only tactical success).

- The absence of clear operational goals, the presence of little data, and a very limited search for alternatives
- The tendency to follow the line of least resistance; innovation and originality being rather scarce
- The concentration of resources on acute and pressing issues to the neglect of long-term considerations
- A tendency to minimize risks and to achieve defensibility

Dror's description will sound familiar to anyone who has had significant experience dealing with organizations. Table 3-2 is a brief summation of the critique of the rational model focusing on the nature of the political system and the nature of organizations.

III. Ideological/Philosophical

Group theory rests on an accepted truism: Groups compete to shape policy. Elite theory suggested elites might make policy different from the policy that the masses might produce. We begin this section by asking a related and simple question. Does it matter who decides policy?

We assume that your answer is "yes, of course" (or perhaps, more colloquially: "duh"). It would matter, if earlier you agreed with the description of a political system that helps set up policy battles due to its pluralistic nature and its failure to produce clear mandates. Or perhaps you accepted our contention that different institutions, different subunits, and different groups of humans could arrive at very different conclusions. It could be you think some individuals are more likely to be wooden-headed, or more intuitive, or better at sorting through volumes of data. Maybe you agreed with the idea that policy problems and facts are subjective and socially constructed, and that they are not objective, not neutral, and not able to "decide" policy. Certainly, the critiques raised earlier do relate to the critiques found in this new category.

TABLE 3-2   SUMMARY OF THE POLITICAL/INSTITUTIONAL CRITIQUE

THE NATURE OF THE POLITICAL SYSTEM	Policy analysts operate in an American political system characterized by pluralism, federalism, fragmentation, checks and balances, incrementalism, and some degree of democracy.
	The political system encourages incremental instead of comprehensive policy change.
	Clear mandates rarely occur.
	Policy occurs rather than is made.
THE NATURE OF ORGANIZATIONS	Decision makers are guided by SOPs that create distinctive organizational cultures, behavioral patterns, and decision premises.
	Different organizations have different interests in policy determination and this contributes to different problem definitions.
	Organizational self-interest and survival come into play.

However, your answer probably did not depend on reading the earlier sections. The final set of critiques argue vociferously that it obviously matters who decides because of the following:

- We have different belief systems and different visions of the future.
- We value and assume different things.
- We make subjective interpretations and judgment calls.
- Policy decisions commonly create winners and losers.

In other words, fundamentally, policy analysis/policymaking is not about rationality, but about competing ideas, alternative views concerning morality and ethics, differing philosophies, and about who should get stuck with the bads, or get rewarded with goods.

We will examine first the less visible ways that the who? affects the data we utilize, and then the more direct ways analysis and decision making are shaped by subjectivity.

Data and Who? Experts and analysts are not exempt from biases, nor are they capable of being dispassionate; that is why it matters who is in the rooms where decisions are being made. Small group theory also has made it clear that not all participants participate equally and that not all participant's contributions are weighed equally.

On juries, for example, social status irrelevant to the task at hand can influence the course of deliberations (e.g., see Bales 1950). Moreover, personality and personal relations play a large role. Deil Wright, author of a seminal article on intergovernmental relations (IGR) cautioned:

> Strictly speaking ... there are no relations among governments; there are only relations among officials who govern different units. The individual actions and attitudes of public officials are at the core of IGR. (1988, 17)

In his discussions of the Bush administration's failures during the breakup of Yugoslavia, Robert Hutchings points to the rejection a priori of military options due to the opposition of the Department of Defense and the Joint Chiefs *and* due to the fact that the recent success of the Persian Gulf War gave their opinions extra credibility (308). As Deborah A. Stone elaborates:

> The rational ideal not only overstates the purity of information, it also exaggerates the rationality of people in using information.... We are as much influenced by the source of information—the person's race, looks, social manners, reputation, and credentials, or whether the source is a person or some other medium—as by the content. (256)

People are, consciously or not, driven by their belief systems, their ideology. Despite the rational model, we cannot and arguably should not, leave our values behind. Our values, models, expectations, and mental constructs precede and shape our selection of the data we then process. Is the problem an economic problem, a legal problem, a political problem, or not a problem? Our answer, the names or categories we apply, will impact which questions we ask and what information we pay attention to.

3-2. Black Letter Law?

In Karl N. Llewellyn's famous work on the legal system *The Bramble Bush* (1951), he discussed the idea that whether or not a particular legal precedent applies is a subjective judgment that depends on taking a strict or loose view. The "loose" view takes the previous ruling as established law without taking into consideration the context and specific facts of the previous case. The "strict" view would argue that very little of the previous case applies in the here and now of these facts and this case. Llewellyn points out that some precedents are welcome, and others unwelcome, to the various judges and lawyers involved in the current case. Students reading Llewellyn are sometimes surprised to consider the idea that precedent (the legal principle of stare decisis) may be just another subjective tool. Those students are often even more disturbed by the writings of Jerome Frank.

Jerome Frank was a judge, a lawyer, and earlier, a teacher. Consider the following points he made in *Law and the Modern Mind* (1963):

- As the word indicates, the judge in reaching a decision is making a judgment. Judges, despite all their professional training, make decisions just like ordinary human beings.
- Just as we do, judges come to a conclusion and then work backwards to find premises that will justify their conclusion.
- Judges pick and choose which precedents to apply to legitimate their decisions.
- The judgments of judges are shaped by their education, race, class, economic background, political background, and moral prejudices.
- Past experiences with "women, or blond women, or men with beards, or Southerners, or Italians, or Englishmen, or plumbers, or ministers, or college graduates, or Democrats" can color one's judgment.
- Something as minor as a smell, a cough, a yawn, or a gesture can decide what the judge hears, remembers, and believes.
- Studies have been done that show that given the same set of facts, different judges decide cases and consequences differently.
- Judges decide based on hunches and are deceiving themselves if they think they can ever escape who they are.

As Kafka's *The Trial* makes clear, the law is not always what it seems. Jerome Frank's words make clear that judges are very human. Llewellyn makes clear that precedent is not something that removes subjectivity from the legal process. More recently, Jonathan Harr's nonfiction novel (and the movie by the same name it inspired) *A Civil Action* portrayed a biased judge whose prejudices had a huge impact on the outcome of this heart rending case. **Black letter law**? Nah.

Sources: Jerome Frank. 1963. *Law and the Modern Mind*. New York: Anchor Books Edition, as edited in *Before The Law*, 6th ed. 1998. John J. Bonsignore, et al.; Franz Kafka. 1998. *The Trial*. Translated by Breon Mitchell. New York: Schoko Books; Jonathan Harr. 1995. *A Civil Action*. Vintage Books Edition. New York: Random House; Karl Llewellyn. 1951. *The Bramble Bush*. Oceana Press, as edited in *Before The Law*, 6th ed. 1998. John J. Bonsignore, et al.

Even the decision to measure something reflects certain beliefs. If, after the appearance of a campus newspaper article on "blow-off" courses, the university or college you attend suddenly decides to measure how many "A" grades are ending up on the grade rosters its professors are turning in, it suggests that a problem does exist and that the number of As is common enough to count. Deciding only to count As also suggests that As are different enough from B+s to count them separately. It also suggests that the grade inflation "problem" is not at the bottom of the scale (perhaps it is even okay to give social promotions and what used to be known as a Gentlemen's C). It may imply that there are questions about rigor in certain departments, and that grades are an accurate reflection of rigor. It implies that the result of this count may tell us how to resolve the problem—reduce the number of As students receive.[5]

"Who?" also affects the data in a way perhaps best captured by the NIMBY syndrome. NIMBY (Not In My Back Yard) reflects the reality that costs are not diffused equally across society, in a geographical sense. Toxic waste incinerators may be a good idea, if they are located in somebody else's neighborhood. The meaning of the data can even be determined by where the who? live.

The issue of discounting (adjusting the cost-benefit analysis of a program over time to reflect the changing value of constant dollars) is another illustration of the power of the who? to affect data. As with decision trees, discounting plugs a subjective determination by the analyst into a formula and creates the appearance of an objective and mathematical fact. The cost-benefit determination is liable to be entirely different if one uses a discount rate of 5 percent rather than a discount rate of 10 percent. (In Chapter 8, "The Positivist Toolbox," we have a much more substantial explanation of discounting.)

This relates to the last point we will make relating to who?, namely, that different individuals shape, select, and omit the facts used to make decisions. A study by the Urban Institute of studies being done on the recent welfare reform noted that differences in how the population who leave the welfare rolls is defined (e.g., length of time off welfare, the reason they left, if they have stayed off) and how outcomes like employment are specifically measured "have led to employment rate differences of as much as 20 percentage points for the same geographic areas (Brauner and Loprest 1999, 3). Braybrooke and Lindblom (1970) point out that "multiple conflicting values are championed by different participants" (17). It is also worth noting that the way we dress up our statistics, the facts we place at the top of the page, and the adverbs and adjectives we use to qualify our findings are reflections of the ideology and interests of the analyst.

To evaluate the argument above, consider a pledge to increase funding by 100 percent. Visualize graphing a five percent improvement in funding (from the base) over the last four years, a total of 20 percent. We drew the first graph using 10 percent increments that go from 0 to 100 percent and that cover the past three years and the next seven years—for a total of ten years—one year at a time. We labeled the

---

[5]Stone's chapter on numbers, 127–46, provided the general basis for this example.

graph "A Troubled Decade" and wrote the following story about the funding situation below the graph:

> At the current pace of funding increases, it will take 16 more years for funding to reach the target level, and by that time inflation will have significantly discounted the value of the funding.

Next, we used 10 percent increments that go from 90 to 130 percent to compare funding four years ago, two years ago, and now (it assumes the same funding increases and base). We labeled this graph "$$$Wow!" and wrote the following story about the funding situation below the graph:

> Significant progress has been made in achieving the goal of increasing funding. It has already increased 20 percent in less than five years.

Both graphs are shown in Figure 3-1. Remember that both presentations are based on the same set of facts. Do you agree that these packages of facts (graph, headline, and story) tell very different tales? This is another way the who? handling the data can impact policy. And, some policy champions are better at this high stakes game than others.

The use of stirring analogies and seemingly apt metaphors, the categorization of this as clearly not that, and the words we drape around our numbers are all designed to persuade, convince, and sometimes bamboozle others into seeing things our way, or as Stone puts it, to see a situation as one thing rather than another (6). Those able to paint a powerful portrait have an advantage in the policy arena.

FIGURE 3-1   SAME FACTS, TWO VERY DIFFERENT TALES

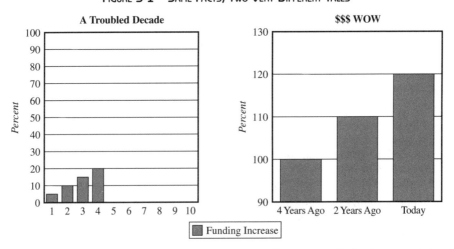

Left: *At the current pace of funding increases, it will take 16 more years for funding to reach the target level, and by that time inflation will have significantly discounted the value of the funding. Right: Significant progress has been made in achieving the goal of increasing funding. It has already increased 20 percent in less than five years.*

Subjectivity's Direct Impact   Even if the facts are presented in a very even-handed way, and even if the facts are consistent rather than contradictory, our differing philosophies and values intervene because the technical question is rarely the key question. Instead, we choose subjectively. We decide the following:

- Whether or not there is a problem
- How significant the problem is
- What the causes of the problem are
- Whether or not it is a public problem
- Whether or not the problem is amenable to a solution
- What solutions will work and are appropriate
- Whether or not the benefits of the solution are worth the costs of the solution
- Whether or not the opportunity costs override the direct cost/benefit equation

Our answers to these questions are based on our beliefs about the nature of human beings, our opinion on the proper role of government, our moral and ethical philosophies, and our interests.

In the policy process we come upon questions that involve making choices where rationality and objectivity simply cannot determine the answer. Answering these questions is about ideology and philosophy, not about rationality and objectivity.

For example, if given a choice between two policies—one where the result is somewhat satisfying and low risk, and one where the result would be significantly better but entails high risk—which one is the rational choice? The answer picked depends on whether or not the decision maker's philosophy is to be a risk taker or a risk minimizer.

In a situation where you must decide who wins and who loses, where the costs or benefits are not distributed equally, or where efficiency is incompatible with **equity**, social justice, or due process, is it possible to come to an objective decision? No. These are questions about your beliefs. Rationality can play a role, and you can try to be as objective as possible, but value questions are decided by your values.

Try to use rationality to answer the following two questions. One, is quantity better than quality? (One colleague of ours feels that way about food, others certainly disagree.) Two, how responsive to organized interests, or to the majority opinion, should government be? Rationality is of little help in determining such answers.

Liberals and conservatives are both generally concerned with the public interest, equity, and efficiency. They disagree, not on the general goal, but on how to get there and the specifics of what it is. In Deborah Stone's classic text on public policy (see Box 3-3 on page 76) she tells a story that drives home this point. The story is about equity and how to divide up a chocolate cake. Besides pointing out that the goal of equity might conflict with other goals (like efficiency), she demonstrates eight perspectives on what would be the equitable way to divide the cake (30–33).

Although it will lose some of its flavor, we will summarize briefly and reduce down to six examples her rich explanation of how people who agree on the goal of equity can still mightily disagree on the definition and path to achievement of that goal.

3-3. The Chocolate Cake in the Classroom Story

1. We could provide equal slices for all students attending. (But is that fair for those who did not know cake would be served?)

2. We could distribute the cake based on group membership instead, giving half the cake to the female students and half to the male students. (But males are only one-third of the students so they will each get more.)

3. We could equalize their overall meals by giving more to those who did not have a chance to eat lunch. (Now the issue is not just how to divide cake, but trying to distribute equity more broadly by increasing the boundary to include external factors.)

4. We could give everyone a fork, line them all up in the back of the room, and let them "go for it." (Resulting in unequal distribution but providing equal starting resources—sort of.)

5. We could cut the cake into eight large pieces and have a lottery to see which students get lucky. (Resulting in unequal distribution but providing everyone with an equal statistical chance.)

6. We could hold an election (one person—one vote) and give the cake to the winning candidate. (Resulting in very unequal distribution, but everyone had an equal vote.)

Subjectivity influences the data we gather, its presentation, the questions we ask, and the answers we arrive at. Gary Orren notes that we are moved to action, and sustained by "a collection of deep commitments and feelings" (cited in Reich 1988, 27). Choosing is about values, not rationality. That is the foremost reason why it matters who decides policy. The following is a brief summary of the ideological and philosophical critiques of the rational model:

- Experts and analysts are not exempt from biases.
- Our values, models, expectations, and constructs precede and shape our selection of the data we then process.
- There is subjectivity in what we decide to measure or decide not to measure.
- We shape, select, and omit facts.

This concludes the chapter's final section, detailing and organizing the extensive and interrelated critiques of the rational-comprehensive model. Underneath the broad category of intellectual/analytical, we discussed the intellectual limits posed by the human factor, as well as the analytical problems stemming from complexity and the problems with prediction, time shortages, and data. In organizing the arguments in the political/institutional category, we utilized two subcategories—the nature of the political system; and the nature of organizations and their impact on decision making and policy—to present the critiques that question the model's descriptive and explanatory power. In the third category, ideological/philosophical, the arguments focused on how the who? affects data and the more obvious ways that subjectivity, not rationality, drives policy.

Concluding Thoughts

The last two chapters have been a thorough introduction to the rational approach. This included: its genesis; a delineation of the rational model; the extensive critiques of the rational model; examples of the power of nonrational explanations; and its use in the case of the small town health clinic (and nonuse in the making of policy for the Vietnam debacle). You have also been supplied with criteria necessary for the evaluation of models. Make sure you don't leave the criteria for model evaluation behind as you progress through the book. What do you think? Has all of this induced you to change your opinion of the rational approach? If you have—who knows—perhaps you will change your mind again before we conclude.

Key Concepts

ethics and role (p. 67)
group think (p. 69)
ideological/philosophical critiques (p. 70)
subjectivity's direct impact (p. 75)
intellectual/analytical critiques (p. 60)
the human problem/the analytical problem (p. 64)
nonrational explanation (p. 58)
organizational decision making (p. 69)
over-quantification (p. 69)
political/institutional critiques (p. 65)
nature of the political system/nature of organizations (p. 69)
positivism, postpositivism, postmodernism (p. 60)

Glossary Terms

black letter law (p. 72)   hubris (p. 61)
critical theory (p. 60)   phenomenology (p. 60)
deductive theory construction (p. 60)   symbolic interactionism (p. 60)
equity (p. 75)

References

Bales, Robert. 1950. *Interaction Process Analysis*. Reading, MA: Addison-Wesley.

Brauner, Sarah, and Pamela Loprest. 1999. *Where Are They Now? What States' Studies of People Who Left Welfare Tell Us*. Published by The Urban Institute. <http://newfederalism.urban.org>

Braybrooke, David, and Charles E. Lindblom. 1970. *A Strategy of Decision*. New York: Free Press.

Crew, Robert E., Jr. 1992. *Politics and Public Management: An Introduction*. St. Paul, MN: West Publishing Company.

George, Alexander. 1980. *Presidential Decisionmaking in Foreign Policy: The Effective Use of Information and Advice*. Boulder, CO: Westview Press.

Gould, Stephen Jay. 1981/1996. *The Mismeasure of Man*. New York: W. W. Norton & Company.

Hutchings, Robert L. 1997. *American Diplomacy and the End of the Cold War: An Insider's Account of U.S. Policy in Europe, 1989–1992.* Baltimore, MD: John Hopkins University Press.

Janis, Irving L. 1982. *Groupthink: Psychological Studies of Policy Decisions and Fiascos.* Boston, MA: Houghton Mifflin.

Jones, Charles O. 1984. *An Introduction to the Study of Public Policy,* 3rd ed. Belmont, CA: Brooks/Cole.

Kingdon, John W. 1984/1995. *Agendas, Alternatives, and Public Policies,* 2nd ed. New York: HarperCollins College Publishers.

Leen, Jeff. 1998. "A Shot in the Dark on Drug Use." *Washington Post,* January 12, National Weekly Edition.

Lindblom, Charles E. 1959. "The Science of Muddling Through." *Public Administration Review* (spring).

Mann, Dean. 1986. "Democratic Politics and Environmental Policy." In *Controversy in Environmental Policy.* Edited by Sheldon Kamieniecki, Robert O'Brien, and Michael Clarke. Albany, NY: State University of New York Press.

Morgenthau, Hans J. Revised by Kenneth W. Thompson. 1948/1993. *Politics Among Nations: The Struggle for Power and Peace,* brief ed. New York: McGraw-Hill, Inc.

Reich, Robert. 1988. *The Power of Public Ideas.* Cambridge, MA: Ballinger.

Simon, Herbert A. 1945/1976. *Administrative Behavior: A Study of Decision-Making Processes in Administrative Organization,* 3rd ed. New York: Free Press.

Stone, Deborah A. 1988. *Policy Paradox and Political Reason.* United States: HarperCollins Publishers.

Tuchman, Barbara W. 1984. *The March of Folly: From Troy to Vietnam.* New York: Ballantine Books.

Wright, Deil. 1988. *Understanding Intergovernmental Relations,* 3rd ed. Pacific Grove, CA: Brooks/Cole Publishing.

CHAPTER 4

THE NONRATIONAL (POLITICAL) APPROACH

Mini-Case

"The Pocatello Prison Siting Story: A Case of Politics"

Case Study

"The Expansion of Human Services in Allegheny County, 1968–95"

This chapter begins by presenting our view of the essence of the policy process and an overview of that process. An important but brief detour on the related topic of the role of individuals in analysis follows, after which you will be walked through the process via a discussion of its component parts. Following that is a story about building a prison, which highlights the political aspect of the policy process. We will then conclude this short but crucial look at the policy process, and ask you to evaluate the nonrational model. What you have learned in the first three chapters, combined with what you will be furnished with in this chapter, provides the background necessary for you to successfully complete the extensive case study that concludes Chapter 4—"The Expansion of Human Services in Allegheny County, 1968–95" (Lewis 1997).

Essence and Overview of the Policy Process

The models, axiom, and extensive critiques in Chapter 3 all point toward the recognition that the policy process is not, at its heart, rational. What then is the essence of the public policy process? We suggest that the answer to the previous question is that the public policy process is essentially a political process.

It is worth reiterating Harold Lasswell's statement that politics is about "who gets what, when and how" (1958). The public policy process is a political process concerned with addressing these same questions. Politics and the public policy process are intricately linked. Not surprisingly, the words *politics* and *policy* both have their origin in the

Greek word *politeia*, a derivative of *polis* (Ayto 1990, 402). In Deborah Stone's conclusion, she states that "Policy analysis is political argument, and vice versa" (1988, 306).

Another important and useful characterization of the fluid and political policy process comes from John Kingdon (1995). Kingdon suggests three separate process streams, which affect each other nonetheless, flowing steadily through society. These "loosely coupled" streams—the problem, policies, and politics streams—occasionally, almost serendipitously, and sometimes with help from skillful work by policy advocates, converge; and in the rush of the confluence, a window of opportunity opens for significant policy development. When they are not in sync, they serve as a constraint rather than an impetus for policy development.

In the *problem stream*, potential catalysts for the perception that problems exist include: policy evaluation reports; budget renewals; comparative data; disasters, crises, and other focusing (or trigger) events; and changed expectations.

Proposals by academicians, elected officials and staffers, think tanks, and other policy analysts and actors generate the *policy proposal stream*. These policy proposals float or sink in a burbling pot of **policy primeval soup** on the basis of their technical feasibility, their cost, the **dominant social paradigm**, and the amount and quality of political opposition or support they set in motion. Some alternatives survive the tides and eddies and are floating about as possibilities to consider; others disappear below the surface, perhaps to wash up on the shores at a later date.

The *politics stream* considers the willingness of our political system's policy institutions to place an issue on the formal agenda. The forces that alter the direction of this stream are perceived changes in opportunities and political mandates. These perceptions are modified as a consequence of election results, perceived changes in the political ambiance, interest group activity, and public opinion polls. In short, the political factors Kingdon considers are "electoral, partisan, and pressure group factors."

The policy process is perhaps best understood by breaking it down into the component parts that occur within the political system, utilizing the policy cycle model. As formulated by Jones (1984), Dye (1984), Anderson (1994), and others, this model posits four to six distinct but interrelated phases. The phases are as follows:

- problem identification/gaining agenda status;
- policy formulation and adoption (including funding);
- policy implementation;
- policy evaluation/adjustment/termination.

"This process is not a sequential, orderly set of stages. It is sometimes defined as being cyclical in nature yet even this definition misses its complexity" (Lewis 1997, 1).

Shortly we will discuss the component parts of the policy process model. As you read about each, note how politics is a constant element. To paraphrase Mao Tse-tung, politics is the water that the policy process swims in. Before we move on, though, we need to pause and take a look both backwards and forwards and discuss the role of individuals in policy analysis.

In Chapters 1 and 2 we discussed how the values of analysts, including their views of power, affect analysis. You read about the role of values in implementation and how Governor Whitman's beliefs are affecting the opportunity to reduce the spread of AIDS in New Jersey. We pointed out the importance of the values of key stakeholders and also that the talents of those using political means could be the difference between whether or not something becomes policy. The subjectivity in the interpretation of data was evident when Robert McNamara mentioned that Walt Rostow was skeptical of any report on Vietnam that indicated anything other than progress. On a related note, the idea that policymakers use fuzzy analogies and rely on their stereotyped suppositions rather than being totally rational was discussed. Yet we also saw the difference a single analyst and his use of the rational method could make in the "Portersville" health clinic case.

Chapter 3 established clearly the importance of the who? making decisions. The fact that some decision makers flee from their cognitive dissonance and that some are more prone to be wooden-headed or intuitive seems equally clear. The effect of inadvertent and unconscious bias on research was obvious. And we saw that the presentation of information, as well as the operationalizing of what is to be measured and the interpretation of the results, is not something that can be ignored. It obviously matters who makes judgment calls—including judges in the legal process. The political skills and willingness to play politics also matters, as it did when President Jimmy Carter failed to sell his rational public policy on energy. In fact, the questions of what is a public problem and of what means to use when we agree on the ends (as exemplified in the chocolate cake story) both point us back to the values of decision makers.

Many of these issues will reappear in this chapter and in the chapters to come. For example, in Chapter 5 the normative views of the analyst regarding power, democracy, who they work for, and what their job really is, are key concerns. We return to the issue of value conflict in terms of problem definition and criteria establishment. You will see your values playing out as you work on a case study involving, of all things, bison. For the sake of brevity, we will just say that Chapters 6, 7, 8, and 9 will also revisit many related concerns.

But, nowhere will the issue of the crucial role of individuals play out as clearly as in the case study, featuring Commissioner Foerster, that follows this chapter. Therefore, before you read about the policy process model, we present "Biography and Policy Analysis" in Box 4-1.

4-1. Biography and Policy Analysis

Imagine that the year is 1939. It is May, and despite the Munich Pact, Hitler has invaded Czechoslovakia. Germany and Russia have not yet signed their secret nonaggression pact that allowed Hitler to invade Poland in September without worrying about fighting a two-front war. You are the top national security policy advisor to the government of a definitely not quite great power located in the southern part of Central Europe. The prime minister wants you to forecast the storyline and outcome of the war that is rapidly evolving into World War II.

Will your analysis be shaped by the excellent psychological profiles you have in your possession of both Adolf Hitler and Joseph Stalin? Will the fact that Neville Chamberlain is still prime minister of England, rather than Winston Churchill, affect your predictions? Will the fact that Franklin Delano Roosevelt (FDR) is president rather than

Herbert Hoover or Calvin Coolidge impact your analysis? We suspect that the answer is yes, yes, and yes.

This is important. National security policy is not made in a vacuum. A major part of decision making in the realm of international relations hinges on trying to predict how other countries will behave. Your country's future, and the lives of your fellow citizens, may depend on your approach to predicting that behavior. In the field of International Relations, analysis is commonly done on three separate levels of analysis.

One level focuses on the nature of the international system (the environment countries operate in—factors external to countries), change, and patterns of interaction. Thus, you would focus on the following:

1. Who the actors are (e.g., countries, the United Nations, NATO, the Organization of African Unity, the World Bank, the International Monetary Fund, the Red Cross, Islam, Zionism)

2. Change in the number of power poles (i.e., how many key players are there? Is it a bipolar world with two superpowers? A tripolar world? A multipolar world?)

3. Patterns of distribution of power assets (e.g., military strength, industrial capacity, natural resources, population, food production, financial resources, technological capabilities, etc.)

4. Behavioral patterns (e.g., arms races, rigid [or fluid] alliances, extensive cultural exchange)

In sum, system-level analysis suggests that countries' policies and their relations will be shaped by the structure of the international system.

Another level of analysis focuses on the nature of the state. The idea here is that states (i.e., countries—like Germany, Japan, Russia, South Africa, Argentina, Mexico, and the United States) are the key actors (it is state-centric) and that they are relatively autonomous. State-level analysis (like geopolitics) tends to view states as logical actors focused on power, resources, and the amoral pursuit of their own national interest … almost as if states themselves decided. This approach is sometimes called the power approach, because a central assumption is that all states seek to preserve or increase their power so that they can pursue their own interests.

One key to behavior that has been extensively written about is the nature of the government of the various countries. In other words, state behavior and relations are believed to be strongly dependent on whether or not the form of government is democracy, theocracy, right-wing dictatorship, or left-wing dictatorship. This is key if, as it has been suggested, democracies don't fight wars with other democracies, you can't appease dictators, totalitarian states are fundamentally different than mere dictatorships, etc.

Thus, state-level analysis concentrates on the size, power, and interests of countries and predicts they will pursue what they believe to be in the national interest.

The third level of analysis, and the one most relevant to our current discussion, focuses on decision making at the level of the individual. In short, it says that Germany and Japan don't decide, people decide. There are three basic approaches that can be subsumed under the rubric of an individual-level approach. We will very briefly touch on two, and then focus on the third.

The first general approach should sound very familiar. It can be called the *humans in organizations* approach. Within this category, scholars and other analysts consider the impact of group behavior factors and roles. Consideration is given to concepts like

SOPs (standard operating procedures), **groupthink**, bargaining, Miles Law (the stand-sit principle), etc. The second general approach can be labeled the *nature of humankind* approach. Herein, two sub-approaches dominate—one focused on psychological factors and the other on biological factors—but neither looks at individuals as individuals. In other words, sociobiology suggests (without much concrete evidence) that humans are genetically predisposed to favor those who are more genetically similar to themselves and that territoriality is also a genetic factor predominant in humans. And this approach believes that human behavior can be predicted based on common psychological traits (e.g., frustration-aggression theory).

The third approach, key for our purposes, is an approach that focuses on *humans as individuals*. Stated simply, the idea is that, since the decision maker's childhood experiences, the tactics used in their first adult success, their ideology, their ego and ambition, and even their habits, suspicions, and physical health will shape their choices, you must study the decision makers to predict accurately.

For example, Harold Lasswell wrote about how private motives (such as hatred of the father) are displaced onto public agendas. Alexander George (drawing upon Lasswell) explained how Woodrow Wilson's drive to power and style of leadership derived from his feelings of inadequacy relating to his father's abusive behavior. James David Barber's classic study of presidential character separated presidents according to a typology based on active or passive approach to their job and the affect toward their job—either negative or positive). Recently, psychobiographies (sometimes psychobabble) of presidential candidates appear even before they are elected.

But none of this is new. One of the oldest clichés about war is the very sound advice the United States failed to heed in Vietnam: that you need to know your enemy. Moreover, in the world of practitioners, it has never become passe (the CIA certainly continues to do research on leaders of other countries). Despite being a very old insight, the importance of biography finds a role in the political world of postpositivist analysis that it could not find under a positivist approach. Perhaps that is one of the key advantages of a postpositivist analyst.

Problem Identification/Gaining Agenda Status

Public policies result after there is a subjective determination that an issue is a public problem. Or, as Fuller and Meyer put it (Chapter 1), the beginning stage is becoming aware of what is perceived as a problem. The work of Hogwood and Gunn (cited in Lester and Stewart 1996, 61–62) strives to explain why some issues never reach agenda status, while others succeed. Issues can succeed by meeting certain necessary criteria. If an issue has "reached crisis proportions and can no longer be ignored," it will be addressed. If the issue has "achieved particularity, that is, it exemplifies and dramatizes a larger issue" it will gain agenda status. Having "an emotive aspect, or receiving media attention because of a human interest angle" helps an issue gain attention. If the issue is seen as having a "wide impact," then it will make it onto the agenda. If the issue raises fundamental "questions about power and legitimacy in society," it will receive attention. Finally, if the issue is viewed as "fashionable," it will work its way onto the agenda.

If a problem is identified and defined in ways that enable it to meet the previously discussed criteria, it will succeed in getting the government to consider acting to respond to the problem. That is what agenda setting is. "Defining the problems of society, and suggesting alternative solutions, is the most important stage of the policymaking process" (Dye, 325).

"In order to define a problem and give evidence to a problem, thus meeting the [previously described] criteria, Deborah Stone, in *Policy Paradox and Political Reason*, presents the subjective nature of the different types of language she claims are used in framing the policy problem. The languages are not objective but are a means to present a version of reality as the framers wish to portray it" (Lewis, 1).

For example, Stone (1988) points out that a "strategic definition" can provide the means to manipulate "the scope of a conflict" by determining who is, and is not, affected (122). Further, she nicely sums up this issue by stating that "There is no such thing as an apolitical definition" (183).

Was the U.S. mission in Grenada an invasion, or a rescue mission? Is social security a welfare program, or money we put away and own? Is a new park entrance fee a tax, or a user fee that will keep taxes down? Were striking air-traffic controllers greedy and a menace to safety, or were they victims of incredible stress concerned for the safety of the public? Are you pro-choice or pro-abortion? Anti-choice or pro-life? Is the issue gun control or gun safety? The words we use to define and describe are indeed both political and powerful.

"The languages used include symbols, numbers, causes, interests, and decisions. Language is used to convey the disparity between the abstract, multi-meaning social goals such as liberty, justice, equity, efficiency, and security, and the current situation.… Added to the types of languages presented by Stone is the language of words. Words are used to tell powerful causal stories that elicit emotive responses and result in action. These causal stories portray a scenario of heroes and villains, good and evil. They provide a version of what is causing the problem and how it can be resolved. The reader should pay attention in the case studies to the many languages used and the intention of the languages" (Lewis, 1).

One example of the power of words relates to the idea of ambiguity. Since government action requires coalitions and consensus, ambiguity can help pull a coalition together (Stone 1988, 123). President Clinton's famous call to "end welfare as we know it" is a great example of an ambiguity that could mean almost anything people wanted it to mean.

Some liberals interpreted it to mean we would finally make available the funds necessary to provide adequate child care, transportation, education and training, and continued help after getting a job—thereby helping people who do want to work. On the other hand, some conservatives interpreted it to mean that government would finally end this costly federal program of handouts, that led to dependency and fraud without requiring able-bodied citizens to work, and that failed to empower states and local jurisdictions to deal creatively with their problems.

This ambiguous campaign slogan helped create the collective action necessary for what proved to be dramatic change. It became the rallying cry that led to the passage of the legislation that replaced AFDC (Aid to Families with Dependent Children) with TANF (Transitional Assistance to Needy Families) and its work requirements, time limits, block grants to the states, and some increases in the support services available during and after the time period of cash assistance.

The political use of language, the portrayal of heroes and villains, and the power of ambiguity are not new. Joseph J. Ellis (1998), author of *American Sphinx: The Character of Thomas Jefferson*, explains Jefferson's well-documented appeal across the political spectrum by describing his genius as being able to "articulate irreconcilable human urges at a sufficiently abstract level to mask their mutual exclusiveness…. The Jefferson magic works because we permit it to function at a rarefied region where real-life choices do not have to be made" (11). Ellis also points to Jefferson's writings prior to the Declaration as having been important primarily for having provided "a story line that brought all American colonists together as innocent victims" (47). Jefferson even wrote a personal history of the United States that cast the Federalists as traitors and corrupt conspirators, himself as innocent, and the revered Washington as being on his side (304–6).

Lewis, evoking Deborah Stone again, wrote that "Stone views problem definition, and subsequently gaining agenda status, as a matter of strategic representation of situations since there are no objective descriptions of a situation" (1). In her own words, Stone put it this way, "Problem definition is strategic because groups, individuals, and government agencies deliberately and consciously design portrayals so as to promote their favored course of action" (106). In sum, people not only fight over ideas, they fight with them, and words are their primary weapon.

The single best work on agenda setting continues to be the Cobb and Elder classic, *Participation in American Politics: The Dynamics of Agenda-Building* (1972). Figure 4-1 on page 86 will graphically walk you through the three-stage model that the following paragraphs will briefly describe.

Stage one witnesses a policy initiator (an individual or group), *possibly interacting* with a *trigger device* (which can also have an affect independent of a policy initiator), to help "create" an issue. Rachel Carson, author of *Silent Spring*, epitomizes the ability of a single individual to be an initiator. Her book, like a disaster at a mine, a plane crash, or—too literally—a shooting at a school, is an example of a trigger device. She told such a powerful story, in such readable words and evocative images, that an issue was born. *Issue creation* is the outcome of stage one.

Stage two involves battles over *issue definition* and *symbol utilization* (both of which determine the perceived *issue dimension* or scope). School shootings by children often not even old enough to drive are frightening tragedies. But what exactly is the issue? Is the problem a permissive society? Is it simply bad individuals? Is it access to guns? Is it the lack of security at schools? Is it the absence of the Ten Commandments on the school walls? Is it the violence endemic to and often celebrated in music, movies, and television?

The portrayed scope of the issue and the effectiveness of the competing campaigns to utilize symbols both affect the amount of emphasis the issue receives in the mass media and the emphasis of the coverage. Issue dimension, symbol utilization, and the *mass media emphasis* determine the *expansion*, or not, of the issue *to a larger public*.

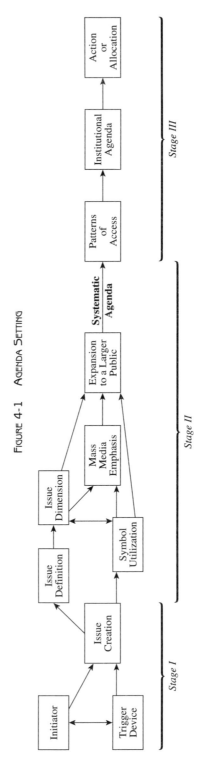

FIGURE 4-1   AGENDA SETTING

Source: Adapted from Roger W. Cobb and Charles D. Elder, *Participation in American Politics*.

Cesar Chavez was successful in expanding the dimensions of how migrant workers in an isolated valley in California were being treated. Part of his success came from the choice of an eagle as the symbol for his organization and the boycott of grapes, and part from his hunger strike and nonviolent marches, which were not only powerful symbols (tying this effort to Gandhi and the larger civil rights issue) but also helped attract the mass media and encouraged sympathetic coverage. If successful, stage two ends with the issue arriving on the *systemic agenda*. In other words, society at large views the issue as important.

Stage three reflects the fact that different *patterns of access* exist. As discussed in Chapter 1, power is not diffused evenly, and not all issues move from the systemic agenda to the *institutional agenda* where government action (in the form of an *action or allocation*) occurs.

Both Carson and Chavez were able to gain powerful governmental supporters who had access to the institutional agenda. Of course, that allocation or action may be merely symbolic, or it may be minor, or it could even be counterproductive and exacerbate the problem. *Silent Spring* and its author altered our thoughts on the environment and the laws of the land. One example was the banning of the use of the pesticide DDT. Chavez's greatest government victory may have been keeping the government from interfering effectively on the side of the growers. To not act is also a policy.

Policy Formulation, Adoption, and Funding

Policy formulation, but not necessarily policy adoption or adequate funding, does occur if an issue achieves agenda status. As Kingdon makes clear, "it is not enough that there is a problem, even quite a pressing problem.... The subject with an 'available alternative' is the one that rises on the agenda, crowding out equally worthy subjects that do not have a viable, worked-out proposal attached.... The availability of a viable alternative is not a sufficient condition for a high position on a decision agenda.... But the chances for a problem to rise on the governmental agenda increase if a solution is attached to the problem (142–43).

Policy formulation involves analyzing policy goals and means, and the creation or identification of explicit alternative action recommendations to resolve, or at least ameliorate, the public problem identified. Remember, Fuller and Myers called this Stage II—policy determination. Although "Policy is designed to remedy the problem and possibly prevent its reoccurrence. Policy rarely solves a problem. (That is not to say that policy does not result in positive change.) The problem is continually redefined, new ideas emerge, competing interests battle for control, and unintended consequences result from the policy implemented. These factors and others lead to the formulation of new policy; thus policymaking is a never ending process" (Lewis, 2).

Policy formulation, as suggested earlier, typically proceeds incrementally, offering changes at the margins by narrowing and limiting the analytical task. As before, using Stone's language, "strategically crafted argument" is used to convince others that a certain course of action should be pursued. Not all options are considered viable or given serious consideration. Due to the values of society, the need for legitimation of policy for and from majority approval, and the goals of the policymakers, only certain programs or policies will be considered.

"The importance of adequate funding to carry out policy may be obvious and yet it cannot be overstated. At the county level, as at the state level, unfunded mandates have presented policymakers and decision makers with difficult dilemmas. In the case study you will soon read, a great deal of effort went into securing funds during Commissioner Foerster's tenure in order to be able implement policy. There were multiple 'legitimate' interests competing for a pot of money too small to go around" (Lewis, 2).

Policy Implementation

Policy implementation refers to organizational activities directed toward the carrying out of an adopted policy by administrative bureaucracies at the national, state, and local levels. Administrators must make decisions about the allocation of the organization's financial and human resources to effect the policy.

Policy implementation begins once a policy has been "legitimized through a legislative act or a mandate from an official with the authority to set policy. Policy formulation and legitimization does not ensure that funds will be allocated to meet policy objectives. Nor does it ensure that action will be taken in an attempt to remedy or prevent the problem. For example, governors who do not favor the National Voter Registration Act (commonly called the motor voter act) are using a variety of strategies to hinder its implementation" (Lewis, 2).

"The stratagems range from simply not instructing eligibility workers to offer to register clients, or telling them to do so only if they have time (and this when cost-cutting is raising worker caseloads sharply), or not supplying the agencies with voter registration forms" (Piven and Cloward 1996, 39–42). As Fuller and Myers indicated, value conflict does not end after a policy is chosen.

There is often great discrepancy between the intentions of a policy and how it is carried out. This is in part due to how the policy is interpreted, the views and expertise of the administrators, and, of key importance, the funding that is actually appropriated (Lewis, 2). The administrative skills of the organizational leaders involved is another key factor, as are the attitudes of the lower level bureaucrats toward the new policy. Political battles through, for example, the use of the media, word wars, definitional struggles, and court cases continue through this aspect of the policy process. Increasingly, the political nature of implementation has become a known reality.

Policy Evaluation, Adjustment, Termination

As the costs and benefits, the winners and losers, and the unintended and unforeseen consequences become clear, the policy creates new demands and supports. The policy process is not only nonlinear, it is continuous, and feedback is inevitable, with or without formal assessment. Especially if policy is implemented without strong legitimization, and even if it possesses it, one common reaction to policy is a political backlash and calls for adjustment.

"Theoretically, policy evaluation takes place as a means to discover the outcomes of the policy. (Did the policy bring about the intended results?) Realistically, as Charles O. Jones states, 'policy evaluation tends to be program justification' (1984, 35). Just as there are no objective descriptions of a situation, nor are there purely objective descriptions of how well the policy is implemented or how well it met its objectives. Ideally, program evaluation also leads to policy change leading to program improvement. Though not the norm, policy evaluation does at times lead to policy termination" (Lewis, 2–3).

So far we have discussed the political essence of the policy process and examined it as a whole. We then examined its component parts and discovered four distinct but interrelated phases of that process. The four phases of the policy cycle model are: problem identification/gaining agenda status; policy formulation and adoption (including funding); policy implementation; and policy evaluation/adjustment/termination. The mini-case that follows will revisit the issues of pluralism, group theory, and elitism as it illustrates the political, rather than rational, aspect of policy formation.

The Pocatello Prison Siting Story: A Case of Politics

What is the best method of deciding where to put a new state prison? Many individuals, desiring rational policy, would argue that a new prison site should be located wherever the study of cost-benefit ratios suggests is most favorable. Perhaps proximity to the major population center of the state would be a major criteria. Or perhaps that would increase the cost of the land too much. A community with an available workforce trained in corrections and law enforcement would tip the scales of rationality. It might even be beneficial to build onto an existing prison rather than build an entirely new prison to reduce duplication of costs. For example, if you expanded an existing prison you would still need only one warden.

However, the process of siting a prison is less a rational process than a political one. Siting is based on state and local politics, on coalition building, on political compromise, on partisan concerns, and on political skill. This is not necessarily to argue that the political path is worse, nor that rationality plays no role. This is the real life story of the siting of a prison in Idaho in the early 1990s. As you read on, notice how rarely rational analysis is the story and how often the story is about political power plays.

In January 1990, the State of Idaho announced it would build a new women's prison. The State Board of Corrections then announced that it would receive bids from Idaho communities. In the first chapter we discussed the fact that in the face of value conflict, government "authoritatively allocates values"—in other words, government decides who gets the goods. To some individuals, a prison may not seem like something a community would want. But to communities reeling from a nearly decade-long recession that had plagued many communities throughout Idaho, a prison is a source of stable (recession-proof) jobs. A new prison pumps additional money into a community's economy through construction and maintenance, and the buying of supplies, as well as the jobs provided.

The City of Pocatello, Bannock County, had been hit extremely hard by the state's economic downturn in the 1980s. Pocatello had lost hundreds of railroad jobs due to deregulation; a major regional trucking firm relocated to Salt Lake City, Utah; a major mining equipment corporation left town after the downturn in the mining industry; and deregulation also led to the loss of major airline service. The retail sector was hit hard and major grocery chains and department stores closed shop and left town. Pocatello's population dropped from 46,000 in 1980 to as low as 40,000 by the mid-1980s. The locals repeated the not very funny joke told in other such distressed communities: "Will the last person leaving *Pocatello* please turn out the lights." It was eagerly decided to put in a bid for the prison.

The principles of pluralism and the very political nature of policy formation, discussed earlier in the text, are clearly illustrated in this tale. Prodevelopment interest groups in Pocatello (e.g., the Chamber of Commerce, the Real Estate Association, the Banker's Association) all strongly supported the city's bid for the prison. These groups all publicly announced their support and worked behind the scene by writing letters of support to the Board of Corrections and using political means to gain the support of Bannock County's state elected officials and of the governor of Idaho.

Early in the process, interest group support was strong because the prison offered **concentrated benefits** (to the community's financial, construction, and real estate sectors) and **diffused costs**. The interest groups wove stories that portrayed the benefits as diffused through a multiplier/ripple effect in the economy that would benefit the community's economy as a whole. In light of this persuasion, clear benefits and vague costs, and given the past economic downturn in Pocatello, citizen opposition to the project was virtually nonexistent. The pro-prison interest group support was highly visible, advancing their position, calling radio talk shows, and writing letters to the newspaper. They gained strong support, indeed sponsorship, from the city's elected officials. They developed a specific plan to bring the prison to Pocatello.

The issue quickly found status on the policy agenda of the Pocatello City Council. They quickly searched for available sites for the proposed prison. With strong interest group support and little, if any, opposition, the city announced that the proposed site for the new prison would be in north Pocatello/Chubbuck. (Chubbuck is a small bedroom community adjacent to Pocatello.) Called the Philbin Road site, this area was, at the time, largely agricultural and there was plenty of room to build a new correctional facility.

The Philbin Road site had one significant flaw, however. The site, located in the north Pocatello valley, was in a U.S. Environmental Protection Agency (EPA) "non-attainment" zone. The EPA designates air quality as either meeting minimum air quality standards (an attainment zone) or as not meeting these standards. Opposition arose quickly from outside the community as the American Civil Liberties Union (ACLU) immediately threatened a lawsuit against Idaho if the Philbin Road site was selected. The threatened lawsuit's basis was an assertion that forcing prisoners to live in an area with significant amounts of air pollution would violate the prisoner's rights to a healthy quality of life.

The State of Idaho, fearing that a lawsuit could delay the siting of the prison for years and increase costs significantly, removed Pocatello from the list of potential locations. The State had, in fact, apparently decided that the state capitol of Boise would receive the siting of the prison. Boise, home of the men's correctional facility, seemed a natural choice, having a highly trained and available correctional work force. Boise, and then Mayor Dirk Kempthorne (R) were 1980s success stories. While Pocatello was suffering, Boise grew tremendously. An economic success, it became a major regional city.

Following the announcement that Boise would be the new prison site, and consistent with pluralism's notion of an open system, the ACLU exited the political system since their interest had been satisfied. However, the progrowth interest groups in Pocatello began their political maneuvering. Under pressure from the pro-prison interest groups, the state legislative coalition from Pocatello traveled to Boise to meet with Governor Cecil Andrus and to cash in a **political I.O.U.**

A political I.O.U. is what we described in the first chapter as a political trade. Cashing in a political I.O.U. occurs when a group of elected officials, interest groups, or elites demand (and subsequently receive) a political favor in return for past political favors or allegiances. Governor Andrus, a Democrat in a heavily Republican state, always relied heavily on Pocatello for votes and support. The Democratic majority in Pocatello had been instrumental in Andrus' very narrow 1986 gubernatorial victory over the Republican challenger David Leroy. The state legislative delegation had faithfully supported Andrus and had literally helped deliver votes in 1986. In fact, the governor's political debts went back to his previous victories in 1970 and 1974. The legislative delegation reminded Andrus of Pocatello's role in his political victories and asked the governor to reconsider Pocatello as a prison site.

At this point, Boise Mayor Dirk Kempthorne announced that since Pocatello had been hit so hard by economic downturn, he would support the new prison being built there rather than in Boise. The mayor's announcement shocked casual observers of politics, but astute students of Idaho's politics knew that Kempthorne was gearing up for a race for an open U.S. Senate seat in 1992 and that his generosity at this time primed him for support from Pocatello.

Meanwhile, Governor Andrus, understanding the political necessity of trading and rewarding, agreed to put political pressure on the Idaho Board of Corrections to "reconsider" Pocatello. Within a week the Board announced that Pocatello was back in the running for the prison. Remember that politics occurs at multiple levels. In other words, the pro-prison interest groups in Pocatello used politics on the state legislators who, in turn, used politics on the governor who, we must assume, used politics on the Board of Corrections.

The City of Pocatello, not only back in the ball game, but the apparent political winner, announced that a new location for the prison had been chosen. Virtually all that had to be accomplished was the "simple" implementation of building the new prison in Pocatello. Yet, as we shall see, politics does not stop at the implementation stage. The new site, Cusick Creek, was on Pocatello's west bench. Consistent with the principles of pluralism, group theory, and the politics of policy formation, an established interest group entered the political system and one new interest group formed to enter the fray.

The established interest group was the local chapter of the Sierra Club. This environmental interest group was resisting the siting of the prison in the Cusick Creek area because the location was in a federally protected watershed that was supposed to be protected from development. The prison violated the group's interests, namely protecting the local environment from damaging development. The Sierra Club mobilized political opposition to the new location and most notably used their political ties to the local congressional representative, U.S. House of Representatives member Richard Stallings (D-Idaho). Stallings, no longer in Congress, had been somewhat supportive of Idaho environmentalists. Because the new prison site would require congressional action to de-list it as a federal watershed, the Sierra Club's connection to Stallings was a strong political resource.

The new interest group that formed was also opposed to the new site. Calling themselves "Citizens to Save the Westbench" this group of local residents feared that the new prison would harm their quality of life and lower their property values. Many of these residents expressed safety concerns and concerns over noise, traffic, and light coming from the prison. This group stressed to the local media that while the prison might benefit the community as a whole, the costs were being dumped unfairly on the citizens in the neighborhood surrounding the new site.

Fearing that the opposition might result in Pocatello once again losing the project, elected officials and pro-prison interest groups engaged in the very political art of compromise. This is also consistent with the principles of pluralism.

First, to remove opposition from the local chapter of the Sierra Club, the city government and prison-backers agreed to zone the rest of Cusick Creek as a 'non-development zone" and to improve hiking trails in the area. The Sierra Club was willing to accept some loss of land in exchange for the assurance of future protection for the rest of the area. The Sierra Club even helped the city receive access to House member Stallings and the city requested and received permission from the federal government to use the land.

Second, to stop the opposition from the Citizens to Save the Westbench group, the City of Pocatello agreed to move the prison location some 500–1,000 yards further up the mountain and away from the neighborhood. Officials also gave assurances to the residents that the new prison would not be an eyesore (no big spotlights, no barbed wire, no tower guards). The neighborhood group, satisfied with the compromise and realizing that they were out of political resources, removed their objections. The path was now clear for the prison to be built in Pocatello.

The mini-case above illustrates the principles of pluralism, group theory and elitism, as well as the political process of policy formation. Is this a good or bad process for American government? The answer depends upon your political values. Many would argue that the siting was simply the result of powerful elites looking out for their own best political interests. Certainly the mayor and the Pocatello City Council received considerable praise and support from local interest groups who wanted the prison. Certainly the governor benefited by maintaining his popularity and support in Pocatello and Boise. Mayor Kempthorne benefited by gaining support for his successful run for the U.S. Senate in 1992. Therefore, some would argue that only these elites benefited from the prison siting in Pocatello. Maybe the rational location for the prison would have been Boise.

There are, though, other interpretations. The hard-hit Pocatello benefited by having new employment and new state money pumped into its economy. The university in Pocatello benefited by getting new programs in corrections. The local neighbors were able to retain the quiet nature of their neighborhood and the Sierra Club traded some development for a promise of no future development on the Westbench. The political nature of policy formation does not necessarily produce bad policy.

Concluding Thoughts

It is our conclusion that the essence of the policy process is much more political than it is rational. Note that the claim is not that rationality and positivist methods have no role to play. This chapter introduced you to the policy process model and its components. When seen as a continuation of the previous chapter, debating the role of rational methods in the policy process, you have been thoroughly exposed to an alternative way to envision how policy analysis and policymaking occurs.

Before moving to the case study, pause again and consider the three criteria for evaluating models presented in Chapter 2. Relate them to both the rational and nonrational policy models. What do you think now?

Key Concepts

agenda setting (p. 85)
agenda status criteria (p. 83)
biography and policy analysis (p. 81)
essence of the policy process (p. 79)
Kingdon's policy process streams (p. 80)
policy cycle model (p. 80)
policy evaluation, adjustment, termination (p. 88)
policy formulation, adoption, and funding (p. 87)
policy implementation (p. 88)
political I.O.U. (p. 91)
problem identification/gaining agenda status (p. 83)
role of individuals (p. 81)
strategic definition/strategically crafted argument (p. 84)

Glossary Terms

concentrated benefits (p. 90)
diffused costs (p. 90)
dominant social paradigm (p. 80)

groupthink (p. 83)
policy primeval soup (p. 80)
political I.O.U. (p. 91)

References

Anderson, James. 1994. *Public Policymaking,* 2nd ed. Boston, MA: Houghton Mifflin.
Ayto, John. 1990. *Dictionary of Word Origins.* New York: Little, Brown and Company.
Carson, Rachel. 1962. *Silent Spring.* Boston, MA: Houghton Mifflin.

Cobb, Roger W., and Charles D. Elder. 1972. *Participation in American Politics: The Dynamics of Agenda-Building*. Boston, MA: Allyn and Bacon.

Dye, Thomas R. 1972/1984. *Understanding Public Policy*, 5th ed. Englewood Cliffs, NJ: Prentice Hall, Inc.

Ellis, Joseph J. 1996/1998. *American Sphinx: The Character of Thomas Jefferson*, vintage ed. New York: Random House.

Fuller, Richard C., and Richard R. Myers. 1941. "The Conflict of Values and the Stages of a Social Problem." Reprinted in Ch. 4 of *The Study of Social Problems*, 4th ed. Edited by Earl Rubington and Martin S. Weinberg. New York/Oxford: Oxford University Press, 1989.

Jones, Charles O. 1984. *An Introduction to the Study of Public Policy*, 3rd ed. Monterey, CA: Brooks/Cole Publishing Company.

Kingdon, John W. 1984/1995. *Agendas, Alternatives, and Public Policies*, 2nd ed. New York: HarperCollins College Publishers.

Lasswell, Harold D. 1958. *Politics: Who Gets What, When, How*. New York: Meridian Books.

Lester, James P., and Joseph Stewart Jr. 1996. *Public Policy: An Evolutionary Approach*. St. Paul, MN: West Publishing.

Lewis, Laura. 1997. *The Expansion of Human Services in Allegheny County 1968–95: A Case Study*. Original Version. Pittsburgh, PA: Institute of Politics, University of Pittsburgh.

Piven, Francis Fox, and Richard A. Cloward. 1996. "Northern Bourbons: A Preliminary Report on the National Voter Registration Act," *PS Political Science and Politics* 29, no. 1 (March).

Reich, Robert. 1988. *The Power of Public Ideas*. Cambridge, MA: Ballinger.

Stone, Deborah A. 1988. *Policy Paradox and Political Reason*. New York: HarperCollins Publishers.

The Expansion of Human Services in Allegheny County, 1968–95

Preface and Introduction

This case study* examines the policymaking process behind the change in the quantity and quality of services that took place in the human service arena in Allegheny County during the nearly three decades Thomas Foerster served as commissioner. It thus can serve effectively as a vehicle for evaluating the ideas presented earlier in the chapter (as well as ideas presented in the first three chapters).

Allegheny County, with a population of 1.3 million people, covers 731 square miles, including Pittsburgh—second largest city in Pennsylvania. Allegheny County does not have Home Rule and therefore has no inherent right to self govern beyond what the state constitution and the General Assembly grant. Three county commissioners serve as the executive and legislative officers of the county, which has 130 municipalities, each with its own government structure. The Second Class County Code adopted by the state legislature in 1933 and modified in 1955 guides Allegheny County government. The functions delegated to the county under this code include: "the management of county finances and property; maintenance of care for dependent children, indigent aged and prisoners; and construction and maintenance of county buildings, roads and bridges." Additionally, numerous legislative acts passed in the 1960s and beyond have either granted permission, or mandated, that county government perform

*Reprinted (with minor changes) by the permission of the author, Laura Lewis. Originally published by the Institute of Politics, University of Pittsburgh, 1997.

services "in the fields of public protection, land protection, land and air transportation, higher education, health, recreation and public welfare."[1]

Simultaneously, the explanation of the policy process that preceded this case study serves as a framework from which to analyze how and why the growth in human services took place from 1968–95. Also to be analyzed is the role that one individual, Commissioner Tom Foerster, played. Although he is often credited as a catalyst for the increase in human services offered, the commissioner is the first to say he is not the one who deserves the credit.[2]

This case study is based on interviews with the commissioner and individuals who worked within his administration, as well as program administrators from outside the administration who solicited and received support from Commissioner Foerster. In addition to interviews, documents and newspaper articles were utilized to gather information. The examination of human services during Commissioner Foerster's tenure should result in increasing students' understanding of the complex, ambiguous, messy, never ending process of public policy, and demonstrate that as Deborah Stone aptly states, "the making of public policy is strategically crafted argument."[3]

Laura Lewis, the author of this case study, did not intend to provide all sides of the story, or a complete story; she provides one perspective and questions designed to help students examine the policymaking process. Despite attempts to remain a neutral outsider in the writing of this case, the author has made her biases evident. One cannot ever remain totally neutral.

Section I discusses who Thomas Foerster is and what subsequently led to his philosophy on the proper role of county government and to his leadership style. Included will be an exploration of the commissioner's early life experiences, his heroes, and their impact on his philosophy. As the key player focused on, Commissioner Foerster provides an opportunity to evaluate the ability of an individual to make a difference in the policy process. Did he impact human service policy and if so how? The stage is then set for a brief examination of how and why policy developed and evolved in the human service arena from 1968–95. The role of the commissioner and other key players is an integral part of understanding this evolution. At the end of the Section I conclusion several discussion questions are presented.

In Section II, three key human services policy initiatives (Kane Regional Centers, Family Support Centers and Mental Health/Mental Retardation) serve as separate case studies to explore in greater depth the complex, ambiguous, and political nature of policymaking. After a conclusion to the entire section discussion questions are again offered.

There is also a brief postscript to the overall case study, offered after the discussion questions as the Case Appendix.

Case Assignment

First, if you are not 100 percent clear on any of the nine following topics, then they need to be reviewed. For maximum learning they need to be kept in mind as you read both sections of the case study. They also serve as guides to the case's discussion questions. Those discussion questions, listed at the end of both Section I and Section II, may be utilized as a case assignment. Your professor may assign some or all of them to you as individuals, or as work teams. Obviously, she or he may also choose to add questions that relate to other materials covered in your course. Overall, the focus should be on what the case says about the critiques of the rational model; the description of the essence of the public policy process as being political; and the policy process model.

1. Kingdon's three streams model of the policy process:
   a. the problem stream
   b. the policy proposal stream
   c. the politics stream
2. Problem identification and gaining agenda status:
   a. How do initiatives gain agenda status?
   b. What are the criteria presented by Lester and Stewart?
   c. The Cobb and Elder model on agenda setting has three stages: Stage I—initiators, trigger devices, and issue creation; Stage II—issue definition, symbol utilization, issue dimension, mass media emphasis, expansion to a larger public, systemic agenda; and Stage III—patterns of access, institutional agenda, action, or allocation.
3. Policy formulation, adoption, and funding. Review why issues "make it" and the impact of funding on policy implementation.
4. Funding, legitimization, administrative support, the values of the implementers, and ongoing political battles affect implementation.
5. The fourth component is policy evaluation, adjustment, and sometimes, termination.
6. Words and (causal) stories are used to define, identify, and persuade.
7. What role do individual's play in the policy process?
8. The use of biography in policy analysis.
9. Politics plays a large role in policy decisions, as seen in the prison siting case.

Section I. Thomas Foerster: Influences on, and of, an Influential Public Servant

Individuals who worked in the human service arena during Commissioner Foerster's tenure refer to him as having a relentless resolve, a deep commitment to creating a level playing field for all, an ability to make things happen, humility, compassion, and wisdom. He is said to put people first and wants to assure that opportunity is available to all.[1]

This glowing rhetoric becomes meaningful when we look at the substantive policy initiatives he supported and promoted for the aged, for children, for families, for person with disabilities, and for veterans. The initiatives demonstrate the definitional meaning the commissioner has given to the goals of equality, liberty, efficiency, and equity.[2] His understanding of what these goals mean, and the role of government in promoting them, began to be determined early in his life.

Commissioner Foerster's Youth and His Beginnings in Politics

Thomas Foerster was born in 1928 to the late J. Edward Foerster and Eleanor (Heyl) Foerster. He spent twelve years attending Catholic schools and recalls vividly the message he heard each school day: "We were put on earth to help one another." He asks, "How can this message not influence anyone who hears it over and over for twelve years?" The message seemed to influence the commissioner as it undergirds his philosophy on the role of government. That is, he believes all levels of government should attempt to create opportunity for all and assure that the needs of vulnerable populations are met.

A significant childhood recollection that imprinted the importance of government intervention was a public works program during the Great Depression. He recalls his mother, and other women in his neighborhood, serving sandwiches they had prepared to Work Progress Administration (WPA) workers who were laying Belgian blocks on their street. The WPA was able to provide jobs for some "and took some of that desperateness away," but others not so lucky would go door to door asking for work in order to get a meal. "People were not just asking for a free handout, they were willing, and preferred to work for it." His mother always provided food for those who asked. At meal time during the warm months she would make sandwiches and set them on the porch where she knew they would quickly be consumed by those unable to secure employment. The compassion his mother and others showed had a lasting effect on him as did his observation of the great benefits of public works jobs. He speaks of the "picnic shelters, the buildings, the underground structure that was built with water lines, dams, all things built by WPA workers, that we are enjoying today." He saw that the opportunity to work was all that these men wanted and if the private sector could not provide the jobs the public sector must. "You have to preserve people's dignity and willingness to work."

The WPA also had a profound effect on Foerster's father. It was one of the factors that led his father to change his political views. His father was a conservative Republican who originally was "not enthralled with President Roosevelt and his programs." Foerster recalls that his father did not hold back from preaching about his anti-Roosevelt views, but after watching the WPA workers pave his street he "really bought into the program." Although his father was not without work himself during the Depression, he was forced to retire on a small pension, leading to financial worries and a recognition of the need for government assistance with things such as health care.

Sports have been a big part of Commissioner Foerster's life since childhood. He had coaches who supported him, who he could talk to, not just about sports but about life. He played that same role for many young athletes during the 23 years that he spent coaching different football, baseball, and basketball teams. Through his coaching efforts he carried out his philosophy that we are here to help each other. Football is his most loved sport and he coached numerous teams over the years. He started coaching grade school football as a hobby while a high school student. After his own practice was over he would go help the younger players. He recalls his first years in the Pennsylvania General Assembly when during the middle of the week he would hurry home at night to his coaching job. He had to give up his coaching position when he was appointed chair of the Clean Streams Committee.

Coaching taught Foerster lessons about the low-income African Americans who lived in his community and played on his football teams. He recalls the "great nobility" of the parents of these kids who would put cardboard in their sneakers because the soles were worn out. "It makes you realize how difficult some people have it. The parents just couldn't find jobs. I got to know the parents, as they would come down and help with the chores at the field. They would never complain but willingly volunteered their time. They were well motivated and loved their kids." Foerster recalls the "determination and hard work these young athletes exhibited." He saw their great potential. Opportunity is all he believed they needed, and they would do the rest.

Another significant part of Foerster's childhood were the many days his family spent at Conneaut Lake, where today the commissioner still spends many hours when possible. The natural outgrowth of his love of the outdoors led to his emergence as a conservationist which in turn sparked his political career in his early twenties. A family friend, Bill Guckert, who was Secretary of the area Sportsman's League, educated Foerster about the damage to the environment caused by strip mining and Foerster says he became determined to do something about it. He took up the cause of fighting pollution long before it was popular to do so.

In 1954, encouraged by Guckert, he ran for a legislative position to put someone in the General Assembly who would speak in support of environmental causes. The backing of the Sportsman's League, and fish and game wardens was not sufficient for this young, unendorsed, Democratic candidate to win the primary. These "groups" were the main supporters of environmental issues in the early fifties. They were upset and wanted something done about strip mining but did not have money, or the power of numbers, behind them. The loss in 1954 did not dampen Foerster's spirit and he ran again in 1956 as the endorsed Democratic candidate. Again he lost.

In 1958 he was victorious, winning by a narrow margin of 342 votes out of the 19,000 cast in his legislative district. He attributes the win largely to two factors. There were a number of women and one in particular, Anna May Wagner, who organized coffee klatches for him as a means to 'drum up' support. Also, the sons of many of these women, who were athletes whom he was coaching, worked at the polls for Foerster. It was a Republican district at the time, and Tom Foerster ran on a single issue—to protect the environment; so these grassroots efforts were vital. "Those women got me elected."

The focus of Representative Foerster's efforts in his early days in the General Assembly was to make good on two promises; which he did. With Leonard Staisey, who was a state senator at the time, he advocated and promoted the passage of the Clean Streams Act and the Strip Mining Act. Staisey and Foerster later ran together for county commissioner where Staisey served with Foerster for eight years, and was Chair of the Board.

During Foerster's tenure as a state legislator, he also sponsored the initial legislation that led to the Community College Act and he was a strong advocate of the Public Defender Act, the Mental Health Mental Retardation Act of 1963 and the Child Welfare Act of 1963. As commissioner, he then put this legislation into action.

The Commissioner's Heroes

Commissioner Foerster's heroes, those people who he has great admiration and respect for, share many positive characteristics, but the one that stands out is that he saw them all as "putting people first." They include his father and mother, mentioned earlier, and local, state, and national politicians.

On the national level the commissioner points to Senator Hubert H. Humphrey (D-Minnesota) as being "the real hero in my book." "Hubert Humphrey really lived and breathed what he preached. He really cared about people and expressed that in many, many different ways." The commissioner's belief in a job for everyone was espoused by Humphrey. "We don't have people who enunciate that philosophy that he (Humphrey) enunciated and Kennedy enunciated and even Lyndon Johnson."

The commissioner got to know Humphrey personally. He worked to get Humphrey elected President in 1968 and recalls the large crowd he was able to get at the Boat House in North Park after being told it's too isolated out there and nobody would show. He recalls how Humphrey just loved everybody in Pittsburgh and in Allegheny County. He expressed admiration for the way Humphrey could "make a speech at the drop of a hat and be consistent and say what he had to say, full employment, jobs for everybody, education for all. He had the philosophy, it was the Vietnam War that ruined him." Like many others, the commissioner thinks that if the 1968 election had been a week later, or if Humphrey would have taken a stronger stance against the war once he became a presidential candidate, he would have defeated Richard Nixon.

In addition, Presidents Truman and Kennedy are named by the commissioner as political leaders who "put people first." He refers to Kennedy as a great speech maker. "He had the same philosophy as Humphrey but could express it better than anyone else and in shorter period of time."

Moving to the state and local level, David Lawrence, powerful boss mayor of Pittsburgh, is another person the commissioner holds in high esteem. He got to know Lawrence through football. When Foerster was in high school, Lawrence came to meet the players in the dressing room after a game. A few years later Foerster was coaching a team of 14–17 year old boys and sent Lawrence, then the mayor of Pittsburgh, a letter inviting him to help in the dedication of lights to the football field. Lawrence started coming to the annual football banquets, a practice he continued even after being elected Governor. Foerster observed Lawrence in this and other settings and admired how well he related to everyone.

The ability to relate to people so well is what enabled Lawrence to leave behind many accomplishments, according to Foerster. "He was a great community person, and people in the communities loved him." As a mayor and governor, "he was one of the most skilled persons I ever met." As Governor he had a great knack for bringing together the Democratic House and Republican Senate, noted Foerster. In Foerster's eyes he was someone who could gain support from the corporate establishment, business establishment and colleges and universities by getting past party affiliation. For example, he enlisted "friendly cooperation" from industrialists in order to combat the air pollution in Pittsburgh caused by the smoke. "Lawrence led the way to get the first smoke ordinance passed. He also led the way to cleaning up the rivers. Raw sewage as well as industrial waste was being dumped into the rivers until 1960." The commissioner goes on to point out that "it was under Lawrence that money was made available for the first time for local libraries like The Carnegie. It may not seem like a big thing but that was a big step forward for state government to move in that field. It was also under Lawrence that the Pittsburgh public schools received a special subsidy as part of a new formula giving the public schools more state money."

Commissioner Foerster credits Lawrence with starting the whole concept of private/public partnership in Allegheny County. He states that "for those of us who grew up in the Lawrence era, it became natural to work with our universities, to work with the corporate establishment, the Allegheny Conference and the Chamber of Commerce. That was inbred in us. You cannot get much done unless you have that kind of partnership with the community." While the commissioner stresses the good that Lawrence accomplished with the aforementioned examples, and mentions "his whole Renaissance Program," Tom does not overlook what he calls the "big failure in those days." He is referring to the people hurt when housing in areas where low-income people lived was demolished and those people displaced.

Leonard Staisey was not only a good friend, he was also one of Foerster's heroes. Staisey was on the conservation team with Foerster and toured a strip mine with him in preparation for passage of a Strip Mine Bill and a Clean Streams Bill. Staisey was badly sight impaired and could see only shadows. Foerster recalls how Staisey "would keep hold of my elbow as we'd walk up and down these strip pits, some of them were 100 feet, 150 feet down a hill. When the strip mine patrol was over, Leonard could really describe what he had seen. He was a remarkable person. When we finally passed the second piece of legislation it was amended in the Senate and sent out for reprinting. The printer left out some crucial, vital language. As Leonard described it, it was like leaving the 'Our Father' out of the Lord's prayer; it made it meaningless. Now here he is, a blind Senator, he had somebody read bills to him; he was the only one who caught the error in the bill. Leonard was so sharp and had a photographic memory."

It was much more than Staisey's razor sharp memory, ability to learn voices, and remarkable ability to compensate for his vision loss that impressed the commissioner. "Leonard Staisey left his footprints behind all over the county in many different ways," states the commissioner. "I think Leonard Staisey can really be attributed with being the father of the whole Mental Health/Mental Retardation system (MH/MR) in the county. He took that under his wing. Leonard saw to it that the MH/MR programs were not centralized under one big bureaucracy that was too far removed from those it served." The county was divided up into nine catchment areas with a base center unit run by the nonprofit and hospital sectors located in each area. Each base-service unit works autonomously and obtains input from its own citizens advisory board. The intent is to ensure that relying on the expertise of the private sector agencies and citizen participation will help to ensure that the program responds effectively. Each base-service unit must submit an annual plan to the county and receives a yearly appropriation from the county.

The commissioner says that Leonard Staisey taught him a lot about human services and people with disabilities. "More people with disabilities had a job opportunity because of Leonard Staisey. Leonard devised a job bank program that was given to the Veteran's Administration to run. It was a relatively small program in which people who had some type of disability because of the Vietnam War were provided with jobs where they acquired a skill."

Such influential people and experiences led the commissioner to become an individual with a strong sense of what he takes for granted as being "right." He believes that "what is right is that people use government as an avenue to create a society with jobs for everybody; to create a society where vulnerable populations, not able to provide adequately for themselves, are provided with services that allow them to live with dignity; to create a society where everyone has the opportunity to an education and job training; to create a society where we show that we value families by focusing on preventative measures rather than reacting to situations that arise when families are not given the support they need; and to create a society where the environment is protected and future generations will have clean air and water."

Tom Foerster was a public servant who started with a single cause, the environment, but who greatly expanded the issues he advocated, making human services a key priority. Lessons he learned by observing the WPA, community people reaching out to feed hungry, desperate people, and political leaders ardently striving to create a level playing field and provide for the elderly, children, and persons with disabilities, all impacted the development of Thomas Foerster and his philosophy regarding the role of government.

Commissioner Foerster's Philosophy on the Role of County Government

Politics is an art where players use strategically crafted argument to persuade others to adopt their policy ideas as the best solution for the distribution and redistribution of goods. Agreement is difficult because of the conflicting ideas people have as to the meaning of basic democratic goals such as liberty, equity, efficiency and equality.[3] One's interpretation of these goals, and beliefs as to how best to attain these goals, determines one's philosophy as to the role government should play in "who gets what, when and how."[4]

As a key political player, how Commissioner Foerster defined these goals and subsequently the policy he supported to arrive at the goals were driven by his world view. The ambiguity of these goals and the difficulty of achieving all goals simultaneously gave rise to the dilemmas he faced in the political arena. For example, let us assume that to create a level playing field, and promote a degree of equality, government funded job training, or some formal post-secondary education, is necessary. Can this be provided without any cost to the liberty of the individuals who will be taxed in order to provide this service? Deborah A. Stone adequately summarizes the dilemmas faced by policymakers with the statement, that "most policy issues can be seen as a question of whether and how the 'haves' should give to the 'have nots.'" The policy issues Stone refers to are redistributive policies which account for most policies in the human service arena. Stone goes on to say that "where one stands on issues of distribution is determined not so much by the specifics of any particular issue as by a more general world view."[5]

The world view held by the commissioner closely parallels that of liberalism. Liberalism holds that the use of government intervention to promote equality and equity is necessary and just. Liberalism views liberty as freedom from dire necessity, which means that there must be a degree of equity, a basic minimal amount of money, and/or goods, that each person is assured. Thus redistribution is necessary to assure fair shares of basic resources such as food and shelter. By assuring basic resources to those who fall through the cracks and by opening up opportunity for all, the entire society benefits and thus individuals. For the liberal, community interests supersede a pure focus on individuals interests.[6]

The conservative view holds that liberty is freedom to dispose of one's resources as one wishes and that government intervention infringes on this liberty. Thus redistribution policy interferes with liberty and takes away individualism. Government becomes a menace and misuses its power. The private sector, not the public sector, is the realm in which social welfare needs must be addressed, especially since most public programs simply cost money but do not solve problems.[7]

The commissioner is not comfortable with being labeled as a liberal. "Trying to categorize someone is all wrong. I don't think it's liberal or conservative to try to create a level playing field; it just make common sense." (He emphasizes that if you can prove to a conservative that a program is cost-effective she or he will buy it.) There are definite dangers in defining anyone as liberal or conservative. To try to fit anyone into boundaries is misleading since one's political philosophy falls along a continuum. The commissioner daily wears a red rose pin on the lapel of his jacket to symbolize his pro-life stance. Another example is that while the commissioner is not a strict fiscal conservative in the sense of opposing all government intervention, he sees himself as fiscally conservative in his attitude toward the county's budget. The operating budget always balanced and the rule he had for the capital budget was that the county could issue no more debt that could be retired over a five year period. Fund raising drives within the corporate community were undertaken in order to comply with this rule. One exception to the rule was made when the county was required to build a new jail by the state.

Commissioner Foerster believes that county government has a vital role to play in enhancing the life of all those who live in Allegheny County. Government's role should not be limited to waste management, engineering and construction of bridges and roads, jails, and parks and recreation. He believes the county government's role is much larger. "Government's key responsibility is making sure that all people are provided with opportunity. All problems circle around lack of opportunity." Another important responsibility of government, according to Commissioner Foerster, is "to speak for those and provide services for those who cannot do so themselves." This includes elderly, people with disabilities, children and infants. He has promoted and supported programs that provide services to exactly these people. He has been a force for programs helping the unborn, infants, children, elderly, and persons with disabilities.

The commissioner exemplifies a person who makes decisions as if he has memorized and been convinced by a mental exercise that John Rawls describes in his book, *A Theory of Justice*. Rawls asks us to imagine ourselves designing rules for a society in which we would live without knowing what our social position would be. We could just as likely be on on the "bottom" as on the "top." Rawls argument is that our knowledge of our talents and probable social status stands in the way of creating fair rules.[8] As we will see, the human service policies the commissioner supported indicate he was able to imagine what he would want the rules to be regardless of social position. As he said "you have to be able to put yourself in the shoes of others." He sought to create fair rules for all, rules that assured that all have opportunity, rules that assured that all have basic necessities and are able to live with a sense of dignity. "When it comes to people, there ought to be some concepts that everybody believes in—here is what we're going to do and here is how we're going to address this problem. Here's how we're going to take care of people and problems effectively. We don't do that. Maybe that's just Utopia and we'll never get that until some day when everybody is in Heaven and the big plan starts to take shape."

Underlying his philosophy is an optimistic view of human nature that is also associated with those who adhere to liberalism. Conservatives tend to believe in a Theory

X view of work as something disliked. Financial need is virtually the sole motivation to work and people must be forced to work and accept responsibility through coercion, control, and threatened punishment. The more liberal view, a Theory Y view, is of people naturally wanting and willing to work and accept responsibility, just needing the opportunity to apply their self-motivation.[9] Foerster has stated he has never met a man or woman on welfare who did not want to work instead of collecting welfare. That is not to say he believes there are not unmotivated poor people, but he does not equate the two, and he basically sees people as wanting to make a contribution to society.

. As Commissioner Foerster's experience in office will demonstrate, no one is purely philosophically driven. There are always pragmatic concerns to be considered. Policymakers are faced with dilemmas based on limited resources, endless demands, and competing interests. He mixed his philosophy with pragmatism. Short term gains were considered, yet so were long term gains. For example, some advocates for the hungry ardently lobbied for county funds to be used for direct services for the hungry, but this was not county policy. The county supplied funding for equipment, such as trucks to haul food items, that indirectly helped the hungry. They also provided funds for low-income individuals for job training so that they could eventually provide for themselves. The commissioner admits to being torn on this policy. He wanted to give needed funds for food. Yet, with limited funds he had to decide how to get the most out of each dollar. Both he and the advocates wanted the same end result but through a different means. He looked at the costs and gains to be had not only today but years in the future.

Leadership

Commissioner Foerster called his style of leadership a "common sense approach." He was a team player. He spoke of the directors working with him, not under him. He believed in delegating. He told his directors to "go manage" and he would be there to support them. "Each unit has its own president" as the commissioner saw it, and he was not there to serve as a micromanager. "I have faith in the capabilities of others, not just the smartest or most skilled." The directors interviewed referred often to the autonomy and support they were given to do their job. Yet, they also expressed that they were aware that each director would be held accountable for his or her area. Foerster, always wanting to build on past initiatives, insisted that each department have a road map, a well-developed plan.

The commissioner quickly credits those in his administration for the "positive progress" that took place in human services during his tenure. His leadership style conveyed not only support and a belief in his staff but also a great appreciation for hard work well done. When discussing initiatives he states, "it is they, not I, who should get the credit for the growth and accomplishments in their respective departments." He credits not only the directors but the staff and citizens who worked on the initiatives. "Anyone can cut ribbons or hold a shovel for a ground breaking" is the commissioner's view.

While comfortable giving credit to others, he is hesitant to take credit for himself. He believes that "if you don't worry about who takes credit for things you get more done." Yet, those who worked with him either directly and indirectly in the human services division, are quick to point out the imperative role that the commissioner played in so many key initiatives that took place not just during his time as commissioner but also during his time in the legislature. Tellingly, they speak of Foerster's accomplishments as he speaks of his hero's accomplishments.

For example, Charles Stowell, past Director of the Department of Aging, states that Kane is a public institution today because people like Tom Foerster cared too much to turn his back on the elderly poor.[10] Vic Papale, the commissioner's executive assistant from 1980–84, considers Foerster as being essential for the implementation of the Kane Regional Centers. Papale says Foerster said a way to fund the building of the centers would be found and would not take no for an answer.[11] Both Laurie Mulvey and Kate Garvey, who work with the Family Support Centers, indicate that the commissioner's active support has been critical.[12] Charlotte Arnold, director of The Program—Alternatives to Incarceration, says it would not be where it is today except for Foerster. She specifically points to how the commissioner personally helped to obtained space to locate its facilities.[13] In describing the positive changes that occurred in the Mental Health/Mental Retardation field, Chuck Peters, the long time director of MH/MR, refers to the free rein the commissioner gave him. Along with the free rein were expectations and strong backing not just in word but in deed. "Commissioner Foerster did not hesitate to go face to face with the Governor and others to obtain funding for human services." Whether it was marches or other dramatic strategies the commissioner was behind Peters.[14] Therefore, while not a micromanager, Commissioner Foerster understood the details and was very involved in the life of the initiatives in the human service arena.[15]

Leo Koeberlein, former executive editor of The Pittsburgh Press, said of Foerster, "He is not a demagogue, but he is dynamic in the sense that he succeeds by using the available tools. Tom's working on the principle that politics is the art of the possible. He's the personification of it." Koeberlein described the commissioner as "a politician who does not routinely throw his weight around and is not one to rant and rave. He just uses a quiet intellectual approach."[16] Vic Papale recalls how articulate and convincing an argument the commissioner could always make to advance an issue.[17] Foerster himself states while discussing issues such as a public works program, that he can sell the idea to the private sector if given the opportunity to sit down and talk with those in the business world.

The importance of listening to others was not underestimated by the commissioner. Listening to the ideas of others was one means the commissioner used to determine community needs which he thought must be continually assessed. "I wanted people to tell me what they thought." He wanted to hear from the opposition as well as supporters. In addition to actively listening, the commissioner "did not hesitate to seek advice."[18]

His staff and others from outside county government were continually presenting ideas. Before acting on an idea, the commissioner said he would almost always seek input from the Allegheny Conference on Community Development. He would also seek input from others outside of government, and although he would listen, he did not always heed the advice given.

One example is the Allegheny Works Program, a public works program, modeled after WPA. "Despite being told you can't do it, it is impossible, we had to try." It was just a "gut reaction" that told Foerster to go ahead with it. "You may not succeed but you have to try." It is not stories told by others of the destitution of people out of work that motivated Foerster. It is the stories he himself tells not only of his hardships during the Depression but also stories of his friends. The closing of the steel mills in the late 1970s and 1980s resulted in friends waiting on his porch steps for him to come home. "They would beg, and that was really discouraging to hear somebody you have known all your life breaking down. The hardest part of the job is that you can't put everyone to work for the county even though you would like to when they can't find other work."

Although politically astute, as is evidenced in his ability to win reelection as county commissioner six times, his style and decision making were driven by ideals. Charles Kolling, who served as the lobbyist for the county from April 1977 to March 1996, speaks of Tom Foerster as "a politician willing to take a stand for goals in which he believed regardless of whether they were politically popular, and an obvious vote getter." Kolling refers specifically to Foerster's decision and subsequent battles to keep the Kane Regional Centers public. Kolling believes this decision, as well as the battles he fought for funding for MH/MR, were not politically driven. "Foerster based these decisions and others on what he felt was morally right, not what he thought was politically advantageous. The vast majority of his constituency are unaware of the struggles encountered trying to get state funding for human service initiatives."[19]

In fact, it can be argued that county government did not market itself to the degree it could have during Commissioner Foerster's tenure. There are things that the Board of commissioners could have done to "toot their own horn." Kolling mentions as one idea that a positive public relations move would have been for the county to have a ½ hour television show to let people know what is available through the county.

It can also be argued that the media was more interested in bad news than positive happenings and did not cover events in an unbiased fashion. Foerster notes that "often the beat reporter would take a news release and shed it in a critical light, even when the editorial page would be supportive." The commissioner does not think that county government got the credit it deserved for all it has accomplished. As staff in his administration admit, many people in the community are unaware of what the county government does, except collect tax dollars. Correctly, Commissioner Foerster claims that people are proud of the Community College of Allegheny County and the airport, to name two examples, yet many people are unaware that it was county government, and (although he does not claim it) Tom Foerster in particular, that made these two things happen.

County Government takes on a New Role— Human Services Becomes Key: 1968–96

Ideas about how people should be treated, what their needs are, and how best to meet these needs, led to legislation which in turn opened the door to change when Foerster stepped into his position as commissioner. Legislation being passed is just one phase of the policy process. The commissioner's strong belief that county government should be actively involved in the human service arena was the driving force behind the funding secured and how these Acts were implemented. A piece of legislation will have little impact if those with power do not see to it that it receives the dollars and support necessary to carry it out.

Policy initiated, authorized, and implemented during the commissioner's tenure was certainly impacted by trends and social and political events that took place across the nation from the 1960s through the 1990s. For example, the 1960s are remembered as a time when people's consciousness was raised as to the condition under which many populations were being forced to live. An unintended consequence of the civil rights movement was the awareness of the rights of not just African Americans but of children, the poor, those with a mental illness, and other populations who did not have a loud voice. There was much optimism in the early 1960s and it was thought that there was enough that everyone ought to get a piece of the pie. Federal and state governments increased funding for human services during part of this time period but there were also times, the 1980s in particular, when funding was being cut.

Events and trends within Allegheny County also led to the perceived need for an increase in human services in Allegheny County. For example, Allegheny County experienced the fall of its economic base, the steel industry. The county also experienced an exodus of people from the city to the county. "In 1950, 45 percent of the county population was concentrated in the City of Pittsburgh and the remaining 55 percent in the rest of the county. In 1990, only 28 percent of the county population was in the city with 72 percent in the county."[20]

The time was ripe to move beyond what Commissioner Foerster recalls was the "biggest event of the year" for the commissioners, the Allegheny County Fair. The legislation that he helped get passed during his time in the General Assembly expanded the functions of county government which he states "were largely limited to dealing with issues of transportation, roads, bridges, county parks, criminal justice, and a county airport." While these functions continue to be carried out today, Allegheny County government has undergone a transformation in structure, role and philosophy. Not only has Allegheny County expanded to play an active role in economic development and a broad range of human services, it is now driven by a philosophy of prevention rather than remediation. This proactive approach has resulted in commissions and committees being formulated by the Board of Commissioners and assigned the task of assessing needs and undertaking long term planning. The intent has been to use the results to inform policy decisions. Ideas grew out of the committees and they grew in part due to an atmosphere the commissioner worked at creating in which people inside and outside of government would "feel free to discuss needs and present ideas." The commissioner's attitude was that "new initiatives should be built upon." Under his tenure, Allegheny County gained state and national recognition for innovative human service programs.[21]

In order to get a sense of the overall change that took place from 1968–96, and avoid the danger of separating out seemingly different arenas instead of looking at the inter-relatedness of all of them, a broad definition of human services will be used for an overview. In the current structure of county government the following areas fall directly under the Human Service unit: Aging, Children and Youth Services, Health, Federal Programs, Kane Regional Centers, Mental Health/Mental Retardation/Drugs and Alcohol/Hunger and Homelessness, and Veteran Services.

Human services broadly defined encompasses all the resources of a community which contribute to the health, welfare, economic adequacy, security, and development of its citizens.[22] Therefore, the following discussion will not be limited to only the previously discussed areas but will touch on specific initiatives that dealt with education, economic stimulation, criminal justice, and employment, since all are essential elements in promoting a community's well-being. The intent is not to give a detailed review of each area but to show the reader the growth of the programs offered, the changing philosophy, and a sense of the process some of the initiatives underwent. (The case studies on Kane Regional Centers, Mental Health/Mental Retardation, and Family Support Centers in Section 2 are a more in-depth review of the policy process).

The Department of Aging, created in 1989 by merging the Department of Adult Service, the Area Agency on Aging, and the Office of Longterm Care Coordination has added many programs, first as separate units and then as a unified department. Following are some examples. There is a Senior Companion Program that serves a dual purpose. It provides employment for low-income elderly as they spend time making in-home visits to frail, homebound elderly.

Westinghouse Valley Services Center, built due to a charge from the commissioners, opened in December of 1982, as an experimental human service center that decentralized county services and provides services to both the young and the old. It was lauded by County Commissioner Cyril Wecht, M.D., as the beginning of "a new and creative era in the field of human services."[23]

Kane-without-Walls, as Foerster refers to it, provides in-home nursing care and enables elderly to remain in their own residences rather than an institutional setting. A family caregivers support program provides some relief to caregivers. In 1988 Allegheny County began a home-care program for elderly persons released from hospitals. The goal of the program was to keep elderly from having relapses. At the time Charles Stowell, Director of the Department of Aging, said that "transitional care is becoming increasingly important, because elderly patients are being discharged from hospitals more quickly than ever before."[24]

Vic Papale, then a staff member, believes that if not for the commissioner, the Lemington Center Nursing Home, which provides nursing care for elderly African Americans, would be out of business today. When the commissioner heard it was going to have to declare bankruptcy in 1983 he said, "we have to do something." He called in his staff and put a group together to see what could be done to save Lemington. As in other situations, many said it was not possible, but as Papale recalls the commissioner would not accept that scenario. Today Lemington Center Nursing Home operates a 180-bed facility that typically is at close to full capacity.[25]

The Volunteer Support Network for Seniors, an umbrella organization that the county formed with private sector partners, was another initiative undertaken by the Foerster administration. The goal of the network is to train volunteers who will visit every frail elderly living alone who expressed a desire to have a contact.[26] These new initiatives for older adults not only have preventative value, making them cost-effective; they also serve to ensure an improved quality of life for the elderly.

Allegheny County Children and Youth Services (CYS) began providing services for 80 children in 1963 and today it serves over 30,000 per year. An initial budget of $250,000 has increased to an annual budget of $79,000,000 in 1995.[27] Its mission, which has remained the same over the years, is to protect children from abuse and neglect; preserve families whenever possible; and provide safe, permanent homes for children. In its 1993 annual report, Celebrating 30 Years of Service, it credited the dedication and commitment of the Allegheny Board of Commissioners for its ability to fulfill its mission. The report thanked the board for its belief that families are important and its "willingness to fight for adequate state and federal resources and to provide funding beyond the county's required mandate. We commend their vision in requiring that services be continually evaluated and revised to meet today's needs." Today it "supports preventive community outreach and education services; family preservation services; in-home services; parent and child therapeutic services; community-based foster care, child care, and after-school programs; residential treatment facilities; and adoption programs."[28] This growth in programs resulted from observation of what other CYS programs around the nation were doing, additional legislation passed, and constant evaluations of what worked and what was needed. A review of the services provided indicate that over 33 years many preventative services were added. Improvements in service delivery and collaborative efforts were also a focus.

Counties are not mandated to run a health department and many do not. Allegheny County Health Department is one of 6 counties out of 67 in the state that made the decision to have one. Commissioner Foerster always advocated the importance of keeping alive the County Health Department when at budget time questions would invariably arise as to why it was needed. His reasoning is that the Commonwealth would not be able to provide the quality of services or respond to emergencies; whether an air collision emergency, a water-pollution emergency, or a flood. He noted that in a recent outbreak of meningitis "our health department responded within an hour." Only a few of its initiatives will be highlighted here.

In 1970 Allegheny County established "the first fully automated round-the-clock air monitoring system in the nation." In Allegheny County, prior to the state taking action, a law was passed that mandated "childhood disease immunizations for all schoolchildren." Foerster notes that although the number of children immunized was high, when he took office, efforts were made to keep increasing the percentage of children immunized, and today Allegheny County is noted as one of the outstanding counties in the nation regarding the percentage of youth immunized.

Despite its positive responses to the community health needs, the commissioner in 1992/1993 gave the County Health Department a mandate to rethink its role and mission. In 1992/1993 "the Department integrated preventive health services with primary care through partnerships with other agencies to improve the range of health care available in economically distressed communities." As a reaction to the studies that showed "persistently high rates" of infant mortality in six areas in the county, the Health Department created Healthy Start.[29] The belief expressed by the commissioner was that Healthy Start needed to be a community based effort assuring that pregnant girls and women receive the necessary services to have healthy babies.

The Drugs and Alcohol Program came into being in 1972 as a result of a decision by the Board of Commissioners, following enabling legislation passed by the General Assembly. Joined to the Department of Mental Health/Mental Retardation, which will be discussed in Section IV, services provided include prevention, detoxification, residential treatment, outpatient care, and methadone maintenance for people of all ages. Intensive lobbying and efforts to educate political leaders at the state and local level have occurred over the years, just as with the MH/MR Program. "Despite these efforts, services for the addicted have never received the recognition and support afforded those with mental and physical disabilities."[30] There are concerns regarding the impact that managed care will have on the treatment of addictions. Despite problems securing funds, the program has grown and prevention has become a key component.

The issues of homelessness and hunger emerged in the 1980s as problems growing in dimension in Allegheny County. Studies were done to try to estimate the increasing number of homeless and hungry individuals. It was estimated that between 1,400 and 1,700 people were homeless at any given moment in 1990 in the City of Pittsburgh and Allegheny County, and "homeless experts who attempt to intervene in this crisis estimate that between 5,000 and 7,000 persons are imminently at-risk of becoming homeless at any given time."[31]

In 1991 a steering committee brought together 70 representatives from government, nonprofit provider agencies, business, foundations, education, religious and medical communities, and formerly homeless individuals to develop the Allegheny County/Pittsburgh Homeless Initiative. It called for a "seamless continuum of care" that will enable the homeless to attain self-sufficiency.[32] Consistent with the new philosophy toward human services, prevention and community awareness were key components, as was participation by consumers. In 1992 the Department of Mental Health/Mental Retardation/Drug and Alcohol was given the responsibility by the Board of Commissioners for the administration, management, and coordination of all county hunger and homeless programs funded by the Pennsylvania Department of Public Welfare's Office of Social Programs. It became the Department of Mental Health/Mental Retardation/Drug and Alcohol/Homeless and Hunger. The homeless programs include emergency shelter, bridge (temporary) housing, subsidized housing, intensive case management, counseling, drug and alcohol support services, a GED program, job training, employment assistance, and specialized residences for the chronically mentally ill homeless.[33]

There are two state funded food programs for which the Department of Mental Health/Mental Retardation/Drug and Alcohol/Homeless and Hunger was given responsibility. One is the Emergency Food Assistance Program which distributes commodity foods provided by the U.S. Department of Agriculture. The other is the State Food Purchase Program which "provides for the purchase, transportation, storage and distribution of food to needy individuals and families."[34] In order to coordinate both homeless and hunger services, the Department of Mental Health/Mental Retardation/Drug and Alcohol/Homeless and Hunger works closely with existing agencies such as the Greater Pittsburgh Community Food Bank and agencies who were already in the business of providing homeless services. Needs and services provided have been continually reassessed. In addition to the state funded food programs about which the commissioner says "we lobbied heavily to get what we got," there are local hunger and nutrition initiatives sponsored by the Allegheny County Board of Commissioners that began in 1990. One initiative expanded the pantry on wheels program to include more public housing communities. Another initiative trained 75 food pantry workers who then developed a food distribution plan resulting in what was determined to be a more equitable food distribution plan.[35]

These hunger and nutrition initiatives fell under the responsibilities of the Director of Human Services, a position created in 1993 to assure the coordination of all human services and create a more efficient delivery system. This position was created in part in response to Allegheny County 2001, a long range plan of action to "enhance human development and to strengthen economic security" in Allegheny County. The plan, set forth in 1992, was initiated by the Allegheny County Commissioners. "The human development panels said: We don't just need more human services, we need to shape a new and just community where basic values of fairness, equality, compassion, and justice have real meaning. Building a stronger sense of community based on true social justice is fundamental to the panel's recommendations."[36] One outgrowth of Allegheny County 2001, which at this point has been stalled, was the move toward one unified information system resulting in each family being assigned to one caseworker, a single coordinator for all services.

Initial steps in streamlining human services were taken during Commissioner Foerster's last years in office. It was hoped that in 1997 demonstration programs would be in place in some regions of the county.[37] Another recommendation that emerged, and that the county programs had already started to focus on, was the "shift from treatment to prevention."[38]

What happens in the economic arena has great impact on the human service needs that arise and how adequately they are addressed. Prior to the Staisey and Foerster team winning in 1967, there was no structure within county government for economic development.[39] The demise of the steel industry was not yet an agenda issue, and proactive measures to solicit new industry and business did not receive what Foerster believed was "adequate attention" prior to 1968. The establishment of a Department of Development soon after the two took office was the beginning of an effort to make economic development a priority.

Both Staisey and Foerster were instrumental in getting the Community College Act passed. They went on to build the community college system in Allegheny County. This was not a mandate. It was the carrying out of a philosophy to level the playing field for all, and it is a program that the commissioner is probably as proud of as anything he has done. As he asserted during an interview with Dianne Jacob, "It (Community College of Allegheny College, CCAC) has had more direct impact than any government program."[40]

Today over 90,000 students attend either the main CCAC campus or one of its four outreach campuses. The school continues to make the guarantee to students that if six months after graduating they have been actively seeking full time work but have not found it, they will receive 15 units of free additional training.

Another initiative, envisioned by CCAC President, Dr. Kingsmore, and supported and backed by Commissioner Foerster, is a scholarship system under which any high school graduate in Allegheny County who cannot afford tuition will be provided with a scholarship. Further, state funds were secured over the years that have enabled dislocated workers and displaced homemakers to receive training at CCAC.

Although CCAC does not fall directly under human services, it has an impact on leveling the playing field. Adequate employment will not result without education and training. Lack of employment then leads to problems that other areas of government such as family crisis and criminal justice will have to get involved in. Commissioner Foerster saw his support of higher education as making good economic sense. It was preventative and proactive rather than reactive. The international airport and all economic development also serves to level the playing field by creating opportunity. Foerster's hope for the airport is for it to create employment and attract employers from all over the world.

In an article by Dianne Jacob, discussing the 1992 Pittsburgher of the Year, Commissioner Tom Foerster, the commissioner is highlighted as the person who made the most positive contribution to Pittsburgh—a new international airport. The airport is the culmination of 24 years of what the commissioner refers to as "friendly persuasion." Jacob describes this accomplishment as the result of the commissioner's "burning desire and determination." He listened to, but was not dissuaded by doubts that this vision could become a reality. As Jacob states, "the commissioner worked ceaselessly on this project with a coalition of leaders from government, the business community, and universities for 24 years to raise support and funds."[41] This statement summarizes the commissioner's mode of operation.

The Program for Female Offenders, Inc., under the auspices of the Allegheny County Probation Department began providing direct services to female offenders in 1974. The origin of the ideas that led to The Program began in 1971 when Charlotte Arnold, the current executive director, met with female offenders in the jails and gained an understanding of their needs. No services were being offered at the time to give the women an increased chance of remaining crime free upon release. At the time Ms. Arnold was responsible for educating the community about the plight of female offenders. The number one need of the women was employment. Ms. Arnold began efforts to secure funds through Law Enforcement Assistance Administration (LEAA) monies to provide job placement and counseling to nonviolent female offenders.

A key challenge faced in the early days was to gain the support of the county commissioners since LEAA funds had to be filtered through the county with a 10 percent match. Commissioner Foerster was hesitant since he knew that eventually LEAA funds might dry up, leaving the county with the future funding costs. None of the commissioners was eager to listen to Ms. Arnold's ideas, so she organized a demonstration with the support of the local branches of the National Organization of Women and the National Association for the Advancement of Colored People to at least get the idea on the agenda. The demonstration worked, and Ms. Arnold was listened to but her idea was not given serious consideration. She persisted and following the meeting began sending the commissioners monthly reports as to the number of women that were worked with and the extremely low recidivism rate of these women. "It was the reports that won me over," says the commissioner.

The tenacious spirit of Ms. Arnold, something the commissioner also exhibits, and her ability to educate the policymakers, proved effective. Commissioner Foerster became an "ardent supporter," according to Ms. Arnold. "It was the commissioner who would go out into communities with me to find facilities to house Alternatives to Incarceration. It was the commissioner who would work with, and negotiate with, community leaders in order to get their acceptance for having a facility in their community." As Ms. Arnold recalls, "Tom was always thinking of how the facility could help the whole community, not just the offenders." (She noted that, as the commissioner predicted, LEAA funds did dry up but that did not dampen the support of the commissioner).[42]

Today this program depends on many sources for funding. Currently a capital campaign is taking place to meet the need of a larger facility. The Program, which has received regional and national attention for its innovative services, began as a storefront operation run by three women who knew that through respect, love and training the majority of these offenders could lead lives free of crime. As this small staff continued to become aware of the needs of the women, more components were added to The Program.

What began as a job counseling and placement program has grown into a model that includes work release programs, child abuse prevention programs, shoplifting prevention classes, life skills training, programs for children and job readiness training. There are residential facilities and most recently added was a drug and alcohol treatment alternative. Men as well as women are now served. The Program makes good economic sense which is often a selling point at the top of the priority list when determining policy. Not only is the cost of having a women live in a residential facility, where she makes a monetary contribution, less expensive than keeping her in jail; her chances of reentering the criminal justice system, or in being in need of Aid to Families With Dependent Children are greatly reduced. A report, released in May of 1995, indicated that the recidivism rate for the random sample of PROGRAM clients is 15 percent as compared to 26 percent for female offenders in Allegheny County who did not receive PROGRAM services.[43]

The mini-WPA program that Commissioner Foerster promoted is yet another initiative that fits under the broad definition of human services. The commissioner's philosophy is that keeping people unemployed is a waste of money as well as human capability. "It is not cost-effective, especially when the indirect costs of unemployment such as crime, youth violence, and drug and alcohol abuse are taken into account." Coupled with this philosophy is his strong belief that when someone cannot obtain employment in the private sector, it is the responsibility of the government to help that person get a job. "That is how people should be treated." This can be done through education, vocational training, and/or a public works job. Foerster sees public works jobs as a way to help people get established and to serve as a building block from which they will pursue employment in the private sector.

As a response to the "massive unemployment" problem in Allegheny County, Commissioner Foerster was a major player behind the creation of a public works program that was patterned after Roosevelt's New Deal WPA Program. A study undertaken by the Pennsylvania Economy League concluded that "depending on the assumptions used, the 'Jobs for Growth' program, designed to give the chronically unemployed work while training them for a career, could save the state almost $16 million in welfare payments over five years or produce $11 million in losses." A county paid consultant conducted a study that indicated that the program would "generate almost $3 in benefits for each $1 invested."[44]

The Mon Valley Commission, set up by the county commissioners to address the unemployment of steel workers, was instrumental in coalition building that raised support for a public works program and lobbying the state for funds for the program. No large source of private funds was ever secured. Governor Casey's support of the program was key in securing state funds that provided approximately half of the budget. Allegheny County Works, Inc., a nonprofit corporation, was established to administer the program.

The program started small and has stayed small. Nonetheless it has provided training and jobs for participants. The commissioner points to three, of the over twenty rehabilitated facilities, as examples of the jobs completed by the program participants. One is an old school in Homestead, one building is being used for a community center with a playground, and one building in Clairiton is used as a Family Support Center. The future of the program is not stable since as of 1995 the state cut the funds it was providing.

The commissioner could "see a crisis and understand the depth of it."[45] The loss of jobs for over 100,000 steel workers left many in jeopardy of losing their homes. Papale recalls that the commissioner "would not stand idly by and let it happen." He therefore helped initiate the Mortgage Foreclosure Prevention Program which provided a 'second' mortgage for unemployed steel workers.

Another small scale work program that began under Commissioner Foerster was a summer work program for people with some type of handicap. The impetus for the program was one special individual, Matt Burda. The commissioner talks with pride of the blossoming of Matt, who worked as a messenger for the county one summer. Matt had been classified as severely mentally retarded prior to his summer with the county. With some individual attention, and a lot of work on Matt's part, by the end of the summer Matt was no longer classified as severely mentally retarded. (It is likely that the original classification was wrong, but a change did occur.) The Commission describes the change that took place because of the opportunity Matt had been afforded. He says that this experience "gave me the idea that we ought to have a special summer work program for people with some type of handicap and we got some people in the private sector to buy into it." The commissioner describes the program as very successful and that for some participants it has resulted in employment at the end of their summer experience.

Jacob, and undoubtedly many others, saw the airport as the commissioner's biggest accomplishment to date as of 1992. Yet, how one defines "biggest" accomplishment (where one stands) depends on one's life situation. The person who was able to attend CCAC because of the commissioner's efforts may see the Community College as his biggest success; the woman who was able to get job training through the 'alternatives to incarceration program' might see that as the biggest success that happened during the Foerster administration; the unemployed individual who obtained employment as a result of the county public works program may see that as the biggest success. Families and individuals who have benefited from the three initiatives discussed in the next section, all of which are part of the human service arena, may claim any one of them as the biggest success. There is a long list of possibilities as to which of the initiatives carried out during Commissioner Foerster's tenure was the biggest accomplishment. What is evident is that there were many initiatives and accomplishments to demonstrate that Allegheny County government took on a new role during Commissioner Foerster's tenure that served to provide opportunity and improve life in Allegheny County. As noted by Vic Papale during the time he worked as the commissioner's executive assistant, he had two primary roles: one being to serve as the gatekeeper; the other charge from the commissioner was to assure the preeminence of human services on the county agenda.[46] Robert Nelkin, who served as executive assistant after Papale, before he became Director of Human Services, was called on by the commissioner to continue to carry out this latter charge.

Section I Conclusion

In sum, the commissioner believes that the problems within a community are community problems best addressed by combining self interest and public interest. As his tenure indicates, he wisely used influence, cooperation and loyalty to bridge the gap between public interest and self interest. "The only way to get things done today is through cooperation." On the other hand, he could play tough and used lawsuits and threats in order to get funds from the state. "He would go face to face with Governor Casey" and Governor Thornburgh and insist that more money should be allocated to human services.[47] The strategies and tactics used by Foerster and his staff to obtain and increase state funding for initiatives, as well as to secure foundation and corporate funds, were a key factor in the transformation of human services in Allegheny County. Commissioner Foerster's leadership style, the support and encouragement he provided, his resilience, and his personal philosophy regarding the active role government should play in creating a just society were also all key factors.

Section I Discussion Questions

1. Did the managerial style of the commissioner lend itself to change or deter change? Why is the commissioner credited by many as the catalyst for change? Can individuals make a difference?
2. What was the commissioner's philosophy as to the role of government in the human service arena and how did it play out in the policies implemented?
3. Were there times when pragmatic concerns appeared to overpower the ideological beliefs of the commissioner?
4. Would a rational public policy approach care about the biographies of major players?
5. Does a postpositivist method of policy analysis lead to an increased understanding of the impact of major players' backgrounds, heroes, ideologies, etc.?
6. How does the use of biography change your understanding of policy development? How can it help you as an analyst?
7. Explain how the case study offered support for, or undercut, the description of the essence of the public policy process as being political.

Before reading Section II you should consider going back and reviewing the list of nine topics listed under the caption: "Case Assignment."

Section II. Three Case Studies in Human Services

Mental Health/Mental Retardation

Introduction

The issue in the mental health/mental retardation field during Commissioner Foerster's tenure was not whether public care should be provided for persons with mental illness and mental retardation but what kind of care should be provided. Policy decisions were made regarding community care versus institutional care. These decisions were, and are, accompanied by related issues such as jobs and programs for this population of consumers to ensure "success" in the community care alternative.

The determination of programs and services needed, and the inclusion of consumers and their families in the decision making process, have been important challenges, as has been securing adequate funding to provide services. Further, community acceptance of community care for persons with mental illness and mental retardation has been an issue that has continuously been addressed.

The 1969–94 Commemorative Mental Health/Mental Retardation, Drugs and Alcohol, Hunger and Homelessness Report explains that the "genesis of the Allegheny County Mental Health/Mental Retardation Program was in the community-driven, broad based, vigorous, participatory, citizens' planning efforts that occurred in the mid-sixties across a variety of human service and neighborhood empowering programs. The slogan of the era was, 'Maximum feasible citizen participation....' In the Mental Health/Mental Retardation (MH/MR) arena the citizen participation effort culminated in the passage of the MH/MR Act of October 1966 by a special session of the Pennsylvania General Assembly. The growth and service innovations that accompanied it were (and are) attributable to the sustained and robust support from the system's volunteers, service consumers, their families, dedicated staff, and the ongoing political backing provided by the Board of Commissioners and the Allegheny County Delegation to the General Assembly in Harrisburg."[1]

Background and Narrative

During the 1800s and first half of the 20th century, persons with a mental illness and mental retardation who needed public help were sent to institutions. This "treatment of choice" changed drastically beginning in the late 1950s as a movement across the nation to deinstitutionalize people with mental illness and mental retardation began. As with any issue that reaches agenda status, and is addressed as a social problem, numerous factors brought the needs of this population to the table and kept attention focused on it. Mental health professionals "formed a coalition, garnered journalistic and philanthropic support, and organized a campaign to influence the President, congressional leaders and the general public about the need for community psychiatry and the treatment of mental illness."[2] Advocates for people with mental disabilities had gained attention and exposed the inhumane conditions that many people encountered while institutionalized. The Civil Rights movement raised the consciousness of many Americans to the rights of many oppressed populations. Ken Kesey's *One Flew Over The Cuckoo's Nest* opened the eyes of many. President Kennedy had a sister who was mentally retarded and was the first president publicly to show concern for the needs of those with mental retardation through the creation of the President's Panel on Mental Retardation. The discovery and use of psychotropic medications decreased the "need" of many for long term care. There was an expectation that community care would carry a lower price tag than institutional care.

The passage of the Federal Community Mental Health Center Act of 1963 marked the first legislation that directly led to deinstitutionalization of persons with mental illness. The Act "provided federal grants to communities for the construction of mental health centers and statewide planning efforts to develop comprehensive service plans." The establishment of community treatment centers would allow for people to be treated close to family and friends rather than in large government psychiatric hospitals. This Act was followed in Pennsylvania by the 1966 Mental Health/Mental Retardation Act which "provided for state-county funding to develop alternative services and for local control of service development and delivery."[3]

From 1968, when the Allegheny County Mental Health/Mental Retardation Program officially started, until 1994, enrollment of residents in mental hospitals dropped from 7,400 residents to about 480 residents. The number of individuals with mental retardation who reside in institutions decreased from 3,200 in 1968 to approximately 750 in 1994. The transfer of persons with mental retardation from institutions to the community did not occur on a large scale until twelve years after the exodus of the mentally ill began.[4] These figures capture the picture of the large numbers of individuals moved to Allegheny County care but do not tell the story of the inevitable struggles and battles that were fought in bringing about the existing system of community living situations and resources. The 1966 Pennsylvania Act was only the foundation and a start. Intensive lobbying, litigation and further legislation furthered efforts to move toward the goal of quality community care.

Charles Peters, director of the program from 1975–96, said much of the success in bringing about quality community care rather than institutional care was because "Tom Foerster aided, abetted, and encouraged" a movement that involved litigation; intensive, and at times radical lobbying; threats; politically unpopular decisions; and unflinching direction to improve services.[5] Peters states that "we were always fighting with the state on how much money Allegheny County got and how it was to be spent." The state called for a 10 percent match on state funds and the commissioner was "always willing to make the match, on all funds available, which resulted in Allegheny County capturing all the money the state offered. This was not typical behavior in many counties. Additional funds were available for Allegheny County to capture because commissioners in many other counties could not (or would not) match funds available to them. Still, struggles ensued because even with capturing all state funds available, the amount fell short of what was considered necessary to meet the needs in Allegheny County.

Although an ongoing problem, funding shortages were more severe during certain time periods for MH/MR, as well as for all other human services. The commissioner never went to Harrisburg without putting in a strong plea for the need of increased funding for MH/MR and other human service programs.[6] In 1988 he requested that Pennsylvania have a statewide conference on human service funding in general. When the state did not respond, he decided to call his own conference. He worked with special interest groups across the state to lobby for increases in human service funding.[7] In May 1988, he joined with other people in the courthouse courtyard to protest low human service funding levels. He sent letters to President Bush on occasion.

The commissioner was not alone in attempts to secure more state dollars. The aggressive efforts of Chuck Kolling, the county's lobbyist, Chuck Peters, and Allegheny County legislators were all crucial in increasing funding, notes the commissioner. "Both Republican and Democratic legislators always bought into the programs. They did what they could to help." He goes on to explain the importance of "fully briefing them on everything and showing that money could be saved eventually by serving people in the community."

The commissioner also recalls how on many occasions Chuck Peters' "outrageous" tactics upset state administrators, the governor included. "They tried to take it out on me as they knew I was quietly behind the scene. Eventually I was able to patch things up."[8] The commissioner could have been referring to many actions taken by Peters to secure funds.

A prime example was action taken after the decision was made in 1989 to retrench and redirect both MH and MR services. The low allocations throughout the 1980s, coupled with significant inflation, left MH/MR very short of funds to provide services in a satisfactory manner. In 1989, the Allegheny County MH/MR Board made a "painful decision" and "announced that it would reduce service capacity, but not contract revenue, by 10 percent a year until the system achieved an adequate level of quality." The board received the overt support of the Board of Commissioners.[9] Knowing that it was not the "politically popular" decision and that there would be some negative side effects, Peters still believed the move was necessary to put pressure on the state through a political, legislative, and legal offensive. "Only Tom's support allowed the volunteer Board and staff to carry out this strategic approach. He was willing to take the heat."

The waiting lists did grow, as did the number of county commitments of mentally retarded citizens to state institutions, but the payoff was increased funding, a doubling of the budget. "This bold decision and firm resolve, coupled with aggressive action in the courts, caught the attention of the general public and the legislature and set the tone for all that followed."[10]

Tactics used by Peters and the provider agencies included sending the governor 2,500 Easter eggs, each with the first name and initial of a client on the waiting list on it; thousands of letters were sent to the governor and key legislators by consumers, families, volunteers and staff; a voter registration drive was undertaken; public demonstrations, as well as wide-spread public forums, were held; mass trips were made to Harrisburg at budget time by consumers, families, volunteers and staff; and Allegheny County sued the state several times concerning mental health and mental retardation funding.[11] Clearly these activities did not endear Commissioner Foerster to the Casey Administration. A simple command from the commissioner to cease would have ended the efforts.

In 1991 the "Unified Systems" project got off the ground. The goal of the project was to oversee the reintegration of Mayview, Woodville, and Torrence Hospital residents with mental illness into community living arrangements. Mayview and Torrence were scheduled for a reduction of residents and Woodville for closure. Originally, the Commonwealth only planned to send a fraction of the money spent on the residents back into the community with them. Peters and others in the field found this totally unsatisfactory. After much discussion, negotiation, and political action, the Commonwealth agreed to move the money, in increments, not spent on inpatient care back into the community. It was believed that this $33,000,000 commitment (the Woodville allotment) over a three year period was necessary to provide the necessary support services. A subsequent evaluation of the project indicated the consumers and their families felt it was very successful in providing them the support they needed to live in the community. Unified Systems led to the doubling of the mental health budget in Allegheny County.

An increase in funds for persons with mental retardation also occurred during the early 1990s, due to a number of law suits. Up until this time funding was based on a set amount per person served, not taking into account different amounts needed, based on each person's needs. Peters says that at first he did not "buy into" the needs-based, very labor intensive (person centered planning) approach to determining funding levels. But, as time went on, and the needs of those served obviously became greater and more costly, a set budget could not meet the needs. It took action on the legal front to gain additional funding that was based on the individual needs of each consumer. Again, without the commissioner's approval, the county would not have sued the state, and this favorable result could not have come to pass. In a time period when MH/MR programs generally were experiencing financial difficulty because of the litigation, the mental retardation budget in Allegheny County more than doubled.

Programs and mandates passed at the federal level also led to increased funding, but not necessarily federal dollars, that impacted services provided at the county level. One key piece of legislation was the Americans with Disabilities Act in 1990. As a result the county Mental Retardation Program was able to increase the number of community based employment programs from three in 1990 to 16 in 1994."[12] Many other community based job initiatives have taken place over the years, with a high degree of coordination with community agencies. These have resulted in jobs for many handicapped people.

Funding issues, while a primary concern, were far from the only difficulty faced in the implementation of legislative acts and the meeting of Tom Foerster's goals for the Department. One of the things that Commissioner Foerster insisted was that when individuals were released from institutions that they be brought back home and not be sent out of the county. As a result, an organization called Residential Resources was created and funded by county government with approximately $1.5 million to locate and acquire homes to house people released from institutions. Residential Resources, which worked independently of county government from its inception in 1988, dealt with the resistance in neighborhoods to locating homes for persons with mental disabilities in their neighborhood. Despite the resistance, by the time Tom Foerster left office, Residential Resources had acquired 143 sites, about one third of the total in the county system.

Education of community members was an important strategy used. For example, it was pointed out that the vast majority of persons with both mental illness and mental retardation "were, and are, always with us." They already reside in "your neighborhood" since most of these consumers are treated primarily on a community outpatient basis, partial hospitalization, or inpatient basis that typically lasts only two weeks.[13] In addition to locating homes and fighting local battles to relocate people back in the community, Residential Resources served to somewhat insulate county government from the local battles that ensued, despite their effort to educate. Peters points out that both before the advent of Residential Resources, and after, no battle to place a residential home in a community was ever "lost." However, there were some compromises made as to how and where exactly the home would be located and how many homes would be located in a particular community.

Once individuals returned to the community, other support services, in addition to housing, were necessary to prevent reinstitutionalization. Inadequate community care throughout the 1970s led to increased recidivism among the growing number of individuals released from state hospitals.[14] Increased understanding of the needs of these individuals and increased understanding of how to meet these needs, due to active family and consumer participation in policy formulation, implementation, and evaluation, has led to initiatives being built on and improved services. One of the difficulties Peters mentions was that as time went on, those released from institutions were more and more difficult to assist in the community. The first people released did not exhibit the severity of "problems" as those released later.

Today "maximizing opportunity" for persons with mental illness or mental retardation includes extensive residential programs, social and vocational rehabilitation, intensive case management and support services for families. As noted earlier, the Drug and Alcohol Program and the Hunger and Homelessness Program were put under the Department of Mental Health/Mental Retardation in order formally to link these services and provide a comprehensive package.

As the previously discussed material indicates, efforts to expand services were continuous under Commissioner Foerster. A new definition of Mental Retardation, that exemplifies the shift in philosophy, was released in 1992 by the American Association of Mental Retardation. This new definition proposed the provision of "supports" rather than "programs" and "focused on supports, abilities, natural environment, and empowerment, not on level of disability."[15] As the Commemorative Report notes, Allegheny County had already embraced this concept prior to that time. "Mental Retardation Blue Ribbon Standards developed by consumers, volunteers, and staff were adopted by Allegheny County. The standards incorporate person centered planning, the transition to independent supports coordination and a shift toward more flexible funding of supports."[16] This same philosophy applies to those with a mental illness.

Kane Regional Centers

Introduction

Providing quality care for elderly indigents who could not afford to pay for in-home care or private nursing home care was an issue surrounded by controversy that was addressed during Commissioner Foerster's tenure. The role that public scrutiny played; the difficulties encountered by omitting individuals who wanted to be involved in the process; attempting to take a holistic approach as to the needs of the elderly; and, as always, funding issues, were all factors that played into the policy decisions made.

John J. Kane Hospital in Allegheny County was an institution that opened in 1958 as a public, government financed, extended care facility for elderly persons who could not afford in-home care or a private nursing home. By 1974–75 John J. Kane Hospital, which had been spotlighted nationally in earlier years for some of its outstanding services, was again in the spotlight. This time it faced both local and national scrutiny for its shortcomings. It was also cited for being in violation of state and federal building deficiencies, such as oversized patient ward areas. Failure to correct deficiencies in order to meet state and federal standards would result in the suspension of its license and subsequently the loss of its major funding sources.

The county commissioners, under whose authority Kane Hospital fell, had to determine what options were available and what the best solution would be. There was a state mandate under the institution district law that, while not specifically calling for the provision of nursing home care for the indigent elderly, states that the county must provide care for the elderly and indigent.[1] At the time Allegheny County was spending approximately 10.1 percent of its budget on Kane Hospital.[2]

Background

In the second half of the twentieth century we have experienced a huge growth in the aging population. At the turn of the twentieth century, persons 65 years of age and older represented approximately 4 percent of the total U.S. population. As of 1980 in Allegheny County the number of persons over 65 was 13.8 percent of the total population. By 1990, 17.4 percent of the population in Allegheny County was over 65 years old.[3] One option that is used for dealing with the segment of this population who cannot manage remaining in the community due to physical limitations caused by illness is institutional care.

John J. Kane Hospital was such an institution. Unmet needs of the chronically ill and aging in Allegheny County led to the construction of Kane which was intended to be used exclusively as a hospital where maximum treatment and rehabilitation would lead to early discharge of patients and their return to the community.[4] For the first seven years of operation, until 1965, there were not a lot of federal or state rules and regulations that had to be adhered to and there was a greater need for short-term care. The passage of Medicare and Medicaid in 1965 diminished the need for public acute and short-term care, but not the need for long-term care. Another result of Medicare and Medicaid was a growing list of regulations that providers were required to meet. By 1978 over 1,200 pages of state and federal regulations controlled nursing homes. These regulations were extremely specific, including such things as how wide the halls had to be and the distance allowable between the patients' beds and a nurse's station.[5] From 1966 through the early 1970s Kane Hospital received little public attention for any deficiencies.

Until the early 1970s Kane Hospital, the second largest institution of its kind in the United States, housing at times up to 2,200 people, enjoyed a positive national reputation. It was spotlighted and used as a guide for similar programs in the field of rehabilitation and restorative care.[6] People came from all over the country to see Kane.[7] Then, in 1973 Kane Hospital began to fall under public scrutiny. That is not to say that government officials and the Hospital's administrators were not aware of problems prior to that time, but that the problems were, or were not, being addressed to a large degree quietly out of the eye and ear of the general public. In 1967, when running for commissioner, Foerster stated that incumbent Commissioner William McClelland had neglected Kane Hospital.[8]

The early 1970s was a time period when deplorable conditions that existed in institutions for the mentally ill, mentally retarded and aged throughout the country started to emerge and gain public awareness. Locally the Action Coalition of Elders (ACE) in 1974 published a document called Kane Hospital: A Place To Die. Claiming that "Kane Hospital is a terrible place" the intent of the document was to draw attention to what ACE described as the inhumane conditions at Kane.[9] (ACE was a group that had sued Allegheny County for not admitting some individuals to Kane Hospital.) Kane officials had determined that these individuals could not be properly cared for at Kane.[10]

The report is full of stories of accounts of poor treatment received by patients due to the shortage of nursing personnel, inadequate supervision of staff, lack of relief personnel, inadequate rehabilitation and restorative services, inadequate support services, inadequate physical plant and accommodations, inadequate medical services, and the failure of grievance and complaint procedures.

ACE used numbers taken from annual reports of Kane Hospital to provide evidence for its argument that Kane is failing to meet its goal of the "restoration to health of the geriatric and chronically ill patient and his return to the community."[11] The annual reports reveal that "of the 2,200 people housed in Kane Hospital, about 200 are discharged each year while nearly 1,100 Kane residents die each year. The average length of stay is two years. This situation has existed unchanged for 10 years."[12] In the 1969 annual report, the low discharge rate is noted as an embarrassment and indicated that many persons eligible for discharge need placement. Reluctance of attending physicians to be involved with families in a discharge process, as well as families' lack of receptiveness to the return of a family member, were cited as key reasons for this situation.

ACE was able to portray an extremely negative picture of Kane Hospital that the media quickly picked up. Pressure for county intervention intensified as the media kept printing horror stories over the next two years. It was this "unfair criticism" and being directly told by Federal officials that "Kane Hospital is a target" that gave Kane Hospital high priority on the agenda, according to Commissioner Foerster. The county commissioners had been working with the Director of Kane, in efforts to address any complaints brought to their attention, but standard operating procedure was not sufficient to quiet the press or appease the state and federal watchdogs. Kane Hospital was by this point operating under a provisional license.

The facility itself, which was state of the art when built, had major physical problems that would be extremely expensive to fix and then to maintain. Cracked and broken window panes were the norm; there was no air conditioning. It was a 2-wire versus a 3-wire electrical system; the elevators were inadequate; the laundry facilities, two floors underground, were a hot box with atrocious ventilation; and the kitchen was a fourth of a mile from where the food was served. The physical plant staff included 10 electricians, 11 plumbers, 10 carpenters, and a 12-person fire department.

Not only were there major problems with the physical environment and staffing surpluses of maintenance personnel, there were staffing shortages of nursing personnel and other staff who dealt directly with the patients. County wages were inadequate to keep on the nurses aides who were trained at Kane through a program set up with the Community College of Allegheny County. Not only was Kane not competitive with private facilities, its location was a problem as far as easy access. "It was hard to get help on board to make sure that the place was properly run," stated Commissioner Foerster.

Narrative

The county commissioners in 1977 decided to conduct their own study to look into the situation at Kane and determine a solution. Note that during this time period Commissioner Foerster, though a Democrat, was a minority commissioner. During his first eight years from 1968–76 he had been a majority commissioner along with Leonard Staisey, who was the chair. In 1976 Jim Flaherty, also a Democrat, aligned himself with Robert Pierce, the Republican commissioner, and was elected chair.

This was an unexpected upset that very possibly impacted action that took place over the next three years.[13]

All three commissioners were very concerned and wanted changes to occur with Kane. While there was consensus on the need for improvements, the process on bringing about the change is what Charles Stowell, a past executive director of Kane, believes would have been different. A committee consisting of county government staff members was set up to look into options available for Kane Hospital. Consultants were hired to provide "expert" opinion to the committee. Stowell says they hired good talent. The architectural firm hired, IKM Partnership, conducted an environmental/behavioral study to be used as one part of the data gathering for the Kane Hospital Master Plan. The "exhaustive multi-volume" study conducted by the committee resulted in the development of twelve options. The option the committee determined to be the best plan was the creation of four different centers spread throughout the county: mini-Kanes they were called.

The committee had ultimately proposed the four centers for a number of reasons. As alluded to before, recruitment and maintenance of staff at Kane was a nightmare. In addition to presenting a hardship in terms of hiring staff, its location was a problem in terms of family members coming to visit. The location also presented a difficulty in recruiting volunteers, which are a vital part of the operation. The committee determined that the high cost of upkeep made staying with one large institution a fiscally bad decision. Four centers could address these problems while maximizing the numbers of patients who could be served.

The original plan was submitted to the Comprehensive Health Planning Agency in June of 1978 and then withdrawn in November after failing to gain full approval from this agency. The proposal could have been sent on to the Commonwealth of Pennsylvania without full approval from the Comprehensive Health Planning Agency, but it was determined it was not worth risking rejection and the waiting period then required before a new proposal would be considered. At this same time, the commissioners were also faced with the threat by the welfare department to stop subsidizing patient care.

In the face of this dilemma, in September of 1978, Charles Stowell came on board as Kane Hospital's Executive Director. He encouraged pulling back the original plan, not necessarily due to the content of the proposal, but because the process had been circumvented and because of the subsequent opposition that arose. The planning committee had left many people out of the decision-making process by not soliciting and including ideas of people in the community who had a vested interest. The decision had come from within government. The price paid for trying to ram a plan through without widespread community involvement was a lot of unhappy and disgruntled people. The committee meetings had not been open. Stowell believes that if Commissioner Foerster had been chair, a more open public planning process would have originally taken place. "That was Tom's style. He was more sensitive to the need for community involvement, including a wide range of interests." He also used finesse in the situation.[14]

Immediately following the withdrawal of the mini-Kanes proposal, the commissioners appointed a committee of over 60 persons to develop a Long-Term Care Plan for the older residents of Allegheny County. This time there was an attempt to have a wide representation of interests on the committee, so it included caregivers, service providers, citizens, legislators, government officials, industry, and the media.

Represented on the committee were individuals who opposed the 1978 mini-Kane proposal. The purpose of this committee was not to look at the 1978 proposal, or determine what should happen with Kane. The purpose was to "identify resources to meet the needs of senior citizens and plan the facilities and services which will most effectively and efficiently utilize those resources."[15] The committee did its work within the six-month framework set by the commissioners and submitted a Final Report on Long-Term Care for the Elderly which was to serve as a working document for community organizations, business and elected officials to pursue actual implementation. Eighty percent of the major proposals in the report were acted on over the years.[16]

Part of this committee's work was to conduct public hearings at which Charles Stowell recalls the "beating" that it received for the original mini-Kane proposal. The committee listened to the comments made and then moved on to focus on its purpose, which was more comprehensive and in need of community solutions. Rather than keeping the planning sessions closed and exclusive, people were being listened to, and it made a difference. Shortly after submittal of the Long-Term Care Plan a committee of approximately 20 carefully selected people who had served on the 60+ member committee convened to draft a new proposal for Kane Hospital. The committee was made up of stakeholders in the community. With citizen participation on the committee the old plan was dusted off, some cosmetic changes made, and a new proposal rapidly drafted.

The concerns that people had with the original proposal were addressed at these open meetings. For example, there was some concern about the quality of the food service to be used, so national "experts" were brought in for advice. Another complaint regarding the original plan was that there were to be four persons to a room. This was changed to two. So while those on one side of the table might have seen the changes as minor and cosmetic, the opposition may have defined these as potentially major problems. Stowell described this latter process as "coopting" the opposition. The final proposal submitted to the Comprehensive Health Planning Agency in 1979 was the result of consensus building. A citizen, not a bureaucrat, presented the final proposal.[17]

From September of 1978 through 1979, while the committees were working on the plan and proposal, the commissioners and Stowell had a terrible situation to deal with. Part of the building was condemned and two strikes took place. Commissioners Foerster and Flaherty made trips to Washington to attempt to get waivers and discuss what was being done to come into conformance with the codes. As always money was a major impediment. The trips did not prove fruitful for, as Commissioner Foerster recalls, the federal government was too interested in making an example out of shortcomings of Kane Hospital. Stowell recalls Senator Frank Church showing up one morning at the front doors of Kane Hospital, camera crew in tow. Church had made the trip to decry the deplorable conditions at Kane.

The commissioners were also working closely with Stowell to make improvements within the constraints of the existing system. They would take Stowell's suggestions and check with others before issuing their decisions on how best to provide adequate care and keep federal dollars coming in while a long-term solution was being worked on. One decision made was to reduce the number of patients being served at any one time from 2,200 to 1,600. Another big change was the restructuring of the staffing of the facility resulting in the division of the building into four separate wings. This was in anticipation of the proposal for four centers becoming a reality.

By late 1979, in less than a year after submission, the proposal was approved, but no state or federal dollars were ever made available for the construction of the facilities. Lobbying efforts were made to the state for construction costs, but to no avail, so if Kane Regional Centers were to be, the county had to raise the money, which amounted to approximately $75 million.

Commissioner Foerster became chair of the Board of Commissioners in 1980 and gave a clear signal to go ahead with the four Kane Regional Centers. He saw the benefits of four separate centers. "You can locate them in different parts of the county so accessibility for staff, volunteers and families is not such a problem. It is easier for school children to adopt a regional center as theirs, and that is what happened. A lot of people adopt one in their region." Additionally, he felt there were many reasons to vacate the old building. One reason he mentioned was that "there were so many doors in and out of the place and a very small minority of workers were responsible for a lot of things disappearing from the facility." The building outlay was such that too many people could find places to sit unnoticed and not do their job.

The minority commissioner was opposed to this plan, but Foerster had a second vote from the other majority commissioner, and secured the necessary funds through the purchasing of bonds. Stowell states that "Tom kept the ball moving." Ground breaking occurred in 1981 for the first new Center and by 1984 the four Kane Regional Centers, each with a 360 person capacity, were completed. But the battles were far from over.

By bringing local opponents to the table, and finding consensus, county officials were successful in overcoming the ardent local opposition to the idea of four centers. Kane Regional Centers have received positive reviews from the community at large and it appears that the horror stories of the old Kane are a phenomena of the past. The environment and overall care provided by the four Regional Centers is an improvement over the Kane Hospital days.[18]

However, one battle to be fought was getting the state to reimburse for operating costs at the rate legislated. Legislation, passed in 1976, sets forth that the state of Pennsylvania is to reimburse the county for 90 percent of the cost of operation of public nursing homes not covered by federal dollars. The state interpreted the law as 90 percent being the ceiling, not 90 percent of the actual total cost. As the saying goes, the devil is in the details. Governors Thornburgh and Casey were each met with personally, lobbying efforts were continuous, and after two years more funds were freed up for nursing homes. Efforts were made to band together with other nursing homes to form a coalition to lobby together. Through the work of lobbyist Charles Kolling and the commissioners, the ceilings were increased, which resulted in more state dollars. Also, using all angles, Allegheny County sued the state in order to recover the reimbursements they believed the Act 135 legislation entitled them to.

Despite the financial costs and difficulties encountered, Commissioner Foerster's commitment to provide indigent care led him to keep at bay those wanting to privatize nursing home care. Many times during the last 15–16 years there have been suggestions to privatize. But Foerster, deeply believing that that privatizing would run against the best interests of poor people did not consider the suggestion as a viable option. "You would not be serving poor people well. There would be long waiting lists for the poor while you took care of private paying patients to make sure the nursing home made a profit." Referring to privatizing, Stowell stressed "Tom would never have let that happen." Yet, some members of the current Board of Commissioners may not share Foerster's views on the role government should play in the care of the elderly indigent. There is currently speculation of a move, within the administration, toward the privatization of the Kane Regional Centers.

Family Support Centers

Introduction

In the public policy arena, policy that is implemented most often leads to additional policy that may improve on past policy, alter it slightly, or even sometimes totally overhaul it. When the latter happens, which is not the norm, a new way of operating emerges. For years the human service arena operated in a reactive, rather than preventive, mode in its relations with families and young children. Following is a story of how the county is redesigning the old way of doing business and has adopted a philosophy of prevention instead of reaction. This philosophy is incorporated in Family Support Centers, founded on a set of mutually held principles with the underlying premise that all families need support. The belief is not that something is wrong with families that needs to be fixed.

Background and Narrative

The Family Support movement has been emerging nationally since approximately 1980. The movement is based on a set of principles. It is a "strengths based," "community and participant governed and designed approach" that builds on "existing individual, family, community, and cultural abilities and vitalities." It is "relationship based, fostering respectful partnerships between and among parents, peers, and professionals." Being community driven means that there is not one model that all family support centers adhere to. "Models cannot be dictated; communities select and design their own. Governance must be a partnership of consumers, providers, and policymakers" within each community.[1] What they all have in common is this set of guiding principles.

It is not possible to identify exactly when the seeds of this movement began to take root in Allegheny County. What is evident is that before gaining the attention of county government, some service providers involved in working with low-income families had adopted the Family Support philosophy and were at work putting it in action. The original program in Allegheny County, out of which the vision of Family Support Centers developed, was Family Foundations.

Family Foundations is a federally funded program designed to provide comprehensive, continuous service to low-income families. From its inception in 1989 the Family Foundations advisory board was very engaged in soliciting the active participation of both policymakers and the participants themselves in a collaborative effort to determine program needs and the means to address these needs.[2] There were also other programs in existence in the county that emulated Family Support principles.

The late Senator John Heinz secured funding to open a Family Support Center in McKees Rocks. The commissioner recalls accompanying Heinz to this Center and witnessing first hand the benefits of the programs. This experience, coupled with a Parent Awareness Panel held in June of 1992, are the two events that the commissioner says made him a firm believer in Family Support Centers. Others involved in Family Support recall that they saw the commissioner's interest sparked as he listened to parents, staff, children, and volunteers tell stories of what the centers had done for them and for their communities. For example, one individual spoke of a picnic, a celebration, that took place in his community because the Center had brought people together. Another gentlemen spoke of his involvement in the care of his child that resulted after visiting the Center in his community. The stories went on, providing powerful visions that captured the interest of a key policymaker. The panel, the vision of Phil Pappas, Director of Community Human Services, Inc. and moderated by Dr. Morton Coleman, of the University of Pittsburgh, was meant to celebrate and increase awareness about the family support movement.[3] "Listening to the community people on the panel left me with a burning desire to support the opening of more centers," recalls the commissioner.

Following the panel, the commissioner began speaking publicly every chance he got about the concept of Family Support Centers. He "endorsed and embraced" family support and said "this is primary." He "set the tone" in the human service department that the idea of Family Support Centers should be valued and the number of Centers increased. He gave the movement "legitimacy and integrity." Laurie Mulvey and Kate Garvey, Family Support staff, stated that Allegheny County is unique in that support from political leaders at the top is not common in many other counties.[4]

It was during this time period that Allegheny County 2001, a planning process sponsored by the Board of Commissioners, was produced. The plan very specifically called for an approach to human services that was preventive. The commissioner not only gave vocal support for Family Support Centers, he gave county dollars to the Centers. When CYS had some money left in its budget at the end of 1995, the commissioner saw that it went to Family Support Centers.[5]

Moreover, the commissioner charged Robert Nelkin, Director of Human Services for the county, with ensuring whatever support necessary to help in the growth of the Centers. Nelkin worked with others to raise nearly $4 million dollars from private foundations to fund Family Support Centers.[6] The commissioner tells of how Nelkin "ensured that every director at every human service department tied their programs into the Family Support Centers." Nelkin spearheaded efforts to secure funds from foundations.

Nelkin also played a key role, along with Christine Groark, codirector of the Office of Child Development, in bringing about the collaboration of centers which basically adhered to the Family Support principles but had programmatic differences and did no networking. After much dialogue, and the adoption of the Family Support principles as a guide, Family Foundations agreed to disband its own policy board and establish one county-wide board for all Family Support Centers. The policy board does not oversee the individual programs, and not all centers are called Family Support Centers.

Due to the vision of Nelkin and Groark, the policy board has brought the different programs together to oversee the crucial components of the overall mission. Despite the centers having the same overarching goals, the struggle between different ideas and different ways of meeting the goals was apparent in the difficulties the centers worked through in coming together. Allegheny County is unique in the nation for its county-wide board.[7]

Another example of the complexity faced by policymakers with this initiative is the friction that has resulted due to the success of Family Support Centers. Some advocates see Family Centers as the place from which the coordination of all human services can take place. The state has pushed for seamless services with Family Centers as the vehicle for coordination. Yet, there is a great question as whether Family Support can stay true to its principles and be a vehicle for the delivery of coordinated services. Some within the movement believe that Family Support is not about services, it is about finding strengths and letting participants decide what happens at the center. There are others who support bringing some services to the sites. How does Family Support maintain its essence and at the same time provide certain services to meet 'predetermined' needs? This tension and tensions that exist between Family Support and social services that still utilize a more traditional approach will be subjects of future debate and policy dilemmas.

One of the Family Support principles is that Family Support is enhanced through evaluations that reflect on the principles and contribute to continuous program improvement. Thus ongoing evaluation is viewed as important, as is a research component for some programs.

To continue to "sell" the concept, thus maintaining its status on the agenda, statistics are used to portray a story of the "cost of failure" if the choice is to not invest in Family and Child Support. Numbers on costs of child poverty, low birth weight births, births to single teens, school dropouts, and juvenile delinquency are just some numbers used to portray a message that the problems are immense, that the old way of "doing business" did not work but that Family Support can make a difference. More statistics indicate the possible cost-savings of investing in "at-risk" populations early in life.

Today there are twenty-one Family Support Centers in Allegheny County, which is another factor which makes Allegheny County unique in the movement. The feeling of community ownership of these centers is strong. As a staff person commented "without the county support provided by the commissioner, the potential for the future of Family Support would be less."[8]

Section II Conclusion

People presenting opposing ideas and approaches, and ultimately working together to find a balance and some common ground between competing forces—that is the process that has led to the adoption of a human service system that:

- believes in community living rather than institutional care for people with mental health and mental retardation;
- focuses on prevention, education and access to service in the area of health;
- has moved from a system that reacts to family crisis to one that is proactive and focuses on prevention;
- started the process of streamlining and coordinating human services so that it is indeed user friendly and so that each family would work with only one caseworker;
- values and depends on citizen participation and input to make changes and improve services.

This process is in place, in part, because of the philosophy of Tom Foerster and individuals he empowered in his administration. It is in place, in part, because of advocates for different populations. It is in place, in part, because the commissioner believed (and believes) that the needs of the community must be continually assessed by listening to people's concerns, studying the current situation, and considering the needs of those without a voice; and that then we must plan for the future in order to give people the life they are entitled to.

The importance of the outcome of this process of how human services has changed its mode of operation should not lead to overlooking the importance of the process itself. The struggle between competing ideas, the struggle to find common ground, the struggle of advocates to obtain resources for their specific population serves to bring people together as a community. These struggles reflect the contradictory interpretations that people have for goals such as justice, equity, efficiency, democracy, and liberty.

According to Stone, the "goals are only aspirations" and while the interpretations divide us, "the aspirations unite us." Except for the pressure "to articulate our wishes, preferences, and visions" in regard to our aspirations, "we could not communicate and would not be a community."[1] The commissioner's philosophy and concomitant practice endorsed democracy and community. As government fulfills its role of "continually responding to community needs"[2] policymaking is a never ending process.

Section II Discussion Questions

1. Did Kingdon's model of the policy process shed any light on how human service policy developed in Allegheny County?

2. Review the chapter section focusing on problem identification and gaining agenda status: (a) How did each of the policy initiatives addressed gain agenda status? (b) Were the criteria presented by Lester and Stewart met, and if so, how? (c) Which elements of the three-stage Cobb and Elder model on agenda setting could you identify in the case study?

3. Who is involved in policy formulation for each of the initiatives? Are the key players within government or outside of government? Does it matter whether key players are within or outside of government? Are the initiatives the result of collaborative efforts? How important were lobbying efforts?

4. What options were not considered? Why not? What advantages did the policies adopted enjoy? What were the funding issues involved and how did they impact policy implementation? What goals were met by the policies implemented? What were the costs?

5. Have policy evaluations led to policy adjustments? If so, what was changed?

6. Overall, what were the most effective words and (causal) stories used to define, identify, and persuade?

7. Explain how, overall, the case study offered support for, or undercut: (a) the critiques of the rational model; (b) the description of the essence of the public policy process as being political; (c) the policy process model.

Case Appendix: Postscript*

It should surprise no one to learn that, in late 1997, two and a half years after finally losing another election, former Commissioner Foerster showed up to testify at a budget hearing about cutting county spending for the Community College, mass transit, and other important services. Nor should his words surprise you:

> If you hurt one of those services you hurt people and their ability to get a level playing field, to earn a living, to get to and from their jobs. The people we hurt, we're going to pay a heavy price for down the road.

Tom Foerster had a different solution. Instead of cutting essential county services, raise the property tax by 1 or 2 mills. Two of the current commissioners agreed. The third attacked Foerster for loving taxes. "Always did. Always will."

Actually, the last budget he and Pete Flaherty passed (1995) cut property taxes by 2 mills and eliminated the personal property tax in favor of a regional asset sales tax of one cent. However, the day Commissioner Dunn came into power, he and Commissioner Crammer froze county assessments and added a 4-mill tax cut on top of the 2-mill cut. With no steps taken to cut costs, they had cut property-tax collections by 20 percent. Within one year of taking office, Dunn and company had used up some $54 million dollars of the reserve in place when Foerster left office.

By the hearing date the cost of bonds had increased due to lowered ratings, the budget director had quit, and county employees were being let go. That's not the end of the story though.

In 1999 Allegheny County switched from a county commissioner system to a county council system. Tom Foerster decided to run for one of the seats on the council and won easily. Unfortunately his health deteriorated and he was hospitalized, but he continued working on issues by phone and was sworn into office in his hospital room.

Shortly thereafter, on January 11, 2000, the former state legislator known as "Little Joe" (because when speaking for or against any piece of legislation he always closed by asking his colleagues to consider its impact on Little Joe—his shorthand term for the average citizen), the seven-term commissioner, died.

His legacy lives on not only in the lives of the family and friends who loved him, but also in the environmental legislation he worked for, in the social service system he helped improve, at the community college he helped found, and at the airport where a terminal was renamed in his honor in February. Individuals can make a difference.

---

*Postscript by Randy Clemons and Mark McBeth. An editorial about the budget hearing appeared in the *Pittsburgh Post Gazette* on December 8, 1997. Obviously, other stories have appeared in the Gazette on a regular basis as well, including a plethora after his death. Personal communication with the case author also was utilized.

Notes

Preface and Introduction

1. County Government Administrative Manual.
2. Tom Foerster: Quotes and thoughts in this section and all other sections taken from interviews on February 7, February 14, February 23, February 28, March 13, March 21, April 4, and June 11, of 1996.
3. Deborah A. Stone, *Policy Paradox and Political Reason* (New York: HarperCollins, 1988), p. 106.

Section I

1. Interviews with Barbara Shorr, Robert Nelkin, Victor Papale, Charles Peters, Charles Stowell, and Kate Garvey, February–June 1996.
2. Deborah A. Stone, *Policy Paradox and Political Reason* (New York: HarperCollins, 1988), pp. 28–29.
3. Ibid.
4. Harold D. Lasswell, *Politics: Who Gets What, When, How* (New York: Meridian Books, 1958).
5. Deborah A. Stone, *Policy Paradox and Political Reason* (New York: HarperCollins, 1988), p. 41.
6. ———— pp. 42–47.
7. ———— pp. 42–47.
8. Alan Ryan, "The Moderns: Liberalism Relived," in *Political Thought from Plato to NATO* (Illinois: The Dorsey Press, 1984), pp. 179–82.
9. Douglas Murray McGregor, "The Human Side of Enterprise," in *Classics of Public Administration,* 3rd ed. (1957/1992), edited by Jay M. Shafritz and Albert C. Hyde.
10. Charles Stowell: Interview on May 15, 1996.
11. Victor Papale: Interview on June 21, 1996.
12. Laurie Mulvey: Interview on May 9, 1996, and Kate Garvey: Interview on June 12, 1996.
13. Charlotte Arnold: Interview on May 13, 1996.
14. Charles Peters: Interview and correspondence June and July 1996.
15. Vic Papale: Interview on June 21, 1996.
16. P. J. Boyle, "Foerster, 30 Years, Career of Persistence and Powers," *Pittsburgh Press*, April 7, 1985.
17. Victor Papale: Interview on June 21, 1996.
18. Robert Nelkin, present at interview with Tom Foerster, 13 March 1996.
19. Charles Kolling: Interview on May 2, 1996.
20. "Preparing Allegheny County for the 21st Century," a report to the Allegheny County Board of Commissioners, prepared by the Committee to Prepare Allegheny County for the 21st Century, p. 2.
21. Our View, Editorial, "Foerster Leaves Legacy of Solutions," *Herald*, January 10, 1996.
22. "Toward a Living Renaissance," A Report of the Allegheny County Human Service Commission, November 1974, p. 9.
23. "Human Services Center Dedicated last Friday," *The Times Express*, December 22, 1982, p. 9.
24. "Elderly to Get Help after Treatment," *Pittsburgh Post Gazette*, February 24, 1988, p. 5.
25. Staff person at Lemington, phone call June 26, 1996.
26. Robert Nelkin, "Some County Human Service Transition Issues," paper for Leadership Pittsburgh, December 14, 1995.
27. *Allegheny County Children and Youth Services,* Annual Report, *1993 and 1995 County of Allegheny Comprehensive Annual Financial Report,* prepared by Frank Lucchinao, Controller, December 31, 1995, p. 140.

28. Allegheny County Children and Youth Services, *Annual Report*, 1993, pp. 1 and 3.
29. "History of Health Department," two-page chronological report of highlights of Allegheny County Health Department.
30. Commemorative Report, 25 Years of Progress 1969–1994: Allegheny County Mental Health/Mental Retardation/Drugs & Alcohol/Homeless & Hunger, p. 24.
31. *Allegheny County/Pittsburgh Homeless Initiative ... An Action Plan*, p. 1.
32. ———— p. 2.
33. Commemorative Report, 25 Years of Progress 1969–94: Allegheny County Mental Health/Mental Retardation/Drugs & Alcohol/Homeless & Hunger, p. 34.
34. ———— p. 37.
35. Video: "Allegheny County Programs Work," published on behalf of Allegheny County Mental Health/Mental Retardation/Drugs & Alcohol/Homeless & Hunger.
36. "Allegheny County 2001," Report by Planning Committee. Sponsored by Allegheny County Board of Commissioners, 1992, pp. 4–5.
37. Robert Nelkin, "Some County Human Service Transition Issues," paper for Leadership Pittsburgh, December 14, 1995.
38. "Allegheny County 2001," Report by Planning Committee. Sponsored by Allegheny County Board of Commissioners, 1992, p. 5.
39. Interview with Tom Foerster and Robert Nelkin, February 14, 1996.
40. Dianne Jacob, "1992 Pittsburgher of the Year: Commissioner Tom Foerster," Pittsburgh, p. 53.
41. ———— pp. 34–37.
42. Charlotte Arnold: Interview on May 14, 1996.
43. Terry Russell, *An Analysis of Recidivism among clients of The Program for Female Offenders, Inc.*, May 1995.
44. Mark Belko, "Report says county program for jobs may save or lose cash," *Pittsburgh Post Gazette*, May 10, 1988.
45. Victor Papale: Interview on June 21, 1996.
46. Ibid.
47. Charles Peters: Interview on May 21, 1996.

Section II

Mental Health/Mental Retardation

1. Commemorative Report, 25 Years of Progress 1969–94: Allegheny County Mental Health/Mental Retardation/Drugs & Alcohol/Homeless & Hunger, p. 5.
2. ———— p. 14.
3. Ibid.
4. ———— p. 19.
5. Unless otherwise specified this and all other quotes and thoughts by Charles Peters obtained in an interview on May 21, 1996.
6. Robert Nelkin, during interview with Tom Foerster, February 1996.
7. Ed Blazina, "Foerster organizing conference on funding," *The Pittsburgh Press*, July 7, 1988.
8. Tom Foerster: Quotes and thoughts in this, and all other sections, taken from interviews on February 7, February 14, February 23, February 28, March 13, March 21, April 4, and June 11 of 1996.
9. C. A. Peters, "Politics Is the Answer—Not the Problem," *Association of Mental Health Administrators Newsletter*, September/October 1991, p. 5.
10. Ibid.
11. Ibid.
12. Commemorative Report, 25 Years of Progress 1969–94: Allegheny County Mental Health/Mental Retardation/Drugs & Alcohol/Homeless & Hunger, p. 63.

13. C. A. Peters, letter to John C. Craig Jr., editor of the *Pittsburgh Post Gazette*, September 16, 1994, p. 2.
14. Commemorative Report, 25 Years of Progress 1969–94: Allegheny County Mental Health/Mental Retardation/Drugs & Alcohol/Homeless & Hunger, p. 50.
15. ——— p. 117.
16. Ibid.

Kane Regional Centers

1. Charles Stowell, Interview, June 26, 1996.
2. Nicholas Stabile, Budget Director, Bureau of Accounts and Statistics, Allegheny County, Pennsylvania as presented in *Kane Hospital: A Place to Die*, Action Coalition of Elders, 1974.
3. *The Social Geography of Allegheny County: Social, Economic, and Demographic Indicators for Allegheny County Municipalities and Pittsburgh City Neighborhoods*. Vol 3. Municipality Profiles, University Center for Social and Urban Research.
4. *Annual Report of the John J. Kane Hospital for the year 1969*, Allegheny County Institution District, Pittsburgh, Pennsylvania.
5. Charles Stowell, Interview, June 26, 1996.
6. *Allegheny County, Kane Hospital Care*, Produced by D. M. Bower and Mary Wolfson Associates in cooperation with Allegheny County Bureau of Public Information, Pittsburgh 1971, p. 5.
7. Charles Stowell, Interview, June 26, 1996.
8. P. J. Boyle, "Foerster, 30 Years, Career of Persistence and Powers," *Pittsburgh Press*, April 7, 1985, p. B-7.
9. Action Coalition of Elders, *Kane Hospital: A Place to Die*, preface, 1974.
10. Charles Stowell, Interview, June 26, 1996.
11. Action Coalition of Elders, *Kane Hospital: A Place to Die*, 1974.
12. *Annual Report of the John J. Kane Hospital for the year 1969*, Allegheny County Institution District, Pittsburgh, Pennsylvania, p. 7.
13. Charles Stowell, Interview, May 15, 1996.
14. Charles Stowell, Interview, June 26, 1996.
15. Charles Stowell, Interview, May 15, 1996.
16. Charles Stowell, Interview, June 26, 1996.
17. Ibid.
18. Linda J. Walker (1984), Dissertation, "Kane Hospital Relocation Project: Attitudes and Perceptions of Patients," University of Pittsburgh.

Family Support Centers

1. Interview with and handouts received from Laurie Mulvey, May 9, 1996.
2. Interview with Laurie Mulvey, May 9, 1996.
3. Interview with Laurie Mulvey, May 9, 1996.
4. Interviews with Kate Garvey, June 12, 1996, and Laurie Mulvey, May 9, 1996.
5. Interview with Kate Garvey, June 12, 1996.
6. Robert Nelkin, September 6, 1996.
7. Interview with Laurie Mulvey, May 9, 1996.
8. Interview with Kate Garvey, June 12, 1996.

Section II Conclusion

1. Deborah A. Stone, *Policy Paradox and Political Reason* (New York: HarperCollins, 1988), p. 310.
2. Interviews with Commissioner Foerster between February and June 1996.

CHAPTER 5

A PRAGMATIC PUBLIC POLICY ANALYSIS METHOD

Case Study
"Playing Politics: Bison, Brucellosis, Business, and Bureaucrats"

In this chapter the discussion balance shifts from *theory* and practice to theory and *practice*, but argues for praxis. It also argues that there is a need for praxis regarding the rational model and its critiques. In a sense we are arguing for a fourth criteria for evaluating models.[1] That fourth criteria is applicability in the field (practicality for practitioners).

As we have already discussed and implied, public policymaking is not a simple technical process. Public policy analysts must not only possess quantitative and other technical skills but must also understand that politics is fundamentally a conflict over interests and values and that policies are ultimately resolved through political power. You know from earlier chapters, particularly Chapter 1, that analysts—either consciously or not—must answer several related normative questions in the process of doing their job. For example:

1. Does the analyst serve the client (elected officials or others), interest groups, or the public?
2. Who has and who should have the power in a democracy—interest groups, elites/experts, or citizens? (See Table 1-5.)
3. Is the role of the analyst to provide a policy recommendation or to educate all stakeholders, including the public, on various options?

This chapter, in addition to providing a five-step method that you can use to "do" policy analysis, lends assistance to students willing to openly confront the tough normative questions. To prepare you, we begin with a discussion that elucidates a public

---

[1]The first three criteria were accurate description (verisimilitude), explanation (ah-hah), and prediction (crystal ball).

policy methodology for analysts. Drawing heavily on the work of Patton and Sawicki (1986), our discussion both presents the process in a step-by-step manner and, strongly relying on the critiques of Danziger (1995) and Stone (1997), establishes further the absolute difficulty of conducting a rational analysis.

The chapter closes with a case, "Playing Politics: Bison, Brucellosis, Business, and Bureaucrats," which deals with rural economies, development, and environmental policy. The case places you in the role of a public policy analyst and requires you to grapple with several important issues. This time you are asked to conduct your policy analysis using the five-step method, which we will introduce to you shortly. In the process you must reconcile conflict stemming from the fact that the case revolves around value conflict and power structures. In other words, the case is very realistic. Indeed, the case, as well as the conflict, is real.

As you recall from the Nightcrawlers and Cappuccino case, the rural west is becoming increasingly divided between two groups. One group is composed of those who want the west to remain tied to an economic, cultural, social, and political system based on extractive commodity industries such as logging, ranching, timber cutting, and agriculture. They view the environment as something to be used for economic survival and profit. The second group is composed largely of newcomers who want the rural west to diversify economically, culturally, socially, and politically. These newcomers view the environment as something to be protected and used for recreation.

As an analyst, you will be asked to recommend policies that will both satisfy the economic survival needs of the rural community and simultaneously protect the natural environment. In doing what appears to be a technical case, you will have to wrestle with issues of power, democracy, and who (as policy analysts) you ultimately serve. The case forces you to decide whether your job is to build consensus or to choose the interests of one group over another. The task, just like real policy analysis, is not easy.

The Rational Public Policy Analysis Method: History and Form

There has always been conflict between those who see government policymaking as consisting of the interaction of power and politics and those who believe that policymaking should be a more rational process. Public administration arose as a discipline in the late 1800s as a response to the corruption and inefficiency of American government. As discussed in Chapter 2, scholars and practitioners such as Woodrow Wilson (1887) believed that government administration should be the same as business administration.

Wilson's belief was that, while policymaking was all about conflict and power, the administration of that policy should be conducted in a rational-scientific manner. Remember that Wilson's ideas are termed the "politics/administration dichotomy." This is the notion, discussed in Chapter 2, that politics should be removed from the implementation and execution of public policy. This ideological construct was a very strong component of the "progressive movement" in American history. Progressives sought to remove the corrupting influences of politics from governmental decisions. According to this philosophy, administrative experts should not make policy, but rather should only use their expertise to implement policy made by elected officials.

In the period from 1880 to 1940, U.S. society changed greatly from a primarily agricultural society to a more metropolitan society. As explained earlier in the text, with these changes came the rise of social problems: crime, poverty, pollution, delinquency, congestion, and others. Governments at all levels were called upon to find creative and innovative solutions (public policies) to these problems. As the problems of society became more complex, the solutions to them likewise became increasingly complex. Elected officials often did not have the expertise to make complex scientific evaluations and decisions about these problems. The policy initiatives most often came not from elected officials but from administrators. The politics/administration dichotomy was a false one, and scholars such as Paul Appleby (1949) suggested that policymaking and administration are not, and have never been, separate.

In fact, with the increasingly complex nature of public problems, elected officials turned to administrative experts to help find policies that would solve public problems. Thus, the "public policy analyst" was born. The roots of public policy analysis come from private management techniques. Businesses attempt to develop policies strategically, based on sound information. Business analysis answers questions such as "Is there a market for our product?" and "Where should we locate our new business?" Business policies are not haphazard. Instead, they are predominantly made on the basis of careful research and statistical analysis. Public policy analysis is premised on the same reasoning. Instead of allowing public policy to simply be the result of power and politics, public policy analysts, steeped in the rational method, attempt to rationally and scientifically determine the most appropriate public policies. (Chapters 6 and 7, and to a lesser degree this chapter, will provide direction on postpositivist methods of analysis.)

The rational public policy analysis methodology is typically based on some variation of a multistep approach: defining a problem, generating alternatives, establishing evaluation criteria, selecting alternatives, and evaluating alternatives. Whatever the variations, some policy analysts believe that the rational approach will produce one "best scientific answer" to policy problems such as poverty, crime, and pollution. This is termed a positivist orientation. Examples of these highly rational and scientific models include Dunn (1981/1994), Edith Stokey and Robert Zeckhauser (1978), and Edward Quade (1975). To help policymakers choose optimal policies, these talented scholars teach—and analysts learn to use—highly quantitative techniques such as cost-benefit analysis (CBA), regression, indifference curves, decision trees, extrapolation, the **Delphi technique**, and other rational models.[2]

This strict approach has received great criticism in recent years from postmodern policy scholars such as Deborah Stone (1997) and Marie Danziger (1995). These scholars argue that rational policy analysis is impossible and instead has largely served the interests of elites. It is argued that the quantitative techniques—the strategic use of numbers, graphs, and scientific formulas—serve as cloaking devices that hide the power politics that determine the outcomes of the value and interest conflicts.

Somewhat of a middle-ground approach, between positivism and the postpositivist and postmodern critiques, is offered by Patton and Sawicki (1986) whose policy analysis method is one of "quick analysis." They reject the notion that policy analysts

---

[2]When addressed, even morality and ethics are often taught as a simple utilitarian calculation, or as a Pareto Optimality (whatever is best for the most, or some win and none lose) that can be objectively determined.

can find the "one best" solution. They realize that policymaking, and hence analysis, is political. Their approach uses the scientific-rational approach but does so to find policies that are politically acceptable and effective. They do not accept a purely positivist orientation that there is one reality, that scientific methods can find it, and that hence we can find the one best policy. Patton and Sawicki (1986, 35) elegantly state:

> Rarely will there be only one acceptable or appropriate alternative. Not only will different options appeal to various interested parties, but two or more alternatives may bring roughly similar results. None of the alternatives is likely to be perfect, as problems are rarely solved. More often their severity is reduced, the burden is more evenly distributed, or they are replaced by less severe problems.

A Five-Step Method

We believe that a five-step method is most commonly used by public policy analysts in practice. Our method is (please read slowly) a postpositivist, postmodernist inspired, nonrational approach to a rational methodology. The form of multistep policy analysis methods suggests a rational, logical, and linear approach. Yet policy analysis, as you learned in Chapter 4 relative to the public policy process, is much more fragmented, subjective, political, instinctual, and nonlinear than the policy cycle model, or a multistep policy analysis methodology, implies.

Step I: Define the Problem and Determine Its Causes

The definition of a policy problem determines what, if any, policies are implemented. We have already established that problem definition is not easy. You know that it is value driven and that nearly all policy problems have complex causes. Take, for example, the problem of drug abuse. Before a government can determine what policies to implement to try to alleviate drug abuse, a public policy analyst must search for the root cause(s) of the problem. Varying problem definitions lead to varying policies. Box 5-1 looks at varying explanations of drug abuse and demonstrates how each one leads toward different policies.

5-1. Different Causes, Different Solutions

Explanation #1   Drug abuse is the result of a breakdown of community institutions such as the family, the church, and the school. These institutions provide guidance to the individual in the form of community norms. The breakdown of these institutions leads to a lack of clear norms, and drug abuse is one result of this breakdown.

Policy #1   Government must institute policies to rebuild these institutions. Examples of such policies could include (a) government mandated employee flex-time that would allow working parents to be at home with their children more often, (b) an expanded family leave act building on the law that was promoted primarily by the Democratic party, vetoed by President Bush, and signed by President Clinton in 1993, allowing workers to take unpaid leave for family emergencies, (c) school uniforms to help restore school discipline and cut back on gang activity in the schools, and (d) teacher-led prayer in public schools as a method to restore religion in the lives of youngsters. (According to the Supreme Court this would be a violation of the First Amendment—policies suggested are often controversial or, in this case, unconstitutional. Note also that there would be a problem putting a coalition together, since the majority of supporters of the Family and Medical Leave Act would quite likely oppose mandated school prayer.)

Explanation #2   Drug abuse, like all behavior, is the result of the individual conducting a cost-benefit analysis on their own actions. Drug users perceive that the benefits of drug use (pleasurable high, social activity with peers) outweigh the costs of the activity (sickness, health risks, the risk of getting caught). Likewise, drug sellers perceive that the benefit of selling drugs (profits) outweighs the risk of getting caught.

Policy #2   From this perspective, government must increase the costs of using and selling drugs. This would include (a) increased penalties like mandatory prison terms for any drug user, and (b) the death penalty for any drug seller. In addition, government could pursue educational policies that inform citizens of the health risks of drug use. Celebrities could be hired to make public service advertisements that persuade citizens that drug use is not socially acceptable or fashionable. These latter activities could help decrease the perceived benefits and simultaneously increase the perceived costs of drug use.

Explanation #3   Drug use is learned through interaction in groups. Individuals learn to become drug users from the people they socialize with. Teenage drug users learn how to use drugs and learn to interpret their effects as pleasurable from their peer group. Corporate executives learn how to use drugs and perceive their effects as pleasurable from other corporate executives who use drugs. Becker's (1953) work on pot smokers found that marijuana smokers learned how to smoke marijuana and even learned that certain effects were "pleasurable" from other marijuana smokers. People who tried pot by themselves without a supporting peer group were far less likely to become pot smokers. In short, when individuals become isolated within one dominant peer group they take on the behavior of that peer group.

Policy #3   Government should implement policies that do not stigmatize users by defining them as part of one peer group. For example, a teenager is arrested for drug use. Policy #2 says that this teen should be punished (to increase costs) by putting him in a juvenile detention center. Policy perspective #3 says instead that the juvenile should not be placed in a detention center because this activity would lead the youngster to define himself as deviant. The youngster's peer group would be other juvenile delinquents who probably also use drugs, and from this peer group the youngster would learn how to use more drugs. The juvenile would accept society's definition that he is a delinquent and this self-perception would lead to more unacceptable behavior. This policy perspective instead suggests that the court system needs to be more lenient and allow the juvenile to remain in school, where he has the opportunity to interact with other peer groups (band, sports, debate, church, etc.) and where he is less likely to define himself as deviant.

Explanation #4   Drug abuse is defined more broadly to include prescription and over-the-counter (OTC) abuse. Capitalism promotes the making of profits and drug companies like to make profits. They make profits by promoting OTCs to consumers, and by pushing their prescription drugs to doctors so that the doctors will prescribe these medications to patients. As a result, the United States has a terrible drug culture. From mass advertising, we learn that if we have even a slight headache we should seek one of the several remedies available at the local pharmacy. If these don't work, we go to a physician who gladly dispenses medication for even minor ailments. Physicians receive all types of inducements from drug companies to prescribe their medications. As a result, doctors make money from office calls, pharmacies make money from drug sales, and drug manufacturers make a lot of money from this activity.

Policy #4   Government could nationalize the drug industry. All drug companies could be owned by the state. This would remove the profit motive and help alleviate drug abuse (this would not be very politically popular in our capitalist system). Other less radical approaches would be to eliminate drug advertisements and instead have public service announcements that promote more holistic health practices such as diet, exercise, and meditation.

Note: Explanation #1 comes from structural-functionalism and systems theory in sociology. See Talcott Parsons (1951, 227). Some of these policies are found in the contemporary works of Amitai Etzioni (1996). Explanation #2 comes from the sociological theory known as "exchange theory." See George Homans (1974). Explanation #3's orientation is from the sociological theory "symbolic interactionism." See George Herbert Mead (1934/1962). Explanation #4 follows a "critical" or "neo-Marxist" line of thought. See Herbert Marcuse (1964).

So there you have it ... four different descriptions of the problem and four different policy suggestions. Perhaps all four explanations are correct or perhaps all four are wrong.[3] And, of course, there are many other policies that could be generated from these explanations as well as other theoretical explanations. But clearly policy choices are derived from the definition of the problem.

How does the analyst go about defining a problem? The following suggestions from Patton and Sawicki (1986, 104–10) are helpful. First, the analyst should research the problem to determine its location, history, and time frame. For example, how long has drug abuse been a problem? What is its history? Is it a national, state, or local problem? Second, the analyst needs to develop a fact base and operationalize terms. For example, what is "drug abuse?" Is it just use of hard drugs or is it pot use, alcohol use, OTC use, or nicotine use? Third, the analyst must conduct a stakeholder analysis. As you recall, in simple terms, stakeholders are those individuals or groups who have an interest in the problem. Remember that, at a minimum, the analyst must also determine the values and interests of each stakeholder. With drug abuse those who can affect, or would be affected by, the policy decision include school officials, parents,

---

[3]Coming from a rational perspective that suggests there is a correct formulation of a problem, William Dunn (1994, 182) writes that "Policy analysts fail more often because they solve the wrong problem than because they get the wrong solution to the right problem. The fatal error in policy analysis is E_{III}, solving the wrong formulation of a problem when one should have solved the right one."

churches, the courts, police officers, doctors, and many more individuals and groups who have direct interests in the problem. These stakeholder groups can provide insights into the problem and provide a great deal of information about what types of policies are acceptable or unacceptable. Fourth, the problem statement should lead to action. Complex theoretical statements often lead to good scientific explanations but do not lend themselves to government policy. Explanation #4 is one such problem statement, since it is doubtful that the U.S. government could ever nationalize drug companies.

Problem definition is not an easy task and it is difficult to build consensus around a definition of a problem. Dunn (1981, 99–100) points out that public problems are (a) interdependent, (b) subjective, (c) artificial, and (d) dynamic. Interdependency means that problems do not stand in isolation. Drug abuse is linked to other problems (e.g., poverty and quality of life) and the causes of these problems are multifaceted and may not be directly linked to the problems that directly cause drug abuse. Subjectivity refers to the fact that policy problems are open to multiple interpretations. Artificiality refers to the fact that, as Dunn (1981, 99) states, "Problems have no existence apart from the individuals and groups who define them, which means that there are no 'natural' states of society which in and of themselves constitute policy problems." Dynamic means that policy problems are constantly changing and do not stay solved.

Step II: Establish Criteria to Evaluate Alternatives

In our first step, it was clear that some of our policy prescriptions would be unacceptable to some. Government control of drug companies is politically unacceptable, state-sponsored prayer in school is legally unacceptable, and mandatory prison terms for all drug users might be socially, as well as economically and administratively, unacceptable. What we have just demonstrated is that there are certain criteria that are used to evaluate all policies. The analyst must be careful to honestly list all criteria.

Patton and Sawicki (1986, 14) point out that elected officials often want to use "naive criteria," which ignores the fact that criteria and objectives are often in conflict. For example, mandatory prison sentences for drug users might meet the effectiveness criteria (it gets drug users off the streets) but it would fail an economic feasibility criteria since hundreds of new prisons would have to be built, necessitating excessive tax increases or ignoring other public issues that citizens expect government action on. Patton and Sawicki (1986, 156–67) argue that there are some universal criteria for nearly all policy areas:

- technical feasibility, including effectiveness and adequacy;
- economic feasibility (costs and benefits);
- cost effectiveness (several policies may work but which one is the cheapest or provides the "most bang for the buck"?;
- political viability (includes acceptability with stakeholders); and,
- legality and ethics (is the policy legal and is it ethical?).

Values affect the choice and ranking of the criteria, as well as the evaluation of how a policy fares against those criteria. Box 5-2 (on pages 140–43) explores these issues further through a series of interesting policy examples.

5-2. The Advice Is Simple, the Reality Isn't

Technical Feasibility

In the heart of the Cold War period, President John F. Kennedy committed the United States to putting a man on the moon before the Soviet Union did. Within a decade all of the technical obstacles had been overcome, and Neil Armstrong took that "one small step for man, one giant leap for mankind." Today, supporters of the space program have other goals and dreams involving sending humans into space, but they can't convince Congress to support them. Outside of the context of the Cold War, would the United States have thought it was technically feasible to go to the moon or would the obstacles have seemed too large?

Another related example from the Cold War shows both how this criteria of technical feasibility is flawed, and how it can be met but will conflict with other criteria and objectives. This is the story of the atomic airplane. For a very long time the Air Force sought a larger piece of the nuclear pie (the Navy had nuclear powered submarines and the army controlled our nuclear missiles). The debate about building a nuclear-powered airplane focused on the question of technical feasibility. It was determined that it was technically feasible—and there was lots of political support from the Air Force, defense contractors, scientists interested in getting research dollars, and Cold Warriors. However, after years and years and tons of taxpayer money they still had not solved the dangers of a plane crash, and the best solution to shielding pilots from radiation that they could come up with was to use older pilots since they wouldn't be having children and any cancer would take a long time to develop. The real point though is that, while technically feasible, it didn't make sense. There was no real mission or need for an atomic airplane.

Economic Feasibility and Cost Effectiveness

We deal with the issue of cost-benefit analysis rather extensively in Chapter 8, but will offer a couple of quick insights. Management of the national forests, like Allegheny National Forest, is the prime duty of the U.S. Forest Service. Yet many critics of their "multiple-use philosophy" accuse the Forest Service of seeing trees as a source of cash rather than being appropriately concerned with preservation, old-growth, biodiversity, and wildlife populations. In terms of dollars, the revenues earned on the sale of timber from our national forests certainly outweigh costs. This also means that a thriving deer population is a bad thing because deer damage and eat trees. The Forest Service has, in fact, consistently argued for lowering the size of the deer population in the Allegheny National Forest. The most cost-effective solution, the most bang for the buck (so to speak), might be allowing a massive hunt with no limits on types of weapons or on the number of deer one can kill, no restrictions regarding does versus bucks, and no protection for fawns. Sorry Bambi, this may not be sport, but it is business. What does cost-benefit analysis really tell us about the competing values at stake? What about possible conflicting ethical, legal, or moral concerns?

These are in many ways the most naive, yet most compelling, criteria. Monetary concerns are politically powerful. Efficiency and cost effectiveness are holy grails in public administration. Can you imagine a politician claiming they weren't fiscally conservative? (Yessiree, I'm all for waste and mismanagement.) Never forget though, that the numbers can be massaged, that not all costs and benefits can be foreseen, and that there are things we should do even if they are not economically feasible or the cheapest option available.

Political Viability

It is obviously true that the authors of this text endorse the importance of political viability, but this is also a concept that can be used as a political weapon. If you declare something politically impossible, if an idea is proclaimed dead on arrival (DOA), or if someone is branded politically naive, then it may be a self-fulfilling prophecy. Recognize though that the political viability of a policy depends mightily on how the entire debate is framed. It depends on how the problem is defined. It depends on how the solutions are packaged and by whom. It depends on whether or not someone is willing to lead an informed dialogue. It depends on advocates who shift the debate through forceful advocacy of ideas outside the middle of the spectrum. Consider the subjective differences in political viability derived from strategic argument relative to two problems that face every major city.

You might not be able to generate public support for "high tech" training programs for inner-city dropouts if you portray it as welfare, but if you sell it as important to our economic future not to waste potential talent and as cost effective compared to a life of crime and long-term dependency, you might.

At one time in the 1980s, concern for the homeless was a hot political issue. The late Mitch Snyder's activism, and his unsupported claim that on any given evening there were 3 million homeless people, helped increase that support. Ironically, the problem is worse today than it was then. (Good economic times can actually be harmful by driving up the price of housing.) The demand for emergency shelter has risen consistently and dramatically since 1985. And so has federal funding for a range of services.

But public support for seriously addressing homelessness depends significantly on whether the cause of homelessness is seen as the fault of the homeless or not. The mood lately seems to be that it is their individual responsibility, not society's. In the eighties, one argument that helped increase support was the fact that many of the homeless were Vietnam veterans. This is a group the nation has long believed deserved to be taken care of. On the other hand, welfare recipients have often been portrayed as undeserving (lazy, giving birth to too many children, and cheats—Ronald Reagan told stories on the campaign trail about welfare queens). Yet, even before reform, most people did not stay on the welfare rolls for more than two years, well over half were children, the average number of children for welfare mothers was less than the societal average, and most of them worked at least part-time. Well, sure, it is political suicide to support spending public monies for people seen as undeserving, but there is political support from the public for helping veterans, those who can't help themselves, and those (like the working poor) who are trying to help themselves.

The main point here is that political viability is a dynamic, not a static concept. It is also tremendously vulnerable to the other criteria. That is, part of the political argument against the Strategic Defense Initiative (popularly dubbed Star Wars—its idea was to protect us from nuclear missiles) was that it was technically not feasible. Cost and benefit numbers are often used to portray something in a way that makes it politically viable or politically not viable. Ethical and legal factors can be used to make an otherwise politically unpopular proposal viable or vice versa. The Americans with Disabilities Act of 1990 legally forced many corporations, schools, and government agencies to do things that (while arguably quite ethical) would not have had winning political support due to cost.

Legality and Ethics

Of course you should consider what is legal, and of course you should consider what is ethical, but neither one is always clear. As you learned in Chapter 3, black letter law doesn't exist, and precedent is often contradictory and may be used strictly or loosely. Also, what could be more subjective than ethics? We certainly have made the argument that value conflict is the rule, not the exception.

Let's briefly visit the issue of cloning. While many people are disturbed by the thought of cloning humans (we are "playing God," this is eugenics ... like what the Nazis and Himmler did, there is a high rate of failure—Dolly was the only sheep out of 277 fertilized eggs to develop from embryo to a lamb, do clones have souls?, we should not tinker with natural selection, etc.) there are also lots of people who support this research as too important to be guided by the yuk factor. Their arguments are also persuasive to many people (academic freedom, natural selection is violated constantly—going back to the domestication of plants and wolves, and continuing to genetically altered tomatoes and in vitro fertilization, trying to stop the shortage of organs for transplant and develop 100 percent matches to stop rejection, twins are clones). Ethics are vital to consider, but not an easily applied criteria. Moreover, we once again must consider the impact of the other criteria on legal and ethical considerations. For our last policy example, let's touch on the reverse aspect of the Nazi's repugnant breeding program, exterminating "undesirables."

The Holocaust is often used (too often and too carelessly) as a metaphor. This is because it is a clear example of evil. However, one of the embarrassing parts of history is how most of the world, the United States very much included, failed to intercede in, and even sometimes abetted, this tragedy. We turned away a ship in 1939 loaded with refugees. We consistently and increasingly turned down applications for visas. We failed to bomb the rail lines transporting people to slavery and slaughter. Why, when Hitler was cranking up his final solution to the Jews, was it so difficult to turn moral abhorrence into a public policy to stop, or at least mitigate, the extermination of six million people? The sad answer is that other criteria and conflicting values won out.

U.S. immigration laws (e.g., the National Origins Act of 1924) were based on ethnic, regional, and religious prejudices. Nativism, fueled in part by anti-Semitism (which was fueled by the radio broadcasts of the Catholic priest Father Coughlin), in part by worries that our Protestant and Anglo-Saxon heritage and values were at stake, in part by Depression-driven concerns about jobs and wages and about the cost of adding people to the public dole, meant there were many hurdles to overcome. We were also worried about a fifth column of Nazi supporters and spies. We didn't divert our bombers, in part anyway, because some believed the best solution for these people was to win the war as efficiently as possible, so other targets were more important. Domestic political concerns (political viability, coalition building for other legislation, and electoral self-interest) were other factors. Crowding out and bureaucratic lethargy were also problems—there was a lot on the agenda. Our own racism and segregation were problems that made speaking out difficult too. In sum, the shame cannot be lessened by this list of other factors, but they do make it clear that, even in the face of unmitigated evil, it is not easy to translate ethics into policy.

Recognizing the role of values, the central importance of political viability, the need to develop policies with legitimacy, and the idea of democracy, it is important that the criteria used in policy analysis come from the selected stakeholders and that stakeholders should represent a strong cross-section of affected parties. Dunn (1994, 307–8) terms such a process "value clarification." He writes:

> The need for value clarification in making policy recommendations is most evident when we consider competing criteria for recommendation (effectiveness, efficiency, adequacy, responsiveness, equity, appropriateness) and the multiple forms of rationality from which these criteria are derived. Value clarification helps answer such questions as the following: What value premises underlie the choice of policy objectives? Are these value premises those of policy analysts, of policy makers, of particular social groups, or of society as a whole?

Beginning policy analysts often believe that evaluation criteria are subjectively created by analysts or policymakers themselves. More advanced analysts realize that the criteria come from stakeholders. As discussed in Chapter 1, the question of who the stakeholders are is directly tied to the analyst's view of democracy and power. The next two chapters also focus on the crucial question of who participates. One issue is that different people see things differently. Another issue is that as an analyst you need to value the instincts, interests, and input of average citizens, not just experts and elites. A simple test is to look not around the table, but under it. You should see diversity in the running shoes, high heels, sandals, wing tips, loafers, and all sorts of other choices on those feet. If you don't, then the talking heads above the table are unlikely to represent adequate diversity.

Step III: Generate Policy Alternatives

Once the problem statement or statements have been developed and the evaluation criteria have been determined, how can policy alternatives be generated? According to Weimer and Vining (1999, 197–98, 278–82) and Patton and Sawicki (1986, 181–92) there are several options:

1. *Best practices search.* The analyst can search for effective policies that other communities or governments have implemented for the same problem. Of course, you are unlikely to find a perfect fit. Weimer and Vining suggest "tinkering." Tinkering involves breaking a policy into its fundamental components to develop alternatives and assembling a combination that fits your community's circumstances.

2. *Use of experts.* Experts can be called upon to offer advice, particularly in highly technical or scientific policy areas. Experts cannot solve value conflict and their values should not carry extra weight.

3. *Client orientation.* What is it that your client wants? If your boss is the mayor, and the mayor wants a policy of increased police visibility in neighborhoods, perhaps even has pledged to increase police patrols on the east side of town, then your policy design should take that into consideration. While we are on the topic, if you don't consider the political power of your client you may design a policy for the state that only the federal government can enact.

4. *Brainstorming.* A group of analysts can simply throw out policy suggestions using their knowledge of the policy problem. Be creative, brave, and willing to have fun. Don't shoot ideas down. Successful brainstorming requires the acceptance of all ideas, regardless of how outlandish they might be. Ideas are often rejected because they fail one criteria. Successful brainstorming requires that all options initially be considered acceptable. While an option might fail one criteria, it might well be acceptable using other criterion. You can also send your ideas up as trial balloons to test their political viability, and this too may generate more ideas as others react to your proposal.

5. *Incremental Approach.* The analyst can look at existing policies and decide to essentially "tweak" the system rather than making large-scale changes. Although a somewhat unappealing theory, incrementalism dominates in practice because it has real advantages, including a solid knowledge base, and political opposition is often lower than for dramatic change.

6. *Use of primary research.* The analyst may conduct mail surveys and focus groups to gather information about acceptable policies.

7. *Generic solutions.* Generic solutions means orienting your search for policies in terms of general policy approaches such as: privatization; trying to stimulate private markets through deregulation; using taxes or subsidies to alter incentives; utilizing regulations or legislation to change the rules; or offering economic protection through subsidization.

8. *Do nothing.* The status quo is always a serious policy option. Analysts must consider whether doing nothing might be the preferred course of action. Other policy analysts thought it was a good idea, and it had the political legs to become policy.

Importantly, the analyst's alternatives should flow from the problem definition. If the problem definition is poor, the policy is likely to be ineffective. Moreover, there are many "no-no"s to keep in mind. David Weimer and Aidan Vining list many of the key ones (280–82). Do not:

- "expect to find a dominant or perfect policy alternative"—you have to operate in the real world
- "contrast a preferred policy with a set of 'dummy' or 'strawman' alternatives"—while this sometimes works, this can anger people, jeopardize your credibility, and is not honest in terms of democracy
- "have a 'favorite' alternative until you have evaluated all the alternatives in terms of all the goals"—this is a common mistake
- produce alternatives that fail to be mutually exclusive; they are supposed to be real choices—this relates to the next point also
- fail to recognize that the number of possible alternatives and combination of alternatives is virtually infinite, but also a waste of time—why offer alternatives that are "too similar?
- offer "'kitchen sink' alternatives—that is, 'do-everything' alternatives"—if there

is one consistent theme in public administration, it is that it is constrained administration (e.g., legal, monetary, ethical, personnel, and time constraints)

- offer alternatives inconsistent "with available resources, including jurisdictional and controllable variables"—time is too valuable; pragmatism matters
- confuse goals with policy alternatives (which are "concrete sets of actions")—increasing employment is not a policy, it is a goal; the question is what actions will assist in reaching that goal

Step IV: Evaluate and Select Policies

Each alternative must be evaluated according to each evaluation criteria. This will include quantitative evaluation, often using extrapolation, regression, discounting, cost-benefit analysis, and discounting techniques. For example, the alternative in our drug abuse example of putting all drug users in prison would require several quantitative applications.

First, the number of drug users in our geographic region of interest would have to be estimated based on court records, interviews with experts, and other sources. Second, based on this, a researcher would have to estimate how many arrests would occur in a given year. Third, this number could be extrapolated over time to take into account anticipated population increases or decreases. Of course, population changes would also have to be estimated. Fourth, the numbers collected so far could help us determine how many new prisons would have to be built over the next ten to twenty years. Finally, once we had the number of new prisons, we could estimate costs using discounting techniques. (There would be several other questions to ask. Our list is suggestive, not exhaustive. Chapter 8 will discuss the sort of positivist techniques needed to perform these quantitative tasks—and the limits of those techniques.)

Several more qualitative evaluations also would have to be made, for example: how do you measure effectiveness, equity, political acceptability, and ethical considerations? Much of this knowledge is subjective but a strong knowledge of social science disciplines such as political science, sociology, social work, and economics can assist the analyst.

The analyst may have to conduct quick surveys, focus groups, or interviews to determine the views of stakeholders on various policy alternatives. In the drug abuse example, how do the different groups evaluate the different policies? What are the most relevant criteria for each group? The analyst must also make some decisions about feasibility. Does the government have the resources to implement a certain policy? Quade, writing in a similar line of argument (1975, 191–98) suggests that when "quantitative models are inadequate," the analyst can use expert opinion, groups of experts, **scenario writing**, and Delphi techniques.

After policies have been evaluated, they should be displayed and scored in some type of matrix. Typically, analysts weigh criteria based on their research of stakeholders. A "Goeller Scorecard" with weighted criteria is the easiest and most useful technique. A simple example is illustrated in Table 5-1 on page 146.

In Table 5-1, Policy A and Policy C are tied with thirteen points each. Policy B can be eliminated for now. In Table 5-2, also on page 146, we score Policy A against

TABLE 5-1   AN ADAPTED GOELLER SCORECARD WITH WEIGHTED CRITERIA

CRITERIA	POLICIES		
	A	B	C
Cost (weight = 3)	$50,000 (2 × 3 = 6)	$60,000 (1 × 3 = 3)	$35,000 (3 × 3 = 9)
Political Feasibility (weight = 2)	Good (3 × 2 = 6)	Fair (2 × 2 = 4)	Poor (1 × 2 = 2)
Administrative Feasibility (weight = 1)	Poor (1 × 1 = 1)	Good (3 × 1 = 3)	Fair (2 × 1 = 2)
Totals	13	10	13

Note: The first score in parentheses is the ranking with a 3 meaning the best alternative; a 2 meaning second best; and 1 meaning the worst. The second number in parentheses is the weighting with a 3 meaning it is the most important criteria; a 2 meaning it is the second most important criteria; and a 1 meaning it is the least important criteria.

Note: The analyst must often make a decision on how to score a tie between choices. For example, what if two policies were rated good under administrative feasibility? Do you give each 3 points or does each receive 2.5 points? In this case the latter choice would be best since you have a total of 6 points to assign to each policy. You could give 2.5 to the two top choices and 1 to the third choice. There is subjectivity in the process, but you must be consistent in your decision making.

Policy C, giving a maximum of two points and a minimum of one point for each criteria. Using this approach, Policy C is the preferred policy.

In reality, it is very difficult to accurately assign points and weights to policies and come up with "one best" policy. But the process is not totally subjective. The assigning of weights is again determined by research of stakeholders. In this example, some stakeholders (taxpayers) believe that cost is the most important criteria while others (administrators) believe that administrative feasibility is the most important criteria.

It is doubtful that you will ever have clear consensus over what are the most important criteria. The analyst must rank the importance of each of the stakeholders and in essence place weights upon their rankings of criteria. As explained previously, her rankings are ultimately tied to her view of power and government. Does the analyst weigh the desires of one interest group higher than another interest group because

TABLE 5-2   BREAKING A TIE

CRITERIA	POLICY	
	A	B
Cost (weight = 3)	$50,000 (1 × 3 = 3)	$35,000 (2 × 3 = 6)
Political Feasibility (weight = 2)	Good (2 × 2 = 4)	Poor (1 × 2 = 2)
Administrative Feasibility (weight = 1)	Poor (1 × 1 = 1)	Fair (2 × 1 = 2)
Totals	8	10

one group is more powerful and influential than the other group, or does the analyst make a decision based on her perception that one interest group represents the public interest more than another group?

The analyst must decide, for interests will conflict, whether they work primarily to serve the political interests of the elected officials to whom they answer, or to serve the public interest at large. These are all value decisions tied directly to the analyst's philosophy of government and beliefs about the role of the policy analyst.

Consistent with the works of Danziger (1995) and Stone (1997), the process is highly subjective and value-laden. However, the evaluation of policies can help eliminate potentially unsuccessful policies and can provide elected officials, interest groups, and citizens with sound information with which to make their choices. As Danziger (1995, 45) writes:

> Students of policy analysis should be taught that their professional goal is not necessarily the attainment of consensus about the nature of the truth in any given policy issue. Rather, they should be concerned that all relevant parties have access to sufficient data and a level of understanding that will enable them to be true players in the policy process.

The goal of the analyst, therefore, might not be one of selecting the best policy using a Goeller Scorecard but rather of presenting information, including how data, criteria, and criteria weightings were derived. In this case, the role of the analyst is one of educator and not just expert.[4] Another valuable technique is to have stakeholders do the scoring themselves. This could range from a committee using Goeller Scorecards, to a community meeting where people put stars on a chart by all alternatives of which they approve.

On a more pragmatic level, we can argue that decisions in government must be made, and while antipositivists may criticize the rational approach, they have really failed to provide better decision-making methods. Postmodernism can be criticized as being comparable to the "lovely lemon tree" of the old folk song. As a theory and critique it is attractive and smells sweet, but its fruit (its pragmatic value) has been impossible to eat. The rational approach, utilized under and informed by the premise that all political decision making is value-laden, is a nice compromise for it provides direction to policymakers who must make decisions in a political environment.[5] The role of the analyst is to help the decision makers see the inherent value-laden nature of the process, how varying stakeholders might disagree with certain policies and support others, how changing circumstances and environments can alter policy decisions (the dynamic process), and the importance of a democratic ethos. (See Chapter 7.)

---

[4]Chambers, Foster, and Clemons (1990), writing about economic development, argued that the key step was community development, and therefore outside experts needed to play the role not of experts who can solve problems (which are about value conflict) but of educators who increase leadership capabilities and help cultivate a sense of ownership and efficacy.

[5]As we will explore further in the next chapter, our approach is postpositivist, but inspired by and reliant upon the postmodern insights, particularly into the power of language. We also recognize—as some other postpositivists do—that there is a role for positivist methods. We are not recommending that analysts abandon the rigor or methods of science, but that it be done with eyes wide open and that other postpositivist approaches and value considerations be given equal or greater attention.

Step V: Evaluate Adopted Policy (Evaluation Research)

Once a policy has been adopted it should be evaluated for effectiveness in meeting its goals. Evaluation research is an important aspect of policy analysis. Many critics of government over the years have complained that many government policies do not work, yet the policies continue year after year. Remember that the fourth component part of the policy process, discussed in Chapter 4, was policy evaluation, adjustment, and termination.

Public policy analysts believe that policies should be continually evaluated in the context of changing social, political, cultural, and economic conditions. Several methods of evaluation research cited by Babbie (1995, 343–48) include the following: (1) experiments (with control groups); (2) nonequivalent control group designs (with comparison groups); and (3) time series analysis. Box 5-3 explores each of these methods.

5-3. Teenage Drug Use

Even if we exclude alcohol, in both urban and suburban schools teenage drug use is widely agreed to be a major problem. Marijuana, inhalants, ecstasy, heroin, blow, speed, and other drugs are serious problems in middle and high schools. Assume that your community had developed and implemented an antidrug program aimed at teenagers. How could you evaluate its effectiveness?

The Experiment

The experiment, or control group approach, is illustrated by testing the success of a teenage antidrug program in schools. Students are randomly selected and then randomly placed into the antidrug program (the test group) or a group that does not receive the program (the control group). You would administer surveys about drug use and attitudes toward drugs to both groups, before and after the program. You would then evaluate the survey data to see if the test group had a greater decrease in drug use and had an increase in negative attitudes toward drugs relative to the control group.

The control group works well in controlled experimental circumstances, but politically it is difficult to administer and often unethical. In our example above, let's say that the antidrug program worked extremely well. Students in the test group had lower rates of drug use and reported more negative views toward drugs in general, when compared to the control group. Parents of students in the test group would be pleased, but parents of students in the control group would most likely wonder why their children did not have the opportunity to participate in the antidrug program. The use of control groups in public policy research is politically and ethically suspect.

Nonequivalent Control Group

Due to political and ethical problems associated with control groups, many evaluation researchers will use what is termed the "nonequivalent control group." Instead of randomizing participants into a test or control group, you would look for a comparison group that approximates the test group (i.e., in the school antidrug program, a drug program would be administered to all ninth grade students in a junior high school and pre- and post-tests would be administered at the beginning and end of the school year). As an evaluation researcher, you would then select a similar junior high school in a similar community and give them the same pretest at the beginning of the year, and the same post-test at the end of the year. You would then compare results between the two schools.

Politically and ethically this approach works. All the students in the first school receive the antidrug training. The second school does not receive the training but does receive information on whether the program works so that they can decide to implement or not in later years. The process is not perfect, nor a true experiment.

In these quasi-experiments, the "control" group is not randomly created, therefore it is nonequivalent. Despite best efforts to find a comparison group that closely matches the test group, in most cases other variables will enter into the picture, making the two groups different and the results less meaningful than if it had been a true experiment.

Time Series

Time series analysis looks at data over a long period of time, ideally before and after a policy is implemented. For example, you could collect data on teenage drug arrests for the past twenty years before the implementation of a teenage antidrug program. This data would typically show some trend. The trend might be that teenage drug arrests are increasing over time, decreasing over time, or are fluctuating from year to year. Data would then be collected each year after the implementation of the antidrug program.

After a period of time adjudged by you to be long enough to be meaningful, you would then analyze the results. If drug arrests were increasing in the years before the antidrug program and they are now decreasing, you would probably infer that the antidrug program was working. If the trend was already decreasing and is still decreasing you could not attribute much effect to the program. Similarly, if drug arrests fluctuated before the program, and are still fluctuating, the program's effectiveness is called into question. If drug arrests have increased since the implementation of the program you would likely deem the program unsuccessful.

However, the analyst is cautioned that use of time series data is often unreliable. We will discuss two of many possible problems with concerns that should sound familiar. First, social data is socially created. Over the years the police department may have changed arrest policies or increased or decreased the number of police officers. This activity could artificially alter arrest numbers. What looks like a drastic decline in teenage arrests could simply be the result of the police department shifting their emphasis away from teenage drug users to what they consider more serious crimes. Second, time series analysis does not control for population changes and cultural changes. Typically, analysts use nonequivalent control groups to help control for these variables. But even when using this approach, many problems remain.

The Politics of Evaluation Research

Analysts must realize that evaluation research is very difficult. Although some agencies will be helpful (feeling they have nothing to hide, wanting to know about problems, and trusting in the evaluation process), that is not the norm. Administrators who implement policies are often very defensive when it comes to evaluating their agency's policies. They may go to great lengths to put up roadblocks to the evaluation process. Many agencies require that the evaluation researcher work through agency personnel when accessing data, files, or clients of the agency. Many evaluation researchers term the person assigned to "assist" the evaluator "the insider" and see this person as a hindrance to securing an honest evaluation.

Agency administrators and personnel are also very defensive about negative evaluations of the policies they implement. This defensiveness is understandable since poor evaluations can lead to budget cut-backs, the ending of programs, or the rare but possible elimination of the agency itself. Analysts should be prepared to defend their methodology, and be prepared for the possibility that their personal integrity will be attacked by agency personnel who work on policies that receive poor evaluations.[6]

Finally, it is often inherently difficult to conduct a fair evaluation. Individuals such as prisoners, drug users, juveniles, and AIDS patients are often the beneficiaries of policies and are legally protected subjects. Evaluation researchers do not easily gain access to these individuals and many times will be denied access to their records. For example, if a researcher was hired to evaluate a teenage drug intervention program, the researcher would most likely want to interview teenagers who have been through the program to measure its effectiveness. However, the researcher cannot legally find out the identity of the teenagers since they are protected subjects.[7] As a result, the analyst would have to interview staff members who work on the project. While this may secure valuable information, ultimately the ones who know whether or not the program works are the teenage clients, and the researcher cannot talk to them.

Summary of the Five-Step Method

Perhaps you now feel you have a methodology; an approach to policy analysis that makes sense and that has pragmatic value despite the important warnings and caveats we offered. This method is neatly summed up in the list below, and the case study that follows (starting on page 152) will let you try it out.

- Step I: Define the problem and determine its causes.
- Step II: Establish criteria to evaluate alternatives.
- Step III: Generate policy alternatives.
- Step IV: Evaluate and select policies.
- Step V: Evaluate adopted policy (evaluation research).

Concluding Thoughts

Most multistep models are presented as ideal rational models. Even our five-step method (despite our warnings about politics, language, value conflict, and subjectivity, and our concerns about broadly defining stakeholders, education, and democracy) comes across as very logical, coherent, linear, and scientific. In practice, public policy analysis is never quite like that. Time frames are short, goals vague, problems ill-defined, and information always imperfect. If a practicing policy analyst was asked

---

[6]For an excellent discussion of the politics of evaluation research, see Earl Babbie (1995, 349–56) and also Carol H. Weiss (1972) cited in Shafritz and Hyde (1992/1987/1978, 397–405).

[7]In some instances it may be possible to secure legal permission to learn their identity, but research with minors always poses additional hurdles.

whether she used the rational model or any of its formal variations, she would probably say no. But if you asked her if she tried to define the problem, identify stakeholders, calculate the perspectives of stakeholders, determine evaluation criteria, generate alternatives, evaluate and choose alternatives, and conduct a postimplementation evaluation—she most certainly would say yes to most, if not all, of this.

Like the policy process, policy analysis in real life is not clean and logical; it does not necessarily flow from step one to step two to step three, and so on. Much of what analysts do is instinctive. Scholars like Patton and Sawicki attempt to rationalize the process and their model is heuristic, which is to say that it helps students of public policy analysis understand the process by providing a sense of coherency and order. Rational models, like the five-step method you just learned, may also help analysts who use them as a blueprint, by helping to prevent them from overlooking an important step.

Unavoidably though, how analysts implement this rather rational five-step method is tied directly to nonrational factors such as how they believe policy problems are created, and their view of the proper role and location of political power. The policy case that follows will help further explicate the processes of policymaking and policy analysis, and once again demonstrates how "value conflict" and views of "power structures" fit into analysis. (You may wish to first review the discussion of these two concepts in Chapter 1.)

As policy analysts in the classroom or on the job you need to recognize the subjective element involved. You must also consider how the role you play fits with the norm of democratic governance. We give it high praise in theory but, all too often, make it a low priority in practice. Good luck.

Key Concepts

analysts as educators and facilitators of democracy (p. 147)
critiques of the rational public policy analysis method (p. 135)
defining the problem and determining causation (step I) (p. 136)
establishing criteria to evaluate alternatives (step II) (p. 139)
evaluating and selecting policies (step IV) (p. 145)
evaluation research (step V) (p. 148)
Five-Step Method (p. 136)
fourth evaluative criteria for models (p. 133)
generating policy alternatives (step III) (p. 143)
Goeller Scorecard (p. 145)
history of the rational public policy analysis method (p. 134)
policy alternative generation "no-no"s (p. 144)
politics of evaluation research (p. 149)
pragmatic evaluation of positivism and its critiques (p. 147)
rational public policy analysis method form (p. 134)
summary of Five-Step Method (p. 150)
universal criteria (p. 139)
value clarification (p. 143)

Glossary Terms

Delphi techniques (p. 135)
scenario writing (p. 145)

References

Appleby, Paul. 1949. *Policy and Administration*. Tuscaloosa, AL: University of Alabama Press.

Babbie, Earl. 1995. *The Practice of Social Research*. Belmont, CA: Wadsworth Publishing.

Chambers, Robert E., Randall S. Clemons, and Richard H. Foster. 1990. "Leadership and Community Revitalization." *Economic Development Review* 8, no. 3 (summer): 29–34.

Danziger, Marie. 1995. "Policy Analysis Postmodernized: Some Political and Pedagogical Ramifications." *Policy Studies Journal* 23, no. 3.

Dunn, William N. 1981/1994. *Public Policy Analysis: An Introduction*. Englewood Cliffs, NJ: Prentice Hall.

Etzioni, Amitai. 1996. *The Golden Rule*. New York: Basic Books.

Homans, George C. 1974. *Social Behavior: Its Elementary Forms*, rev. ed. New York: Harcourt Brace Jovanovich.

Marcuse, Herbert. 1964. *One Dimensional Man*. Boston, MA: Beacon Press.

Mead, George Herbert. 1934/1962. *Mind, Self, and Society: From the Standpoint of a Social Behavioralist*. Chicago, IL: University of Chicago Press.

Parsons, Talcott, and Edward A. Shils, eds. 1951. *Toward a General Theory of Action*. Cambridge, MA: Harvard University Press.

Patton, Carl V., and David S. Sawicki. 1986. *Basic Methods of Policy Analysis and Planning*. Englewood Cliffs, NJ: Prentice Hall.

Quade, E. S. 1975. *Analysis for Public Decisions*. New York: American Elsevier.

Shafritz, Jay M., and Albert C. Hyde. 1992. *Classics of Public Administration*. Pacific Grove, CA: Brooks/Cole Publishing Company.

Stokey, Edith, and Richard Zeckhauser. 1978. *A Primer for Policy Analysis*. New York: W. W. Norton & Company.

Stone, Deborah. 1997/1988. *Policy Paradox: The Art of Political Decision Making*. New York: W. W. Norton & Company.

Weimer, David L., and Aidan R. Vining. 1999. *Policy Analysis: Concepts and Practice*, 3rd ed. Upper Saddle River, NJ: Prentice Hall.

Wilson, Woodrow. 1887. "The Study of Administration." *Political Science Quarterly* (June): 197–222.

Playing Politics: Bison, Brucellosis, Business, and Bureaucrats

A Policy Analysis Case Focusing on the Yellowstone Interim Bison Plan

Prelude

In 1895 the world learned that Yellowstone National Park, the world's first area dedicated to wilderness and wildlife protection, had only 185 bison remaining (Grinnell, quoted in Bartlett). One hundred years later, in January 1995, the Yellowstone bison herd stood near 4,000, prompting many conservationists to proclaim the restoration of the Yellowstone herd as an "American wildlife restoration success story."

However, by mid-1998, following three years of intense political controversy, the Yellowstone bison herd was estimated to be only around 2,200 animals. Sharpshooters and bureaucrats working for the State of Montana had shot, or sent to slaughter, over 1,500 North American bison since the 1994–95 winter season. More than 1,100 bison were killed by Montana during the brutal winter of 1996–97 alone. In addition, during the winter of 1996–97, some 800 bison died of natural causes due to the severe Yellowstone winter.

During the past few years, environmental politics and policy in the Greater Yellowstone ecosystem had been dominated by the controversy generated by the killing of free-ranging bison by the Montana Department of Livestock. To understand the bison controversy, one must understand the important symbolic and historical role of bison inside the park. Additionally, it is important to understand the larger context and issue cleavages surrounding park management, and how the bison controversy fits into the larger philosophical and political controversies of Yellowstone National Park Management.

Case Assignment

The "Greater Yellowstone Interagency Brucellosis Committee" (GYIBC) has hired you to conduct a policy analysis of the situation and come up with policy recommendations. You are to do the following:

Step I: Define the Problem and Determine Its Causes

1. How will you define the problem when the interests and values of the interested parties are so disparate?
2. Who are the major stakeholders here? What are the values and interests of each of the stakeholders? How do you decide which stakeholders to include or exclude? What are the "stories" of the major stakeholders?
3. How does your view of power structures lead to a problem definition? Who is your client here?

Step II: Establish Criteria to Evaluate Alternatives

1. What are your major evaluation criteria?
2. How are your criteria tied to major stakeholders? If stakeholders have conflicting criteria, how will you reconcile this?

Step III: Generate Policy Alternatives

1. What are some possible policy alternatives? How do you generate alternatives in this case?
2. Do these alternatives eliminate the problem without favoring one group over another?

Step IV: Evaluate and Select Policy

1. What policies do you recommend and why? A table showing the pros and cons of each considered policy would be helpful.
2. What criteria did you use to weight criteria? Was your decision ultimately based on some view of power and democracy?

Step V: Evaluate Policies

1. Detail a plan to evaluate each recommended policy. What problems do you anticipate in evaluating these policies?

Introduction: History and Context

Yellowstone National Park (YNP), located in parts of Wyoming, Montana, and Idaho, was established in 1872 as America's and the world's first national park. The majority of the park is located in the state of Wyoming but the communities that surround the park's boundaries are located in Montana. YNP was established for the benefit and enjoyment of citizens of the United States and to protect the beautiful natural resources of the area, including pristine rivers, rugged canyons, geothermal features, and wildlife.

Yellowstone sits in the middle of traditionally resource-based economies. With the popularity of YNP, however, the economy has grown increasingly dependent on tourism over the past few decades. The park has survived a tumultuous past with its surrounding communities and residents. The "gateway" communities of West Yellowstone, Gardiner, and Cooke City, Montana, rely almost exclusively on the park for tourist dollars. In addition, much of the private and public land surrounding Yellowstone is used by local ranchers for grazing cattle.

The environment of YNP and the economy of the region have always been intertwined. There have always been calls to increase tourism in the park even with the knowledge that increased tourism leads to increased environmental stresses on Yellowstone and its larger ecosystem. Early visitors to the park after 1872 were mostly poachers who decimated elk, bear, deer, and bison populations, selling their meat and hides for easy profits from eastern businesses. Early tourists also vandalized the park's natural features. For example, they tried to clog the Old Faithful geyser with garbage and various other debris, and scraped off mineral deposits from the terraces at Mammoth Hot Springs (Bartlett 1989, 19–35). Regulations against hunting and vandalism did not arrive until 1877 and these new regulations were difficult to enforce until the U.S. Army arrived in 1886 (1989, 257).

These pioneer tourists, like modern tourists, created great environmental stress on the ecology of the park. Bartlett (1989, 36–37) makes the point that each year the winter season in Yellowstone healed the wounds left by summer's visitors. Discussing a Yellowstone adventure of the Earl of Dunravan in late fall 1874 (before the 1877 act and the appearance of the U.S. Army), Bartlett (1989, 36) writes:

> Soon the earl left, and before many days the cold wind would die down, and a blanket of velvety white cover the ground, hiding the tourist's dead campfire, covering the old newspaper, the tin cans, the stones that traced the site of the tourist's tent.

The few buildings would be frosted, their unpainted sides clashing with the white of roofs and surrounding land. The bears would sleep, the little rodents would go about their business beneath the safety of snow cover, the elk and deer and buffalo would drift down the valleys, paw away the snow and munch the dry grasses underneath. And, months later, the land would look new again.

Pressures on the ecology of Yellowstone caused by tourists would multiply significantly during the end of the 1800s, as the United States expanded west and railroads and roadways led directly to Yellowstone. Yellowstone National Park became, both in the United States and internationally, a major summer tourist attraction. Today, over the course of the spring, summer, and fall seasons, over three million people visit Yellowstone.

The visitors have created a tremendous tourism economy in the gateway communities. New hotels, restaurants, and other tourist accommodations have been built in recent years in the communities that directly or indirectly border Yellowstone. These communities include West Yellowstone and Gardiner, Montana, Jackson Hole, Wyoming, and Island Park, Idaho. However, resource-based groups like the livestock industry remain politically powerful.

Conflicts between the environmental needs of Yellowstone and the economic needs of nearby communities have been a constant. The National Park Service (NPS) has always vacillated between trying to ecologically maintain YNP and meeting the economic needs of both local business owners and ranchers. Sometimes, trying to simultaneously please environmentalists, ranchers, the business community, Congress, and its own mandates and mission has proven difficult, if not just plain impossible.

There has also been a longstanding controversy over how the park should be managed. In some ways, the overarching dilemma faced by YNP policymakers has been whether to follow a natural management policy or one that allows for more active human intervention. Many have argued that Yellowstone should be managed "naturally" without human intervention. Others believe that YNP exists within a human sphere of influence and that management must always take into account how humans impact park ecology. Over the last thirty years, three examples of YNP management illustrate the tension between human and natural management of the park and how very difficult it is for the NPS to please all constituent groups in the region. These recent controversies include bear management, fire suppression management, and wolf reintroduction.

Yellowstone is famous for its bears. The first controversy involved the feeding of bears. Humans were originally allowed to feed bears and hungry bears would gather by the hundreds along Yellowstone roadways begging for food. This practice made Yellowstone famous as "bear country" and allowed many visitors to see bears up close. Unfortunately, the practice also led to many deadly encounters between humans and bears. In addition, grizzly bears were allowed to enter dumps inside the park and in areas surrounding the park. In West Yellowstone, a nightly tourist attraction for decades was the arrival of mighty grizzlies at the community's garbage dump. Tourists would turn on their car headlights and watch the great bears feed from the garbage. These practices ended in the 1970s after concern that feeding practices had habituated bears to human contact and that the garbage dumps and human feedings created an "abnormally" large population of bears that the system could not naturally sustain.

The practice of feeding bears was seen as "unnatural" and the new 1970s policy emphasized the idea that bears should live naturally within the ecosystem and without human feeding (Chase 1986, 142–69). The ending of bear feeding was controversial at the time because some contended that it had reduced the numbers of bears inside the park and at least temporarily (from a tourism-community perspective) reduced tourist interest in YNP. Only in recent years have bear numbers increased to a point where bears are once again a major tourist attraction. However, bears have also moved outside of the park in larger numbers and increases in subdivision development near the park's borders has increased human-bear contact. Many state officials in Idaho, Montana, and Wyoming have contended that grizzly bear numbers have increased to a point at which the grizzly should be delisted as an Endangered Species. Environmentalists contend that bear numbers have not increased and that increased bear sightings are simply the result of increased competition for bear habitat, making bears more visible to humans.

Second, massive wildfires in 1988 burned much of the park. The fires were initially allowed to "burn naturally" despite the fact that many fires were caused by human conduct. The National Park Service had implemented a natural burn policy that stated that all naturally created fires would be allowed to burn unless they threatened human settlements (Chase 1986, 70). It was difficult to determine what fires were lightning-caused and what fires were human-caused, especially when different fires joined together. Many local communities contended that the Park Service should have fought the fires from the beginning in the hope of saving the 1988 tourist season for area communities. On the other hand, the fires were a tremendous ecological event for Yellowstone, and in the past decade YNP forests and range lands have been virtually reborn.

Finally, the reintroduction of wolves in the winter of 1995 created great controversy among YNP officials and local ranchers. With increased and increasing numbers of elk and bison, the NPS and environmentalists wanted the wolves reintroduced to the ecosystem in efforts to restore ecological balance. Wolves had been exterminated in YNP in the early 1900s to protect area livestock interests. Wolves prey on elk and bison, and therefore help control the populations of these herds.

Ranchers, however, feared that wolves would eat cattle and sheep. The political battle was tremendous, but ultimately wolves were reintroduced to Yellowstone (Fischer 1995). Battles over the role of the wolf in Yellowstone and the impact of wolves on local ranching interests, however, remain a weekly source of controversy in the region.

Despite all of the controversies, tourism continues to grow in Yellowstone. As already mentioned, in the summer of 1988 Yellowstone experienced terrible human-started fires that ravaged the dense forests of much of the park. Afterward, the "word of mouth" throughout the region was that Yellowstone, as a tourist destination, was finished for at least the next few decades, as tourists would not want to see thousands and thousands acres of burned forests. In response to this, YNP and local communities began an intense advertising campaign to promote tourism in the park.

The advertising campaign worked, as tourism boomed in the late 1980s and through the 1990s. In addition, the fires actually made the park more beautiful, with open vistas revealing meadows of long green grass and fledgling lodgepole pines. Increased visitors, combined with a general migration of urbanites and others to the rural west, led to tremendous building booms in West Yellowstone, Jackson Hole, and many other communities in the Greater Yellowstone Ecosystem.

Despite, and partially because of, the increases in tourist numbers, Yellowstone is facing several problems. The park is in disrepair and federal budget cuts have led to major problems in maintaining even the most basic of services. Roads in YNP are full of potholes, campgrounds are in deteriorating conditions, and in the summer of 1996 some campgrounds and visitor centers did not open because of budget woes.

Consumer Reports, in a 1997 rating of the National Parks, revealed that visitors to Yellowstone rated the park low on many features because of deteriorating infrastructure and overcrowding. All the while, gateway communities continued to build more and more hotels and restaurants. Yellowstone Park Superintendent Mike Finley shocked many local communities when, in 1996, he "floated" the idea of having "daily caps" on the number of tourists that could enter the park. Finley's suggestions brought outrage from some tourist-based businesses.

In addition, beginning in the 1970s, snowmobiles have been allowed inside Yellowstone from late December to early March. Snowmobile tourism has increased greatly over the years and West Yellowstone has become the self-proclaimed "Snowmobile Capital of the World." Shops, restaurants, and hotels that once closed up for the winter season now thrive during the winter months. Snowmobiling, however, has environmental consequences. Snowmobile users themselves have complained that winter use of the park was spoiled by noisy snowmobiles and noxious emissions from the machines. Superintendent Finley has called for a study into the environmental consequences of snowmobile use, and it seems clear that the Park Service wants to end winter-time snowmobile use of the park. West Yellowstone officials are very concerned about losing their winter season.[1]

A Political History of Bison in Yellowstone National Park

No other issue—not bear management, not fire management, and not even wolf reintroduction—has created the national political controversy caused by the killing of Yellowstone bison by the Montana Department of Livestock. As you will see, bison occupy an important and special place in the history of Yellowstone. The controversy over how to manage bison, however, falls into the same general controversy over natural versus human management of the park. The bison controversy also demonstrates the multitude of interests that the National Park Service must try to accommodate.

The American bison, a symbol of the precowboy American West, has long been caught in the middle of a political and cultural struggle that makes western politics a seed-bed of bizarreness, ideological warfare, and violence. The current slaughter of Yellowstone National Park bison is best understood not in the biological or scientific realm but rather in the world of power politics, economics, cultural identity, and postmodern symbolism. The slaughter is only indirectly related to brucellosis, the virus that infects some Yellowstone bison and that the ranching community publicly worries will be transmitted from bison to cattle. The history of politics surrounding Yellowstone bison is a long one, dating back to the founding of the American West.

---

[1]See "Winter Visitor Use Management: A Multi-Agency Assessment." Greater Yellowstone Winter Visitor Use Management Working Group. Greater Yellowstone Coordinating Committee. National Park Service and U.S. Forest Service. April 1997.

The evidence is that bison long ago made the 2,200,000 acres of Yellowstone and the 19,000,000 acres of the Yellowstone ecosystem home. Schullery, Brewster, and Mack (1997) cite a Yellowstone National Park study that found bison blood residue on a 9,000-year-old knife found in the park. In 1600, Haines (1995, 157) states, there were so many bison in the Yellowstone River Valley that the animals were forced to migrate into Idaho's upper Snake River plains. Haines (1977, 2:81) found that in 1870 an explorer, A. Bart Henderson, reported seeing thousands of bison above Hellroaring Creek in northern Yellowstone (the area now known as the Buffalo Plateau).

Therefore, we know that bison lived in Yellowstone and its ecosystem before 1872, when Congress established Yellowstone National Park as "a public park or pleasuring ground for the benefit and enjoyment of the people." Unfortunately, thousands of bison had been killed in the years since John Colter first "unofficially" discovered Yellowstone in 1807. The establishment of the park did not end the carnage. Yellowstone Park Superintendent Philletus Norris reported that thousands of deer, elk, moose, and bison had been poached, since the park's enabling legislation did not specify that hunting or acts of vandalism were prohibited. In 1882, the Park Improvement Company (a park concessionaire) had contracts with professional hunters to kill 20,000 pounds of elk, deer, mountain sheep, and bison. The meat was used to feed concessionaire employees (Bartlett 1989, 137).

The larger problem facing wildlife, bison in particular, was poaching. Over 7,000 elk, deer, bighorn, and bison were killed in 1875 alone. By the mid-1880s, the near extinction of the bison drove the price of a bison head up to between $300 and $500 (Bartlett 1989, 316; Haines 1977, 2:60) and made bison a prime target of poachers. The history books often romantically use an 1870 campfire meeting of the famed "Washburn Party" at Yellowstone's Madison Junction to explain the park's origins. According to this history, near the end of their exploration of the area, the Washburn Party discussed the beauty of the region and decided that Yellowstone's lands should be placed aside as a preserve and left "as is." Sadly, this ideal was not realized with the creation of the park. Yellowstone National Park was instead founded under the ambiguously symbolic phrase of "for the benefit and enjoyment of the people." The debate over the passage of the act that created Yellowstone National Park reveals that environmentalism was a concept still far from the minds of the U.S. Congress. On January 30, 1872, Senator Cornelius Cole of California was quoted in the Congressional Globe. Cole stated:

> I have grave doubts about the propriety of passing this bill. The natural curiosities there cannot be interfered with by anything that man can do. The geysers will remain, no matter where the ownership of the land may be, and I do not know why settlers should be excluded from a tract of land forty miles square. (quoted in Haines 1977, 169–70)

Luckily, Cole's objection was in the minority in the Senate. Still, supporters had to address Cole's objection by promising that the law could be repealed later (Haines 1977, 170). Interestingly, the strongest support for the new park came not from idealistic nineteenth-century environmentalists who wanted to protect resources, but from enterprising eastern and western businessmen who knew the park would encourage the development of a branch track from the Northern Pacific Railroad. However, the Forty-second Congress that passed the act also wanted a park without federal expenditures.

The debate and eventual passage of the organic act creating Yellowstone assumed that the area could be managed at no cost to the federal government. Haines (1977, 179) writes:

> The reasoning behind this conclusion evidently paralleled that of the maid who took her eggs to market in a basket on her head, 'counting her chickens before they were hatched' without considering what a fall would do to her plans. From the commonly held supposition that the Northern Pacific Railroad would be extended into Montana in a year or two, opening an easy route for large numbers of tourists whose coming would create many business opportunities attractive to concessionaires, it was presumed franchise fees would accumulate which would be more than adequate for the support of the Park.

Major tourism trade did not arrive for several years and the park existed for its first fourteen years with a skeleton crew whose main job was to map the area and build a human infrastructure of roads and buildings. It took several brave U.S. military officials, the actions of some outrageous poachers, and the eastern U.S. media to bring wildlife protection to Yellowstone.

Stories of bison poachers spread throughout the region and many became ingrained in Yellowstone folklore. According to Bartlett (1989, 317) in 1882, "A U.S. Geological Survey party was accused of killing an old buffalo in the park and packing out about a hundred pounds of meat, the skin, and hooves. One man took the animal's penis, dried it, stretched it, and made a walking stick out of it."

Without a National Park Service, the only government institution large enough to protect Yellowstone's resources was the U.S. Army. The Army arrived in 1886 and quickly tried to end bison poaching. Acting Park Superintendent Captain George S. Anderson, in 1891, apprehended E. E. Van Dyck of Cooke City, Montana, who was poaching in the northeast corner of the Park. Later in 1892, Anderson captured Charles Pendelton, Cooke City poacher and butcher. Anderson also spent considerable time patrolling the area west of the park near Henry's Lake, Idaho, where several buffalo poachers were thought to base their operations (Haines 1977, 61–62). Anderson's actions helped slow the poaching and perhaps saved the remaining bison.

Increasingly, the national media became involved in promoting the protection of Yellowstone bison and wildlife in general. During the winter of 1893–94, an Army scouting party went into the Pelican Valley to look for buffalo and found a sledge trail headed toward Cooke City (Haines 1977, 62). An earlier trail had been associated with known bison poacher Ed Howell, so Captain Anderson sent out another party to look for poachers. On February 13, 1894, the party found Howell with six bison scalps. The soldiers escorted Howell back to Fort Yellowstone at Mammoth Hot Springs despite the fact that there was no law to hold Howell or any other poacher. On the way to the Fort, the party encountered Emerson Hough, Frank J. Haynes, and T. E. "Billy" Hofer of the New York weekly magazine *Forest and Stream*. Hough, an early nineteenth-century environmentalist, clearly recognized the symbolic importance of the event, wrote a story on the spot, and telegraphed it east (Haines 1977, 2:63–64). According to Haines, George Bird Grinnell, *Forest and Stream* editor, took the article to some important friends in Congress who used the bill to push passage of the Lacey Act, which would ban the killing of animals in National Parks.

The Lacey Act was signed by President Cleveland on May 7, 1894. The act prohibited "all hunting or the killing, wounding, or capture, at any time, of any wild animal or bird, except dangerous animals when it is necessary to prevent them from destroying human life or inflicting injury" (The Lacey Act, U.S. Statutes at Large, 28:73). Importantly, for future Yellowstone history, the act excluded predators such as wolves, coyotes, and cougars from protection. While the act was clearly a method to save all the wildlife in the park including elk, moose, mountain sheep, and deer, the act more than anything was the result of the near-extinction levels of the American bison. The bison thus played an essential role in the preservation not only of wildlife but of the parks themselves. Without the outcry that surrounded the possible extinction of bison from Yellowstone (since they were nearly extinct elsewhere on the continent), the Lacey Act probably would not have had the necessary political momentum to be passed and signed into law.

With bison now protected in Yellowstone, several offers, some of which were sincere and others of which were money-making schemes, were made to help save and grow the herd in the park. Charles Jesse Jones, known in the history books as "Buffalo Jones," offered to become Yellowstone buffalo keeper in 1895 but was denied (Bartlett 1989, 333). During that same time period, the Smithsonian Institute provided some money to build a buffalo enclosure in Yellowstone. That money built an enclosure on Alum Creek in the Hayden Valley. The enclosure used hay to bait bison inside where soldiers would then close a gate behind them. Unfortunately, only a few bison drifted in around the enclosure and none of these were captured (Haines 1977, 2:69).

Other unsuccessful efforts were attempted. E. C. Waters was given permission to buy four bison from a private herd in Texas (two cows and two bulls) and place them on an island of Yellowstone Lake. There, the bison would become prime tourist attraction for Waters' Yellowstone Lake Boat Company. His "game show" attracted visitors between 1896 and 1907. After 1907, the park regained control of the small bison herd that had been built up on the island (Haines 1977, 2:77).

Dr. Frank Baker, superintendent of the National Zoological Park at Washington, informed the park that capturing adult, wild bison was normally unsuccessful as the wild bison typically resisted restraint and died. (Haines 1977, 2:71). Haines writes of Baker's remarks, "His statement provided the basis for future efforts to save the Yellowstone bison. No further attempt was made to entrap the Hayden Valley herd; instead, funds were sought to purchase a semidomesticated buffalo suitable for establishing a captive herd—which could be augmented with calves from the wild herd in the spring" (Haines 1977, 2:71–72).

In 1901, with Captain John Pitcher as park superintendent, Congress appropriated half of a requested $30,000 for buying between thirty and sixty bison and establishing them in a corral. The $15,000 was authorized by Congress on July 1, 1902. Buffalo Jones, after establishing a domestic herd of bison in the midwest, sought and was awarded the title of "game warden" for the park. An enclosure was built one mile south of Fort Yellowstone and fifteen bison cows and three bulls were respectively purchased from domestic herds in northwestern Montana and Texas (Haines 1977, 2:72).

By 1902, only 22 bison were found in Yellowstone's once bison-rich area of

Pelican Creek (Bartlett 1989, 333). By 1904, 11 calves were born in the Mammoth corrals. In addition, the size of the domestic herd was enlarged with the purchase of 21 bison from Howard Eaton's herd in North Dakota (Bartlett 1989, 334). By 1905, Pitcher moved some of the Mammoth herd to a new corral (to be later named Buffalo Ranch) located in the Lamar Valley (Bartlett 1989, 336). Meyer and Meagher (1994, 65) report the establishment of the Buffalo Ranch in Lamar in 1907. Bartlett (1989, 336) reports that the domestic bison population grew from 74 bison in 1908 to 276 by 1916. Near this time, brucellosis first appeared in the Buffalo Ranch herd. According to Meyer and Meagher (1994, 650), the most likely source of the brucellosis was infected milk cows kept at Buffalo Ranch.

The first park rangers arrived in Yellowstone in 1915 during the same time that automobiles were first allowed inside Yellowstone. The National Park Service Act, which set in motion the establishment of the National Park Service, was signed in 1916. The role of the U.S. Army was then phased out and the rangers and the Park Service then took over the management of the bison herd. Some of their wildlife management techniques would have detrimental environmental consequences. The U.S. Army began killing predators from the time of their arrival in the Park. Between 1908 and 1917, 23 mountain lions, 1,188 coyotes, and 18 wolves were killed (Phillips and Douglas 1996, 15), The Park Service continued the extermination of predators such as coyotes, cougars, and wolves in the false belief that the killing of these animals would help preserve elk, bison, moose, and deer. Park Superintendent Horace Albright wrote in 1922, "It is evident that the work of controlling predators must be vigorously prosecuted by the most effective means available" (Phillips and Douglas 1996, 15). By the mid-1930s, the last wolf pack had disappeared from Yellowstone.

During the 1930s, Yellowstone rangers actively managed the Bison herd. Haines (1977, 2:311–12) writes:

> In the off season the rangers managed the elk and buffalo in the northern part of the Park. They cut hay in the meadow at Yancey's (Pleasant Valley, near Tower Junction), on Slough Creek, and on the bottom lands along the Lamar Valley at the Buffalo Ranch, stacking from 500 to 800 tons for the park horse herd and for feeding elk and buffalo during the worst part of the winter. The hope was to prevent large loss of elk and buffalo by holding them in the Park during very hard winters. The ranching operations were handled by a chief buffalo keeper, who had an assistant, one or two herders and an irrigator, and the help of rangers for feeding and for such big operations as slaughtering excess animals, castrating, and inoculating calves.

Using such control techniques, the bison herd was maintained at between 425 to 650 bison from the late 1920s until 1967. In that time period, 9,000 bison were killed or transferred (Bison Fact Sheet, State of Montana Department of Livestock 1997). The National Park Service changed their bison management in the late 1960s in response to the influential Leopold Report that advocated natural regulation of wildlife. According to this philosophy, bison numbers would be reduced only through natural deaths caused by winters, disease, or age. Under this new management philosophy, bison herd numbers increased significantly. In the fall of 1996 the bison population was estimated at between 3,400 and 4,000.

The Case: The Interim Bison Management Plan

The 1996 season was a difficult one for Yellowstone Park officials. Problems began during the late 1995 winter season when government shutdowns forced the closure of the park and hurt local tourist economies. The Park Service then floated their plan to cap day use and hinted at making changes to winter use, further outraging local tourism communities.

Park officials were probably looking forward to a quiet off-season as the summer drew to a close in August. Much of the political discussion surrounding the park revolved around wolves, capping day use, and snowmobile restrictions. Very few foresaw that one of Yellowstone's most abundant creatures, the bison, would dominate the next few months (and years) of Yellowstone politics.

In August 1996, Yellowstone National Park Superintendent Mike Finley approved what was termed the "Interim Bison Plan." For years there had been conflict between local ranchers and the park over the question of whether Yellowstone bison infected with brucellosis could transmit the disease to domestic cattle. Elk in Yellowstone are also infected with brucellosis, a disease which causes female animals to prematurely abort calves. The U.S. Department of Agriculture's Animal, Plant, and Health Inspection Service (APHIS) is responsible for classifying a state as a "brucellosis class-free state." Idaho, Montana, and Wyoming are classified as "brucellosis free" states. The classification is important for it allows a state's ranchers to sell cattle across state lines. APHIS has in recent years threatened to withdraw Montana's brucellosis-free status because of its proximity to Yellowstone's bison (Keiter 1997, 5).[2]

The Interim Bison Plan was developed after a lawsuit was filed by the State of Montana against the National Park Service (NPS) and the U.S. Department of Agriculture's Animal, Plant, and Health Inspecting Service (APHIS). The plan called for bison who were prone to wander outside the park to be corralled and tested for brucellosis. The plan replaced the "zero tolerance" policy that had guided the State of Montana for several years. Under this policy, any bison that wandered outside the park was shot. According to the Yellowstone Journal (Glover 1996, C-7), more than 400 bison were killed in the winter of 1995–96 near Gardiner and West Yellowstone, Montana. Bison killings are typical each winter, with kills ranging from 200 to 400.

The Interim Bison Management Plan found the National Park Service operating a capture facility inside the park near Gardiner, Montana. Unlike the previous zero-tolerance policy in which bison were shot by State of Montana officials once they left the park, this new policy instead had NPS personnel corral bison who were headed for private land inside the park. The Montana Department of Livestock operated a capture facility at the park boundary near West Yellowstone. Both facilities would test all bison and send those who tested positive for brucellosis, and pregnant females,[3] to slaughter houses.

---

[2]Ranchers and policymakers are less concerned about elk spreading the disease to cattle. Some have suggested that this is because elk are hunted outside the Park and thus have a strong political base of support.

[3]Female bison are considered the highest risk bison (since brucellosis is theoretically transmitted by infected placentas being licked by cattle). Brucellosis testing is imprecise, producing huge numbers of false-positives and false-negatives. Montana's answer to this uncertainty is to "play it safe" and just kill all pregnant bison cows. This is also an effective form of bison population control and, it could be suggested by skeptics, possibly part of a not-so-hidden agenda.

Bison normally stay inside the boundaries of Yellowstone National Park during the spring, summer, and fall months when grasses for grazing are long and green. During mild winters the vast majority of bison continue to stay inside the park. In the northern part of the park near Gardiner, Montana, the winters tend to be relatively mild in a climate that is essentially high desert. In the Madison River Valley near West Yellowstone, Montana, wintering bison tend to migrate toward the Firehole River Valley where geyser basins melt snow and keep some grasses and foliage available for grazing.

In October, a lawsuit was filed against the National Park Service, APHIS, and the U.S. Forest Service by the Greater Yellowstone Coalition, the Jackson Hole Alliance for Responsible Planning, the American Buffalo Foundation, the Gallatin Wildlife Association, and a private citizen. The plaintiffs were represented by the Sierra Club Legal Defense Fund (now known as the Earthjustice Legal Defense Fund). The suit charged that the NPS could not participate in the capture and slaughter of bison since it was a "fundamental betrayal" of the National Park Service mission (West Yellowstone News, October 31, 1996:1). The suit was filed against federal agencies and not the State of Montana because the plaintiffs argued that the activities would take place on federal lands and that the activities would violate the "National Environmental Protection Act" (Mansfield, October 31, 1996:14).

Meanwhile, the winter of 1996–97 in YNP arrived later than normal. October remained unseasonably warm. The park remained open to motorized vehicles until early November. The period between early November and mid-December is a closed season for the busy park. In mid-December, the park opens for snowmobiles and the season lasts until mid-March. Snows finally arrived in November and by early December the park was a beautiful winter wonderland of deep and fluffy snow. The Park Service began grooming trails into Yellowstone from the park's west entrance near the community of West Yellowstone and throughout Yellowstone.

Snowmobile trails follow roadways and run from West Yellowstone through the Madison River Valley, and then at Madison Junction the trail splits into two directions. One trail breaks north and east and heads to Norris Geyser basin and the Grand Canyon of the Yellowstone. A second trail leaves from Madison Junction and heads through large bison herds down the Firehole River Valley to Old Faithful. The northern entrance of the park is open year round since a major roadway travels from Gardiner, Montana, through Mammoth Hot Springs to the Lamar Valley and to Cooke City, Montana. (See Case Appendix A, which features a map of YNP.)

Around Christmas 1996, a major warming trend hit Montana, Idaho, and Wyoming. Temperatures rose to nearly 50 degrees (Fahrenheit) and the snow inside the park began to melt. The situation became so severe that park officials had to temporarily suspend snowmobile travel within YNP. It seemed as if the winter of 1996–97 would be an unusually mild one.

In January 1997, the "Greater Yellowstone Interagency Brucellosis Committee" (GYIBC) met in Bozeman, Montana, to discuss solutions to the bison problem. Apparently, according to the West Yellowstone News (Mansfield, January 16, 1997:4), a feud had been going on for about thirty years about the risks of brucellosis to cattle. The GYIBC is made up of the State of Montana livestock and wildlife agencies, the federal Fish and Wildlife Service, the National Park Service, the U.S. Forest Service, and APHIS. The group began meeting in 1994. They had been charged with the task of beginning an Environmental Impact Statement (EIS) addressing various options for bison management including: continuation of slaughter, public hunting, and vaccinations.[4]

By mid-January 1997, 52 additional bison had been killed in West Yellowstone, 113 were shipped for slaughter in Gardiner, and approximately 220 bison were seen near Gardiner and were expected to be captured shortly. Over 200 more bison were roaming near West Yellowstone. At this point, it appeared that the bison slaughter would be "minimal."

However, winter returned to Yellowstone in January, as heavy snow and severely cold temperatures hit the region. The melting in December had created a thick block of ice on Yellowstone grazing areas. Bison, even in the thermal areas of the Firehole, could not break through the ice to reach food. As a result, bison began migrating by the thousands toward what they hoped would be better feeding areas. The Firehole River Valley bison used the groomed snowmobile trails that led directly to West Yellowstone and the capture facility. The park's northern herd headed toward the deserts of northern Yellowstone and Gardiner.

By late January, the West Yellowstone News (Mansfield, January 23, 1997:14) had reported that over 585 bison has been killed. An article in the paper quoted Paul Pritchard of the National Parks and Conservation Association (NCPA), an eyewitness to the slaughter:

> The scene at the northern border of the Park is tragic. Animals are goring one another as they are crammed into pens and trucks to be shipped to slaughter. Three calves had their horns broken off and were bleeding profusely. An adult female arrived at the slaughterhouse badly gored and with broken ribs. Meanwhile, more bison are stacking up near the pens so another 100 bison could be killed next week at the north entrance alone.

Yellowstone National Park Superintendent Mike Finley wrote a letter to Montana Governor Marc Racicot expressing concern about "humane treatment" for the bison and about the "number of animals being killed." Finley asked the governor to invoke "contingency plans" to retain the integrity of the herds. The harsh winter of January, interacting with the melting of December that preceded it, was turning the Interim Bison Plan into a policy of bison extermination. Many bison did not move toward the capture facility, but were starving as the winter range was iced over.

Environmental groups such as the Fund for Animals and Biodiversity Legal Foundation called for an environmental impact statement to investigate the effects of snowmobiling on the park wildlife and other features. Environmentalists had noted for years that heavy winter use of the park was detrimental. Many environmentalists contended the groomed snowmobile trails were providing easy access for bison to leave YNP. The community of West Yellowstone, however, depends heavily on snowmobiling inside the park for its winter season.

Over 700 bison had been killed by the end of January 1997.

The USA Today newspaper ran an advertisement paid for by the "Fund for Animals" that stated in part, "Boycott Buffalo Butchery.... The State of Montana has zero

---

[4]The EIS was released in 1998 and the public comments on it were subsequently released in 1999. See Case Update.

tolerance for buffalo so we need you to have zero tolerance for Montana." The ad asked readers to contact Montana Governor Racicot and "tell him that you won't spend a dime in a state that doesn't give a damn about the one animal, of all animals, everyone should have a conscience about." In response to the ad, Racicot blamed the bison incident on the federal government and accused the Fund for Animals of false advertising (Mansfield, January 23, 1997:1, 8).

In late January 1997, Yellowstone National Park officials temporarily suspended the killing of bison at the Gardiner facility because of the harsh winter. Instead, officials tried to haze animals away from the park boundaries. By early February, YNP officials resumed capture operations after hazing efforts failed. Montana officials continued to shoot bison near West Yellowstone during this period. In February, Governor Racicot, facing severe national criticism, invited federal officials to Helena to discuss contingency measures.

Interest groups soon began proposing their own bison policies. In early February 1997, seven conservation groups outlined a bison management plan that included the following concepts:

- The NPS should honor its commitment to protect wildlife.
- The NPS should eliminate the grooming of several snowmobile trails.
- Bison should be allowed the full use of the national forest lands outside the park.
- A hunting season for bison could be implemented to control populations.
- Livestock could be vaccinated against brucellosis.
- Private landowners must realize their stewardship responsibilities.

In early March 1997, Montana's congressional delegation and Governor Racicot met with Interior Secretary Bruce Babbitt and Agriculture Secretary Dan Glickman to discuss the bison problem. Montana Senator Conrad Burns made it clear to federal officials that he wanted the NPS to manage bison within the park (Mansfield, March 6, 1997:3). The parties seemed to disagree on ownership of the bison problem but agreed to work together to create an Environmental Impact Statement by the end of July 1997.

By early March 1997, 1,049 bison had been killed under the policies of the "Interim Bison Plan." In an editorial printed in the West Yellowstone News (Racicot 1997), Governor Racicot called the shooting of bison "a tragic reality." He blamed YNP for not controlling the population of bison and stated that his job, as governor, was to protect the interests of Montana's main economic asset … ranching. In late March 1997, a woman from Bozeman, Montana, threw bison entrails at Governor Racicot as he spoke on the bison issue at a public forum in Gardiner.

Spring finally arrived in Yellowstone in late March/early April, even though 35 inches of snow remained at West Yellowstone in mid-April. The surviving bison slowly returned into the core of the park. An aerial count of the herd in early April 1997 found the bison's numbers in the park to be 1,089 compared to the 3,400 to 4,000 estimated count in the fall of 1996.

The recorded slaughter of bison in Yellowstone National Park left many environmentalists and citizens concerned. Many felt that, while it was unfair to penalize the ranchers and the State of Montana for this disease that was beyond their control, it was equally unfair to kill a magnificent, recognized symbol of the United States and the American west. This led to public outcry and a reassessment of the situation.

Update of Bison Case: Spring 1997–Summer 1999

In May 1997, the National Academy of Sciences began a study that looked at the following issues: the extent of bison infected with brucellosis in the greater Yellowstone area and the potential of developing a vaccination program; the transmission of *B. abortus* among cattle, bison, elk, and other wildlife; the relationship, if any, between bison population dynamics and brucellosis; the ability of serology testing to establish true infectiousness; the efficacy and safety of existing vaccines for target and nontarget species and the need for new vaccines (including bison-specific vaccines); the nature and likely successes for limitations of a wild animal vaccination program; and key factors in reducing risk of transmission from wildlife to cattle and among cattle.

In November 1997, the Academy's findings were presented to the public. The major findings were as follows:

- Seronegative results do not necessarily establish the absence of infection, because some seronegative animals in chronically infected herds are carrying live *B. abortus*.
- Due to testing insufficiencies, seropositive animals should be assumed for management purposes to be carrying live *B. abortus*.
- The risk of bison or elk transmitting brucellosis to cattle is small, but not zero.
- If infection rates are not substantially reduced in elk, reinfection of bison is inevitable.
- *B. abortus* is unlikely to be maintained in elk if the elk winter feeding grounds are available.
- Brucellosis is not a major factor in herd survival for elk or bison … winter mortality is most important.
- Bison leave the Park as a result of an increasing population and harsh winter weather, and under current management practices, the bison herd numbers will continue to grow.
- The U.S. Department of Agriculture and the Department of Interior should develop a plan to maintain a series of Yellowstone National Park perimeter quarantine zones with progressively increasing disease surveillance, vigorous monitoring, vaccination, and contact reporting programs as one nears the Park. The boundaries of the zones and management needed to maintain the zones should be determined jointly by the U.S. Department of Agriculture, the Department of Interior, and the states surrounding Yellowstone. The plan should remain in place until brucellosis is eliminated from Yellowstone National Park.
- A long-term, controlled vaccination study must be conducted to assess the complete role of vaccination in brucellosis control and eradication.
- Any vaccination program for bison must be accompanied by a concomitant program for elk.
- If the current vaccination program in elk feeding grounds are continued, it should include collection of serologic and culture data and appropriate epidemiological analysis.
- Research priorities with sufficient funding need to be determined cooperatively and with support of the secretaries of the U.S. Department of Interior and the U.S. Department of Agriculture. (Cheville, et al. 1998)

On November 24, 1997, adjustments to the Interim Bison Management Plan were made public. The revised plan addressed the early bison situation for 1997 first. The count for that winter dropped from 3,500 bison in the beginning of winter 1996–97 to 2,200 bison for early winter 1997–98. The adjustments to the plan were then addressed, with the goals and objectives consistent with the 1996 Interim Bison Management Plan. The overall objectives of adjustments to the interim plan were to reduce the number of bison killed as part of the interim bison management actions at or outside of the Yellowstone boundary, and to provide for a generally stable bison population at its current levels.

In the winter of 1997–98, a less lethal approach was taken with bison management. Most of this had to do with the December 1997 federal court decision that required the court's permission before more than one hundred bison could be killed. That winter was also mild in comparison to the previous winter. A total of only eleven bison were slaughtered, although hundreds of bison were outside of Yellowstone National Park boundaries. However, most of the bison did not enter into the state of Montana until late in the winter.

In the spring of 1998, the State of Montana, the Department of Interior, National Park Service, U.S. Department of Agriculture, the U.S. Forest Service, and the Animal Plant and Health Inspection Service came forward with an action plan known as the "Preferred Alternative." This plan was included in the Environmental Impact Statement (EIS). The plan was difficult to distinguish from the Interim Bison Management Plan. First, bison would continue to be killed as they left the park. The animals would be shot, or trapped, tested, and shipped to slaughter. Second, many groups felt an unreasonable target number for the number of bison living in Yellowstone National Park had been established. Many argued that the numbers being proposed were based on "politics, not science." Third, the plan did not make a commitment to modify public grazing allotments or to acquire critically important land from willing sellers, such as the Church Universal and Triumphant north of the park. And lastly, it called for continuing to kill bison because of brucellosis, while ignoring the fact that elk carry the disease also.

The "Citizen's Plan" came about in the summer of 1998 due to the protests against the "Preferred Alternative." The Citizen's Plan, according to its supporters, had the support of sportsmen, Native American tribes, ranchers, conservationists, scientists, park visitors, business people, and others. Proponents also supported the Citizen's Plan because it managed bison as wild animals, minimized human interaction in wildlife dynamics in Yellowstone National Park, and accommodated buffalo on winter range outside of the Park while taking reasonable efforts to protect private property and livestock interests.

The fall of 1998 saw a flurry of activity with all the various management plans, comment periods, and land negotiations regarding the bison. An October aerial survey found 2,239 bison in Yellowstone National Park, which was an increase of 18 percent from September 1997's count of 1,896 bison. (Remember that the number of bison in YNP is only an estimate and that numbers from season to season rarely add up.) The fall of 1998 also marked Phase I of the Church Universal and Triumphant (CUT) land purchase being approved by Congress. This agreement among the Church, the U.S. Forest Service, and the Rocky Mountain Elk Foundation was announced in 1997. The Church Universal and Triumphant has 7,850 acres adjacent or close to Yellowstone National Park's northern rim in the Gardiner, Montana, area. The asking price for this land was $13 million. The Department of Interior saw this purchase as part of a policy creating "bison easements" allowing bison more room to wander when they leave the park. Hundreds of bison had been killed in previous years on the acres owned by CUT.

In the spring of 1999, the comments generated from the Environmental Impact Statement were released to the public. The public comment period was June 12, 1998, through November 2, 1998. Approximately 47,000 comments voiced support for the Citizen's Plan, which had the backing of the Inter-tribal Bison Cooperative, the National Wildlife Federation, and the Greater Yellowstone Coalition. This represented 86.7 percent of all comments supporting the Citizen's Plan over various other management plans (National Wildlife Federation, 1999). There were 25,000 objections to the Preferred Plan (also known as the draft Environmental Impact Statement), which would limit the number of bison to 2,500 bison and would continue with hazing and slaughter. Over 67,000 letters were received ... including letters from every state, sixty-six countries, federal and state agencies, nongovernmental agencies, and tribal governments.

In November 1998, the State of Montana requested $500,000 from the U.S. Department of Agriculture to construct and operate a bison capture facility near Horse Butte (north of West Yellowstone). The capture facility opened in the spring of 1999. Its purpose was to capture and test bison that leave the park. The 100 x 300-foot facility is owned by the U.S. Department of Agriculture, but it was installed, operated, and maintained by the Montana Department of Livestock. The capture facility created much controversy since it was built on an area that included three nesting pairs of bald eagles. In addition, environmental groups contended that the facility threatened other animals in the areas, including bears, woodpeckers, owls, swans, and wolverines. Environmentalists feared that the facility would disrupt the animal and bird habitats due to increased human activity. Environmentalists also contended that capture and testing of bison was unnecessary in the winter since cattle do not arrive on the public lands until mid-June of each year.

On January 2, 1999, thirteen bison were sent to slaughter. Tests conducted in an Ames, Iowa, lab revealed that only two of the thirteen dead animals tested positive for brucellosis. In mid-January 1999, thirteen more bison were killed. Also in mid-January 1999, the Buffalo Field Campaign (formerly known as Buffalo Nations) constructed five thirty-foot-tall tripods of logs blocking access to the bison capture facility near Horse Butte. These tripods were manned twenty-four hours a day by the group's members. On March 18, 1999, twenty law enforcement officials ended the two-month blockade by arresting Buffalo Field Campaign protestors.

Symbolic protests and legal decisions also dominated the busy 1999 spring. On February 7, 1999, one hundred members of the various Native American tribes began a pilgrimage of more than five hundred miles from Rapid City, South Dakota, to Gardiner, Montana. On March 25, 1999, a federal judge rejected a request by the Inter-tribal Bison Cooperative and several conservation groups to limit the slaughter of bison for the winter of 1998–99. Judge Lovell stated, "Plaintiffs have failed to show irreparable harm to their aesthetic, emotional, religious and cultural interests arising from the 1997 interim plan, which in fact serves to reduce bison mortality" (Anez 1999).

On April 14, 1999, the Department of Livestock hazed and captured sixty bison in their capture facility, resulting in the killing of forty-five bison. In an April 24, 1999, press release, Buffalo Field Campaign announced that bison calves were starving north of West Yellowstone because their mothers had been slaughtered. Finally, in May 1999, the National Federation of Wildlife offered to pay for brucellosis vaccinations for all cattle that graze on public and private land in Montana adjoining Yellowstone National Park. The environmental group offered to pay up to $12,000 a year for at least the next five years. The Montana Department of Livestock and Montana Stock Growers did not accept the offer because, according to Montana Stock Growers Association Executive Vice-President Jim Peterson, the solution did not do much to address the "big picture problem of eradicating brucellosis for good" (McKee 1999). On May 6, 1999, the 9th U.S. Circuit Court of Appeals upheld a decision allowing the State of Montana and the National Park Service to continue the current management plan for bison.

Finally, in what was a surprise to environmentalists, businesspersons, and recreationists, the National Park Service in April 1999 suggested that snowmobile traffic from West Yellowstone to Old Faithful be ended. Instead, the NPS would plow roads, and cars and buses would be allowed to drive from West Yellowstone to Old Faithful. Local West Yellowstone businesses opposed the plan, snowmobile interest groups were unsupportive, and some environmentalists wondered whether the plowed roads would make it significantly easier for bison to leave Yellowstone in the winter.

In short, three years after the signing of the Interim Bison Management Plan, no end to the controversy was in sight. A summary of citizen views is found in Appendix 6-3 (page 229), and Case Appendices B, C, and D (pages 171–73) are examples of public comments that surfaced.

Case Note

As of spring 2000, there had been only a handful of documented cases of a wolf killing a bison. Bison herds have been successful in protecting their newborn calves and the size and power of adult bisons have deterred attacks from predatory wolves. Wolves have preyed mainly on elk herds. This has been a disappointment to environmentalists who had hoped that the wolves would provide a natural means of herd management. (*The authors would like to thank Ashley Ford Rudel, whose writing and research played a major role in the bison update section of the case.*)

Discussion Questions

1. Does Kingdon's policy model shed any light on what might or should happen here?

2. The rational actor model (public choice theory) suggests people are rational actors weighing out costs and benefits and pursuing their own best interests. As a whole, does this case study support this view?

3. In Chapter 4 we discussed implementation. It has often been stated that the way public policy decisions are made has a substantial impact on their legitimacy. How would that play out in this situation?

4. Democracy is a recurring theme throughout this text. Would an analyst with a strong commitment to public involvement in policy analysis make a difference?

5. We have also focused on the impact of individuals and argued that personality, personal relations, propensity to take risks, and the quality of leadership are important factors in the policy process. In your opinion, in this case, what has been and what should be the role of individuals?

6. On a related note, in Chapter 3 we quoted Gary Orren as saying that what motivates people to sustained action is a "collection of deep commitments and feelings." How does his point relate to this case study?
7. To put it bluntly, we have insisted that the essence of policy analysis is political—that it is about power and objective facts viewed subjectively based upon value conflict and interests. One key we have also stressed is the role of what Deborah Stone called "strategically crafted argument." Does this case study support our view of the essence of the policy process and the argument made by Stone?

Case Appendix A:
Map of Yellowstone National Park

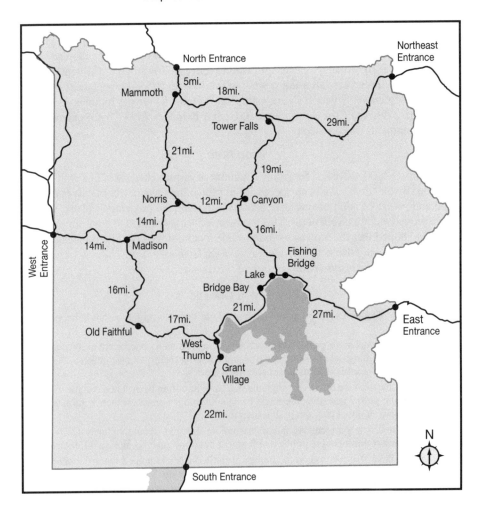

Case Appendix B:
Hypothetical Letter from an Environmentalist

January 17, 1997
Mike Finley
Superintendent
YNP

Dear Mr. Finley:

I am writing to let you know that I strongly disapprove of the current rounding up and slaughter of the Greater Yellowstone bison herd. The bison are a symbol of the American West. Some of the fondest memories of my childhood are the first times I saw large herds of bison in YNP. The herding of bison within the park for testing and slaughter is unacceptable. Yellowstone National Park, I do not have to tell you, was created to protect wildlife from the senseless slaughter advocated by special interest groups like ranchers. There is no scientific proof that bison can transmit brucellosis to cattle. While I understand your political concern of working with ranchers, there are alternatives to this problem other than slaughter. The Park Service should not engage in the rounding up of wild animals or the slaughter of animals.

Keep the bison free, make policies based on science, not interest group politics, and restore Yellowstone to a wildlife sanctuary.

Sincerely,

Frances Green
Pocatello, Idaho

Case Appendix C:
Hypothetical Letter from West Yellowstone Business Owner

February 2, 1997
Mike Finley
Superintendent
Yellowstone National Park

Dear Mr. Finley:

In recent days, I have heard scuttlebutt around town that some environmentalists are proposing that YNP end snowmobile use in the park to keep bison from migrating into West Yellowstone where they are then killed. While I personally hate to see the bison killed this way, I can assure you that bison have always migrated outside the Park during bad winters. When I was about six years old in the late '60s, I remember seeing hundreds of bison in West Yellowstone during bad winters. This was long before the park was open to snowmobile use.

If you closed the Park to snowmobiling, my small motel would not survive. The summer competition has increased greatly and my summer season is not what it used to be. In the winter, however, I have a large and faithful clientele and now make about half of my yearly profit in the winter season. I am not a wealthy woman and cannot influence politics like these rich environmental and ranching groups. But I strongly encourage you to keep the winter season open to protect the small business owner in West Yellowstone.

I hope that you find some solution to the bison problem. I am tired of the bad publicity. Last week a California couple left the area after seeing a bison shooting. The dragging of dead bison behind pick ups is not a big attraction for our tourists. But I do support my ranching friends who for centuries have tried to make a living raising cattle in the tough climate of Montana. I think that this is a Park Service Problem. Take care of it, but don't stop winter tourism.

Sincerely,

Bev Mulder
West Yellowstone

Case Appendix D:
Hypothetical Letter from Rancher

February 15, 1997

To: All local newspapers:

I've been reading the terrible remarks that have been aimed at Montana ranchers by environmentalists and other outsiders. We ranchers have been called "butchers" and "murderers." Last week a group of California tourists made rude gestures toward my family as we were going to buy groceries in Gardiner. I would like this opportunity to express the rancher's point of view in this situation.

I was born on a ranch about 15 miles north of Yellowstone National Park. My father was a rancher and staked out a living in the rugged Montana climate. We are a small ranch and make a modest living. We and nearly all of our ranching neighbors are small, independent ranchers. We are not "corporate ranchers" like environmentalists like to call us. I get up each morning at 4:30 A.M. to check on my cattle, and tend to their sickness. I have cattle both on private land and on public land. I pay money to use the public land.

The National Park Service is not a friend of the local rancher. The reintroduction of the wolf into Yellowstone has caused me great anxiety as I wait for my cattle to be attacked by wolves. Wolves are terrible and vicious creatures.

Bison in Yellowstone have brucellosis. A study has shown that bison can transmit brucellosis to cattle when they come into close contact. If my cattle were to get brucellosis, I would have to destroy them and Montana would lose its brucellosis-free status. This means that I could not sell my cattle across state lines. This means that my neighbors and I would go bankrupt. Ranching is how I make a living. Tourists and environmentalists can come and see the Park and take pictures of bison, wolves, and grizzlies and then return home. Yellowstone is like an amusement park for these people, but ranchers must live with bison, wolves, and grizzlies and the damage they do to our economic interests.

I do not want all the bison killed. But the economic interests of Montana revolve around ranching. Thanks to Governor Racicot and Senator Burns for standing up to outside interests and protecting our way of life.

Sincerely,

Joe Jones
Gardiner

Case References

Anez, Bob. 1999. "Judge Upholds Management Plan for Park Bison." *Billings Gazette*, March 26 <http://www.billingsgazette.com/region>.

Bartlett, Richard A. 1989. *Yellowstone: A Wilderness Beseiged*. Tucson, AZ: University of Arizona Press.

Chase, Alston. 1986. *Playing God in Yellowstone*. Boston, MA: Atlantic Monthly Press.

Cheville, Norman F., Dale R. McCullough, Lee R. Paulsen, Norman Grossblatt, Katherine Iverson, and Stephanie Parker. 1998. *Brucellosis in the Greater Yellowstone Area*. Washington, D.C.: National Research Council.

Consumers Union of the United States. 1997. "Rating the Parks." *Consumer Reports* (June): 10–17.

Fischer, Hank. 1995. *Wolf Wars*. Helena, MT: Falcon Press.

Glover, John. 1996. "Interim Bison Management Plan Approved." *Yellowstone Journal* (September/October): C-7.

Haines, A. 1977. *The Yellowstone Story: A History of Our First National Park*. Vol. 2. YNP, Wyoming: Yellowstone Library and Museum Association.

Haines, X. 1995. *The Buffalo: The Story of American Bison and Their Hunters from Prehistoric Times to the Present*. Norman, OK: University of Oklahoma Press.

Keiter, Robert B. 1997. "Greater Yellowstone's Bison: Unraveling of an Early American Wildlife Conservation Achievement." *Journal of Wildlife Management* 61, no. 1:1–11.

Lacey Act. 1894. *U.S. Statutes at Large* 28:73

Mansfield, Gayle. 1996. "Local Man Joins Others in Lawsuit on Bison Plan." *West Yellowstone News*, October 31, p. 1, 14.

Mansfield, Gayle. 1997. "Officials Debate Future Bison Plan." *West Yellowstone News*, January 16, p. 1.

Mansfield, Gayle. 1997. "Number of Bison Killed Surpasses record of '88–89. *West Yellowstone News*, January 23, p. 14.

Mansfield, Gayle. 1997. "Bison Plan Revisited." *West Yellowstone News*, February 6, p. 1, 8.

Mansfield, Gayle. 1997. "Officials Parley over Bison." *West Yellowstone News*, March 6, p. 3.

Mansfield, Gayle. 1997. "Bison Meeting Interrupted." *West Yellowstone News*, March 27, p. 1, 6.

McKee, Jennifer. 1999. "Bison Battle: Wildlife Groups Offer to Pay Ranchers for Vaccinating Cattle Against Disease." *Billings Gazette*, May 4 <http://www.billingsgazette.com/region>.

Meyer, M. E., and Mary Meagher. 1994. "On the Origin of Brucellosis in Yellowstone National Park: A Review." *Conservation Biology* 3, no. 8:645–53.

National Wildlife Federation. 1999. "Bringing Buffalo Back: National Park Service Report Reveals Public Overwhelmingly Supports Ending Slaughter of American Buffalo." March 15 <http://www.nationalwildlife.org./buffalo/pcomment.html>.

Phillips, M. K., and D. W. Smith. 1996. *The Wolves of Yellowstone*. Stillwater, MN: Voyageur Press.

Racicot, M. 1997. "Governor's Statement on Diseased Bison." *Montana Online*, March 3 <www.mt.gov./governor/press/bison.htm>.

Schullery, Paul, W. Brewster, and J. Mack. 1997. "Bison in Yellowstone: A Historical Overview." Pp. 326–36 in *International Symposium on Bison Ecology and Management in North America*. Edited by L. Irby and J. Knight. Bozeman, MT: Montana State University.

State of Montana Department of Livestock. 1997. *Bison Fact Sheet*.

CHAPTER 6

POSTPOSITIVIST PROBLEM
DEFINITION AND PRAXIS

Case Study
"School Shootings and Focus Group Research:
A Postpositivist Method of Problem Definition"

This chapter revisits the bison case study in Chapter 5 and uses this political controversy to demonstrate postpositivist problem definition. Problem definition is arguably the most crucial step in policy analysis and the essential insight in the postpositivist model is the subjective and conflictual nature of problem definition and the key role of language and stories in that process. In addition, we extend our study of postpositivist and postmodern theory and examine three methodological tools used in postpositivist analysis. The final inquiry for this chapter concerns the pragmatic value of the postpositivist model. Can it provide analysts with guidance for doing policy analysis? Are there useful postpositivist analytical methods? Can deconstruction of political rhetoric help democracy?

The Two Tracks of Policy Analysis

Society and government, at all levels, have grown apace in terms of size and complexity, making public policy and our need to understand the process by which it is made, prima facie more relevant. Yet, even as the salience of policy analysis became clearly recognized, the parochial walls erected between scholars also grew. For example, scholars of national and state level policymaking use substantially different approaches and bodies of literature. These stout walls inhibit cross-fertilization.

Instead, policy analysis theory building[1] and the teaching of policy studies have largely run along two tracks that rarely intersect. One track is the positivist, rational, value-neutral, quantitative track that has dominated the field. In recent years, however, the field has increasingly become interested in a second track of policy analysis. The second track is a postrationalist, postpositivist, and postmodern approach to analysis (Danziger 1995; deLeon 1997; and Stone 1988/1997). This qualitative track features social construction of reality and argues that subjectivity is inevitable. Its inroads, however, have been much more substantial in terms of theory than in practice.

Public policy analysis has been dominated by positivist approaches since at least the 1970s. The seven tools described in Chapter 8 illustrate this approach. Positivism, in theory, is a rational, value-neutral, and quantitative approach to policy analysis. In the classroom, students taught in this approach learn the rational choice model and public choice theory,[2] microeconomic concepts, statistical analysis, and other forms of probability and risk assessment. This approach is useful, for it provides a tangible methodology for future analysts. It is also rather easy to teach in the classroom since there are specific steps and methods to learn. While used extensively in public policy education, the positivist method is used less often in the field, and it is of questionable value for democracy and in the political system where policy is determined. Most often the complex models and mathematics of the positivist approach do not parallel the even more complex world of democratic policymaking.

Most importantly, many issues policy analysts deal with are political issues that involve normative values. Positivism is most useful only when political issues are framed as technical questions such as: "Can bison graze on public lands without the risk of brucellosis transmission to cattle?" However, these "technical issues" often involve much larger normative questions. For example,"Should bison be allowed to graze on public lands?" or "Should cattle be allowed to graze on public lands?" Policymaking is political and positivist tools leave the analyst severely lacking in their ability to grasp the complexity of politics. The positivist approach to policy analysis emphasizes efficiency at the expense of democracy. The positivist approach is tied to bureaucratic decision making with its emphasis on calculability, generalizability, stability, rationality, and proceduralism. Peter deLeon (1997, 81) writes that the most important problem with positivism is that it falsely presents an appearance of "truth." It does so by assigning numbers to a variety of decision-making criteria and producing what appear to be definitive answers to political questions. It does so because of the bureaucratic imperative

---

[1]In 1997, Kim Quaile Hill, Paul Sabatier, and Edella Schlager engaged in a scholarly exchange of ideas in the journal *Policy Currents*. Their focus was the development status of systematic and generalizable theory in the field of policy studies. Sabatier and Schlager both identified the advocacy coalition framework and the institutional rational choice model as the two most developed theories. Hill initiated the debate with the call for greater attention to theory building, including the use of what he labeled ambitious case study scholarship and use.

[2]The rational choice model and public choice theory are both models for explaining and predicting behavior of individuals in a society. Both assume that individuals are goal seeking and will always seek to improve their position in life. The individual seeks to maximize. Therefore, we can view policymaking as equivalent to individuals pursuing private goods in a marketplace. Individuals will pursue their own interests and only support using tax dollars in so far as the public project delivers benefits that exceed the tax dollar investment made by the individual.

to reduce emotional and conflict-ridden political questions to neutral, scientific, and technical ones. Bureaucracies are designed to deal with nonpolitical issues. Once political questions and issues enter into the bureaucracy, the bureaucracy deals with them by methods that ensure efficiency, procedure, and predictability. The positivist method of policy analysis is very much part of bureaucratic culture.[3]

Generations of policy analysts have learned in the classroom that their work should be nonpolitical, technical, and scientific. The politics/administration dichotomy is still the dominant overarching theory of public policy analysis. Discussed previously, the dichotomy asserts that administrators merely execute laws and implement policies passed by elected officials. Fox and Miller (1996) describe this as the "loop theory" of democracy. Loop theory asserts that at the core of democracy is a sovereign citizen with political preferences. Political parties then form that put together various packages to meet these preferences. Citizens vote for the parties and candidates that meet their preferences. Elected officials then pass laws and citizens vote to retain them in office or remove them. The key is that there is a direct connection in loop theory between the citizen and the elected official. The administrator does not stand between the citizen and the elected official. Instead, the role of the administrator is simply to technically execute policies passed by an elected body. The policy analyst's role, under loop theory, becomes the positivist role of using rational, scientific, and neutral methods to define problems and evaluate policies. It has you working directly for elected officials.

As Fox and Miller (1996) explain, loop theory has been severely undermined. In contemporary American politics, even at the local level, elected officials act more as "symbols" raising campaign dollars, finding wedge issues, and producing interesting soundbites. Much of the legislation passed by elected officials is symbolic, vague, and ambiguous. So the bureaucracy is left to deal with all of the politics of both policy generation and implementation.[4] Unfortunately, generations of public administration students have been trained to assume that their job is to be efficient and that they should not and cannot deal with political issues. But, as you now know, public policymaking is very political. Thus, policy analysts, trained in the politics/administration dichotomy school, use "neutral" positivist methods on policy questions and issues that are still ripe with political conflict. Their number calculations appear scientific and truthful but often the numbers intentionally or unintentionally hide values that are inherent in policies. There is no "objective truth" when the questions asked are political and normative ones.

Yet, even as we enter a new century, the graduate classroom is still dominated by positivist teaching techniques. Fischer (1998, 143) writes, "still dominated by an outmoded conception of scientific **epistemology** [boldface added], the social and policy sciences ill equip their students (especially doctoral students) for the world they are sent out to confront." Lawlor (1996, 111) reemphasizes the point by adding, "Mainstream

---

[3]For an excellent discussion of the imperatives of bureaucratic culture, see Hummel (1994), Chapter 2.

[4]It is interesting to note that "bureaucracy" is a symbol that over the last two decades has been the enemy of both liberals and conservatives. Bureaucracy-bashing is very much part of elected official rhetoric. Calls for government reform consistently focus on bureaucratic reform instead of electoral or campaign finance reform. Bureaucracy has become the symbol for all that is wrong with American government. Yet elected officials are the ones passing vague legislation and leaving the real work of government to experts in bureaucratic agencies (see Box 6-1 for a closer look at how citizens view public bureaucracy).

policy analysis has not kept pace with advances in relevant social science. Many curricula and texts seem frozen in intellectual time, circa 1970, with heavy emphasis on straight cost-benefit analysis, decision analysis, and public choice."

In response to these and other criticisms, there have been calls for changes in policy analysis pedagogy. If loop theory and the politics/administration dichotomy is indeed dead, it would seem that new approaches and methods of teaching and practicing policy analysis are needed. These new methods must be democratic, must explicitly recognize the workings of politics, and must be based on the latest social science techniques. Danziger (1995, 435) argues in this vein that policy analysis must be made more democratic and sophisticated and that the graduate classroom is the beginning focus of this effort. Danziger (1995, 447–48) adds that "students need to be encouraged to examine the inescapable narrative element in policy analysis" and taught that the weapons in policy wars are "hidden presumptions, underlying ideologies, emotional arguments, powerful metaphors and analogies, moving personal narratives, economic models, and the striking presentation of statistics."

In addition, like most of academia, the field of policy studies has not been immune from the powerful influence of "postmodernism." The positivist approach has received great criticism from scholars such as Deborah Stone (1988/1997) and Marie Danziger (1995). These scholars, while not necessarily true "postmodernists," argue that rationalistic policy analysis is impossible and instead largely serves the interests of elites. These scholars use postmodern techniques such as deconstruction to demonstrate that politics is subjective and that what rational techniques identify as the "truth" may in fact be the product of some deep, hidden ideology. Analysts socially construct facts and these subjective interpretations are contested by stakeholders. Postpositivism suggests that the role of the analyst is not to find the truth, but rather to be suspicious and distrustful of all policy claims and ultimately to provide access and explanation of data to all parties, to empower the public to understand analyses, and to promote political issues into serious public discussions (Danziger 1995). In short, this view of analysis seeks to turn the expert policy analyst into the democratic facilitator.

The idea is that, just as different answers derive from different questions suggested by different models,[5] different policies are likely to stem from different problem definitions; fueled in part by the inescapable subjectivity of the various advocates, agents, institutions, and analysts. The postmodern focus is on the crucial role of language, rhetorical argument, and stories in framing debate and changing the context in which policy is made by affecting public opinion, coalition building, and the perception of who is potentially affected.

We can conclude that a major contribution of the second track of policy analysis (whatever we call it—postpositivist, postrationalist, postmodern) is in regard to problem definition. This track clearly demonstrates the subjective, value-laden, and conflictual quality of problem definition. As you remember from Chapter 5, different problem definitions lead to different policy solutions.

---

[5]Graham Allison's recently revised 1971 classic of decision making and the Cuban Missile Crisis, *Essence of Decision* (1999, 2nd edition) is still perhaps the best example of this phenomenon.

A second type of postpositivist policy analysis involves the actual participation of citizens in the formation of problem definitions, the generation of policy alternatives, and eventual determination of policy. This second type is referred to as "Participatory Policy Analysis" (PPA) and it emphasizes a brand of deliberative or participatory democracy. It is highly critical of the proceduralism and legalism of contemporary American democracy and instead attempts to tap into the Tocqueville and Jeffersonian view of American democracy.[6]

But for now our focus is on whether postpositivist methods, with their emphasis on problem definition and democracy, have made inroads into the graduate classroom. Certainly these approaches provide an excellent theoretical critique of traditional positivism. But positivism remains the dominant teaching method in the policy analysis classroom. Part of the problem is that much of the literature of postpositivism is solely theoretical in its scope. These works often provide excellent theoretical criticisms to positivism but provide little guidance for applied policy analysis since they often lack mention of specific and teachable skills. Danziger (1995, 445) writes of "postmodern policy analysis" in this regard:

> There is a sense, after all, in which the "postmodern" seems fuzzy and inefficient by comparison, without the lure of quasiscientific models for reducing complex data, and the issues surrounding them to some degree of measurability. Then too, methods of teaching rationalist models almost inevitably are more clearcut. Concepts in economics and statistics can be demonstrated quite effectively through lectures, graphic displays, problem sets, and software, while the teaching and learning of elusive deconstructive insights, not to mention persuasive writing and speaking, do not lend themselves to any surefire classroom formula.

6-1. Bureaucratic Horror Stories: Public versus Private

One of the book's coauthors likes to have students discuss their worst experiences with public bureaucracies. We all have our own bureaucratic horror stories, or have heard the stories of others (e.g., the student who spent four hours going from line to line trying to get financial aid). One such story related by a student goes as follows:

> All I needed was a new driver's license. I had just moved to town from out of state and I needed a new license. I went into the courthouse and stood in a line that said "Driver's Licenses Here" for about one hour. After I reached the front of the line, the clerk told me, "You are in the wrong line. For new driver's license issues to former out-of-state folks, you need to stand in line over there and take a longer examination." Unfortunately, there was no clerk at this station. I asked why there was not a clerk and the first clerk stated, "Well, it's because it is the lunch hour. You shouldn't show up at lunch time and expect to get service." Well, of course, I had showed up at 11:00 A.M. but stood one hour in the wrong line. After a wait of another hour and fifteen minutes, a clerk showed up and it looked like I was going to be

---

[6]This approach will be discussed in Chapter 7, and we will provide some actual democratic tools of analysis and policymaking.

waited on. However, the clerk could not wait on me because his job was only to process the driver's licenses, not to give the examination. The examination person would not be back from a post-lunch meeting until 1:45. I asked the person whether he could give me the exam and he stated, "Sorry, that is not my job." Finally, at about 1:50, the examination clerk arrived, and by 2:30, I had my new license. I had spent three and one-half hours in the courthouse, however. Don't these bureaucrats realize that my time is valuable? I have more to do each day than just boss people around, telling them to stand in line and fill out forms. Why don't these people get a real job?

In a typical class, your author gets several stories like this. He then leads the class through a discussion of how we view public bureaucracy. Students use terms like "incompetent," "useless," and "stupid" to describe bureaucracies and bureaucrats. Many students then argue that government should be privatized or at least "run like a business."

Then the students are asked to relate their worst experience with a private organization or bureaucracy. At first they are hesitant but soon the stories start flying. We hear tales of flies in sandwiches, people paying for services never received, inconsiderate sales clerks, dishonest car salespersons, and so on. The author usually relates his favorite private horror business stories: how he wanted to buy a new computer but the clerk would not take the time to order him one, how he once sat unattended at a local restaurant for one hour waiting for a piece of pie, and how a clerk at a sporting goods store didn't know what a first baseman's glove was.

Your author then asks the students, "Why don't we call for the end of capitalism and private enterprise? It seems our bad experiences with private organizations actually surpass the number of bad experiences with public organizations. However, somehow we want government to be run like a business? What is going on here?"

From here, the author tells several good examples of service provided by public agencies: how the city arrived in only fifteen minutes late one night to unfreeze a frozen pipe; how financial aid clerks worked overtime to process a late financial aid request; how a police officer once stopped to help change a flat tire, etc. The point is that public bureaucracy has become the symbolic target of government hatred. Yet, American bureaucracy is one of the most efficient and effective in the world.

In a similar exercise in his American Government course, the other author reframes the original question, asking, "Think about your most recent dealing with bureaucracy (getting your license renewed, temporarily stopping mail delivery, dealing with financial aid here at the college, etc.). How did that experience go?" Most students admit it went smoothly, that they were treated with respect, that no favoritism or corruption was evident, etc. Part of the image problem for the bureaucracy is that we don't tell those stories. Of course not—they're not very interesting.

Much of the difficulty of applying postpositivist methods, according to deLeon (1997, 85–86), is that, unlike conducting rationalist methods like cost-benefit analysis, there is no endpoint. In short, deLeon (1997, 86) argues that with postpositivist methodologies, the wider spectrum of opinions and perspectives tend to complicate the analyst's task of making a final decision. In addition, he adds, policy analysis becomes subjective, dynamic, and there are no clearly defined parameters. In the final analysis, deLeon (1997, 86) writes, "One may ultimately achieve 'clarity' but many would ask at what cost and in what time frame?"

Postpositivism often leaves the student in a sea of doubt and subjectivity that, just like positivism, fails to equip the student for the real world of policy practice. For example, while Lawlor (1996, 111) fretted over the outdated epistemological standards of policy analysis, he pessimistically concludes in his review of postpositivist works that "postpositivism and so called postmodernism in policy analysis is a swamp of ambiguity, relativism, and self doubt. The new argumentation framed as an integral part of the policy process and with an unapologetic normative agenda, creates more problems for the policy analysis business than it solves."

So professors of public policy analysis are usually stuck with a dilemma. Teach positivism that provides the students with tangible skills, but which is undemocratic and often not useful in the political morass of public policymaking; or teach postpositivism which, while theoretically superior both in its epistemological and democratic orientation, provides little guidance for practitioners in the field. Positivist approaches do not help to end the conflict that occurs over problem definition in policymaking. Instead, positivism inserts a **hegemonic lifeworld** view into the decision-making process that stifles democracy. However, postpositivism seems to just confuse the issue of problem definition. It is more democratic, but does democracy mean anarchy? What is needed is a fusion of the tangible analytical skills provided by positivism with the democratic aspirations of postpositivism. What is needed is praxis.

The abstract of Marie Danziger's article (1995, 435), "Policy Analysis Postmodernized: Some Political and Pedagogical Ramifications," states her call "for the academic preparation of more democratic, more rhetorically sophisticated 'postmodern' policy analysis." What Danziger seeks is the translation of postmodern insights into analytical skills. She urges the writing of "new case studies focusing on the kind of inevitable professional conflicts" that practicing analysts face and the deconstruction of existing case studies, helping students to "identify unheard voices, missing criteria or policy alternatives, hidden assumptions, contradictory findings, uncertain outcomes, and suspicious numbers." The pedagogical difficulty that Danziger sees is that "often the only means of learning such skills and values is the trial and error of concrete experience."

We begin our search for teachable and useful postpositivist knowledge and techniques by first examining the subjective nature of problem definition. From here, as promised earlier, we introduce you to some tools of postpositivist analysis and return you to Yellowstone National Park and the controversy over bison (where we will demonstrate a postmodern approach to problem definition.)

The Ambiguous and Subjective Nature
of Events in the System

At the heart of the postmodern method is the belief that social events are socially interpreted and thus the meaning of these events are socially created. The rational approach to policy analysis asserts that certain events occur in the political system and that these events lead to policy implementation or change. These events are usually referred to as "triggering events" and every beginning policy analyst knows that these triggering events lead to calls for policy change and implementation of new policies.

A famous example from American history was the assassination of President Garfield by a disgruntled job seeker named Charles Julius Guiteau.[7] Public personnel textbooks nearly always mention that the passage of the Civil Service Act of 1883 (the Pendleton Act) was a response to the shooting, since Guiteau had been denied patronage by the Garfield administration. These textbooks assert that this event gave civil service reform (which was already being discussed in Congress), the necessary momentum to be passed and signed into law.

It is interesting, however, that Guiteau's actions were portrayed by the media and others at the time as the work of a "disgruntled job seeker." In contrast to the simple media story, Guiteau had a long history of mental instability, including several bouts with syphilis. He expected patronage for simply publicly reading an old speech supporting Garfield that he had written originally for Horace Greeley. Guiteau was never asked by the Garfield campaign to deliver the speech. Guiteau was, in fact, unknown by the campaign. Certainly, no rational person would expect patronage in this situation. The media of the time did not tell the entire story of Guiteau's action.

Thus, another interpretation of Guiteau could have been that he was simply deranged and that the shooting was an isolated action having no larger social and governmental implication. This interpretation would have meant that the patronage system did not encourage the killing of a president and, if it had become the dominant story, reform movements would not have been able to use the assassination to mobilize support for civil service reform.

Compared to the 1880s, contemporary events in American society are perhaps more likely to produce multiple interpretations. Modern society is fed by 24-hour television news channels, tabloids, news magazines, talk shows, and internet chatrooms; providing citizens with a plethora of views, facts, half-truths, conspiracy theories, opinions, and advice about the latest happenings in American society. The well-publicized school shootings of the late 1990s generated much discussion among citizens and policymakers alike. What, if anything, these shootings represent, however, is a subject of debate in a highly fragmented and individualistic American society. There are many interpretations of the causes of, and appropriate lessons from, these shootings.

---

[7]Tragically, many "triggering events" in American history have been literal triggering events.

School Shootings and Problem Definition

After a disturbing 1997–98 school year, the 1998–99 school year had been relatively quiet. The year closed with a flurry of arrests, suspensions, bomb threats, canceled events, rumors, jitters, additions of law enforcement officers, increased security measures, establishments of tip-lines, redoubled efforts to identify troubled youths, and budget requests for physical security measures. What set this tidal wave of activity into motion was Littleton—a strongly Republican, wealthy, overwhelmingly white, bedroom community of Denver.

On April 16, 1999, in Notus, Idaho, a high school sophomore fired shotgun blasts, but no one had been injured. Four days later it was a very different story. On April 20 the media turned its cameras, and the nation its eyes, upon a Jefferson Colorado High School where victims, some of them wounded, were fleeing the deadliest school shooting rampage of the nineties. Two boys at Columbine High School opened fire and killed thirteen people and then themselves. Reportedly laughing and taunting victims, one of their weapons was a Tech DC 9 (assault style, semiautomatic weapon). Tens of thousands attended the funeral services and millions of Americans watched on television. We mourned the heroic teacher and freshman who helped others flee, the junior who refused to deny her faith, the inspiring senior apparently a target because he was both an athlete and black, and eleven more lives tragically ended.

Sadly, this wasn't the end of the school year's violence. In Conyers, Georgia, a 15-year-old boy was arrested after he shot six students. None died, as the shooter apparently wanted it; they were all shot below the waist. According to reports, unlike the ostracized Columbine High Trench Coat Mafia shooters, the suspect was a clean-cut, average student who attended church every week with his family, and the night before the shooting, had even attended a Catholic youth group meeting. Working backwards, chronologically speaking, let's review the year before:

- On May 20, 1998, a fifteen-year-old in Springfield, Oregon, was suspended from school for carrying a gun to school. He killed his parents and then returned to school on the 21st and killed two students; another twenty were injured.
- On May 19, 1998, in Fayetteville, Tennessee, a student was shot in the school parking lot—allegedly by an eighteen-year-old male classmate.
- On April 28, 1998, a thirteen-year-old boy was taken into custody following an after-school shooting at a Pomona, California, elementary school basketball court. Two teens were killed and a third was wounded.
- On April 24, 1998, at Nick's Place (a banquet hall outside of Edinboro, Pennsylvania) a General McLane High School science teacher and coach, father of three, was shot and killed at the eighth-grade graduation dance he had helped plan and volunteered to chaperone. Two male students were shot, another had a bullet pass through his shirt sleeve, and a female teacher was grazed by a bullet. The fourteen-year-old shooter, Andrew Wurst, had told people he was going to make the dance "memorable." He reportedly played with Legos and had Raggedy Ann dolls, but called Hitler and Napoleon heroes, used marijuana and whiskey, loved the movie *Spawn*, and was nicknamed "Satan."
- On March 24, 1998, two young boys in Jonesboro, Arkansas, pulled a fire alarm in their elementary school, hid in the nearby woods, and opened fire on classmates,

teachers, and school personnel. The two boys shot twenty-two rounds in four minutes. Five students were killed and ten were wounded.

- On December 1, 1997, in West Paducah, Kentucky, students were gathered in the morning for a prayer circle in a Heath High hallway when a fourteen-year-old student, who had warned his classmates that "something big was going to happen," opened fire. Five students were wounded and three were killed.
- On October 1, a sixteen-year-old in Pearl, Mississippi, killed his mother and then went to school and shot nine students, two fatally, including his ex-girlfriend.

It is no wonder that the nation's attention had been drawn toward juvenile violence in public schools after Littleton and the previous year. For the record, according to the National School Safety Center, in the last seven school years (1992–93 through 1998–99) there have been slightly over 250 school-related violent deaths and a little over 75 percent of those deaths were caused by shootings.

Gun Access   According to some groups and individuals, the shootings are primarily the result of easy access to guns combined with a culture that glorifies gun use. This has led to calls from this group for fines and prison terms for gun owners who fail to secure them, and at the 1998 U.S. Conference of Mayors there was a lot of discussion about suing the manufacturers of assault weapons. Barry Krisberg, president of the National Council on Crime and Delinquency in San Francisco offered *Time Magazine* (Labi 1998, 39) this quote, "The violence in the media and the easy availability of guns are what's driving the slaughter of innocents." In *Newsweek*, Geoffrey Cowley (1998, 25) commented that among other possible causes, "It's possible, of course, that young boys have always nurtured bizarre revenge fantasies but lacked the means to carry them out." He then quotes Geoffrey Canada, president of the Rheedlen Centers for Children and Families. Talking about the possibility that teenage boys may have always concocted revenge fantasies, Canada argues that easy access to guns make fantasies become real. He states, "It would be a pain, but it wouldn't be mass murder." The article goes on to cite a National Institute of Justice study that found that one-half of all guns are unlocked and sixteen percent are both unlocked and loaded (Cowley 1998, 25). A more recently published study appeared in June 1999, in the journal *Archives of Pediatrics and Adolescent Medicine*. In a national survey of over 5,000 households they discovered that about 20 percent of households stored an unlocked, loaded gun in the home. More specifically, 11 percent of the homes with both guns and children under eighteen admitted that they kept unlocked and loaded guns in the home. The study also mentions that in 1995 almost 36,000 people died from firearms in the United States, including over 5,000 children and teens (Uhlman 1999). Further, editorial writer Bob Herbert (1999) quoted the following statistics on murders by handguns, by country, in 1996: New Zealand = 2, Japan = 15, Great Britain = 30, Canada = 106, Germany = 213, United States = 9,390.

And an April 21, 1999, Gallup Poll showed that a majority (60 percent) of adults believe the availability of guns bears a great deal of the blame for school shootings (*Erie Daily Times* 1999). Polls also show that students are concerned about both guns and troubled classmates. According to a Washington Post/ABC News poll done in April 1999, 40 percent could think of a student at their school who could do something like the Littleton Shootings, 20 percent knew students who had brought guns to school, 54 percent reported that it was very or somewhat easy for them to get a gun, and 42 percent thought schools should do more to prevent violence (*Washington Post Weekly Edition*, May 3, 1999).

Supporters point to recent figures released by the U.S. Justice Department demonstrating the success of the federal law known as the Brady Bill. Pre-sale checks of prospective handgun buyers blocked sales of nearly 70,000 guns, while allowing over two and one-half million sales. Approximately 62 percent of those rejected had felony convictions or indictments. Nearly 10 percent had been convicted of misdemeanor domestic violence and another 2.1 percent were under restraining orders to prevent their stalking an intimate partner or harming a child. Thirteen percent (13 percent) were either fugitives from justice or prohibited by various state or local restrictions. Drug addiction and mental illness denied handgun purchases to another 2.5 percent and the remaining rejections (11.7 percent) were barred under a 1968 federal law whose restrictions included illegal aliens, people who renounce their U.S. citizenship, dishonorably discharged military personnel, and juveniles (Fari, 1998:6A.).[8] In sum, the problem is defined as allowing youths today, in our culture, to have easy access to so many deadly weapons.

Concealed Gun Advocacy   Others believed that the shootings could be prevented if teachers and school administrators were allowed to carry concealed weapons. In a *Wall Street Journal* article posted on an internet site <http://www2.ari.net/mcsm/arkansas.html> John R. Lott Jr., a professor at the University of Chicago School of Law (1998) discusses a study with a colleague in which, "we examined a whole range of different gun laws as well as other methods of deterrence, such as the death penalty. However, only one policy succeeded in reducing deaths and injuries from these school shootings—allowing law-abiding citizens to carry concealed handguns." This view suggests that responsible adults should carry concealed weapons and when mass shooting occur, these adults can put an end to the violence by shooting the shooters. Lott's policy recommendation is therefore stated, "Attempts to outlaw guns from schools, no matter how well meaning, have backfired. Instead of making schools safe for children, we have made them safe for those intent on harming our children. Current school policies fire teachers who even accidentally bring otherwise legal concealed handguns to school. We might consider reversing this policy and begin rewarding teachers who take on the responsibility to help protect children." According to the *New York Times*' Barry Meier (1999), on the day before the Columbine shootings, Professor Lott was in Colorado advising supporters of concealed weapons legislation that some legislators and lobbyists were trying to pass. The NRA and other groups have been pushing such legislation in state legislatures around the country. Charlton Heston, the president of the NRA, said the day after the massacre in Littleton, that even one armed guard at the school might have prevented the tragedy." (He didn't know yet that there was an armed guard at the school.)

---

[8]The manufacture and sale of nineteen specific assault weapons were banned by the federal legislation signed into law in 1994. This gun control legislation got a momentum boost from another tragic triggering event at a school when a twenty-four-year-old drifter with a AK47 assault rifle opened fire on a Stockton, California, school yard, killing five children and wounding thirty more.

More support for this view was cited in an April 23, 1999, *New York Times* article (A-16). Governor Jesse Ventura (Reform Party) of Minnesota, also on the day after the shootings, said that Littleton demonstrated the need for more gun permits and/or conceal-and-carry laws. Ventura ventured that "had there been someone who was armed, in this particular situation, in my opinion, it may have been stabilized." And Bill Dietrick, an NRA member who lives in Colorado and had lobbied hard for the legislation to loosen concealed weapons permit restrictions, stated, "When you make places like schools off limits to the honest gun-carrying people ... you create a killing ground for those inclined to do so."

But perhaps no one has been as actively opposed to any and all restrictions on any and all weapons as Larry Pratt, the executive director of the Gun Owners of America organization. Mr. Pratt was forced out of his role in Pat Buchanan's 1996 campaign for the Republican nomination for the presidency, when his ties and associations with white supremacist groups, militia movement extremists, and militant antiabortion fringe groups were revealed. The week of the shootings in Colorado, Pratt said, "We're saddened that there were not teachers and principals who had access to a gun, who might have been able to stop the mayhem" (Bruni 1999).

Part of this argument is that, since there are already an estimated 200 million guns owned privately, we should not restrict gun access to criminals and thus inadvertently endanger the public we are trying to protect.

Media Violence   The shootings are the result of popular culture's glorification of violence, approval of ridicule, encouragement of getting even and demanding respect, and perpetuation of cynicism. Several individuals and groups call for government regulation and control of the internet, video games, television, and music. Stanton Samenow was quoted in *Time Magazine* right after the Arkansas shootings. Samenow argued, "Television and the movies have never in my experience, turned a responsible youngster into a criminal." He added, however, "But a youngster who is already inclined toward antisocial behavior hears of a particular crime, and it feeds an already fertile mind" (Labi 1998, 38). Representative Henry Hyde (R-IL) in June of 1999 fought for a House bill that he introduced that would have curbed access to violent and explicitly sexual material in movies and video games. Hyde said his measure would "slow the flood of toxic waste into our kids minds." Representative Jo Ann Emerson (R-MO) said on the House floor, "Anyone who thinks (school violence) has nothing to do with the media is an idiot" (*Erie Daily Times*, June 17, 1999). Wayne LaPierre, executive vice-president of the NRA, said that the killings at Littleton could be blamed on Hollywood's obsession with violence and the moral breakdown in society (*New York Times*, April 26, 1999).

Some critics of television violence do distinguish between types of violence portrayed. A study of nearly 10,000 hours of television programming, from late 1994 to mid-1999, discovered that factors such as whether or not the perpetrator of the violence is shown to be punished, whether or not the aftermath of pain and suffering of the victim is shown, whether it was provoked or random, etc. do affect the impact of watching violent shows (Fari 1998, 21).

What are the consequences of rap songs about killing cops, video games like Doom (which also teaches hand-eye shooting coordination and tactics), movie heroes who get even, and hours and hours of TV violence? According to critics, the result is people who are desensitized to violence, who are convinced it's a "mean world" and that they are owed their due, and who see those who use violence as heroes and people of significance. A related argument is that it is the parents' fault for not doing their jobs and for abandoning the task of teaching values to their children to the media.

Religious and Moral Values and Conspiracy The violence is seen as an outgrowth of the government's own liberal values, which, according to individuals telling this narrative have "outlawed prayer in school," "disallowed corporal punishment," "taught students to sue their parents," and "authorized the murder of babies." The solution from this perspective is governmental and societal return to what these individuals believe are fundamental Christian values. Consider this posting on the internet: An individual identified only as Roger argued that the shootings were, among other things, the result of the following:

- "Children taught that they are just accidents of mindless evolution with no purpose and no future beyond this life."
- "Children taught that it is alright to murder babies if they are not wanted."
- "Children taught that there are no moral absolutes but that what ever they think is alright is."
- "Children taught in our liberal propaganda schools that it is more important to feel good about one's self than to learn anything of value."
- "Children taught that casual sex is the norm and they should be participating, or there is something wrong with them." <http://www.techmgmt.com/restore/shooting.htm>.

On the same website, an individual identified only as Brian, wrote:

The LIBERALS and Socialist Scum have been teaching a godless behaviorism to our school children for 20+ years. Now it is they who reap the Whirlwind of out of Control children, they have turned into sociopathic killers! They ARE to BLAME Not the GUNS! The true Atrocity here is not the fact that they stole the guns to be used in the Crime of murder, but rather the responsibility of the LIBERAL Scum who taught the children their values! Goal 2000 + other communist propaganda is to blame! They are a Godless people who use an appalling shooting to further their communist goals of disarming all of America! <http://www.techmgmt.com/restore/shooting.htm>

A Letter to the Editor that appeared the day of the Littleton tragedy (therefore obviously written before it happened) promised to answer for readers this question: "What is the matter with our country?" The answer was obvious, he wrote, by looking at the front page of the paper a week before. It had shown a baseball player, during the national anthem, blowing a bubble with his gum (*Erie Daily Times*, April 20, 1999). Within a week, another Letter to the Editor appeared in the same paper (April 26, 3B). This author: (1) blamed abortion (while we protect Bald Eagles); (2) claimed we took Jesus out of Christmas, prayer from school, and God out of the country; (3) named evolution as the foundation of racism and communism; (4) summed up the problem by saying the solution to what happened in Littleton was to "turn back to God."

Prominent politicians hitch their wagons to this explanation as well. Representative Tom DeLay (R-TX), one of the most powerful members in the House at the time of the debate on gun control and school shootings, produced a litany of causes other than guns. Texas-based, nationally syndicated columnist Molly Ivins sums his argument up well. "DeLay blames all of this—the theory of evolution, birth control, small family size, day care, abortion and moral relativism—for the shootings in Littleton. He does not blame guns. He does blame liberals" (Ivins 1999, 46).

Absent fathers often get blamed too, as well as easy divorce and single moms, and even Jack Kevorkian; but religion is often the central focus. Representative Bob Barr (R-GA) captured the extreme end of this explanation with a statement he made during the debate of an amendment to a juvenile justice bill (that passed the House). This probably unconstitutional legislation allows states to post the Ten Commandments in schools. As seen on C-SPAN and widely reported, Barr said that the Columbine killings would not have happened if the Ten Commandments had been posted there. Also the week of the massacre, Representative James Traficant (D-OH) was also seen calling for lifting the ban on organized school prayer because (to paraphrase) "it is unlikely that people who prayed together would kill each other."

Liberals have their own argument that evokes the notion of values and cultural learning. Some have argued that statistically speaking, parents are much, much more likely a threat to kids than their classmates. The problem is that in the world, and in their homes, we teach them that violence is an acceptable way to deal with problems. As a government, if we don't like what the leader of another country is doing, we bomb them. As a parent, if we don't like what you are doing, we spank you. Many individuals contend that we have given conflicting messages to the young, "Don't hit your brother or I'll tan your hide." Or, "If you don't stop crying I'll give you something to cry about." In addition, liberals tend to cite violence in sports, history books praising warriors, and the God of the Old Testament smiting Israel's enemies cruelly. All of this, the liberal community contends, promotes the value of violence to children.

Isolated Events/Bad Kids   Finally, some view the shootings as isolated incidents of "bad kids" or "attention-seeking kids" who should be held individually responsible for their acts. *Time Magazine* quotes a neighbor of the Arkansas school boys as saying, "These are cold-blooded, evil children, and I don't care how bad that sounds" (Labi 1998, 36). These citizens argue that individual responsibility is the key and the only public policy matter to consider is making sure that states put juvenile killers on trial as adults and that discipline in the school is returned. Gun access is not seen as the problem, nor the media, nor liberals and the separation of church and state, nor the lack of enough guns; rather the problem is the bad seeds who misuse guns. The goal of society should not be to ban guns or censor media because these solutions would restrict the freedoms of all Americans, even those who are highly unlikely ever to commit an act of violence toward another human. This message about the Littleton shootings from an internet chat board is illustrative:

> I had only wished they had caught those freaks alive. They should hang them in the middle of town and let them swing for a couple of days. Then parade every little two bit crook or sack of crap by their bodies and let them see what happens to people like that.... We should be strong enough to say that it was those kids that did this. It was not the gun, the bomb, or some movie, or some other factor that gets the blame away from them. We are so afraid of responsibility that we start making excuses for our behavior. What happened was the fault of the kids and nothing else. <http://talk.channel2000.com/cgi-bin/webx?talkback-14> (KCBS Channel 2000, Los Angeles, California)

6-2. *South Park* and School Shootings

Y ou might have expected that an essay connecting the two topics of the title would be blaming the casual and excessive violence of *South Park*. (Poor Kenny, episode after episode, killed again and again by some @#$$#@$$@$.) But guess what? You would have been wrong. Often attacked as obscene, sacrilegious, foulmouthed, raunchy, and crude—*South Park*, the popular television show spawned (pun intended) a film version—"Bigger, Longer, and Uncut"—that hit the theaters in the summer of 1999.

The plot was, perhaps shockingly, not only evident but very ambitious. A film reviewer (M. V. Moorhead, in *Showcase*, a supplement to the *Morning News*, July 22, 1999) accurately noted that the plot involved "war, bigotry, censorship, nationalism, true-versus-false patriotism, and the cosmic fate of the earth, and it all hinges on that most American of ideals, freedom of expression."

Sure, the boys are incredibly foulmouthed, and guest characters Satan and Saddam Hussein are having an affair in Hell, and the Chef (voice of Isaac Hayes) is about the only intelligent, wise, and semiconcerned adult. The other adults tend to be oblivious, hypocritical, racist, and consumed with sex. Moreover, they all find horrific, deplorable violence okay as long as no one says any naughty words. And, yes, the songs (including "What Would Brian Boitano Do?") tend to be lyrically inspired by studies of scatology. However, this movie's connection to the school shootings relates to the blame game (and we don't mean the MTV show about embittered couples willing to be embarrassed on camera for their fifteen minutes of fame). Once again, Moorhead scored in the conclusion of the movie review:

> The point of it all, of course, is that the grown-ups of South Park—thus in microcosm, of the U.S.—are willing to plunge society into any degree of panic, fury, and bloodshed in the name of "protecting our children" from the sort of language and crude culture that makes grown-ups uncomfortable. Yet all of the adults except for Chef pretty much ignore the children during the whole affair. In the media-critic opportunism and blame-shifting to which the post-Columbine climate has given rise, this mockery is a breath of vulgar fresh air.

In one song about who is to blame for the kid's behavior, they alternatively blame the government, society, images on television, and Canada. Late in the movie Kyle suggests his mom overlooked the possibility of blaming him. Hmmm. Maybe they're all to blame (well, except for Canada).

What Is the "Truth" and How Are Policies Generated?

So what is the truth? What lessons do these shootings have for the American political system? What should government do or not do? The answers to these questions are complex. Analysts and experts will collect data on juvenile shootings and produce hundreds of studies on why children kill. Gun control advocates will produce similar policy briefs on gun use in juvenile crime. Other studies will examine the linkages between popular culture and youth violence. The safety of children at school will be compared with the number of children killed by their parents at home. All of these scientific studies will most likely still produce conflicting interpretations of causes and therefore conflicting policy recommendations.

While empirical studies are used by policymakers, eventually definition of what happened in Jonesboro, Edinboro, Springfield, and other places occurs in the political system as activists are mobilized, coalitions are formed, rhetoric exchanged, elections held, and propositions passed (or not passed) that ultimately produce a public policy. At the end of this chapter, a case dealing with the school shootings is presented. In this case, you will be given a first-hand opportunity to actually conduct a postpositivist analysis. First we must further examine the political creation of public problems and introduce you to some methodologies used in postpositivist/postmodern policy analysis.

Types of Public Policies and Policy Interests

Stone (1997) uses James Q. Wilson (1973) to provide a matrix that assists in the understanding of American public policy. Using a rational approach, Wilson argues that there are four types of public policies and the type of policies are determined by whether benefits and costs are concentrated or diffused. In addition, the type of policy determines how politics is played (see Table 6-1). Wilson asserts that concentrated benefits lead to mobilization on the behalf of interest groups, elites, and other groups. Conversely, diffused benefits (because they are necessarily smaller) will not give rise to such concentrated political efforts. Similarly, concentrated costs will give rise to intense political opposition from elites and interest groups who will bear the concentrated costs. Diffuse costs will not bring much political opposition since the costs are small and mobilization less likely.

TABLE 6-1   WILSON'S POLICIES AND INTERESTS

	BENEFITS	
	DIFFUSED	CONCENTRATED
COSTS		
Diffused	1 Incremental	2 Pork-Barrel
Concentrated	3 Regulation	4 Stalemate

Source: Adapted from Stone (1997, 223).

In Quadrant #1 of Table 6-1, policies have benefits that are diffused broadly among many citizens and groups, and costs that are likewise diffused. These policies are termed "incremental." They are marked by the fact that the benefits and costs are both diffused. Such policies do not normally create much positive or negative political mobilization. Many public goods have these characteristics. For example, the National Weather Service gives benefits to many dispersed groups and theoretically to everyone. The Weather Service benefits farmers, sailors, tourists, fisherman, and just about every citizen. However, the benefits that we receive are not so great that any one group would mobilize to expand the service, although some would if the Weather Service was going to be terminated. Likewise, because costs are diffuse, no groups are going to mobilize to have the Service's budget cut. Policies in Quadrant #1 expand or decline in a gradual or incremental fashion.

In Quadrant #2 of Table 6-1, we have policies by which benefits are concentrated and costs diffused. These policies are what we term "pork-barrel." The goal is to redistribute money from a large group (the American people) to a recognizable group that benefits directly. For example, federal irrigation projects in Washington State and federal urban renewal programs in Michigan are paid for by all Americans, not just by Washingtonians and Michiganites. Benefits, however, are concentrated to Washington and Michigan respectively and the level of benefits is still more concentrated for the agricultural sector in the Columbia River Basin region in Central Washington state and in the city of Detroit. Costs are diffused to all Americans. There is less likely to be significant opposition to such policies because there is a concerted effort among those who will receive the benefits to sustain the policies. For example, if you were a New York state citizen and you discovered that $1.35 of your taxes were going to an irrigation project in Washington or a urban renewal project in Michigan, would you bother to take time to mobilize against the project? The answer is that almost certainly no one would expend energy, time, and financial resources to kill a project when the costs are so diffused. On the other hand, because benefits are concentrated, citizens, interest groups, and elected officials in the states, regions, and cities that will benefit are going to spend a great deal of time maneuvering for the policy. Money will be spent, favors granted, and political I.O.U.s called in to bring the irrigation system to Washington and the urban renewal package to Michigan. The political contest is uneven since there is a strong coalition promoting the policy and literally nobody opposing it.

The prime example in Quadrant #3 of Table 6-1 is regulatory policy. In this quadrant, political opposition rules the day since the costs (as with any regulatory policy) are focused on a specific group. Any environmental regulation has specific industries that bear the brunt of regulatory costs. These groups often spend millions and millions of dollars fighting attempts to regulate. In contemporary American politics, the attempts to regulate the tobacco industry have been thwarted by well-organized and well-financed tobacco interest groups. In addition, interest groups, and the Motion Picture Association of America, and its president Jack Valenti, fought Henry Hyde's amendment discussed earlier that would have restricted the motion picture industry.

At the same time, benefits in Quadrant #3 are diffuse so there is little incentive to mobilize support. It is difficult to individually determine how much, if at all, one directly benefits (or is harmed directly) by pollution or by reductions in teen smoking. The rise of environmental groups since the 1970s can be seen as an attempt to organize individuals who receive diffuse individual benefits—but large collective benefits—from clean air, clean water, and wildlife preservation.

In Quadrant #4 of Table 6-1, both benefits and costs are concentrated and political support and opposition are strong. This situation most often creates a "policy stalemate" because neither side is strong enough to win, or a situation occurs in which victories alternate from policy to policy. The current struggle over bison and brucellosis in Yellowstone National Park could be seen as such a policy. Because Yellowstone politics draws national attention and thus national environmental constituencies and interest group mobilization, pro-bison groups have successfully countered the local and regional ranching industry that still dominates regional politics. Neither side is strong enough to dominate, and emotions and symbolism have kept compromise and win-win solutions off the policy agenda. The box below uses Deborah Stone's ideas about strategic representation to reinterpret Wilson's matrix.

6-3. Air Regulation: Wilson versus Stone

The rational model of politics introduced by Wilson assumes that policies in Quadrant #1 and Quadrant #2 are most likely to be supported. Conversely, policies in Quadrant #3 and Quadrant #4 are more likely to find political opposition. But how do we really know where a policy fits in the matrix? For instance, take the example of regulating air pollution. In the rational model it would seem that air pollution regulation is something that rational citizens would mobilize to support, since the benefits of regulation seem concentrated to individuals who do not want the health consequences of dirty air. Interestingly enough, however, unless the pollution is easily visible or can be smelled, rational citizens may not bother to mobilize to support air regulation. It is easy to gain support for obvious environmental problems like hazardous waste sites that leak into watersheds. It is easy to get citizens to support regulation when rivers are on fire and people are choking on the smog. It is more difficult to find support to regulate pollution whose potential detrimental consequences are not immediate to the population. As a result, the politics of air pollution regulation are best explained by the use of the postmodern view of strategic representation.

Who will benefit from air regulation and who will pay the costs? The answer to this question seems simple. We can say that this policy belongs in Quadrant #3 because benefits will be diffused among the general population and costs concentrated on the polluting industry. With diffuse benefits nobody, it would seem, is going to get too excited about mobilizing to support the policy.

For example, as a citizen, why would I spend my time and money to support a policy that, while it may benefit me, does not benefit me in a direct and tangible way? My rational choice may be to free-ride. That is, even if I don't mobilize to support the policy of regulation, I will still get the benefits of the regulation once the law is passed. The costs of mobilization are high (time, money, opportunity costs) and the individual benefits are small. On the other hand, the affected industry has concentrated costs and it is very rational for them to oppose the regulation. They will oppose the regulation by lobbying, giving money to political candidates, and conducting a public information campaign. The issue's salience is presumed to depend on a rational calculation of costs and benefits.

In reality though, as the postmodernist approach suggests, Wilson's 2 x 2 box may be of only minimal help in understanding problem definition and policies. As Deborah Stone (1997, 133) writes, "Problem definition is a matter of representation because every description of a situation is a portrayal from only one of many points of view."

In the case of air regulation, we can imagine that the industry may want air regulation policy to remain defined as a regulatory policy, since regulatory policies tend to not attract a well-organized and financed group of people in support of the policy (since benefits are diffuse). But since costs are concentrated on the industry, many citizens may be indifferent to the regulation and hence would not oppose the regulatory policy. Therefore, the industry may well want to redefine both costs and benefits. Through a well-financed media campaign, the industry might well argue that "industry" really means "family." That is, the industry is really made up of workers, stockholders, and others who are just common people with kids, mortgages, and car payments. Therefore, costs are now perceived as diffuse, which may make the policy seem irrational or at least unpopular in the rational model. The industry may attempt to attract community support for the industry and thus create or stimulate community opposition to the regulation. The industry could argue that regulation will increase costs on the industry and this will lead to lost jobs that in turn will lead to losses in tax revenue for the city government, government cutbacks, and general social unhappiness.

The industry would likewise try to make benefits concentrated instead of diffuse by portraying environmentalists as wealthy elites who do not understand or care about the workers in the industry or the community at large. A common rallying cry would be to term environmentalists as "elites" or "Yuppie-Tree Huggers." The point is that the industry might try to make environmentalists seem out of touch with economic realities. In Jonathan Harr's tale of a courtroom battle resulting from polluted water and leukemia deaths, John J. Riley, one of the businessmen involved in the lawsuit in Harr's book, is described as making "no secret of his belief that environmentalists were conspiring to drive him out of business" (Harr 1995/1996, 92). The industry avoiding regulation will portray environmental groups as composed of social elites, such as university professors, attorneys, and physicians who really "don't have to work for a living."

The strategy of the industry is to make costs seem diffuse and benefits concentrated. This would portray the policy as being in Quadrant #2 and make it a pork policy. According to Wilson's logic, this would be a bad move since policies in Quadrant #2 are likely to be passed into law according to the principles of diffuseness and concentration. However, on another level the actions of the industry are politically smart because they turn the regulatory policy away from a definition of a collective good and toward the definition of a good that benefits only a select few. A major part of contemporary American political ideology rejects pork barrel policies because they favor special interests over collective interests.

In a similar manner, in our example, environmental groups will try to either concentrate or diffuse the portrayal of benefits. For example, they will react to the industry's charge that environmentalists are elites by painting the industry as "greedy and selfish" and interested in profits at the expense of local health. Environmentalists will emphasize that the corporation is headquartered not in the local community but in a far-away and wealthy urban area. Statistics will be released that link air pollution with a variety of deadly diseases. The environmental group will appeal to collective interests and simultaneously will try to make the individual citizen see the individual benefit to them from regulation (better health and a longer life).

At the same time, environmental groups may argue that lack of regulation on this industry will ultimately concentrate costs on the larger community. Under this scenario, wood stove, barbecue, and lawn mower use may have to be curtailed, economic development efforts curtailed, other industries will have to be regulated, and even car use may be affected. Environmentalists will argue that costs should be imposed on the industry since air pollution is an externality whose cost is a spillover to the larger community while the profits from polluting are concentrated.

The point is that problem definition does not exist independent of political definition. Policies are not sitting objectively in the political system but rather are created through political language and representation. This line of reasoning is at the heart of the postmodern contribution to a postpositivist policy analysis method.

Stone's Symbolic Representation of Problem Definition

Now, having better explained how policies are created through political language and strategy, we can look specifically at how postmodern scholars view problem definition. Stone (1997, 154–55) argues that "Problem definition in the polis is always strategic, designed to call in reinforcements for one's own side in a conflict" and that "problems are not given out there in the world waiting for the smart analyst to come along and define them correctly. They are created in the minds of citizens by other citizens, leaders, organizations, and other agencies, as an essential part of political maneuvering."

As we discussed in detail in Chapter 4, Stone (1988, 122) points out that a "strategic definition" can provide the means to manipulate the "scope of a conflict" by determining who is and is not affected. In addition, players often present a Hobson's Choice, and strategically portray problems using four types of symbolic representation: narrative stories, **synedoches**, metaphors, and ambiguity.

Stone (1997) also argues that in their efforts to define problems, analysts, politicians, interest groups, and others are essentially trying to identify causes of the problem. Recall that Fuller and Myers (1941) discussed the evolutionary and political nature of social problems. Discussions of the life cycle of social problems became common after that. Robert Ross and Graham L. Staines (1972, 18) in a journal article entitled "The Politics of Analyzing Social Problems" summarized that process succinctly:

> Private or interest group recognition of the social problem; political recognition of the problem as an appropriate issue for public discussion; *public debate and social conflict about the causes of the problem: a set of political outcomes of this sequence* (emphasis added).

In their cogent elaboration of the article by Ross and Staines and its discussion on the debating of causes and solutions, Neubeck and Neubeck (1997, 14–15) write the following:

> This stage is extremely important for perceived causes have a definite relationship to the types of solutions that are considered. Ross and Staines distinguish between two different causal interpretations commonly brought to bear on social problems. On the one hand, a problem may be given a *systemic attribution*.... On the other hand, a problem may be blamed on the people involved.... This second causal interpretation is termed *personal attribution*.... Different groups find either systemic or personal attributions in line with their perceived self-interest.... As Ross and Staines put it: "Since causal diagnoses of social problems are reached by different people in different political situations, conflict between alternative patterns of attribution becomes inevitable." (Emphasis in original)

When causes are found, blame and responsibility can be pinpointed, assigned, and then solutions offered. Stone (1997, 189) writes, "In politics, we look for causes not only to understand how the world works but to assign responsibility for problems. Once we think we know the cause of a problem, we use the knowledge to prevent people from causing the problem, to make them compensate other people for bearing the problem, and to punish them for having caused suffering." Stone goes on to explain how causal definitions are, in the end, stories told carefully using symbols and numbers. Stone argues that there are four type of causal theories and she uses a two by two matrix to detail these (see Table 6-2).

Using consequences and actions as her two dimensions, Stone's four types of causal theories are important for demonstrating that multiple interpretations of causes are likely and that causation is ultimately socially created rather than just existing in the political system and waiting for a positivist policy analyst to find it. The four types of causes are common in political debates.

Accidental causes have unintended consequences and unguided actions. Examples include winter blizzards, earthquakes, and generally anything attributed to "mother nature." Since they are outside of human control, accidental causes are often the representational story told by those accused of causing a problem. For example, as has happened in many communities that have experienced rapid and extensive growth, a

TABLE 6-2   STONE'S CAUSAL THEORIES

	CONSEQUENCES	
	INTENDED	UNINTENDED
ACTIONS		
Unguided	1 Mechanical	2 Accidental
Purposeful	3 Intentional	4 Inadvertent

Source: Stone (1997, 190).

particular western community has recently had several flash floods that have sent tons of sediment down city streets and often into homes. Many local residents believe that the problem is caused by both unfinished and finished development at the base of the community's eastern foothills. The local government and local developers, however, claim the floods are simply the result of too much rain coming down at one time and therefore the problem is outside of governmental control and human intervention.

Inadvertent causes are essentially unintentional with unintended consequences and purposeful actions. Here policies are implemented that have unforeseen side-effects, sometimes due to carelessness. In the flooding example mentioned earlier, residents believe that the city's foothill development policy has had the unforeseen side effect of causing soil erosion. In addition, carelessness by the developer in not landscaping the newly developed properties has led to more problems. In politics, individuals accused of intentionally causing a problem will often use the inadvertent cause as a fallback. When accused, the first line of defense is to claim the causes of a problem as accidental, but if this fails, "inadvertent" causes become a convenient fall-back for the accused.

Intentional causes are actions that are purposeful and with intended consequences. Successful conspiracies would fall in this category. Intentional causes are the strongest form of accusation made in politics. In the flooding example, a small number of residents have accused the city government of being "politically in bed" with the primary developer who has torn up ground on the eastern foothills. These residents view some city leaders as having a personal interest in the development at the expense of the larger community who must deal with the soil erosion and flooding.

Mechanical causes are found in technological and institutional systems. In many examples of mechanical causes, human control is at dispute. For example, the "Millennium Bug" problem involving computers demonstrates how reliant the human system is on technology. The doomsday scenario was that as of January 1, 2000 (Y2K), many computers that did not have the year 2000 in their memory system would shut down, causing bank accounts to disappear, traffic lights to quit working, electrical grids and medical equipment to shut down, and a variety of other problems to occur, which would bring our everyday life to a screeching halt.

In addition, mechanical causes come from institutional systems in which organizations see problems as a result of what Stone (1997, 195) terms "a web of large, long-standing organizations with ingrained patterns of behavior." In this latter case, conflicting organizational mandates lead to problems in determining direct causes or may be a barrier to finding solutions. Mechanical causes are often used as a defense by those accused of causing a problem. In the community flooding example, developers have blamed conflicting regulations, laws, and requirements for slowing the development process that has left many lands undeveloped and therefore susceptible to soil erosion.

Other Critics of Positivism

Beyond Stone's contribution, a series of studies on public policymaking have been highly critical of positivist policy analysis. deLeon (1997) argues that policy analysts have relied too much on quantitative analysis and in doing so, have become elite technicians separated from the lives of real people. deLeon (1997, 7) cites the failure of Clinton's health proposal as evidence of policy that "was embedded in its closed council, nondemocratic genesis, giving unwitting sustenance to the perception that too often important policy work is the privileged domain of distant and detached policy elite." Instead, deLeon argues, policy analysis must rediscover its roots found in the work of Harold Lasswell who said the aims of policy analysis are "directed toward knowledge to improve the practice of democracy" (Lasswell cited in deLeon 1997, 7). deLeon believes that a more participatory policy analysis framework is found in the postpositivist models of social science research including phenomenology and critical theory.

Majone (1989, 7–8) contends that policy analysis is essentially about language and how individuals are persuaded of the truth through political language. The voices of common citizens, he argues, must be heard in the political process. For example, he writes on the nuclear issue, "the consciousness of the dangers inherent in nuclear engineering in the United States and Western Europe is largely the result of public debate. Where nuclear technology has been allowed to develop according to its own logic, unhampered by criticism and public concern, as in the Soviet Union, it has produced few of the safety features (such as containment shells for pressurized water reactors) that are standard in the West" (Majone 1989, 5).

The implication of Majone's work is that policy analysts cannot just engage in purely objective and technical assessment of various policies. Instead, analysts must engage in a public discourse and produce policy arguments that are, finally, based on value judgements.[9] The audience of the analyst is not just the client, decision maker, or stakeholder but rather what Majone calls the "audience." He writes that audience, "a term with a long tradition in rhetoric—is a better, more flexible, and more neutral characterization of the set of actual or potential recipients and users of analysis than more familiar terms like 'client' or 'decision maker.' It also reminds us that the main justification of advocacy and persuasion in democratic policymaking is their function in a continuous process of mutual learning through discourse." (Majone 1989, 41)

Finally, Yanow (1996) severely criticizes positivist policy analysis in favor of what she terms an "interpretive approach." Outlining an interpretive methodology, Yanow (1996, 5) argues that "Our social institutions, our policies, our agencies are human creations, not objects independent of us." Using the case of the Israel Corporation of Community Centers (ICCC), she examines its history from a realist (objective) perspective and then from a variety of postpositivist methods focusing on symbolism, language, metaphors, myths, and other stories. The key is that the policy analyst must understand the nonrational methods including language that citizens use to understand and interpret public policies.

---

[9]Critics across the political spectrum have raised the issue of policy relevance. For example, the late social historian Christopher Lasch (1995) and political pundit E. J. Dionne (1991) have both suggested that the reason for public apathy and antipathy to politics is that citizens rightly perceive that today's fierce political battles center on peripheral issues that fail to address that which affects people's daily lives and concerns.

Postpositivist Tools

The key to postpositivist analysis is that the methodology used must not rely solely on quantitative analysis and that the analyst must seek a political understanding of problems. The postpositivist analyst, in determining problem definitions, looks for rhetoric, ideologies, symbols, and metaphors and tries to understand how these socially construct the definition of the problem leading to action or inaction. What type of methodologies can the policy analyst use to produce these postmodern/subjectivist analyses? While there are many techniques and this is not a research methods text, we will discuss three major postpositivist research techniques: narrative analysis, focus groups, and content analysis. At the end of the chapter a case is presented that will ask you to actually apply these methodologies while utilizing the theoretical orientations explained in this chapter.

Tool #1: Focus Group Methodology

Since the 1950s, focus groups have emerged as a popular form of qualitative research. Focus groups (or discussion groups) allow a facilitator to ask questions of persons in a group. The discussion therefore occurs within a social system and individuals can react to the statements of other group members. According to Morgan (1996):

> Focus group methodology is an interview style designed for small groups. Using this approach, researchers strive to learn through discussion about conscious, semiconscious, and unconscious psychological and socio-cultural characteristics and processes among various groups.

Morgan (1988) identifies five unique qualities of focus groups not found in other forms of social research, such as surveys. First, the focus group provides a way to learn about the implied, unspoken, and incidental knowledge that informs people's opinions. This is possible because focus groups, unlike surveys, do not generally lead participants but, rather, collect unfiltered and open-ended responses and discussions.

Second, focus groups similarly provide researchers access to the opinions of the participants in their own words, rather than in the closed-ended expressions of a researcher. Traditional techniques, like survey research, use questions and, most importantly, response options to the questions, that are predetermined by the researcher. Essentially, the researcher using traditional techniques is testing only concepts that she believes are important. The postpositivist view, of course, holds that there are many different interpretations of events, issues, and policies. Focus groups ask general questions and then allow the group discussion to flow into a variety of areas.

Third, focus groups provide an approach to examining people's intent and meanings in the phrases, words, and expressions that they use in social interaction. This symbolic analysis is essential to the postpositivist method. Unlike other forms of social research, particularly survey research, researchers can probe and follow up in ways impossible in the more traditional methods.

Fourth, the focus group provides researchers with opportunities to study the individual as part of a larger group. This aspect is essential since individuals do not form opinions about public issues in isolation but rather their opinions are formed in the context of group life. An important criticism leveled by postpositivists against the positivist school is that the latter uses an economic (market) view of the atomized individual. According to postpositivists, the individual cannot be the sole unit of analysis and instead the unit of analysis has to be the larger entity of the community or polis.

Fifth, the focus group can be combined with surveys and interviews. Small discussion groups are invaluable when researchers wish to design survey instruments based on valid opinion categories. Listed below are some general suggestions about setting up focus groups and facilitating focus groups:

1. Group size should be between ten and fifteen members.
2. Focus group composition should be representative of the studied population. For example, a study of local elected officials may include a city council member, a mayor, a county commissioner, and an elected county sheriff. A group with all city council members would not be representative of local elected officials.
3. The facilitator must be trained. A good facilitator redirects questions back to the group and does not contribute their own opinion in the group process.
4. A trained facilitator does not allow one or a few participants to dominate the group.
5. Other than the facilitator and perhaps an assistant, nobody other than focus group members should be allowed at the focus group sessions. Outside members are a distraction and their inclusion will violate the rules of institutional review boards that govern research with human subjects.
6. Each focus group should be tape-recorded and then transcribed by a trained transcriber.

Criticisms of focus groups include financial expenses for facilitators and participants' incentives, the time involved in forming and facilitating groups, and the difficulty of generalizing results since sampling is less random and systematic than that used in survey research (Babbie 1992, 255). The latter concern about generalization is the most significant criticism of focus groups. Phone and mail surveys allow large numbers of randomly sampled individuals to participate in research. With these surveys, sophisticated sampling techniques can be employed that provide results that are highly generalizable to the larger population. It is fairly easy to sample 5,000 citizens in a mail survey and, with follow-up mailings, expect at least 2,500 respondents. Focus groups are necessarily smaller and most often use sampling techniques that are far from random. For example, with an average focus group size of 10 participants, it would take 250 focus group meetings to produce the 2,500 number responding to a mail survey. This number of meetings would be time-consuming, expensive, and probably impossible over a large geographical area. Even if a researcher did conduct 250 focus groups, the generalizability of the sample is not guaranteed since random sampling is far more difficult with focus groups.

Focus groups are often a more effective method to research disadvantaged groups such as the poor, minorities, or other special populations. These groups usually do not respond in great numbers to mail surveys. Focus groups are more friendly to these populations. However, these groups, unless aggressively recruited, are still unlikely to attend focus group sessions. Sadly, focus group discussions on important issues like health care, nuclear waste, and school violence most often include only community elites and exclude those whose voices should be heard under the philosophy of postpositivist research. Appendix 6-2 provides an example of how focus groups could be used in the Yellowstone bison and brucellosis controversy.

Tool #2: Content Analysis

Content analysis is an approach used by researchers to examine written documents or transcripts of recorded interviews, such as focus groups and other types of communication. Content analysis revolves around classifying or categorizing unfiltered information into a conceptual framework. Babbie (1992, 318–19) and others differentiate between manifest and latent content. Manifest content is visible and clear. An example of coding manifest content would be to simply count the number of words describing the phenomenon that you are studying. For example, in a study of citizen trust of government, the researcher would count the number of times a citizen in a focus group transcript uses adjectives like trustworthy, believable, and confidence to describe their interactions with government. Conversely, the researcher would also count words like "untrustworthy," "unreliable," and "corrupt" used in a similar context. Manifest content is reliable since it is easy to count words.

Latent content refers to the language's underlying meaning. Latent content is more valid than manifest content but also less reliable. One researcher's interpretation of a sentence may differ greatly from another researcher's interpretation. Babbie recommends using both manifest and latent methods and then comparing your findings. Ideally, the two methods will produce similar results. If not, the researchers need to rethink their coding strategies.

The key to content analysis is defining categories. Both deductive and inductive methods should be used. When studying people's trust of government, for example, the researcher may want to examine the level of trust. He may produce categories such as very trusting, trusting, neutral, untrusting, and very untrusting. The researcher would then read the focus group transcripts or open-ended survey comments and classify each statement into one of the five categories. Each category needs to be defined for coding. The "very trusting" category could include responses that use several words to describe strong trust (words like honest, responsible, faith) and just a general interpretation that the person strongly trusts government. The trusting category would have responses that used fewer adjectives of trust and seem subjectively trusting. All five categories would be defined and coded (see below).

Question: Give me an example of why you trust or don't trust local government.

Answers and Coding

1. "I have for a long time believed that my local government is better than most businesses. I have had several discussions with the mayor and city council about problems and each time they have kept their word, told me the truth, and even when they can't help me I believe that they strongly care about me and are honest. I have faith in them." (Coded: Very Trusting)

2. "I really have no views on this question. I really don't think much about local government." (Coded: Neutral)

3. "I think that there are some problems with our local government. I am not sure but I think that some of the city council members are looking out for their own interests. This might not be true, I don't know." (Coded: Untrusting)

4. "Local government is a joke. They say one thing and then do another. I quit going to public hearings because the council will do whatever they want anyway. This is a major problem for our town. (Coded: Very Untrusting)

5. "My few interactions have been mostly positive and I think I trust them. I might be wrong but I haven't had any problems with the local government." (Coded: Trusting)

Realistically, an inductive approach would be used also. After coding all responses, the researcher may find that the five categories do not fit with the responses and that he needs more categories, less categories, or altogether different categories. A common approach is to use a pair of scissors and cut transcribed responses into strips of paper. Then sitting on the floor or at a large desk, the researcher lumps similar responses together. Only through the reading of all responses can the researcher get a feel for the types of responses and the commonalities of each. At this point the researcher names the categories of responses.

Importantly, in content analysis at least three researchers should classify responses independently of each other. For example, perhaps one researcher may have found that the five categories of trust were adequate and successfully classified responses into these predetermined categories. A second researcher also uses the five categories but comes up with slightly different results. A third researcher abandons the five categories and instead decides to use a new classification scheme based on whether the respondent had interaction with government and whether that interaction was positive, neutral, or negative (see Table 6-3). When this occurs, the first two researchers need to examine their coding sheets and compare how they classified each response. Then these two researchers must listen to the third researcher and decide if her new categories are more valid than the five categories produced through deductive research. A simple tool is to determine the inter-rater reliability by dividing the total number of agreements (in coding) by the total number of agreements plus disagreements. When there are disagreements the process provides no fast and hard rules. Instead, the process is very much one of negotiation, discussion, and common sense (this process, after all, is as subjective as the concept of public opinion).

TABLE 6-3   AN EXAMPLE OF DIFFERENT CONTENT ANALYSIS OUTCOMES

RESEARCHER	VERY TRUSTING	TRUSTING	NEUTRAL	UNTRUSTING	VERY UNTRUSTING
A	9	13	29	22	17
B	9	17	25	28	11
	NO INTERACTION	INTERACTION- NEUTRAL	INTERACTION- NEGATIVE	INTERACTION- POSITIVE	
C	25	15	40	10	

Content analysis is an effective method in conducting postpositivist policy analysis. It should be reemphasized that content analysis is used for not only focus group transcripts but also for classifying open-ended survey responses and social artifacts such as newspaper articles, magazines, and public documents. Appendix 6-3 provides examples of the use of content analysis in the Yellowstone bison controversy.

Tool #3: Narrative Policy Analysis

Brian Fay (1996) distinguishes between three different philosophical views of narrative analysis: (1) narrative realism, (2) narrative constructivism, and (3) narrativism. These three approaches have differing views of the relationship between the storyteller and the other. Fay (1996, 179) writes, "What is the relationship between me the storyteller and you the other about whom I tell a story as a way of comprehending your thoughts and deeds?" Fay is asking a very important question. Can we truly understand others or do we merely interpret other peoples lives by imposing standards and stories that are common to us? Fay (1996, 179) asks again:

> When I come to tell a story of someone else who is quite different from me as a way of understanding that person, am I looking for something which is a property of that person's life—its dramatic structure or plot? Or am I inventing a pattern which is significant for me given who I am but which may not be significant for the person I am trying to understand in part because it is not contained in that person's life? Am I trying to discover something which is already there, or to create something which isn't? The possibility of genuine understanding of others, and of what such understanding consists, rides on the answers to these questions.

The three different philosophical views answer these questions in different ways. Narrative Realism asserts that stories are indeed real and that social scientists merely find them. Narrative Constructivism asserts that stories are not real but instead represent social scientists imposing structures on random events. Narrativism attempts to find a middle ground between Narrative Realism and Narrative Constructivism. Fay (1996, 194) writes:

> A proper view of the relation of narrative and life needs to capture what is correct about realism (that narrative form is not accidental, nor a mere representational device; and that our identities as agents embody narratives) without including what is erroneous about it (that each person's life just is a single enacted narrative of which the agent is the partial author and the biographer a mere reporter). Moreover, it needs to do justice to the insights of narrative constructivism (that the narrative account of any life is continually and infinitely revisable) without making its mistakes (that narratives and the form of narrative are mere creations imposed on material which is non-narrative).

Narrativism tries to capture the positive elements of the realism and constructivism approaches while eliminating their negative elements. Fay (1996, 195) writes of narrativism, "But the stories we think we are living and the stories we or others come to see ourselves to have been living are not necessarily the same." In other words, although people live their lives through stories, these very people and others may rightfully reinterpret their stories since "told narratives" may not equate with "lived narratives." Narrativism seeks to analyze stories while placing them within contexts of larger meaning.

We clearly subscribe to a narrativism philosophy of policy analysis. It is quite possible that individuals tell stories without fully connecting their story to a larger lifeworld. A rancher or environmentalist telling their respective stories about the Yellowstone bison controversy might not fully connect how their individual stories are really narratives of their respective interests, values, and life experiences. An individual might tell a story that he or she asserts is "nonpolitical" and only desires "a fair and neutral resolution to the problem." However, a trained postpositivist analyst can deconstruct the narrative and find significant issues of power and interests.

Consider the following narrative surrounding the seemingly nonpolitical decision of performance evaluation and salary allocation in a government agency. Let's say, for example, that the agency has received an extra $5,000 and must decide how to allocate the money. Frank has a tenured position in the agency and has worked in the agency for fifteen years. Frank states about the decision, "We should allocate the money fairly, base it on merit; politics and the buddy system should have nothing to do with the allocation decision." Frank's narrative is one of merit and fairness. He clearly wants to indicate that he does not like what he sees as the unfairness of politics. While we could take Frank's narrative as the truth, the careful narrative analyst would search further and try to place his views within a larger context. First, we must learn how Frank defines "merit."

Perhaps we will find that he defines merit as years of service, number of clients served, knowledge of procedures, etc. Clearly, this definition of merit will benefit someone who has had a long career in the agency. Thus, built into Frank's definition of merit is a bias toward length of service. His definition of merit has political interests in it. An even more careful analysis might find that the manager of the agency has traditionally allocated extra money based on factors that include service to clients, evaluations of peers, and attendance at voluntary training sessions. The manager (Chamique) states, "I always try to allocate money in a method that rewards performance in a variety of ways. I really try to reward those who have given quality service to our clients." Maybe we can conclude that Frank has interests and that he sees himself as losing in the battle for these interests in the past. He may not realize that his definition of "merit" is tied to his interests and that other equally possible definitions of merit are possible. Instead, he sees the manager as using the buddy system. The analyst, of course, would also have to analyze the narrative of Chamique and determine whether her told narrative equates to her lived narrative.

We have oversimplified to make a point. The point is that narrative analysis is subjective. The analyst has to attempt to place narratives within larger lifeworlds and look for issues of power and interests. It is important for the analyst to try to be prudent and not "invent" interpretations. Remember there are always tradeoffs in approaches and the problem with narrative analysis is that it invites subjectivity on the part of the analyst. Using narrative analysis as a methodology can be as subjective and undemocratic as the use of positivist methods.

Roe (1994, 156–62) offers a distinctive method of narrative analysis that re-volves around the development of a **metanarrative**. Roe sees narrative analysis as a process that occurs in four steps:

1. "The analyst starts with the conventional definition of stories and identifies those policy narratives in the issue of high uncertainty that conform to this de-finition; if they are stories, they have beginnings, middles, and ends, as in sce-narios; if arguments, they have premises and conclusions."
2. "Identify those other narratives in the issue that do not conform to this defini-tion or run counter to the controversy's dominant policy narratives, that is the non-stories or counter-stories." Roe (1994, 53) differentiates between "stories" that have beginnings, middles, and ends and "non-stories" which he views as cri-tiques that "tell us what to be against without completing the argument as to what we should be for. Critiques, to put it sharply, simply don't have their own beginnings, middles, and ends."
3. "Compare the two sets of narratives in order to generate a metanarrative 'told' by the comparison."
4. "To determine if or how the metanarrative recasts the problem in such a way as to make it more amenable to the conventional policy-analytical tools of micro-economics, legal analysis, statistics, organizational theory or public manage-ment practice."

The uniqueness of Roe's approach is his use of the "metanarrative." Accord-ing to Roe (1994, 156–62), (1) a metanarrative embraces the major opposition in a controversy but does not slight any of the opposition; (2) the metanarrative cre-ates a new and more insightful story for a policy controversy; and (3) the meta-narrative captures the "intertext" or the story between the major narratives. Roe uses case studies of the California Medfly controversy, animal rights, irrigation, and other issues to demonstrate his approach. His approach, especially the idea of a metanarrative amenable to positivist analysis, would be anathema to many post-modernists, some of whom might also object to our harnessing it in the service of practicality.

Narrative analysis is the major tool of postpositivist problem definition. You should view narrative analysis in relation to the two other tools that we have dis-cussed in this chapter and everything you have learned in the earlier chapters about language, numbers, stories and subjectivity. The focus group method is a major tech-nique to generate narratives. Content analysis is a method to analyze and report dif-ferent narratives. In addition to focus groups, there are other ways to generate narratives. Sources of policy narratives include letters to the editor, public speech-es, transcripts of public speeches, public policy statements of elected officials and agencies, qualitative mail surveys sent to citizens, internet chat boards, and other public documents. In short, in most policy analysis areas, there are many sources available to create narratives. The discussion that follows will demonstrate how your authors used narrative analysis to recast the problem definition of the Yellowstone bison controversy that you worked on in Chapter 5.

Using Language in Problem Definition: The Yellowstone Bison Controversy

In the last chapter, the Yellowstone bison and brucellosis controversy was used in conducting a pragmatic policy analysis utilizing a five-step method that combined the rational and political approaches. In this chapter, we added to your knowledge about problem definition using postmodern perspectives. With this new knowledge, we now revisit the bison case and use it to illustrate postmodern problem definition and how it can be used by policy analysis practitioners. The bison controversy provides a lot of excellent examples of how stories, symbols, and metaphors are used in the policy process, how they are subjective, and how they are used to misrepresent or to shape the definition that will, in turn, shape policy. Like all practicing analysts, we were faced with the question of how to gather information. We chose a combination of three methods. First, public documents from elected officials and interest groups were content analyzed. These included position papers, public speeches, government documents, and newsletters. Second, newspaper editorials and letters to the editor printed in local newspapers were examined. Third, a mail survey was sent to 225 residents in the communities of West Yellowstone and Gardiner, Montana. One hundred twenty-four (124) citizens returned the survey that included their written comments concerning problem definition. These responses were then content analyzed. Notice that focus groups would have been the preferred methodology to gather citizen views. However, time constraints and budgetary constraints often lead analysts to use other methods. We used a traditional mail survey that combined quantitative and open-ended questions. The method was effective, but as researchers we did lose the group interaction that would have been valuable for our understanding of problem definition.

Major Stakeholder Narratives

After reviewing all the materials and using an inductive approach, five major categories emerged from our analysis. Each category or story told by various actors in this public drama portrayed the bison issue in a different way, either by emphasizing some aspects of the case at the expense of other aspects, by using captivating metaphors, by misrepresenting facts, by searching for causes, and ultimately by trying to spin a story that favors a problem definition that would lead to a policy favorable to their interests.

Story A: "Hidden Agendas and Heroes" This narrative involved citizens, wildlife activist groups, and a few experts. It revolved around two major themes. First, suspicion existed that a conspiracy was at work as the stories from this perspective asserted that brucellosis was only a smoke-screen used to hide a true agenda. The true agenda, according to this narrative structure, was that the ranching community and the State of Montana were fighting against the National Park Service and the environmental community to maintain exclusive control of public lands.

Many citizens questioned the nonscientific basis of brucellosis transmission from bison to cattle. One citizen survey respondent wrote, "Where's the problem? Since cattle are vaccinated, the problem is coming from politics, people, and misinformation."

There has never been a documented case of a cow contracting brucellosis from a buffalo." Paul Pritchard, spokesperson for the National Parks and Conservation Association related a similar theme in a press release: "The Park Service has abandoned seeking scientific evidence and has completely given in to scare tactics used by the cattle industry to create an irrational fear of brucellosis. The fact is that there has not been a single case of bison transmitting brucellosis to cattle" (Pritchard 1996).

The citizen activist group Buffalo Nations (now called Buffalo Field Campaign) also belongs in this category, as they questioned whether brucellosis was the real issue. In January 1997, members of the group video-taped the corralling and eventual slaughter of two hundred Yellowstone bison. This emotionally charged video included a striking presentation of a statistic when it showed the slaughterhouse owner explaining that only two of the two hundred slaughtered bison that day had tested positive for brucellosis. In addition, consider the following statement from a Buffalo Nations flier:

> The slaughter was conducted under the guise of grossly exaggerated fears that the growing herd, roaming traditional range outside of the park, would spread a disease called brucellosis to cows. Many old time ranchers in the valley think this is absurd. Testing of the carcasses showed that although some had been exposed to brucellosis, they were not necessarily infected. The butchers worked bare-handed and left hundreds of gut piles scattered across the hills—not what you'd expect from state officials who were truly concerned about 'infected' animals. (Buffalo Nations 1998)

More suspicion of hidden agendas was evidenced in the form of questions as to why elk were not being slaughtered along with bison. Many citizens surveyed pointed out that 50 percent of the elk in the Greater Yellowstone Ecosystem (GYE) were infected with brucellosis, yet there had been no calls to slaughter elk. Elk hunting, many citizens suggested, is a major Montana cultural pastime and significant revenue source. Hunting interest groups, according to these citizens, had put pressure on elected officials to ignore elk. Bison, who are not hunted in Montana, lack similar interest group support.[10]

Furthermore, suspicion of a hidden agenda was evidenced by many citizens who asked why bison were being killed some seven to eight months before the arrival of cattle on public lands. They argued that no study had indicated that the bacteria can live more than sixty days in exposed conditions. As one survey respondent asked, "Why kill the bison in November, December, and January when cattle don't arrive on the range until June 15th?"

A second major theme in this narrative was to portray bison as heroes in a political drama. One letter to the editor in a local newspaper tried to make the reader empathize with the bison by asking: "Could you raise a family, try to keep out of harms way of humans in the long cold winter?" (Letter to the Editor 1997). Throughout the letters to the editors, survey responses, and public documents, bison in this narrative

---

[10]Elk have high levels of brucellosis in the southern regions of Yellowstone. In this area, elk migrate out of the park and feed on the National Elk Refuge near Jackson Hole, Wyoming. Cattle graze in fairly large numbers in this region during summer months. Yet, there have been no calls to kill infected elk or the small Grand Teton National Park bison herd.

structure were portrayed as "magnificent," "free," and "noble" creatures that symbolize the American West. Ranchers, elected officials, and the livestock industry were portrayed conversely as "selfish," "greedy," and having a "me-first attitude."

The problem definition consistent in "Hidden Agendas and Heroes" is summed up by wildlife scientist Virginia Rvandal (1998) who wrote of the "true" motives behind the bison slaughter:

> Bison represent the pre cattle (and perhaps the post cattle) West. They are the symbol of the environment movement and the emblem of the equally unpopular (in the eyes of many stock growers) federal Department of Interior. Yellowstone bison are 'owned' by the federal government, the same entity that is blamed for hardships resulting from restrictions on livestock grazing, predator control, water rights, and more recently, for reintroducing the wolf.

Story B: "Winter Ghost Towns and a Hobson's Choice"   Proposals to regulate or end winter snowmobiling predated the Interim Bison Management Plan (IBMP). In August 1996, the first public notices of park interest in studying winter use in Yellowstone appeared. The snowmobile issue and the bison issue were quickly entangled when environmentalists in January 1997, pointed out that bison were using groomed snowmobile trails to migrate inside the park and eventually leave its boundaries, where they were then shot by Montana livestock officials.

Importantly, bison are ambiguous symbols to local businesspersons. First, bison are a popular tourist attraction and local businesses are tied to Yellowstone tourism. The slaughter of bison had already caused a national controversy and created a potential backlash against the Montana tourism industry. Second, local businesses are equally reliant on winter snowmobiling in the park. Before the National Park Service (NPS) opened Yellowstone to snowmobiles, gateway communities closed down after the summer tourist season ended in September.

An editorial presented a common story from the business perspective (Costello 1997). The symbolic representation of the problem was quite revealing for what was included and excluded. The narrative was one of decline aimed at political mobilization. The tale emphasized that the ending of Yellowstone snowmobiling would negatively affect everyone in West Yellowstone and therefore everyone should pay attention. The strategy was to remind citizens how bad things used to be before the NPS allowed winter use in Yellowstone. The editorial made West Yellowstone citizens look into a potentially gloomy future. For example, the narrative asked the reader to consider the following consequences of closing snowmobiling: "Services provided to local residents: the library, emergency medical services, fire protection, police protection, summer recreation, and snow plowing, to name a few, would have to be scaled back or eliminated." In addition, the narrative continued, in a future without snowmobiling, "You get your prescriptions filled 90 miles away because the drug store can't stay open. You travel to Bozeman or Rexburg, or farther, because the clinic can't afford to be open." Lastly, the argument stated, "You might have one choice for movie rentals, three places to eat instead of 12 like last winter and no live lounge entertainment."

Interestingly, nowhere in the editorial did the author mention the bison issue. This is interesting since by early 1997 the bison issue and snowmobiling had become inseparable. The story's careful avoidance of bison seemed aimed at keeping citizens focused on the negative impacts of snowmobile closure and not on the more immediate and emotional subject of bison slaughter. Everyone would agree, holding larger environmental values aside, that turning West Yellowstone into a winter ghost-town was not something to be desired. This story of decline implicitly presents the reader with a Hobson's Choice between a vibrant economy and an economic crisis.

Story C: "Two Goliaths and Little David (Montana)"   A press release written by Montana Governor Marc Racicot (see Appendix 6-1) told a story of helplessness (Racicot 1997). First, the governor, reacting to the February 1997 ad in *USA Today*, proclaimed, "Yellowstone National Park and every one of its wild creatures are national treasures for all Americans, not just those who live far away," and "We really need no lectures about valuing wildlife; it was Montanans who 60 years ago saved grizzly bears when the federal policy was extinction." Trying for a positive tone, in these early statements the governor proclaimed himself and his constituency as the environmentalists. Next, unlike the pro-bison stories, in which people used words like "magnificent," "free," and "noble" to describe the Yellowstone bison, Governor Racicot consistently used adjectives like "sick," "diseased," and "unmanaged" to describe Yellowstone bison. The governor also argued that APHIS had "threatened to revoke Montana's hard-won brucellosis free status if we allow one such diseased creature into the state to potentially infect livestock,"[11] and that this would devastate industry and family.[12]

The governor found a villain for his narrative. He stated: "What we have here are too many unmanaged, diseased bison leaving an overgrazed park to mingle with protected livestock in violation of the Department of Agriculture ban." Later he wrote, "The Park Service is responsible for the park's bison. Yellowstone refuses to manage its wildlife. This has resulted in a drastic overpopulation of bison who must flee the park." Throughout the argument, Racicot contended that Yellowstone is overgrazed and cannot support the current number of bison. For example, using a metaphor that is easily understood, he stated, "If any citizen tried to keep several thousand animals on land that might support 1,500, they would properly be in trouble with animal abuse officers."

The governor then used another simple metaphor that ordinary citizens can relate to and portrayed the Park Service as a "bad neighbor." Montana, according to the governor, was "left to manage its neighbor's unmanaged herd of wild animals choosing to leave the park because there is nothing left to eat there." The governor ended

---

[11]APHIS loosened its standards in August 1997, and allowed "low risk" bison on the public ranges. The State of Montana, however, opposed this more liberal policy. Montana Chief Veterinarian Arnold Gertonsen wrote the forty-nine other state veterinarians and asked them to reject the new federal proposal that allowed low risk bison (yearlings, bulls, mother cows who had already dropped their young) to leave the park. Gertonsen was quoted in *High Country News* (McMillion 1998, 8) as saying that if bison are allowed to leave the park, this would equal, "defacto expansion" of the park's borders.

[12]Racicot's disaggregation of "industry" into "family" is a common political tactic mentioned by Stone (1997, 224–26).

his narrative with the following statement of helplessness: "We have written count-less letters, attended countless meetings, even gone into federal court. We use noise-makers and helicopters to frighten the animals back. We will continue to try to stop this ridiculous—and expensive—spectacle of federal policy paralysis." In short, the gov-ernor stated that the federal government and its unresponsive bureaucratic agencies, not the actions of the Montana Department of Livestock, constituted the real problem.[13]

In our survey, 36 percent of the citizens of Gardiner and West Yellowstone shared the governor's general views and blamed the problem on the Park Service's natural regulation policies. These citizens portray Yellowstone National Park as a closed ecosys-tem and want herd management to control the park's wildlife. Consider the following actual responses to a question asking for potential policy solutions:

* "maintain the herd at numbers the park can handle."
* "keep the bison in the park."
* "control the herd."
* "bison need to stay in the park."

In addition, 15 percent of respondents offered comments that suggested environ-mental groups, in addition to the Park Service, were to blame. One respondent wrote a typical response, "Wildlife groups are unwilling to compromise, they spend a lot of money that should be used to manage wildlife. The rights of animals should not come before property rights." Others viewed environmental interest groups as outsiders try-ing to push environmental agendas on local communities. One respondent comment-ed, "The lack of wildlife management has devastated YNP and now these same people (environmentalists) want to do the same to surrounding states."

Causation in this narrative is either mechanical (that complex and differing man-dates of APHIS and NPS led to the bison slaughter) or inadvertent (only a few hundred bison were expected to be killed but the bad winter drove thousands outside the park). Officials and citizens here attempt to evade responsibility for the problem. Instead, they try to pin causes on other agencies and groups.

Story D: *"Blue Ribbons, a Mercy Harvest, and Anti-Recreationist Conspir-ators"*   This analysis was taken primarily from a speech given by Clark Collins, ex-ecutive director of the Blue Ribbon Coalition (BRC).[14] The BRC is an interest group that promotes the off-road use of motorized vehicles and became important in the Yellowstone bison controversy because of a lawsuit filed by an environmental group that would have halted winter use of Yellowstone Park and, according to these envi-ronmentalists, would have stopped or slowed the out-migration of bison from the park.

---

[13]This portrayal of the bad government (national) and the good government (state) is also an example of the creation of a dichotomy from a continuum, wherein, through the linguistic construction of a differ-ence, one half is depicted as natural, superior, and more important than the other half. Further, the signifi-cant relationship between the two artificially created binary categories and the important differences within the categories are downplayed (Tavris 1992; Wonders 1999).

[14]Mr. Collins' talk was held on February 10, 1998, at Idaho State University in Pocatello, Idaho. The authors thank Mr. Collins for sharing his views on the bison subject with an ISU public policy analysis course.

The name Blue Ribbon Coalition is itself symbolic and ambiguous. When asked about the title of the group, Clark Collins, executive director and founder, said it was chosen simply because it "sounded good, like motherhood and apple pie."[15] Collins began his two-hour presentation with an argument similar to the one used by Governor Racicot in the previous narrative. Collins, trying to define his group as environmentalists, argued that snowmobilers had for a long time realized their responsibility to wildlife. He contrasted his group with the "so-called environmentalists," who according to Collins, cannot have it both ways. That is, according to Collins, "they" (mainstream environmental groups) had stated for years that motorized recreation made life difficult for wildlife and now these groups are saying that the groomed snowmobile roads makes life too easy for bison. When quizzed about whether the groomed roads provided easy routes for the bison to leave the park into the waiting shooting lines of Montana Livestock officials, Collins responded that he had information that bison used the Firehole and Madison rivers and not the groomed trails to leave the park; but he offered no evidence to support this claim.

Next, Collins used a metaphor to define the bison problem. He stated, "If I had a horse with a broken leg, I would be expected to shoot it. It is the same situation with bison; if they are starving we should shoot them." Finding a villain, he then contended that the "so-called environmentalists" would rather see them starve to death. He also responded, when asked, that the carrying capacity for Yellowstone bison was about 1,000 head and that only the boundaries of the park should be considered as bison territory. He stated that the bison herd was too large and that the actions of 1996–97 were a harvest. He carefully avoided the more emotional term of "slaughter" used consistently in Story A.

During questioning, he also suggested that the antirecreation people had been waiting for an issue that would assist in their agenda to end Yellowstone snowmobiling. Seeing a hidden agenda and conspiracy, he claimed that when the bison killing started, "they" (the antirecreationists), tried to use the issue to end snowmobiling. Collins stated about environmental groups, "These folks don't want competition for trails. They want to close off public lands."

Story E: "Wild Bison and Wild Bureaucrats"   The "Greater Yellowstone Coalition" (GYC) is a nonprofit advocacy group formed in 1983 and is based in Bozeman, Montana. Their spokesperson, Marv Hoyt, stressed five major themes in a speaking presentation.[16] First, he started his presentation by asserting that bison are wild creatures—even though the majority of bison in the United States are domesticated. He firmly argued that the Yellowstone herd was the last wild herd in the continental United States, or "our last lineage to the last wild bison." He then argued that Americans want Yellowstone to be a wild area where animals are free to migrate.

---

[15]The reader should note that the use of the term "Blue Ribbon" by this group is ambiguous since it is often used to portray clean and natural trout streams.

[16]The speaking presentation of Mr. Hoyt was held on February 17, 1998, at Idaho State University in Pocatello, Idaho. The authors thank Mr. Hoyt for sharing his views on the bison subject with an ISU public policy analysis course.

Second, Hoyt challenged industry numbers.[17] The GYC contended that only about 2,000 cattle were located within a seven- or eight-mile area of the park. Agricultural interests had used numbers that show over 100,000 cattle are in the two counties that border Yellowstone Park. Hoyt's point was that only 2,000 cattle were close enough to Yellowstone to be affected by infected bison and, more important, he stressed a theme found in Story A: "These 2,000 cattle are not on the range in the winter time when bison are likely to be on the same public land."

Third, Hoyt contested a scientific study that was used consistently by elected officials to justify bison slaughter. He noted that only one study (Davis et al. 1990) had demonstrated that bison cows could transmit brucellosis to cattle. According to Hoyt, the study was not conducted in a natural setting, however, but in a closed corral. The bison cow in the study was additionally injected with high doses of brucellosis. For these reasons, according to Hoyt, the study was flawed and not relevant to the wild bison of Yellowstone.

Fourth, Hoyt, unlike the other narratives, offered solutions and wove a story that suggested the interests of the ranchers and environmentalists are not in conflict. Rather than being beyond our control or a Hobson's Choice, his story was one of potential mutual winners (win-win). He stated that GYC was purchasing several thousand acres (10,000 to 15,000) from a church group that owns a large ranch north of the park. Utilizing the Cambodian example, Hoyt referred to this land as a Killing Field during the bison slaughter of 1996–97. The purchased land would become a buffer zone between YNP and ranchers. He stressed that the interests of ranchers and the GYC were compatible and also challenged ranchers to move toward compromise. He noted that ranchers were becoming increasingly viewed as antienvironment and that national polls revealed that the American public "love" wildlife. He said that if the Farm Bureau and other groups were successful and were able to fence in Yellowstone's wildlife, the American people would revolt against the ranching industry. He noted that Americans now consume more chicken and fish and that beef consumption was declining. He stated, "When American citizens are asked 'what do you want on your public lands?' they will choose wildlife." This, according to Hoyt, would effectively destroy the ranching industry in Montana, which in turn would lead to the large-scale development of subdivisions as ranchers sell off their lands to urban immigrants, who then would use the land to build "trophy homes." These lands where ranchers currently keep open spaces are crucial wildlife habitat along river valleys, and further development would greatly harm Yellowstone wildlife. Therefore, he claimed that the GYC had an interest in preserving the ranching industry in the area.

Finally, while the problem was not "beyond control," he asserted that APHIS and Montana officials were completely "out of control" during the winter of 1996–97. To stress his point, Hoyt closed his presentation with a story of a single bull bison that had migrated onto a private ranch. The ranch owner, a wildlife supporter, was upset because

---

[17]Stone (1997, 163) writes of numbers in problem definition, "And just as there are infinite ways of describing a single object in words or paint, so there are infinite ways of describing with numbers. Numbers are a form of poetry."

this single bull attracted several sharpshooters with rifles, the state livestock industry, and several other bureaucrats who had surrounded his ranch. According to Hoyt, the rancher did not want the bull bison shot but the bureaucrats advised him that if necessary they would get a court order to enter his land. The rancher gave up and allowed the bureaucrats and sharpshooters to enter his property. By this time the bison had become agitated because of the attention and bolted out of the ranch through fences and toward open lands. The sharpshooters were unable to get a clear shot at the bison. A key to this final point in his narrative is the argument that bull bison cannot transmit brucellosis to cattle. According to Hoyt, even the Montana State Veterinarian had said that bull bison pose a 1 in 10,000,000 chance of transmitting brucellosis to cattle.

An Evaluation of the Postpositivist Model

Herein we followed the lead of the postpositivist model and focused on the crucial analytical step of problem definition. Assuming conflicting problem definitions, we actively sought the narratives told by stakeholders (including regular citizens) and utilized the insights of postmodernism in general, and Deborah Stone in particular, to analyze their stories. We discovered stories with heroes, victims, and villains with hidden agendas and conspiratorial plans, as well as stories of decline, helplessness, and hopelessness. We identified evocative metaphors, striking statistics, scare tactics, and witnessed battles over—and with—words like slaughter and harvest, wild and domesticated, and noble versus diseased. Each story emphasized certain aspects of the policy controversy and intentionally left out potentially harmful information. There were examples of varying representations of causes. Storytellers presented us with a Hobson's Choice, foretold of economic disaster, used a foreign genocidal disaster to label the land near the park as the Killing Fields, and referred to themselves or others as "bad neighbors," "victims," "true environmentalists," "so-called environmentalists" and "out of control."

A key advantage of the postpositivist method is that it demonstrates that ambiguity and subjectivity are involved. Another benefit is that the focus on concepts such as metaphors, symbols, and stories suggests that analysts need to think critically about language being carefully crafted by stakeholders to frame problem definition. If one accepts the ideal of democracy, there are positives associated with the postmodernist demand that we seek input broadly so that we can hear the voices usually unheard. Democracy also benefits when we make the various stories both available and assailable. Importantly, an analysis of the conflicts evident between the different narratives raises several questions. At least nine questions crucial in problem definition emerge from the analysis of the bison stories:

1. Is there scientific proof of bison-to-cattle brucellosis in natural settings?
2. Why were bison that were not infected being killed?
3. Why is it that the elk are not considered a problem?
4. Why are the bison killed some six to eight months before cattle are on the same range lands?
5. What is the empirical evidence of bison using snow trails in the winter?

6. What is the economic composition of Montana?

7. What exactly is the policy position of APHIS in this matter?

8. Is there an agreed-upon scientific carrying capacity for bison in Yellowstone and is this question ultimately tied to the bison using public lands outside the park?

9. Are Yellowstone ranges overgrazed and are bison starving to death in the winter?

While definitive answers may be an impossibility, and while all answers will be partially political, not all stories, numbers, and claims are equally well-supported by the available evidence. Nothing in the postpositivist approach forbids the use of positivist methods (informed by the postmodernist critique). One may not be able to prove whether or not brucellosis transmission is possible, but you can gather the scientific evidence, trying to objectively evaluate the sources, and pass your research findings along. Statistics are obviously vulnerable to manipulation, but we can count the cattle potentially impacted, compare the economic contributions of tourism and ranching, and examine public opinion on the relative importance of each. And, while the question of scientifically evaluating carrying capacity hinges on the political question of what land to include in the carrying capacity equation, we can at least lay out the questions.[18]

In the spirit of postmodernism, the reader is the final arbiter of the value of the postpositivist model, but it seems to inform problem definition in a way that makes it more comprehensive, more democratic, and that accounts for the role of politics better than does the positivist method.[19]

Concluding Thoughts

Positivist methodology has its place. As Hagan (1997, 1–5) effectively points out in his excellent *Criminal Justice Research Methods* text, social science research—like scientific research in general—has revealed that the obvious and what is considered "common sense" are often patently false. Making social policy based upon, for example, myths about crime, welfare, education, or immigration is not unlike making ocean exploration plans based on the idea of a flat earth. It may seem obvious to you that church attendance and delinquency would be related (negatively), but Hirschi and Stark (1969) found it to be a very weak relationship (and promptly had their study attacked as inadequately done, false, and stupid by those whose values and common sense objected to their findings).

If policy is made based not upon solid research but upon the obvious, taxpayer

---

[18]Wilkenson (1997, 8) writes of the bison killings: "That slaughter has dramatized a fundamental conflict over the management of wildlife in and around Yellowstone National Park: Should the park be a sort of zoo, in which bison, grizzlies, and other animals are confined? Or is the park just one part of a larger ecosystem, with the animals free to move onto neighboring national forest and private land? It's a question no one wants to confront, but that the bison slaughter raises starkly."

[19]The authors thank the *Administrative Theory & Praxis* journal for granting us permission to quote extensively from the McBeth/Clemons article published in June 1999 (vol. 21, no. 2), pp. 161–75.

money will often be wasted, successful alternatives not chosen, and the problem left unattended or exacerbated. Arguing for a scientific methodology, Hagan is persuasive:

> ... verbal description of phenomena are a little different than numerical measures of some entity; while thinking through the concept under study in a more disciplined manner. Thus, common sense and the experience certainly serve an important function in sensitizing us to a subject; however, our separate experiences might better be viewed as limited case studies of a subject matter that may not be entirely generalizable to the universe of such subjects, or as observations that may be limited by time, place, and the subjective biases of the observer.

But your authors believe that it is simply not enough. The words we have acquired and arranged, the stories we tell and believe, demand more. You are given the opportunity to test the usefulness of the method yourself and reflect critically about postmodern problem definition in the case that closes this chapter.

Key Concepts

ambiguous/subjective nature of events in the system (p. 182)

content analysis (p. 200)

evaluation of postpositivist methods (p. 212)

focus group methodology (p. 198)

how policies are generated (p. 190)

Language in Problem Definition: The Yellowstone Bison Controversy (p. 205)

major stakeholder narratives in the bison case (p. 205)

narrative policy analysis (p. 202)

Stone's symbolic representation of problem definition (p. 194)

two tracks of policy analysis (p. 175)

types of public policies and policy interests (p. 190)

Glossary Terms

Epistemology (p. 177)

hegemonic lifeworld (p. 181)

metanarrative (p. 204)

synedoches (p. 194)

References

Allison, Graham C. 1971. *Essence of Decision: Explaining the Cuban Missile Crisis*. Boston, MA: Little, Brown.

Allison, Graham C., with Philip Zelikow. 1999. *Essence of Decision,* 2nd ed. New York: Addison Wesley Longman.

Babbie, Earl. 1992. *The Practice of Social Research*, 6th ed. Belmont, CA: Wadsworth.

Buffalo Nations. 1998. Informational Flier. Buffalo Nations, Gardiner, MT or <http://www.wild rockies.org/bison>

Bruni, Frank. 1999. "Speaking Up for Guns, Lots of Them, for Nearly Everyone." *New York Times*, April 26, A-14.

Collins, Clark. 1998. Speaking Presentation, Pocatello, Idaho. February 10, 1988.

Costello, John. 1997. "Some Thoughts about West's Winter Economy." Guest Editorial in the *West Yellowstone News*, February 2.

Cowley, Geoffrey. 1998. "Why Children Turn Violent." *Newsweek*, April 6, pp. 24–26.

Danziger, Marie. 1995. "Policy Analysis Postmodernized: Some Political and Pedagogical Ramifications." *Policy Studies Journal* 23, no. 3:435–50.

Davis, D. S., J. W. Templeton, T. A. Ficht, J. D. Williams, J. D. Kopec, and L. G. Adams. 1990. "Brucella Abortus in Captive Bison, Serology, Bacteriology, Pathogenesis, and Transmission to Cattle." *Journal of Wildlife Dis.* 26, no. 3:360–71.

deLeon, Peter. 1997. *Democracy and the Policy Sciences.* Albany, NY: State University of New York Press.

Dionne, E. J. 1991. *Why Americans Hate Politics.* New York: Simon & Schuster.

Dunn, William N. 1981. *Public Policy Analysis: An Introduction.* Englewood Cliffs, NJ: Prentice Hall.

Erie Daily Times. 1999. "House Ok's Posting of Commandments." June 17, p. 9A.

Erie Daily Times. 1999 "Letter to the Editor:"Here Is the Problem with Our Country." April 20, p. 3B.

Erie Daily Times. 1999. "Who's to Blame? What to Do Now?" April 24, p. 13A.

Erie Daily Times. 1999. "Letter to the Editor: Getting Back to Basics." April 26, p. 3B.

Fari, Paul. 1998. "TV Violence: It's Not All the Same Wavelength." *Washington Post National Week Review*, June 22, p. 21.

Fay, Brian. 1996. *Contemporary Philosophy of Social Science.* Cambridge, MA: Blackwell Publishers.

Fischer, Frank. 1998. "Beyond Empiricism: Policy Inquiry in Postpositivist Perspective." *Policy Studies Journal* 26, no. 1:129–46.

Fox, Charles J., and Hugh T. Miller. 1998. *Postmodern Public Administration.* Thousand Oaks, CA: Sage Publications.

Glover, John. 1996. "Interim Bison Management Plan Approved." *Yellowstone Journal* (September/October): C-7.

Hagan, Frank E. 2000. *Research Methods in Criminal Justice and Criminology*, 5th ed. Needham Heights, MA: Allyn and Bacon.

Harr, Jonathan. 1995/1996. *A Civil Action.* New York: Vintage Books.

Herbert, Bob. 1999. Editorial, "Addicted to Violence." *New York Times*, April 22, p. A-31.

Hill, Kim Q. 1997. "In search of policy theory." *Policy Currents* 7, no. 1 (April): 1–9.

Hirschi, Travis, and Rodeny Stark. 1969. "Hellfire and Delinquency." *Social Problems* 17 (fall): 202–13.

Hoyt, Marv. 1998. "Greater Yellowstone Coalition." 1998. Presentation by GYC field representative, Pocatello, Idaho, February 17.

Hummel, Ralph P. 1994. *The Bureaucratic Experience: A Critique of Life in the Modern Organization*, 4th ed. New York: St. Martin's Press.

Http://www.techmgmt.com/restore/shooting.htm. 1998. "People Are Asking Why These School Shootings Happen." Internet site available on July 22.

Ivins, Molly. 1999. "The Wrath of DeLay." *The Progressive* (August): 46.

Keiter, Robert B. 1997. "Greater Yellowstone's Bison: Unraveling of an Early American Wildlife Conservation Achievement." *Journal of Wildlife Management* 61, no. 1:1–11.

Labi, Nadya. 1998. "The Hunter and the Choirboy." *Time Magazine*, April 6, p. 28–37.

Lasch, Christopher. 1995. *The Revolts of the Elites and the Betrayal of Democracy.* New York: W. W. Norton & Company.

Lawlor, E. F. 1996. Book review in *Journal of Policy Analysis and Management* 15, no. 1:110–21.

Letter to the Editor. 1997. "Killing Bison Is a Montana Tragedy." *West Yellowstone News*, February 22, p. 4.

Lott, John R. 1998. "The Real Lesson of the School Shootings." *Wall Street Journal.* Article posted on the internet at <http://www2.ari.net/mcsm/arkansas.html>. Site available on July 22.

Majone, Giandomenico. 1989. *Evidence, Argument, and Persuasion in the Policy Process*. New Haven, CT: Yale Press.

Mansfield, Gayle. 1997. "Number of Bison Killed Surpasses Record of '88–89. *West Yellowstone News*, January 23, p. 14.

Mansfield, Gayle. 1997. "Bison Plan Revisited." *West Yellowstone News*, February 6, pp. 1, 8.

Meagher, Mary, and Margaret E. Meyer. 1994. "On the Origins of Brucellosis in Bison of Yellowstone National Park: A Review." *Conservation Biology* 8, no. 3:645–53.

Morgan, David L. 1988. *Focus Groups as Qualitative Research*. Newbury Park, CA: Sage Publications.

Morgan, David L. 1996. "Focus Groups." Pp. 129–52 in *Annual Review of Sociology*. Palo Alto, CA: Annual Reviews, Inc.

New York Times. 1999. "Advocates of Guns Are Put on the Defensive." April, 23, p. A-16

New York Times. 1999. "Renewed Battle Over Weapons Control Both Side Uses School Attack to Advance Agendas." April 26, p. A-16.

Neubeck, Kenneth J., and Mary Alice Neubeck. 1997. *Social Problems: A Critical Approach*, 4th ed. New York: McGraw-Hill Companies.

Pritchard, Paul. 1996. Quoted in "Interim Bison Management Plan Approved," John Glover. *Yellowstone Journal* (September/October): C-7.

Quade, E. S. 1975. *Analysis for Public Decisions*. New York: American Elsevier.

Racicot, Marc. 1997. "Governor's Statement on Diseased Bison." *Montana Online*, March 3 <www.mt.gov./governor/press/bison.htm>.

Roe, Emery. 1994. *Narrative Policy Analysis*. Durham, NC: Duke University Press.

Rosin, Hanna, and Claudia Deane. 1999. "Teens Feel the Threat of School Violence." *Washington Post News Weekly Review*, May 3, p. 34.

Ross, Robert, and Graham L. Staines. 1972. "The Politics of Analyzing Social Problems." *Social Problems* (summer): 18–40.

Rvandal, Virginia. 1998. "Eradicating Brucellosis is Feasible." *Yellowstone Net Newspaper*, Monday, February 2, vol. 2, no. 12 <http:www.yellowstone.net/newspaper/news020298.htm>.

Sabatier, Paul. 1997. "The Status and Development of Policy Theory: A Reply to Hill." *Policy Currents* 7, no. 4 (December): 1–3.

Schalager, Edella. 1997. "A Response to Kim Quaille Hill's 'In Search of Policy Theory.'" *Policy Currents* 7, no. 2 (June): 14–17.

Stokey, Edith, and R. Zeckhauser. 1978. *A Primer for Policy Analysis*. New York: W. W. Norton & Company.

Stone, Deborah. 1988. *Policy Paradox and Political Reason*. New York: Harper Collins Publishers.

Stone, Deborah. 1997. *Policy Paradox: The Art of Political Decision Making*. New York: W. W. Norton & Company.

Talk Back. 1999. "Is School Violence Out of Control?" Internet chat board. KCBS Channel 2000, Los Angeles, CA. (available in July).

Tavris, Carol. 1992. *The Mismeasure of Women*. New York: Simon & Schuster.

Uhlman, Maria. 1999. "Survey Finds One-Third of Households Have a Gun." *Erie Daily Times*, June 18, p. 6A.

Wilkenson. Todd. 1997. "No Home on the Range." *High Country News*, February 17, vol. 29, no. 3, pp. 1, 8.

Wilson, James Q. 1973. *Political Organizations*. New York: Basic Books.

Wonders, Nancy A. 1999. "Postmodern Feminist Criminology and Social Justice." Pp. 111–28 in B. A. Arrigo, *Social Justice/Criminal Justice: The Maturation of Critical Theory in Law, Crime, and Deviance*. Belmont, CA: West/Wadsworth.

Yanow, Dvora. 1996. *How Does a Policy Mean?* Washington, D.C.: Georgetown University Press.

School Shootings and Focus Group Research: A Postpositivist Method of Problem Definition

The Case

A focus group researcher was interested in finding out the views of parents of school children toward the recent school shootings. The focus group researcher arranged for twelve parents to show up at 7:00 P.M. to discuss the shootings. Only nine parents actually arrived at the school cafeteria for the session. Due to scheduling problems, the focus group lasted for only one hour. After introductions, the discussion began and the following transcript has been produced.

Read the following transcript and be prepared to answer questions.

Focus Group Transcripts

7:00 P.M.

FACILITATOR (F): Question: "What are your thoughts on the recent school shootings?"

PARTICIPANT #1 (P1): "I believe that the media really glorifies these events and that basically we have these kids who are looking at trying to make a name for themselves by doing these horrible things."

PARTICIPANT #2 (P2): "Yeah, I agree maybe if the media just would stop reporting these things maybe the killing would stop."

PARTICIPANT #3 (P3): "But the media is really responsible in much larger ways, such as their glorification of violence to teens. I saw a show the other day on television where 15 people were killed in 45 minutes. You can't tell me that this doesn't lead to violence. Kids sit and watch this stuff for hours."

PARTICIPANT #4 (P4): "Yeah, but that is the parents' responsibility to make sure they monitor what their kids watch. I don't let my kids watch anything without me knowing what it is."

P2: "Yeah, but do you watch your kids 24 hours a day? What happens when they go to someone else's house or to school? You can't be a 24-hour-a-day watchdog."

P4: "Well, I know what my kids are doing all of the time."

P2: "Oh yeah, what are they doing now while you are here?"

7:08 P.M.

FACILITATOR: "I think we are getting off topic here. Let's get back directly to the school shootings."

PARTICIPANT #5 (P5): "I think the point about violence on television is okay but maybe what we are missing here is the central point. Guns! How do these kids kill? They kill with guns. Why does this society need so many guns? I really get frustrated with our cultural love of killing machines."

PARTICIPANT #6: "I don't like your tone. Guns are about freedom. I have owned guns for years and I don't kill people. Anyway, people kill people, guns don't kill people. Why not ban rocks, they can be a weapon?"

P5: "But guns sure do make it a lot easier, can you imagine somebody throwing rocks at their fellow students and really killing them. Can you imagine Oswald throwing a rock and killing a president? Get real."

P6: "Yeah, but people will find a way, I tell you that the bigger problem is the justice system. People get away with murder now days. The Bill of Rights has become a hiding place for these thugs. What we need is a death sentence for one of these thugs. That will make others think about whether killing is really the cool thing to do."

PARTICIPANT #7 (P7): "I agree that guns are not the problem."

P6: "Voting for gun control is a violation of the oath our elected officials take to uphold and protect the Constitution. In my heart, I believe that the handgun used to shoot that teacher and those students in Edinboro was no more responsible for that tragedy than the automobile involved in a drunk driving death. My prayers and heart go out to the families, but when a drunk kills somebody the law goes after the driver of the car; why do they go after the gun when somebody shoots somebody?"

P5: "There are big differences, the car is not something that is designed to intentionally kill. The NRA and gun manufacturers should be responsible."

P6: "Remember, the NRA is the biggest advocate of teaching kids how to handle guns safely."

FACILITATOR (TO P5): "What was your point again?"

P5: "The NRA says it would be terrible to limit guns, to not be able to buy them, to have to wait to buy them, to not be able to have quick access to a loaded gun, to not be able to use automatic weapons when hunting. That's not terrible. Kids at a dance diving under the punch bowl for safety is terrible. A dead father of three, who was there because he was the most giving teacher in the school, is terrible. School kids in bodybags is terrible. I'm tired of the NRA portraying anybody who favors any gun regulations—no matter how reasonable, how narrow, and how carefully cast as an elitist, anti-American, soft-headed, constitutional traitor. This isn't about gun control; it is about gun safety."

P3: "I think if gun owners let their guns fall into the hands of anyone else they are both responsible for what happens and grossly negligent. The Second Amendment was about keeping the states free from armed invasions. It is about a well-regulated militia. Two hundred years ago we had muskets not automatic weapons. We also didn't have video games, movies, and television glorifying violence or the internet and talk radio preaching hate. Moreover, the Constitution allows the government to protect us. It is very American to protect the innocent from reckless individuals. If they go back to using muskets then I will support the abolition of all gun control."

7:13 P.M.

FACILITATOR: "Okay, I think what we have in this first discussion is the question of causes. What exactly is the cause of the problem. We will get back to this, but first let's try and determine if there is a problem in the first place. Are these school shootings something for us to be concerned about?" (What do you two think?—points to Participants #8 and #9)

PARTICIPANT #8 (P8): "Well yeah, kids killing kids is a big problem."

PARTICIPANT #9 (P9): "Certainly, I worry about my kids going to school with all of this violence."

P1: "Yeah, but come on these things are isolated incidents, it is the media who makes it a big deal. If a school house shooting happened 100 years ago halfway across the country, most of us would never hear about it. Today, the media is so nationalized that everything becomes national news. These 24-hour-a-day news channels need something to keep them going."

P6: "100 years ago these kids would had been strung up. Today, we coddle them, bring in the counselors, find excuses. Talk about how their parents are to blame, blah, blah, blah."

P3: "I guess we need as a society to actually find out how many killings and shootings happen each year and then decide if it is really a problem."

P9: "That is what the media does. The media just tells us what happens. Don't blame the media."

P8: "I read in a magazine that there had been 10 killings in the last 18 months or maybe it was 10 separate shooting incidents at schools."

P4: "I heard that it was only 8 shootings."

7:18 P.M.

FACILITATOR: "So is this a problem that society needs to be concerned about? I personally think that it is, but I want to hear from you."

P7: "No, there are just bad kids and bad people, always have been. Just because there are some bad people doesn't mean that we should gut the Constitution. These are isolated events. We shouldn't take several school shootings and then use these to find a large national problem. That is poor reasoning. These shootings don't affect me."

7:20 P.M.

FACILITATOR (TO R7): "So is the problem just natural or is it subject to human control? I guess that is the central question."

P7: "It is just natural, part of human nature. We cannot control the evil that lives inside of some of us or perhaps all of us."

P4: "You sound like Captain Kirk." (brings laughs).

P7: "Yeah, but seriously, how come liberals get so worked up about a few dead school kids, but don't care about hundreds of thousands of murders of unborn children."

P5: "This is not about religion or abortion and it's not about taking away guns. It's about limited and practical anti-crime measures that most Americans and most cops support."

P7: "Give me a @#@$#$#$ break. The term 'practical anti-crime measures' is just some fancy liberal talk for 'gun control' and your appeal to cops is funny since liberals always support criminals and now suddenly want them for allies to stop guns."

FACILITATOR: "Let's watch our personal attacks."

P8: "This is a child issue, not a gun issue. We are raising troubled kids. We abandon and alienate them."

P5: "So you don't think that giving guns to desensitized, angry, tense, and immature teens is a mistake? I think it's like giving gasoline and a lighter to a pyromaniac. We can't just ignore these events. All events have a larger meaning. We have to take a hard look at how we raise our kids, what our priorities are, and what we want our children to grow up believing."

P2: "The school is a symbol for me. It is a place that characterizes community, learning, respect, friendship. It is an experience that we all share together. All of us in this room went to school. I think anyway. So the shootings do affect all of us. We can all relate to the horror that the kids must face when there is a shooting. We all have an interest in trying to stop the violence."

P1: "Yeah, there is a problem. If we don't stop school violence it will spread to other areas. This is like a disease that has to be nipped in the bud. We must contain the problem now."

P2: "I agree."

7:22 P.M.

FACILITATOR: "It seems that there is some consensus that these shootings are a social problem. If so, what can government do about it? I guess this gets us back to the question of causes."

P6: "If the problem is things like values, can government really play a role? How can we expect passing a new law to solve a problem of the heart? Kids without hope or shame are the problem. It may be a cliché but people kill people. I'm more upset at the tobacco industry than gun manufacturers."

P1: "Absolutely, government can play a role. They don't have to condone murder like they do with abortion, they don't have to ban prayer in school, they don't have to glorify pot smoking like they do."

P2 TO P1: "What does that mean?"

P1 TO P2: "What does what mean?"

P2: "The government glorifying pot smoking."

P1: "I mean that Bill Clinton was a pot smoker in college. Do you think that is a good symbol for our children. Plus, he is a liar and a womanizer. Can you imagine Ronald Reagan smoking pot and sleeping around? All of this is part of a larger agenda. The government is trying to change our values into accepting the philosophy of anything goes."

P2: "Clinton maybe tried pot once and I heard that so did Reagan back when he was an actor."

P1: "That is not true."

P2: "It is, and George Bush Jr. used cocaine."

7:25 P.M.

FACILITATOR (TO P1): "So do you believe that the problem is intentionally caused by a hidden government agenda? Please clarify what you mean here."

P1: "Do I think that this is intended? Well, I believe that since the 1960s that the generation that grew up smoking pot and dropping acid have waited for their time in power. Once in power, they would legitimize all of the stuff that happened in the 1960s. So yes, I think that Bill Clinton's escapades are intentional."

P5: "Wow, a conspiracy, I guess we better call in Scully and Mulder (brings laughs). Now Bill Clinton is the cause of the problem. What ever happened to individual responsibility in this country. A kid goes nuts and shoots some fellow students and suddenly it is Clinton's fault. Give me a break! I say it is the families' and the kids' fault."

7:28 P.M.

FACILITATOR: "Okay, I think we need to get back on subject here." What is the cause of these school shootings?

P7: "What we haven't talked about is the economy today. Many years ago my parents only needed to work 40 hours a week. That is, my Dad worked and my mom stayed at home and took care of the kids. Dad had all but the 40 hours to spend with us. Today, I work, my husband works, and it is not just 40 hours for each of us. I get home and there are phone calls to make, faxes to respond to, e-mails to answer, etc. In addition, I am tired of single moms getting blamed. Those two kids in Littleton both grew up in two-parent households and with stay-at-home mothers."

P1: "That is what you feminists wanted. Maybe the intention of feminism was to give women freedom but the consequences have been family decay and violence."

P7: "I work out of economic necessity. We live from paycheck to paycheck. It doesn't have a lot to do with feminism."

P4: "What does this have to do with school shootings?"

P7: "This is where I think the shootings are important to understand. Maybe we need to look at who these kids are. Do their parents work all the time or does the stress of work lead to divorce?"

P8: "Yeah, but what can the government do?"

P7: "How about mandated governmental child care on the work site? How about raising the minimum wage so we can make ends meet?"

P6: "How about not raising my taxes to pay for all of these social programs? This issue only affects people who have children go to school where there is violence. I feel bad for them but why should my tax dollars be used to help a few. I don't buy all of this talk about larger interests and meanings being at play. It doesn't affect me."

P2: "As American citizens, we all have an interest in this. Something must be done, the shootings are not just isolated events. They are events that are happening in our schools and are important to all of us. We are all paying the price of this violence."

P5: "I think the cause is really complex and that maybe all of us are kinda right. It is like this huge complex system of values, laws, politics, culture, media, and it all interacts and in some ways are outside of our control. But easy access to guns and the glorification of guns is what I am concerned about. Government outlaws dope why not outlaw guns? Some guns might be okay but let's get real here."

P1: "Once you start banning some guns, all will be banned."

P6: "I do think that people should be more responsible with their guns. Keep them locked up and stuff."

7:40 P.M.

FACILITATOR: So if we were to give advice to government in terms of public policy what would this advice be? (looks at P8).

P8: "I don't know, government can't really do much"

FACILITATOR (TO P8): "But certainly, government must play some role."

P8: "Well, how about putting gun detectors in schools. That is practical and makes sense. That is why all of the shootings have happened in rural and suburban schools. The big city schools already have them. I really have a tough time with all of this social engineering. A kid kills two kids and suddenly we need governmental mandated childcare, gun control, and economic reform. Pretty soon government will control our lives totally. I heard the other day that they want to collect DNA samples of all Americans. Once we allow government into our lives a little bit we are on the road to total government control and domination. We have to draw the line somewhere and prevent government intervention in our lives."

P6: "We need to reform the juvenile justice system. If you are old enough to kill you are old enough for capital punishment. Quit all the plea bargaining and make these kids responsible. Its like when I was a kid and did wrong. My parents would whip my butt and pretty soon I figured out that it wasn't worth being bad because the whippings really hurt."

P4: "This sounds good, but in reality, I doubt whether a kid is going to be rational and say 'I am not going to kill because I don't want to be put in prison or face the electric chair.' These kids are not rational in the first place. I have never bought the death penalty as a way to stop crime. Crimes of violence are not rational and the death penalty or any deterrence only works if the person committing the crime has rational ends or goals."

P1: "That is why government must teach values from an early age. When I was young and did bad, my Dad spanked my butt. Now days, when a parent spanks a kid, the kid probably has a lawyer and sues the parent (laughs in the group). I know that you think this is funny but I read just the other day about a kid who was suing his parents for spanking him. What they now call 'abuse,' my Dad called 'discipline.' I whip my kids good when they need it and they are good kids not hoodlums."

P2: "I am glad that you are not my Dad."

P1: "Yeah, I wouldn't put up with your lifestyle" (brings moans from the group).

7:50 P.M.

FACILITATOR: "Let's get back to what we want the government to do in regard to the school shootings."

P3: The government won't do anything because we haven't fixed the campaign finance laws. Was it coincidence that senators like that Sanitorium guy from Pennsylvania and Slade Gorton from Washington (both of whom have received thousands of NRA dollars) even opposed background checks. At least, the government should play a stronger role in regulating what is on TV, the Net, and CDs. Have you seen some of the video games that they put out? My gosh, people are biting each others heads off and there is violent murder. In my time, we played video games like Frogger, Asteroids, and Pac-Man. These were harmless and fun games. But things have changed today. I also think that we need mandatory ratings of shows and the outright banning of some acts like violent murder on any media outlet. I know all about the First Amendment, but this is the late '90s and we need some value clarification."

7:52 P.M.

FACILITATOR: "What do you mean by 'value clarification'?"

P3: "I mean that government does, and should, play a role in what is accepted and not accepted. Blowing someone's head off with a gun on TV is not what I want my kids watching after dinner and before bed. The Constitution is not a "free pass" for violent people and perverts. It is just a set of values that says we basically support free speech, it says nothing about supporting violence, hatred, and so on."

P9: "I think the focus really has to be on schools and not on these larger issues. I think schools have to play a larger role in counseling students and identifying these problem kids earlier in the process. I know it is a family responsibility but families are breaking down, we live in a mass society now and government, in this case the schools, have to take a stronger role."

P4: "Yeah, I've heard about a really successful program in Seattle called the Second Step program that teaches little kids about taking turns, conflict resolution, and anger management."

P8: "I don't think that we are going to solve the problem tonight. But just talking about this has been helpful. I guess there are a lot of different views on the subject. I am surprised. But how can society possibly solve this problem when we all have such different views? Maybe the experts can sort things out. I don't know."

8:00 P.M.
FACILITATOR: "I guess our time is up; thank you all for participating."

Questions/Problems

Note. The professor may choose to have you answer all of these questions or only some, depending on time limitations, but please read all of them and think about the issues raised.

Conduct a Content Analysis of Problem Definitions

What are the major categories of respondents' views toward the causes of school shootings? How are their views of causes related to policies. Are the respondents always consistent in their views?

   a. What type of method did you use to conduct your analysis (deductive, inductive, a combination)?
   b. Did you look for manifest or latent content or both?
   c. In your opinion, how reliable and valid are your findings?
   d. How do your results compare with other classmates conclusions?

Critique the Facilitator

Critique the performance of the facilitator in this discussion.

   a. Did the facilitator intervene at the right moments? Are there examples where the facilitator should have intervened but did not or where the facilitator intervened inappropriately?
   b. Are there examples of the facilitator using leading questions?
   c. Did the facilitator ever inappropriately interject his or her own opinion into the discussion?
   d. Were the questions asked appropriate? If not, what questions would have you asked and why?

Surveys and Focus Groups

Having read this transcript, what do you believe are the strengths and weaknesses of focus group research as compared to what you know about mail survey research? If you were to design a survey based on the results of this focus group session, what questions would you ask, and what responses would you let them choose from?

Symbols and Metaphors

Can you find examples of participants using symbols or metaphors in their responses? What about their use of causes and Stone's discussion? Does the understanding of Stone's symbolic representation help in understanding the responses?

What Next?

From a practical perspective what could a policy analyst do with this information? Is this approach more democratic than other types of policy analysis or is it merely an exercise in postmodernism that takes us nowhere?

Appendix 6-1:
Governor's Statement on Diseased Bison

Montana Online <www.mt.gov./governor/press/bison.htm>

March 3, 1997

Governor Marc Racicot

Note: Italicized words and phrases are used by the authors to illustrate the use of narrative argument, metaphors, and symbols.

Let's get one thing clear right off: Yellowstone National Park and every one of its wild creatures are national treasures for all Americans, not just those who live far away. Those who live next door to the Park value its beauty, wildness, and diversity at least as much as those who choose to visit it now and then.

Indeed, Montanans treasure those qualities so much they have over the years sacrificed opportunities and income to live in such a grand isolated place where wild creatures are everyday neighbors, outnumbering humans many times over. We really need no lectures about valuing wildlife; it was Montanans 60 years ago who saved grizzly bears when the federal policy was extinction. [Note. These first two paragraphs are aimed toward outsiders who had been very critical of Montana's slaughter of bison—most notably in the ad in *USA Today* that called for a tourist boycott of Montana.]

I speak specifically now about the bison in Yellowstone National Park or, rather, the bison that are leaving Yellowstone National Park. Here's the problem. Many are *diseased*, probably from the day their ancestors were herded into the park decades ago.

It does not matter how many are *diseased* or how they got *sick* because one branch of the federal government—the Department of Agriculture—has threatened to revoke Montana's *hard won* brucellosis-free status if we allow one such *diseased* creature into the state to potentially infect livestock. This—the infection or the revocation—could devastate a *major industry* and its many *families*.

Another branch of the federal government—the Park Service—is theoretically responsible for the Park's bison. Unlike every other national park, however, Yellowstone refuses to manage its wildlife, specifically to control overpopulation and combat *deadly diseases*. This policy was instituted some 30 years ago but, unlike the previous policy of wildlife management, appears difficult to change.

This has resulted in a drastic over-population of bison which cannot find sufficient food in the Park. So they seek it elsewhere. Is this really the humane policy we want in force? To revere these animals so much that so many are kept in one place to starve try to flee their *alleged sanctuary*. [Note. Tests on slaughtered bison have consistently revealed that they are not starving. Instead, they simply could not break through the Yellowstone ice to find forage and therefore left the Park looking for food.]

What we have here are too many *unmanaged, diseased* bison leaving an overgrazed park to mingle with *protected livestock* in violation of an Agriculture Department ban. *If any citizen tried to keep several thousand animals on land that might support 1,500, they would properly be in trouble with animal abuse officers.* In fact, the Park's chief bison researcher recently confirmed in a published report, "The drop in numbers is exactly what the system needs." [The metaphor using animal abuse officers defines the problem from the governor's viewpoint effectively.]

Still, Montana is in the *crossfire*, in effect, *left to manage its neighbors unmanaged herd of wild animals choosing to leave the park because there is nothing left to eat there*. We have no desire to shoot some of these *magnificent* creatures, living symbols of our wild heritage and walking reminders of last century's profligate slaughter. But, according to the other federal department, we cannot allow these *diseased* creatures in.

Feeding the bison in the park would be a short-term solution. But that is not possible, according to "natural regulation" and could help spread the disease by encouraging mingling. Vaccination of healthy animals and removal of diseased ones would be a longterm solution. But that too would violate "natural regulation." What about taking the animals away? That would violate disease control rules.

So Montana is left as the *victimized* neighbor to harvest the *sick animals* of one federal agency to protect the state's largest industry, agriculture, against the sanctions of another federal agency. It *is preposterous*. And it is the hard, sad reality.

The answer is not to *fan the flames* of adverse public opinion to *fuel emotional membership drives*. Montana, Wyoming, and Idaho have spent years working with federal authorities on a solution. It's been eight years now since Yellowstone started the environmental impact statement. Still, none is in sight.

Our suggestion was for the federal government to establish a quarantine facility, ideally within the park or perhaps on a Montana Indian Reservation. This would avoid interstate shipment of possibly diseased animals and provide needed economic development opportunities while diseased animals were removed and healthy ones inoculated.

We have written *countless letters*, attended *countless meetings*, even gone into federal court. We use noisemakers and helicopters to frighten the animals back. We will continue to try to stop this ridiculous—and expensive—spectacle of federal policy paralysis. Meanwhile, it seems to us that public criticism and threats might more appropriately and effectively be directed at the host agencies which refuse to address the real problem and not at the adjacent state that can only attempt to treat the symptoms.

Appendix 6-2:
Focus Groups and the Yellowstone Bison Controversy

Note: This appendix should be read after reading the problem definition case of the bison controversy. If you remember, we identified nine empirical questions from our narrative analysis. This write-up gives the reader a general look at the use of focus groups but also provides some idea of how focus groups could be used to help develop discourse on the nine questions posed by our narrative analysis.

In the Yellowstone Bison Controversy, focus groups could have been used in a variety of ways. We believe that they would have been an interesting follow-up to the narrative analysis that we discussed in Chapter 6. In addition, they could have been used to generate narrative analyses.

First Round of Focus Groups: To Generate Narratives

Hold separate focus groups with the following groups: (1) Buffalo Field Campaign, (2) National Park Service administrators, (3) APHIS administrators, (4) Greater Yellowstone Coalition, Sierra Club, Fund for Animals, (5) West Yellowstone and Gardiner business owners, (6) West Yellowstone and Gardiner citizens, (7) Montana State Livestock officials and ranchers, (8) recreation groups like the Blue Ribbon Coalition.

Questions
1. Tell me the history of this problem? When did it start?
2. What exactly is brucellosis and how is it transmitted?
3. Why is this a problem?
4. Who are the potential winners and losers in this issue?
5. What are the solutions to the problem?

These focus groups would provide a detailed qualitative history of the bison controversy from the perspective of each of the groups. Importantly, each group would have a different view of the history of the problem, brucellosis transmission, what the problem is, winners and losers, and solutions. In addition, the analyst may find some areas of agreement that could lead to solutions.

Second Round of Focus Groups:
As a Follow-Up to the Narrative Analysis

The analysts would spend time researching these questions and would probably provide a presentation of their results to each participating group. In addition, each focus group participant would receive an information packet that he or she would take home and read before the focus group session. The same groups invited to the first round of focus groups are invited to these sessions.

Questions

1. What about the question of transmission of brucellosis to cattle in the wild? Based on what you read and discussed with others, what are your views?
2. Many have contended that bison that were not infected were killed. Based on what you have read and discussed, why did this happen?
3. Many have argued that elk carry brucellosis but they have not been killed by livestock personnel. Based on the information that we provided, how do you deal with this issue?
4. Why are bison killed in the winter months before cattle arrive on the range?
5. Do bison use the snowtrails in the winter? What is the evidence? How would we want to study this issue?
6. Many have contended that ranching is the dominant economic base of Montana. Based on the information that you were presented, what do you think?
7. What is the current position of APHIS in regard to bison leaving Yellowstone National Park and grazing on public lands? At what point, would APHIS pull Montana's brucellosis class free status?
8. How many bison can the park handle? Is there scientific evidence to support any answer?
9. Is the park overgrazed? Do bison starve to death in the winter?

The goal of these focus groups is to provide detailed and informed answers to the questions that were raised in the narrative analysis. These questions were once again considered to be pivotal in explaining why the bison controversy had continued year after year. The provision of information by the analysts helps move the discussion away from mere opinions to some serious discussion of facts. However, we can expect wide disagreement over many "scientific facts." The process would be very long and tedious. Analysts would need at least two to three hours to present their findings. Participants would need time to read collected materials. Each focus group would last at least three to four hours. We would expect disagreement between the groups. However, we might find some areas of agreement.

Third Round of Focus Groups: Combined Groups

This third round of focus groups will combine members from the eight groups. Two members from each of the eight groups will be invited to participate. Some questions would be repeated from the first focus group session. Most questions would be derived from the analysis of the second round of focus groups. The facilitator will explore areas of commonality and agreement. In the end, the group's responses will be considered as indicative of the stakeholders' views.

Analysis of the Use of Focus Groups as a Policy Tool

This approach would obviously be very beneficial since a lot of new information would be secured from each stakeholder group. The approach would allow the analyst and elected officials to understand the often widely differing viewpoints of stakeholders. In addition, the focus groups would provide some areas of agreement. The analyst would be left with a huge amount of information that could be analyzed, coded, and reported. Unlike a survey, the focus group results would come from the stakeholder themselves and not from preconstructed questions and answers that are typical of surveys. After the asking of the general questions, the focus group participants have a great deal of say over the direction of the focus group.[1] No doubt policymakers would obtain a rich treasure trove of information.

There are drawbacks, however, to the use of the focus groups. The most obvious is time and resources. Focus groups take a great deal of time to set up. Meeting rooms must be scheduled, individuals must be invited and reminded several times of the focus group sessions, facilitators must study the background of the issue, facilitators must be trained, assistants and transcribers must be found and trained. As a rule, there are at least five hours of preparation before each focus group (this includes inviting members, sending out invitations, sending reminders, etc.). Then each focus group lasts an average of three hours. Following the focus group, there are approximately ten hours of transcribing, content analysis, analyzing, and reporting. As a result, each focus group requires around eighteen hours to prepare, execute, and report. This means that the first round of focus groups would require 144 "person hours," the second round would require an additional 144 hours, and the third round (with only one group) would require eighteen hours. Thus, the three rounds of focus groups would require 306 hours of work. This, in addition to the time required to research and report the information collected around the nine questions, would put a tremendous strain on any governmental agency.

The second problem with focus groups is that they require active and informed participants. The interest group and administrative agency focus groups would be the easiest to conduct in this regard. They would consist of individuals who get paid to be advocates and staff members. It would be more difficult to recruit citizens and small business owners. Citizens live busy lives and often do not have time to attend three rounds of lengthy focus group sessions or read information collected by facilitators. Business owners, likewise, have a difficult time leaving their businesses for such activity. The real danger of focus group recruitment is that facilitators often end up with convenience samples. That is, the focus groups consist of those who have the time and interest to attend the sessions.

---

[1]There is some disagreement among experienced focus group facilitators about whether facilitators should operate as "weak" or "strong." A weak facilitation style allows the participants to move answers in directions that the group controls. The facilitator only intervenes when the activity strays totally off target or when personal insults are being thrown around. A strong facilitation style keeps respondents answers narrow and to the point. Generally, the weak facilitation style is more democratic and not time efficient. The stronger style is more efficient but also tends to cut off what might be important discussion in favor of facilitator-led discussion.

Appendix 6-3: Content Analysis and the Bison Case

Note: The purpose of this appendix is to provide you with an application of content analysis using the Yellowstone bison case. It can also be useful as a source of information in completing the bison case in Chapter 5.

Unlike the focus group example where we could only provide hypothetical use of focus groups, here we can provide a real example of the use of content analysis in the bison controversy. Surveys were mailed to 225 citizens and businesses in the Yellowstone border communities of West Yellowstone and Gardiner, Montana, in the spring of 1998. One hundred twenty-three respondents returned the survey for a 55 percent response rate. Not all respondents, however, completed the qualitative section. In the qualitative section of the survey, respondents were asked to contribute their open-ended comments on the cause of the bison problem and solutions. This section reports the results of this qualitative section. Comments on each question were sorted into distinct categories and then analyzed.

Problem Definition

The National Park Service Is Not Managing Wildlife

Twenty-eight (36 percent) respondents believed that ultimately the bison problem rested with the National Park Service's lack of wildlife management. One respondent suggested, "The Park should regulate the size of the herd, make the Park Service take responsibility for the problem it creates." Another citizen offered the following metaphor, "If I starved my dog or horse I would go to jail; they (NPS) need to control the problem." Many respondents felt that the NPS had made the State of Montana the "bad guy" in the issue. One citizen offered the following, "Decide upon a carrying capacity for the YNP ecosystem and then sterilize, slaughter, or transfer excess animals. This should be done by the Park Service, not by the State of Montana. The Park Service has given Montana a bad rap."

Most respondents in this category believe that Yellowstone is overgrazed and that the Park cannot sustain a large herd of bison. One respondent argued, "Yellowstone is overgrazed and the herd size needs to reduced." Another stated, "The real problem is not disease but overpopulation, the Park Service needs to be responsible for the problems they create."

In addition, some citizens were concerned about the public safety and property damage issues raised by the large bison population. As one West Yellowstone citizen noted, "Bison are not like the other animals in the Park. They like to lay down in the roads, somebody is going to get killed. Bison also cause a lot of property damage that insurance does not pay for." Another stated, "I don't think it is fair to people driving down the road to have to put their lives at risk because you cannot see bison at night. I also do not like to have to see them starve to death in my front yard." These citizens do not want Yellowstone bison leaving the park. Many made comments about how they like the bison but only if they stay inside the boundaries of Yellowstone. A common theme running through all of these narratives is one of control (to be discussed in detail later). These citizens believed that the Park Service has a duty to control its wildlife and keep bison (and presumably other animals) inside the park.

The Problem Rests with Ranchers, APHIS, and Montana

Twenty-six comments out of seventy-eight (33 percent) were directed against the trio of ranchers, APHIS, and the State of Montana. One respondent wrote, "It should not be a controversy, money is the highlight here." "Where's the problem?" commented another citizen, "Since cattle are vaccinated, the problem is coming from politics, people, and misinformation. There has never been a proven case of a cow contracting brucellosis from a buffalo." Another respondent suggested, "What we have here is a greedy (me first) attitude with the public lands."

The lack of scientific evidence was cited by many citizens. For example, "There is no scientific study saying bison can transmit brucellosis" and "use real science, drop the pretense about brucellosis being the rancher's concern. Vets who are extremely intelligent have published works that state the bison/cattle brucellosis transmission is nearly impossible, it has never happened in the wild but instead only in corralled areas." Still another wrote, "It is impossible for cows to get brucellosis from bison, experts need to bring out strongly the false ideas of Racicot, the Montana Department of Livestock, and the ranchers who senselessly killed thousands of bison."

Another citizen noted that "Montana has killed hundreds of young and marked (uninfected) bison and bulls—I have seen their guts in the snow." Another citizen wondered, "If the ranchers are so concerned about brucellosis infected bison on the cattle ranges then why do they leave bison entrails and remains all over the public lands?" Others commented, "The cattle aren't on the public range until mid-June so why did they kill bison in the winter?" Many respondents suggested that the Yellowstone elk herd have higher rates of brucellosis yet, "We ignore the elk because they are a source of revenue."

The Problem Rests with Environmental Groups

Twelve comments (15 percent) indicated that the problem rested with environmental groups that according to these respondents wanted to use the bison issue to raise money, refused to recognize property rights, and wanted to stop snowmobiling. One

TABLE 1   CITIZEN PROBLEM DEFINITION

PROBLEM DEFINITION	FREQUENCY	PERCENT
Problem rests with environmental groups	12	15%
Problem rests with ranchers, APHIS, Montana	26	33
Problem rests with the National Park Service and the non-management of bison	28	36
Problem rests with media coverage	3	4
Problem rests with the lack of scientific studies	8	10
Problem rests with snowmobile trails	1	1

Note. There were a total of 78 comments from respondents offering problem definitions.

respondent from Gardiner wrote a typical response in this category, "Wildlife groups are unwilling to compromise, they spend a lot of money that should be used to manage wildlife. The rights of animals should not come before property rights."

Other respondents picked up on the theme of environmental groups using the bison issue to raise money. A West Yellowstone respondent suggested, "If the people trying to use the bison to raise money would get out of it the problem would solve itself."

Others viewed environmental interest groups as "outsiders" trying to push environmental agendas on local communities. One respondent commented, "The lack of wildlife management has devastated YNP and now these same people (environmentalists) want to do the same to surrounding states." Another respondent wrote in regard to the problem definition, "Quit putting animals before man, read your Bible." Another commented, "We love this place like anyone but there are limits to what we can have shoved down our throats by outsiders."

Other respondents in this category believed that the real problem rested in environmental groups who wanted to use the bison issue to end winter snowmobiling in Yellowstone. As one citizen stated, "I believe the Fund for Animals and other groups will do anything to stop snowmobiling."

Solutions

Respondents offered several solutions to the bison-brucellosis controversy (see Table 2). There were ninety-six comments made by citizens concerning possible solutions. Seven major categories are reported and analyzed here.

Control the Herd/Determine a Carrying Capacity

This solution, offered thirty-six times (38 percent) was that scientists and experts needed to determine the carrying capacity of bison inside the park and then use "herd management" techniques to keep bison at this scientifically determined number. Not surprisingly, these solutions came almost exclusively from respondents who believed that the National Park Service is the source of the problem. These respondents believe that bison should be kept in the park and their statements demonstrate that they view Yellowstone as a "closed ecosystem. Consider the following responses:

- "Maintain the herd at numbers the park can handle."
- "Keep the bison in the park."
- "Regulate the size of the herd and make the Park Service responsible for the problems they create."
- "Control the herd; we don't need more than 1,000 head."
- "The park must control its bison herd; the park is way overgrazed."
- "Sterilize the bull bison and cows; control the number of bison so forage can return."
- "Bison need to stay in the park."
- "If the Indians and the environmentalists want them they can keep them; I am tired of fixing fences that they crash into."

TABLE 2   CITIZEN SOLUTIONS TO THE BISON CONTROVERSY

SOLUTIONS	FREQUENCY	PERCENT
Keep bison within a carrying capacity/herd management	36	38%
Science and research on whether Brucellosis can be transmitted	14	15
Create buffer zones	10	10
Ethical hunting	15	16
Capture, testing, slaughter	7	7
Vaccinate cattle	6	7
Vaccinate bison	4	4
Leave bison alone	3	3
Feed bison inside yellowstone	1	1

Note. There were a total of ninety-six comments from respondents offering solutions to the crisis.

An analysis of respondents who believed that the bison herd needs to be controlled revealed that respondents came disproportionally from West Yellowstone rather than Gardiner, that they had lived a higher percentage of lives in their current community, and that they were more likely to be business owners.

Science and Research

Fourteen respondents believe that the solution rests in scientifically determining whether brucellosis can be transmitted from bison to cattle in wild settings. Again, as stated earlier, no scientific studies have documented transmission in the wild. Serious students of this issue, which has led to the slaughter of over 3,000 bison since the mid-1980s, must question why research has not been conducted on this subject. If bison cannot transmit brucellosis to cattle in wild settings, the problem disappears. At least the problem would disappear if the problem really was one of brucellosis transmission.

Create Buffer Zones

Ten respondents favored the creation of buffer zones for bison and other wildlife around the park. This would include the acquisition of private lands and not allowing cattle to graze within a twenty-mile radius of the park.

Ethical Hunt

Fifteen respondents wanted Montana to reestablish a bison hunt. Most respondents noted that the hunt should be regulated and that it must be ethical.

Capture, Testing, Slaughter

Seven respondents wanted a return to the original idea of the Interim Bison Plan. According to these respondents, the plan's goal was to capture bison, test them for brucellosis and then kill pregnant bison and those testing positive for brucellosis.

Vaccinate Cattle

Six respondents believed that ranchers should take responsibility for vaccinating cattle.

Vaccinate Bison

Four respondents favored the vaccination of bison. (Currently, there is no effective bison vaccine for brucellosis but research is ongoing.)

CHAPTER 7

DOING DEMOCRACY: A NEW FIFTH STEP

Mini-Case

"Southern-Fried Analyst"

Defining Democracy

> Sesame Street teaches third-graders about democratic elections in the following manner: You have three dollars to spend. Some people want crayons, others juice. You vote what to buy. If the majority wants crayons, you get crayons, and vice versa. (Amitai Etzioni [1996, 115])

Our view of democracy is too often an understanding of voting and majority rule. Despite our society's tremendous respect for democracy and freedom, it is common to denigrate and underestimate the public. Pundits do it all the time in clever editorials. Jay Leno does it with his interviews of people on the street. Newspapers generally aim stories at "the lowest common denominator." After hearing the percentage of votes that Ross Perot received, a colleague of one of the authors joked that anyone who voted for him should have their voting privileges revoked for five years. Is this fair and accurate? Or is it a self-fulfilling prophecy? Are people responding to the expectations of the elites and the lack of opportunities for meaningful participation? Consider the following two related stories.

In the fall of 1991 the *Philadelphia Inquirer*, one of the nation's best newspapers, ran a nine-part series of articles. The focus was not about sex in the oval office, but the economic patterns of the 1980s. Specific issues included corporate debt, the savings and loan bailout, tax policy, the bankruptcy code, and all sorts of other stuff people supposedly can't fathom. Yet crowds gathered in the lobby of the newspaper's building for reprints—so many people, in fact, that security guards were called in to control the crowd. Word got out and people around the country began asking for reprints of the series. In the first eight months the number of reprints exceeded 400,000. Seven years later *Time Magazine* ran a three-part series on corporate welfare. Once again, the overwhelming response from the supposedly apathetic public was genuine interest. As with the nine-part series on the '80s, the writing was crisp, clear, vivid, and informative, without being oversimplified or demagogic. Perhaps there really is such a thing as "democracy" and perhaps we should listen to the public.

This chapter examines democracy and the role of the citizen in policy analysis. It is not the concluding chapter, but it will serve to pull together several loose ends (and clear up areas where, with good intentions, we deviously misled you). There is one more chapter in this section of the book, in which the focus has shifted more toward practice and less toward theory, but this chapter represents the end of our introduction to postpositivist methods of analysis. Its primary focus, as suggested by the title, is on the role of the public policy analyst as custodian of democracy—not only in theory, but also in practice.

In completing the cases in this book, you have probably dealt with questions of democracy. In your role as a policy analyst, you have had to wrestle with questions of who should and should not be your stakeholders, how evaluation criteria should be determined, and who you as an analyst work for. In the classroom your authors and their students have certainly confronted these questions, as Box 7-1 will show.

7-1. Teaching the Bison Case and Democracy

The bison case introduced in Chapter 5 and discussed in Chapter 6 typically brings out several discussions of what democracy is and is not. The case was completed by students of one of the authors in a public policy analysis course. Guest speakers from interest groups came to class and gave their spin on the bison controversy. Original surveys of citizens were conducted, public documents analyzed, and letters to the editors clipped and scrutinized. The students completed the case using a combination of the pragmatic model introduced in Chapter 5 and the postpositivist model used in Chapter 6. After several weeks, it became clear that this course on policy analysis was not simply a course where students learned a technical process. Instead, infused by the postpositivist method, the course became one focused primarily on democracy. Questions were discussed on the class email list concerning whose "facts" should be believed, whose interests satisfied, and whether it was possible or even desirable to attempt to please all stakeholders.

One vocal student, Pat (not the real name of the student), after listening to several interest group speakers and reading bison literature, proclaimed that the whole postpositivist approach and its emphasis on democracy was "a waste of time," since, to quote Pat, "Democracy is simply majority rule." The student held this belief with almost religious conviction and believed that postpositivism was part of a left-wing liberal agenda that had already destroyed "the rights of the majority." The student's point was that it did not matter what citizens, animal rights advocates, or even ranchers had to say about the bison issue. Instead, to this student, socialized in the Sesame Street manner, democracy was a process of majority rule and voting. The job of the analyst, Pat informed the class, was to "find out what the majority of the people wanted and then suggest this majoritarian policy." Pat boldly proclaimed that the views of "Buffalo Nations," "the Greater Yellowstone Coalition," and the "Blue Ribbon Coalition" did not matter because they had only a few thousand members between them. In addition, citizen views were "full of beans" and their views had to be discounted.

In latter weeks, in a argumentative debate with the professor on an email list, the student claimed that the U.S. Constitution was a majoritarian document. The professor, trying to temper his anger, argued that the Constitution was full of antimajoritarian biases (e.g., the U.S. Senate, the U.S. Supreme Court, the Bill of Rights, the Electoral College). The student discounted this evidence by making such arguments as "the court uses a majority voting procedure as does the Senate and U.S. House of Representatives."

None of the students in the class really had a strong grasp on the concept of democracy, but they did have a different definition of democracy than Pat's. Other students became outraged at the majoritarian arguments of Pat and suggested that democracy was really about protecting the rights and viewpoints of the minority. These students were excited about the postpositivist approach and were glad that common citizens were being heard in the process. Many of these students believed, however, that the five-step method was undemocratic. They thought that the only method used to determine solutions should have been the active facilitation and participation of all stakeholders.

There were still other views of democracy. Some students felt that the varying viewpoints produced by the postpositivist approach were interesting but uninformed, and that it would be better for experts to make policy unencumbered by the rhetoric and misinformation of common citizens. They also felt that, in the long run, this elite policymaking might be more democratic since uninformed citizens could really make bad policy that would hurt minority interests.

The discussions were often intense, and students and the professor alike spoke passionately about their views of democracy. Unfortunately, perhaps, the class never came to any consensus on defining democracy. As they worked on the case, some students followed citizen views, others followed the lead of experts, some wanted a popular referendum on bison management, and still others saw no possibility of democratic consensus, given the large number of views and conflicting interests and values.

Democracy is a symbol that almost all Americans cling to with great resolve. We know that the United States is a democratic experiment. We know that men and women have fought and died for democracy and we agree on the principle. But just what is democracy? After teaching policy analysis from a postpositivist perspective, we are forced to conclude that democracy is an ambiguous symbol. We all espouse democratic rhetoric but have a difficult time articulating and agreeing on exactly what democracy is and is not. An underlying theme of this book is that we want public policy analysis to be democratic, but what exactly is the value of this if we cannot come to a common definition of democracy?

Discovering first-hand the ambiguous nature of democracy was an unsettling finding for the professor. He struggled along, but the students never really found an agreed-upon definition of democracy or its role in policy analysis. This chapter provides guidance for prospective policy analysts. While we cannot claim to provide a

definitive definition of democracy, we believe we ask the right questions, provide our
view of what democracy is and is not, and advocate for its inclusion in your policy
analysis methodology.

Democracy as an Ambiguous Symbol

Fortunately, if you feel frustrated by defining democracy in policy analysis, you are not
alone. Democratic theorists have for years debated exactly what democracy means.
Democracy is derived from *demokratia*, meaning rule by the people. "Rule by the people" may appear an unambiguous concept, but appearances are deceptive. The history of democracy is complex and marked by conflicting interpretations. According to
Held (1988, 2), definitional problems emerge with each element of the phrase: "rule,"
"rule by," and the "people." Held's questions about democracy (1988, 2) appear below:

The People
- Who are to be considered the people?
- What kind of participation is envisioned for them?
- What conditions are assumed to be conducive to participation? Can the disin-
  centives and incentives, or costs and benefits of participation be equal?

Rule
- How broadly or narrowly is the scope of rule to be constructed? Or what is the appropriate field of democratic activity?
- If "rule" is to cover "the political," what is meant by this? Does it cover law
  and order? Relations between states? The economy? The domestic or private
  sphere?

Rule By
- Must the rules of "the people" be obeyed? What is the place of obligation and
  dissent?
- What mechanisms are created for those who are avowedly and actively "nonpar-
  ticipants"?
- Under what circumstances, if any, are democracies entitled to resort to coercion
  against some of their own people or against those outside the sphere of legitimate rule?

What Counts as Rule by the People
- That all should govern, in the sense that all should be involved in legislating, in
  deciding on general policy, in applying laws and in governmental administration?
- That all should be personally involved in crucial decision making, that is to say
  in deciding general laws and matters of general policy?
- That rulers should be accountable to the ruled; that they should, in other words,
  be obliged to justify their actions to the ruled and be removable by the ruled?
- That rulers should be accountable to the representatives of the ruled?
- That rulers should be chosen by the ruled?
- That rulers should be chosen by the representatives of the ruled?
- That rulers should act in the interests of the ruled?

Held's questions are very important to us as policy analysts. His question "who are the people?" relates to our question "who are the stakeholders?" Besides those who can affect adoption and implementation, should those directly affected by policy have a say? And should only those directly affected by a policy have a voice in the policy process? In a policy issue involving a state, local communities, and a national park, should the stakeholders be limited to local interests, or should American citizens living in Florida have as much to say (or at least some say) regarding National Park Service wildlife policy as citizens living in communities that border that particular national park?

Once we have dealt with this question, we as analysts must consider what level of participation is appropriate for the stakeholders. How do the people rule? Do we simply send surveys to citizens and hold open public meetings and then say that we have included the "people" in our democratic process? Or do we actively seek citizens to sit on policy boards and make decisions? Listed below are additional questions of democracy for policy analysts, followed by an examination of the advantages and disadvantages of various techniques of gathering citizen input. Should we seek input of citizens if they are uninformed and uneducated about issues? Why should analysts spend hundreds of hours studying an issue and then allow uninformed citizens to make final decisions? Of course, if we agree that the uneducated should not rule, we are left with other troubling problems. Does this mean that we should only listen to the "educated," when in most policy issues the educated are going to be special interest lobbyists? Further, this begs the question: Why are so many citizens uneducated? Could it be that it is in the interests of the "politically educated" and powerful to keep the uneducated in the dark? If so, should the analyst try to "educate" citizens? This sounds good, but how do analysts separate their own subjective biases from their educational function? Would analyst education really be analyst propaganda? Moreover, we are left with the troubling notion of majority rule versus minority rights. How do we listen to the views of the minority and still make good policy? If the people make policy, does this oblige all to obey?

Additional Questions
- Should the "politically uneducated" rule?
- Should only the "educated" rule?
- Why are the "people politically uneducated?"
- What does it mean to be "politically educated?"
- How do we separate "education" from "propaganda?"
- Should the majority of the people rule or should we protect the minority from the tyranny of the majority?

Mail Survey Research: Advantages
- It is relatively quick.
- It produces generalizable data.
- It is relatively inexpensive.
- It can be used for both quantitative and qualitative data generation.

- It can be used to gather sensitive data since anonymity of respondents can be guaranteed.
- Quantitative data is easy to report.
- Quantitative data can be used to produce statistical tests.
- Quantitative data can be used to track changes in citizen attitudes.
- It does not require a lot of time from respondents.

Mail Survey Research: Disadvantages

- It requires a trained and skilled survey writer.
- Questions asked are preselected by the survey writer.
- Poor question construction can lead to misleading or confusing responses.
- It yields generally poor response rates without multiple mailings (which drive up costs).
- There is a response bias.
- Interpretation requires a skilled statistical analyst or content analyst for qualitative data.
- It is often difficult to draw good random samples.

Focus Groups: Advantages

- They allow researchers to secure answers in the context of group and social interaction.
- The flow of the discussion is determined to a great extent by the response of the participants rather than by the researcher.
- Information gathered typically provides a relatively deep understanding of a public issue or controversy.
- Researchers are able to explore the context of respondent's views.
- Focus group members have more latitude in their responses.
- Responses occur within a social setting.

Focus Groups: Disadvantages

- They are costly.
- They require a trained focus group facilitator and someone trained in content analysis.
- They are difficult to use in situations calling for sensitive information since anonymity cannot be guaranteed.
- The information generated is more difficult to report.
- Representative samples are difficult to draw.
- Longitudinal analysis is more difficult to achieve.
- They require a substantial time commitment.

Public Hearings: Advantages

- They satisfy legal requirements.
- They provide the appearance of public forum.
- They give citizens more input into the political process.

Public Hearings: Disadvantages

- They frequently turn into shouting matches.
- There is little evidence that bureaucrats or elected officials listen to public comments.
- Citizens participating are usually not representative of the general population.
- They turn public policymaking into "us" versus "them.

Citizen Advisory Panels: Advantages

- Provides a forum for citizen participation.
- Creates an educated citizenry.

Citizen Advisory Panels: Disadvantages

- There are questions about whether citizen advice is used.
- "Citizen advisory" is redundant in a democracy.
- They can be used by elected officials for impression management or manipulation.

Finally, we need to consider the descriptive question: How democratic is policymaking? Postmodernism offers input on this as well as staking out a normative prescriptive position.

The Postmodern Critique

Postmodernism is a worldview that recognizes that elites manipulate the public through symbols, through their dominance of the media, through insistence on positivist techniques and "rational" dialogue, and through "selling short" both the competence and community-mindedness of average citizens.[1]

One of the postmodernist critiques of teaching positivist methods of supposedly rational and neutral policy analysis is that the positivist model fails to facilitate democracy and, in fact, lends legitimacy and support to the status quo (which, it is argued, is controlled by elites and interest groups, rather than citizens). Danziger, as we have previously discussed, suggests the role of the analyst is not to find the truth but to provide access to, and explanation of, data to all parties; to empower the public in regard to understanding analyses, and to promote serious public discussions of political issues. Peter deLeon, in his book *Democracy and the Policy Sciences* (1997) focuses specifically on the issue of public participation and advocates a "minipopulist" procedure to increase citizen participation.

Of course, the critique that the making of policy is not very democratic is not unique to postmodernism. Concerns over this issue are prominent within the mainstream. At the 58th National Conference of the American Society for Public Administration, July 28, 1997, Herbert Simon delivered a speech subsequently transformed

---

[1]Ironically, citizens are portrayed in the positivist rational choice model, and even in newer more postpositivist models such as Advocacy Coalition (AC) and Institutional Analysis and Development (IAD), as being self-interested, and predominantly (if not perfectly) rational. The irony arises from the fact that it is also common among elites, elite theorists, and advocates of positivism to describe the average citizen as irrational, easily swayed by emotions, ill-informed, apathetic, and not committed to democracy.

into a Guest Editorial in the January/February 1998 *Public Administration Review*. Consider his words:

> Of course, it is not enough that a society work efficiently and productively. We also expect a society to distribute goods and services fairly, however vigorously we may debate and disagree about the criteria of fairness. *In particular, we cannot expect fairness of distribution, measured by almost any criterion, unless all members of the society are represented in the distribution process.* (emphasis added)

Professor Simon even argues that "democratic society is only sustainable if power is dispersed." Moreover, the American Society for Public Administration (ASPA) Code of Ethics calls for those who work in the public sector to do the following:

1. Recognize and support the public's right to know the public's business.
2. Involve citizens in policy decision making.
3. Respond to the public in ways that are complete, clear, and easy to understand.
4. Assist citizens in their dealings with government.
5. Respect the public.
6. Enhance organization capacity for open communication.

The democratic ethos that public servants are ethically bound to follow is simply not limited to majoritarianism. It includes openness, access to representativeness, and responsiveness.

Recall that in Chapter 1 we made it clear that democracy is much more than merely having the right to vote and having the majority rule. Two of the elements we discussed as part of an ideal democracy were effective participation and citizen control of the policy agenda. Let's briefly revisit these ideas and take them forward a bit by quoting from Chambers, Clemons, and Foster (1990, 29–30, 34):

> Effective participation means that throughout the decision making processes, including the stage of putting issues on the agenda, citizens in the community must have adequate and equal opportunity for expressing preferences as to the final outcome (Dahl, 6; Barber, 203–12). The further assumption is that participation will lead to public conflict and that democratic processes need to be utilized to resolve the conflict (Dahl, 10–11). Barber sees this "strong democracy" as offering an alternative model to "thin democracy" of which majoritarianism democracy is an illustration. He argues that "Those who identify democracy with decision making through choices or voting capture the urgency of action without which politics becomes an abstract process that touches neither power nor reality. Yet to limit democracy to a selection among preferences and to think of efficient decision-making as its sole measure is to ignore all but the thinnest features of democracy (p. 198). In the literature there is often a nod to a participatory process and occasionally there is evidence of a very real commitment to it. Yet the reality often is that the citizen feels left out of the decision making with the consequences that she or he becomes less articulate and makes fewer contributions to decisions shaping the collective destiny (Biddle and Biddle 1965, 2–4). This sense of no "control" promotes conflict, divides the community, and spawns bitterness.

As we explained in Chapter 6, postmodernism and postpositivism call for the reinvigoration of democracy, and call on policy analysis to play a key role in that process. Danziger (1995, 445) writes, "If public deliberation is to remain democratic in any meaningful sense of that word, then policy analysts must accept the rhetorical challenge shouldered by the ancient sophists: to promote the 'truth' in public policy debates, all the contenders need to be well armed. If most professional analysts work behind closed doors in the service of political and economic elites, they will breed widespread public mistrust of their profession, of their technocratic paradigms, and of the powerful interests who sponsor them." In addition, deLeon (1997, 124) concludes, "If participatory policy analysis is taken seriously by citizens, analysts, and policymakers, it might well extend to a revitalization of social capital and to what many observers have called a flagging faith in democracy and its governance."

Although he was clearly not a postmodernist, the articulate concerns, descriptions, and prescriptions of social historian Christopher Lasch (1995) correspond closely to the postmodern position. Box 7-2 offers you a sampling from Lasch's last book, which wondered about the possibility of resuscitating democracy.

7-2. Democracy: Problems, Descriptions, and Solutions

Fierce ideological battles are fought over peripheral issues. Elites who define the issues, have lost touch with the people. (3)

Democracy requires a vigorous exchange of ideas and opinions. Ideas, like property, need to be distributed as widely as possible. Yet many of the 'best people,' as they think about themselves, have always been skeptical about the capacity of ordinary citizens to grasp complex issues and to make critical judgments. Democratic debate, from their point of view, degenerates all too easily into a shouting match in which the voice of reason seldom makes itself heard. (10)

According to Walter Lippmann ... the 'omnicompetent citizen was an anachronism in the age of specialization.' Lippmann argued ... the public idealized by the progressives ... was a 'phantom.' Substantive questions could safely be left to experts, whose access to scientific knowledge immunized them against the emotional 'symbols' and 'stereotypes' that dominated public debate. Lippmann's argument rested on a sharp distinction between opinion and science. (10–11)

In the 'age of information' the American people are notoriously ill informed. The explanation of this seeming paradox is obvious, though seldom offered. Having been effectively excluded from public debate on the grounds of their incompetence, most Americans no longer have any use for the information inflicted on them in such large amounts. They have become almost as incompetent as their critics have always claimed—a reminder that it is the debate itself, and debate alone, that gives rise to the desire for usable information. In the absence of democratic exchange, most people have no incentive to master the knowledge that would make them capable citizens. (11, 12)

Mickey Kaus, a *New Republic* editor, has advanced an interpretation ... that has a great deal in common with the interpretation advanced in these pages.... (That) the most serious threat to democracy in our times, comes ... from the decay or abandonment of public institutions in which citizens meet as equals. (19)

[The Progressives] took the position that government was a science, not an art. They forged links between government and the university so as to assure a steady supply of experts and expert knowledge. But they had little use for public debates. Most political questions were too complex, in their view, to be submitted to popular judgment. (167)

Lippmann had forgotten (that) ... it is only by subjecting our preferences and projects to the test of debate that we come to understand what we know and what we still need to learn.... It is the act of articulating and defending our views that lifts them out of the category of 'opinions,' gives them shape and definition, and makes it possible for others to recognize them as a description of their own experience as well....

    The attempt to bring others around to our own point of view carries the risk, of course, that we may adopt their point of view instead. We have to enter imaginatively into our opponents' argument, if only for the purpose of refuting them, and we may end up being persuaded by those we sought to persuade.... [A]rguments are not won by shouting down opponents. They are won by changing opponents minds—something that can happen only if we give opposing arguments a respectful hearing.... In the course of this activity, we may well decide that there is something wrong with our own. (170–71)

Of course, it is one thing to call for civic-mindedness, careful listening, active promotion of community discourse, cultivation of inclusive citizen participation, empowerment and education of citizens, the breaking down of boundaries, and working toward justice without paternalism—and quite another thing to operationalize these goals. Postmodernism, as previously explained, is often criticized for its lack of applicability.

Zanetti and Carr (1999, 211) state that, "... this postmodernism can only tear down the world; it cannot build it back up. The political consequence is a Hobbesian version of society as a war of all against all." They then quote C. Fred Alford who argues that postmodernists don't even write about

... politics. Not one word about how resources might be distributed, disputes settled, legitimate claims to authority determined, and collective amenities, such as hospitals, schools, parks, and roads funded and organized. Not one word about power and authority. Not one word about leadership. In part this is because an abstract, metaphysical approach to political theory leaves no room for such details (133).

Although this surely overstated the situation, postmodernism has been vulnerable to criticism echoing the fourth criteria we introduced for model evaluation—practicality. It is one thing to reveal tyranny, another to topple it. To some degree, this text is an attempt to remedy that problem. Thus, Chapters 5 and 6, in particular, sought to find pragmatic value in postmodernism for policy analysis, just as throughout the book we have made it clear that for postpositivist analysts there is still a place for a rigorous methodology and positivist techniques. As Lasswell (1962, 12) wrote in the mid-1960s, democracy will be both "blind and weak" if it lacks a scientific policy process—but it will not be a democracy if the sort of critiques offered by postmodernism remain solely in the realm of theory. But how does one actually structure democracy? How can a policy analyst "do democracy?"

Structuring Democracy

Democracy, from this perspective, is not about voting and polling, but an ongoing, inclusive participation that leads to real outcomes. If participation is not genuine, empowered/facilitated, and potentially meaningful, then it merely provides a fig leaf for nondemocratic policy decisions, and will end in increased cynicism (like the corporate suggestion box stationed squarely over a trash container). Rather, the postmodern perspective suggests that public discourse, that is to say real dialogue, is essential to the development of shared values and visions. It is a belief that civic engagement can end the political posturing, conflict, and name calling that characterize modern policy debate; thereby leading to win-win solutions and an end to the we/they, us/them stories.

Once again, these criticisms are not limited to postmodernists. There is an entire school of writing (with important distinctions developing about viewing people as customers or citizens) regarding government reinvention and reform that aims at increased citizen participation (e.g., Hindy Lauer Schachter 1997; Guy Peters 1996; Edward Lawler 1996; David Carnevale 1995; David Osborne and Ted Gaebler 1992). The May/June 1998 edition of *PAR* (*Public Administration Review*) featured a symposium on Leadership, Democracy, and the New Public Management, featuring articles with titles like, "What Right Do Public Managers Have to Lead?" and "An Inclusive Democratic Polity, Representative Bureaucracies, and the New Public Management." The next edition of *PAR* (July/August 1998) had an article titled "The Question of Participation: Toward Authentic Public Participation in Public Administration." Moreover, practitioners are making efforts to implement these ideas.

Likewise, the ideals being operationalized are neither radical nor necessarily driven by postmodernism. The ideal sort of democracy postulated by postmodernism is an older view of democracy and civic life; invoking a time when there was a set place and time where people deliberated together, face-to-face, voicing hopes and fears, and working together on common problems. The Greek city-states (although limited to free men), the indigenous peoples of North America (whose models of democracy influenced the founding of our democracy), and the idealized small town hall in New England are the examples people desire to imitate. Box 7-3 provides numerous concrete stories of implementation efforts that are being hailed as evidence that this is not a utopian dream.

7-3. Changing the Game

The Innovations in American Government program, an awards program sponsored by the Ford Foundation, has, for more than a decade now, recognized innovative government programs. At least once a year there are stories in the newspapers praising, rather than bashing, bureaucracy. A common theme among winners has been responsiveness to citizen participation that goes beyond voting, that builds partnerships with nonprofit organizations and the private sector, and that treats the citizens and groups that are affected by that governmental agency as insightful customers. Impressive federal, state, and local programs are nominated every year, and very worthy winners identified.

Similarly, Douglas Watson (1997) authored a text titled *Innovative Governments: Creative Approaches to Local Problems* that uses case studies from small- and medium-sized local governments in the southeastern United States. Coverage ranges from affordable housing to storm water management, and from public safety to changing the form of government in a small town. His central point is that the success of these programs hinged on the sense of shared ownership created by real participation of the various citizens and constituent groups.

Columnist Neal Peirce has written numerous times about this topic. Perhaps the most memorable was an article he wrote (1998, 5A–6A) that began by telling the tale of Clark County, Washington, where the government responded to allegations by Ross Perot's United We Stand members that they were cooking the books and using secrecy and murkiness to hide the facts. Rather than fight the battle in a traditional way, they decided to make the budget process as open and accessible and participatory as possible. They had citizens vote on funding for various departments by distributing beans. They used surveys asking how citizens would allocate 100 dollars among the thirteen primary services provided by the county. To create a dialogue, they created citizens panels, funded mailings, put people together who disagreed, etc.

Peirce then goes on to argue that budget processes across the United States could be demystified and improved, and explains that a task force in December 1997 created a framework for doing just that. A Government Finance Officers Association publication that explains how to do this is available at <www.gfoa.org>. According to Nancy Kopp, vice chair of the task force, the central point is that "A budget is only superficially numbers. Think of it as a meeting point of the shared needs, the common goals, the available resources, of a state, county or city." Kopp also is quoted as noting, "In a way, open and participatory budgeting is dangerous to the near monopoly on knowledge—and power—many government officials often use and possess." She also feels this can dissipate public cynicism, and that with "public debate, special interests lose some of the clout they most effectively exercise behind closed doors." Another benefit, according to Kopp, is that, "If people are fully informed and consulted they'll often consent more easily, even to final decisions they disagree with." Moreover, Peirce points out, this all parallels "the more open, participatory, team-driven management styles now increasingly popular in corporations."

Last, but certainly not least, among our changing-the-game examples, is the large number of organizations and communities that are concerned with reinvigorating democracy. One of the more interesting structures being implemented is known as a study circle. The Study Circles Resource Center (SCRC) was created to advance deliberative democracy and helps communities, through materials and other assistance, organize study circles. These are democratic, high participation discussions, in small, diverse groups. You can read success stories and access publications at <http://www.studycircles.org>. A fall 1998 publication told of study circles and the changes they had brought about in places like Lima, Ohio; Elkhart, Indiana; Pflugerville, Texas; Waterloo, Iowa; Wilson, North Carolina; Inglewood, California; Burbank, California; Dover, Delaware; Northeast, Connecticut; Hampton County, South Carolina; Warren County, Iowa; Tacoma, Washington; Buffalo, New York; and ten sites each in Arkansas and Oklahoma. The organizing topics have varied (included education, crime and violence, race, diversity, jobs, solid waste disposal, and economic development) and have led to tutoring programs, expansion of a Soup Kitchen's operation, rebuilding a church that had been burned, arranging financing for a new supermarket in a city neighborhood, a cultural awareness festival, programs to improve race relations, and increased community input into a new county land use plan. They are currently working with nearly two hundred communities.

Communitarianism and Democracy

Our first and more minor deviousness goes all the way back to Chapter 1. In this chapter, when we introduced you to stakeholder mapping, we intentionally downplayed those "affected by or interested in the policy or issue" and instead focused your attention on those "with power over its adoption or implementation." Along the way, we hope we have made it clear that some stakeholders have different resources and capabilities when it comes to representing their values and interests. In this chapter we are asking not only that the downplayed stakeholders be brought more fully into the picture, but also that you be aware of the power differences and try to bring this into better balance. The real challenge isn't recognizing that different actors have different interests (by now that should be obvious); the challenge is to try to find common ground, common purpose, and common agreements. But, considering what you know about politics and value conflict, is that possible?

The communitarian movement has found its voice in the last ten years, primarily in the well-publicized works of sociologist Amitai Etzioni. Communitarianism sees itself as a moderate- and middle-ground alternative to what it terms "radical individualism" and "excessive moralism." As Lasch (1995, 109) explains, Etzioni, who founded the prominent communitarian journal *The Responsive Community*, convincingly argues the following:

> There is more consensus than at first seems to be the case. The "values we share as a community" include a "commitment to democracy, the Bill of Rights, and mutual respect among the subgroups." Americans believe in fair treatment for all and in the "desirability of treating others with love, respect, and dignity." They believe in the virtues of tolerance and truth telling. They condemn discrimination and violence. It is the breadth and depth of this agreement ... that makes it possible to envision a "reasonable intermediate position."... Unfortunately the inordinate influence wielded by special interest groups, the media's vested stake in conflict, and the adversarial mode of justice embodied in our legal system promote conflict rather than consensus.

One major critique of the communitarian view is that it would lead to social pressure to conform to the majority's values, including the various communities' parochial and often intolerant morality. More telling are two other critiques. The first relates to what we might call the Fulcrum Principle (Archimedes already has his own "principle" regarding the displacement of water, so we won't name this the Archimedes Principle, but his is the name most associated with fulcrums).

The idea is that choices must be made and it is not always (perhaps rarely) possible to choose in a way that balances the lever on the point on which it pivots. Values like individual rights and the welfare of the community may not always, or completely, be conflicting or mutually exclusive, but they are not easily balanced either. Time is a good example. You can try to balance your time between studying for this class and having a social life, or between work and family, but in the end you must make a choice that is somewhat a zero-sum choice, at least in the short run. Another example can be found in the power of unions. Without strong unions workers often find themselves taken advantage of, placed in dangerous working conditions, and unable to share in the profits they generate. With strong unions though, we often see competitiveness hurt, the protection of the incompetent, and corruption. A final example is deciding on the size and number of groups you engage in the policy process. Small groups almost always favor active participation. Big groups are, by definition, more likely to be representative. Unless you have unlimited time, staff, and money, you can't have both. One choice tips the scales one way; the other choice tips the scales the other way. So, we must choose. We must pick our poison. We must decide what to sacrifice. We must favor one side or the other. Politics is about deciding who wins and who loses. Any other view of politics is a utopian delusion.

The second idea has two parts, both of which relate to an acceptance of the fact that the values Etzioni cites do unite us. First, although true, these values cannot determine policy—only process. This hearkens back to the definition of democracy that parallels Lippmann's view that what the public is interested in is the rules for (the process), not the substance of, policy. Second, certainly most of us agree with general principles like "freedom of speech" or "democracy," but when we start deciding what is protected speech and what isn't (flag burning?) and what democracy really means (majority rule versus minority rights?) we disagree—sometimes violently.

Communitarians find modern democracy inadequate because of its emphasis on procedural democracy, individualism, and lack of concern for community. Etzioni's most recent book on the subject, 1996's *The New Golden Rule: Community and Morality in a Democratic Society*, includes an important chapter for policy analysts called "Sharing Core Values." In this chapter Etzioni argues that current democratic practices that emphasize rational, deliberative thought are insufficient. Deliberation is a belief in democracy which assumes that by using democratic procedures, such as public hearings, as a forge, emotion and popular outrage will be tempered into policies that are well-reasoned. He quotes Jack Knight and James Johnson who write, "We view deliberation as an idealized process consisting of fair procedures within which political actors engage in reasoned argument for the purpose of resolving political conflict" (Etzioni 1996, 98). He then quotes Philip Selznick who adds, "If deliberation is taken seriously as a guiding principle, it is bound to check populist impulses. Deliberation is an appeal to reason rather than will, including popular will" (Etzioni 1996, 98). Etzioni, oddly agreeing with many of the principles of postmodern policy analysis, argues that deliberation is inadequate because information is insufficient, group values influence individuals, and because public issues are primarily normative, not empirical, questions. He then chastises both the right and left for their use of inflammatory language, in what Stone would call "strategic representation." Instead of procedural deliberation, Etzioni suggests a form of civic engagement that allows citizens to engage each other not as enemies using democratic procedures but rather as citizens with responsibilities and obligations to each other. Etzioni (1996, 104) provides several rules of what he terms "moral dialogues:"

1. "Contesting parties should not 'demonize' one another; they should refrain from depicting the other side's values as completely negative, as when they are characterized as 'satanic.'"
2. "Do not affront the deepest moral commitments of other groups."
3. "Use less of the language of rights and more of that of needs, wants, and interests."
4. "Leave some issues out of the debate."

In Etzioni's world of moral dialogues, the postmodern world of symbolism and strategic representation is replaced by one of honest discussion.[2]

Another communitarian who provides interesting guidance for policy analysts is Daniel Kemmis. Kemmis, in his 1990 book, *Community and the Politics of Place*, uses his experiences as mayor of Missoula, Montana, to promote his own brand of civic engagement. In the book, Kemmis provides several examples of political controversies that were resolved simply by making people engage other people. He is highly critical of Madisonian democracy with its emphasis on mechanistic checks and balances that keep citizens from factious politics. Instead, Kemmis (1990, 17) argues that Madisonian democracy was an approximation of **Smith's Invisible Hand**, where individual interests were merged into the public interest. He argues that Madison had abandoned the idea of citizens acting upon the public interest. Kemmis (1990, 17) writes of Madison, "It was their private interests which he wanted them to behold, to understand, and to pursue." Kemmis then reviews the political philosophy of Thomas Jefferson who believed that democratic government had to build a sense of mutual responsibility among citizens for each other through the development of civic virtue. Kemmis (1990, 21) writes, "Jefferson was appalled by the thought of large numbers of people making their living by depending solely upon the choices of other people with whom they had no social or moral ties of any kind. Yet it was this very disconnectedness which lay at the heart of Adam Smith's doctrine of the 'invisible hand' of the market."

Kemmis then reconceptualizes democracy based on Jefferson's civic virtue and Friedrich Hegel's view that American democracy would only be possible when the space of the country had been filled and the occupants of the land forced to deal with each other. Hegel had argued that the frontier in American history had always acted as an escape valve for the development of a real civic culture. With this notion and the frontier of the western United States filling up with human populations, Kemmis suggests a new democracy based on a commitment to place and each other.

As a practitioner of policy and not just a theorist, Kemmis provides many examples of his theory of civic engagement. One example (111–13) is of a community group trying to secure a community development block grant to build a laundromat that would

---

[2]Again, many contend that communitarianism tries in vain to take the "politics out of politics." Some would even argue that the political world portrayed by Deborah Stone (1997) is the natural and inevitable outgrowth of hedonistic humans who want to win in the political arena.

help generate income for a solar-powered greenhouse that would provide work for disabled, elderly, and unemployed Missoula citizens. The city's private laundromat owners were outraged that public monies were going to be used to subsidize competition. Mayor Kemmis arranged a meeting at which the laundromat owners could meet with the nonprofit greenhouse group. At the beginning of the meeting, Kemmis asked the laundromat owners to explain why they were mad and then allowed the director of the solar greenhouse project to talk. Kemmis notes that, at first, both sides wanted him to make a decision, but after some coaxing he encouraged them to talk with each other and offer compromise solutions. After some time, the greenhouse group leader decided that even though he had the votes on the city council to win, he could not go through with his revenue-generating idea. This revelation did not produce victory yells from the private laundromat owners. Instead, they were impressed by the long planning efforts of the group's director and tried to encourage him and the mayor to find other sources of revenue for the group's endeavors.

The traditional approach to this problem would have been for both groups to go before the city council and have each testify to the council members and mayor. This body would then make a decision and someone would walk away angry. Voting produces winners and losers, but the engagement approach of Kemmis made both sides take responsibility for what should be done.

We are not suggesting that you transform yourself into a facilitator of democracy because it is easier than playing the role of neutral expert. Inclusion of those not normally included in the policymaking process is, of course, no panacea. (See Box 7-4, which revisits the school shooting at Columbine High School.) In fact, it significantly complicates—and often slows—policy analysis. Still, including them in steps I–IV is essential.

7-4. Big Hearts, Cold Cash, and Value Conflict

Humanitarian aid by the U.S. government, as a percentage of GNP, has long been embarrassingly low compared to other developed economies—yet money for humanitarian aid from citizens and private sector organizations in the United States consistently leads the world. When tragedy strikes within the United States, money also flows into charity coffers in a most impressive fashion. Time and again, when the media covers a heartbreaking story, wallets open. Littleton was no exception.

Big hearts responded. Within two months, over $5 million dollars had poured into Colorado. Over two-thirds of the aid was directed to the United Way. But cold cash has a way of making people anything but united. Controversy over how to spend these funds also arose.

Some believed the money should go to the families of the victims of the shootings, especially to the families of those killed. Others wanted to include the families of those who were wounded, especially those seriously wounded. Still others thought all of those who attend or worked at the school, more than 2,000 people, should benefit.

Disagreement also centered on the question of what to use the money for. Should it only pay direct costs (funerals, medical bills, etc.) or should it be used as partial compensation for the losses? Would it be appropriate to use the money as partial compensation for the losses? Would it be appropriate to use these funds to set up programs for all of those suffering from the terrible trauma they experienced? Could it be used to make sure this sort of thing didn't happen again through an education and prevention program?

One family of a victim who died wanted only the amount of money necessary to pay for the funeral expenses, saying they didn't want to profit from what had happened. Another family argued that the money had been raised for them under the pretense of helping them, and that therefore it should go to them. Some families were upset about not being involved in the process of deciding how these funds should be allocated.

And, oh yeah, different agencies who received money had different ideas and priorities as well. Moreover, we would bet our bottom dollar that within the different agencies there were differences of opinion too. Who decides what to do with these gifts of the heart? Who should be part of the process that makes those decisions?

Value conflict, a topic we first introduced in the opening chapter, does not disappear when good people are involved. Sometimes an inclusive process helps ameliorate it; but it is ever present. It does not disappear even when there is a tragedy and big hearts respond. It is part and parcel of decision making. It is part of community. Logically, and somewhat coldly, cash tends to exacerbate it.

Democratizing Steps I–IV and the New Fifth Step

We're sorry. We apologize for our deceit, but it was quite important. In Chapter 5 we introduced you to a five-step methodology for policy analysis. Did you notice that the fifth step was about evaluation following the policy decision? Of course, in one sense, all policy analysis begins after a previous policy choice. History matters, nondecisions are decisions, and defining a problem as not being a public problem still creates a policy. Yet, in another sense, formal policy evaluation after adoption is as different from the first four steps as it is infrequent. If you want, you can, of course, call it the sixth step or Step V-B. We, however, prefer you think of evaluation research as separate from the five-step policy model, even though that was the appropriate, and common, place to locate its discussion. The inverse of the above is true as well. Before reading Chapter 6, and Chapter 7 up to this point, you weren't fully primed to grasp or evaluate our proposed fifth step. Before we explain our step five, let's back up for a minute and review the first four steps.

- Step I: Define the Problem and Determine Its Causes
- Step II: Establish Criteria to Evaluate Alternatives
- Step III: Generate Policy Alternatives
- Step IV: Evaluate and Select Policy

Postmodern policy analysis, as explained in Chapter 6, was incorporated into the five-step method before its introduction in Chapter 5. Now that you are more familiar with the language of postmodernism, we must rephrase and reemphasize its role.

The stories of the stakeholders, their narratives, are central to problem definition—as is your narrative and the determination of who is a stakeholder. This chapter has suggested that democracy demands an inclusive and democratic discourse. The stakeholders' stories, and the values they encompass, will also drive debates about evaluation criteria, and influence the generation of policy alternatives. During the fourth step, you were encouraged to use positivist methods to study the stakeholders' use of facts. Chapter 6 suggested that you would deconstruct the rhetoric and ideology and provide "facts" that were relatively more truthful than the facts presented by some stakeholders. But now what? The new fifth step argues that, while essential, it is not enough to just invite to the table voices too frequently ignored, to treat the speakers and their narratives with respect, or to work with their stories, utilizing both the insights of postmodernism and the techniques of positivism. No, our fifth step suggests you haven't done enough democracy yet. Informally, we call step five "returning to the table"; formally, we call it Civic Engagement.

Step V: Civic Engagement

Allow us to return to Etzioni and company for a minute. Can communitarianism play a role in the pragmatic work world of the public policy analyst? While communitarianism and postmodernism are drastically different in many ways, we have shown—as befits communitarianism perhaps—that there is a surprising amount of common ground as well. Additionally, while positivism and postmodernism/communitarianism may seem diametrically opposed, in the world of pragmatic policy analysis the two approaches might work well with each other. We offer, in essence, a hybrid step of analysis that blends communitarianism, postmodernism, positivism, and postpositivism. Let's see how it would have worked in the bison case.

In Chapter 6, we examined "postmodern" policy analysis, by which we used postmodern methodology to examine various narratives in the Yellowstone bison case. That analysis closed with several questions arising from rhetoric and symbolism. In that chapter, we stated that "while definitive answers may be an impossibility, and all answers will be partially political, not all stories, numbers, and claims are equally well-supported by the available evidence." We then suggested that positivist methods could be used to answer questions about brucellosis transmission, the number of cattle, economic impact, and public opinion. In short, perhaps some "facts" are more reliable than other "facts." With this information collected, positivism would suggest that the analyst now make a decision. After all, we have listened to the stakeholders, we have analyzed their views, and we have answered questions. Communitarianism, however, would suggest that we take this further. The principle of civic engagement and moral dialogues would encourage the analyst to take the newly collected data and facts to the very stakeholders whose narratives were analyzed in the first place.

At this point, the analyst facilitates sessions with the stakeholders at which the new facts deconstruct many of the ideological arguments of the stakeholders. The analyst can present the information and then allow the stakeholders to digest and recycle it. Of course, in the postmodern reality, many of the findings of the analysts are going to be disputed by some stakeholders. For example, in the bison case, it is true that there have been no scientific studies documenting transmission of brucellosis from bison to cattle in the wild. However, some ranching groups will state that there have been no attempts to study the issue and that they have evidence that transmission exists. The analyst may find that only 2,000 cattle graze in the public lands near Yellowstone, but the ranching community will say that if these cattle are infected the economic impact will go far beyond the park, as sanctions would impact all of Montana.

The analyst should follow Kemmis's lead and not allow the stakeholders to engage each other as enemies but rather as citizens occupying a common place. Through discussion, perhaps common political interests will arise. Perhaps rhetoric will be replaced by honesty and the real political and cultural issues dividing the stakeholders will finally be addressed honestly. Environmentalists, ranchers, and the business community may find that they share a common political interest in the protection of Yellowstone's lands.

Ranchers need to make profits so that they can keep their ranches and not be persuaded by big dollars to sell their land to subdivision developers. Environmentalists need to protect key wildlife habitat and migration routes found mainly in the area's riparian zones. Interestingly, many of these areas are on private lands owned by ranchers. If ranchers sell their lands to developers, key habitat and migration routes will be destroyed. Businesses rely on outside tourist dollars, and tourists come to Yellowstone to see wildlife and open spaces, not condominiums and trophy homes. Under this scenario, all three major stakeholders would have a common political interest. Out of the common interests, perhaps over time common values would emerge as the three groups worked cooperatively on projects that preserve ranching, wildlife, and open spaces. Controversies would still arise but they would be less likely to spiral into all-out political wars, since the groups would have developed interpersonal relations and modes of communication that make villainization unnecessary.

In sum, throughout the process of the first four steps, stakeholders' narratives play a key role. They also raise questions and make facts amenable, at least in part, to positivist analysis. Recognizing the limits and subjectivity of the positivist approach, you as an analyst answer those questions and study the stakeholders' use of facts. This involves weighing the evidence, conducting focus groups (refer back to Appendix 6-2), content-analyzing surveys, reading census data, searching out and evaluating scientific studies, analyzing trends, etc. You prepare a narrative of your own that deconstructs their rhetoric, clears up "factual" misunderstandings, and provides facts that are relatively more truthful than facts presented by some stakeholders.

It is then time for civic engagement. Rather than hearing the stakeholders out and then playing Solomon the wise king, return to the stakeholders. Strive to make the presented information as accessible as possible and to reveal the methodological pitfalls, assumptions, and biases associated with your research. You seek to educate (and, yes, persuade) stakeholders and tell, shall we say, your analyst story—striving to keep your personal story in the background. If you have strong feelings on the issue, someone else should probably handle the task, or you should state your bias up front and ask the stakeholders to monitor your fairness.

Civic engagement must engage. Rather than merely presenting the information, you engage the stakeholders again and facilitate another discussion, wherein the participants may reconstruct their narratives. This time (it is hoped) the dialogue is based more on "concrete information" and less on emotional rhetoric, half-truths, misunderstandings, and claims unsupported by evidence. You do not attempt to remove values from the discussion. Values are certainly a valid matter for stakeholders to raise. This is not a purely rational/scientific dialogue. On the other hand, just because one endorses the idea that people socially construct reality does not mean moving away from rational dialogue. As Lasch put it, "pragmatism holds that the impossibility of certainty does not preclude the possibility of reasoned discourse—of assertions that command provisional assent even though they lack unimpeachable foundations and are therefore subject to revision" (188–89).

The discourse must be facilitated by a trained facilitator (you); and the goal must be consensus. You do not have to have expertise in the substance of policy, but you do need to have expertise in process, and understand that positivist methods cannot be your methodology. The process is key and it is more political than empirical. Your position means that you have to do the following:

- Try to pull together differing narratives.
- Help brainstorm.
- Point out that there may be weaknesses and limits to their individual stories.
- Draw them beyond their parochial picture to focus on the larger context.
- Be perceived as a fair arbiter.

The rest of the chapter consists of advice, rules, and tools (and examples) on doing democracy. The approach you will be offered is crucial to the successful use of all five of the steps in our policy analysis model and, we would argue, to democracy.

Doing Democracy: A Postpositivist Approach

Tool #1: Discourse Rules for Achieving "Some Talk"

A major problem for the postpositivist approach to policy analysis is that, as an approach, it may replace the elite tendencies of positivism with the equally unwanted reality of anarchy. Fox and Miller (1996) argue that, in essence, typical bureaucratic policymaking is exemplified by monologic discourse or what they term "few talk." They see the postmodern world of talk shows, twenty-four-hour news cycles, and internet chat boards as "many talk." Fox and Miller (1996, 139) write of their view of many talk:

> The many-talk model is mostly random bits of phraseology and unconfirmable gossip, with no situation to channel discourse. There is no object of intentionality; no "what do we do next" question that would lend itself to policy deliberation and effective action, no situation providing contexts to the conversations. Participating in babble, however uncoerced, deflects the prospects of collective will formation and frustrates the circulation of coherent public opinion.

Fox and Miller (1996) instead suggest that public policy must be made within the context of what they term "some talk." Some talk can be seen as a middle ground between the elitist tendencies of traditional positivist policy analysis and the anarchic tendencies of real postmodern policy analysis. How can the policy analyst use postpositivist methods (which are more democratic) without falling prey to the chaotic and anarchic notions of many talk? Using Habermas, the authors provide "rules of discourse." These rules (Fox and Miller 1996, 120) include the following:

1. sincerity of the speaker
2. situation-regarding intentionality
3. willing attention
4. substantive contribution

An explanation of these rules (Fox and Miller 1996) is provided below. "Legitimate discourse" is discourse that meets the rules discussed below. The problem, of course, is that at some point there is the danger of returning the policy analyst to the position of an elite, since who is to say "what is and what is not legitimate discourse?" To counter this criticism, the authors use Hannah Arendt's "agonistic tension." To quote Fox and Miller (1996, 11), "In the discourse we can expect a struggle over meanings, we expect argumentation, claiming, and counterclaiming, not harmonious consensus, as the participants try to resolve what to do next. But discipline is needed in such discourse." The discipline is found in the rules provided by Habermas and informed by Arendt's agonistic tension.

Sincerity

Fox and Miller (121–22) argue that there are three classes of insincere claims: (1) insincere claims that betray the trust of discourse participants, (2) lame excuses for having made an insincere claim, and (3) calculated, consciously devious claims.

Situation-Regarding Intentionality

Fox and Miller (123) write, "Speakers with a situation-regarding intentionality will take into account the context of the problem, the lives of those affected, and the public interest." Claims must be connected to a situation and this avoids "the danger of levitating into postmodern hyperreality" as the "concreteness of the problematic increases."

Willing Attention

Fox and Miller (125) define this as "a spirit of vigorous, active, even passionate engagement" but at the same time "a caring for the substance, process, and results of deliberation at another level." Participants must listen and understand others viewpoints, they must be informed, and they must question the honesty or "veracity of an unwilling colleague."

Substantive Contribution

Here the authors (125) write, "Warrant for discourse can also be obtained by virtue of one's proximity to the situation, by offering a unique point of view, specific expertise, generalized knowledge, or pertinent life experience, or by being able to express the concerns of groups or classes of citizens that one (actively or passively) represents." They argue for an inclusive view of discourse where "People learn to be competent discourse participants in a developmental process that occurs over time and with ample opportunities to practice."

How does the analyst turn Fox and Miller's views into concrete tools for analysis? One method would be found in the facilitation of public meetings by policy analysts. The participatory democracy approach to policy analysis asserts that analysts must allow stakeholders to generate policy criteria, generate solutions, and ultimately choose solutions. Unfortunately, this approach is very inefficient since such an approach would invite a wide-ranging scope of voices and opinions. However the use of the discourse rules by the facilitator would help eliminate "useless discussions."

It has been asserted that a major problem with postmodern policy discourse is that most individuals are not held accountable for what they argue. Analysts send anonymous surveys to respondents who then can take verbal shots at anyone they please since they are protected by anonymity. Internet chat-boards allow users to use screen names that protect their real identity. Call-in talk shows allow citizens to argue their facts without ever having to face up to the responsibility of what they say.

A policy analyst facilitating a participatory session would want to carefully implement Fox and Miller's rules. Maybe the following example will be helpful in moving Fox and Miller's ideas from the theory book to the practice of policy analysis. After setting the discourse rules of Fox and Miller, the analyst (facilitator) proceeds as follows:

ANALYST (FACILITATOR): We are here today to discuss options for ending school violence.

PARTICIPANT #1: I think that the school shootings are a manifestation of a government conspiracy to eliminate guns. The government is training kids to kill in the hope of finding ways to ban guns.

ANALYST: Do you have any proof of this?

PARTICIPANT #1: I heard it on a talk show yesterday.

ANALYST: Did the talk show provide any proof?

PARTICIPANT #1: No

ANALYST: Then we are not going to go in this direction. (Participant #1 violated the rules of "sincerity of the speaker," "accuracy of what is claimed," and "relevance of utterances to the context of the discussion).

(15 minutes of authentic discourse occur.)

PARTICIPANT #2: There is no way that I would ever want any more regulation on my guns. It would be too time consuming and expensive for me.

PARTICIPANT #3 (TO PARTICIPANT #2): But what about the school shootings? Doesn't this justify some regulation for the good of society? Aren't you willing to sacrifice a little for a common good? (Participant #3 is enforcing the rules of discourse, #3 is making the speaker confront "situation-regarding intentionality" and "substantive contribution.")

(30 more minutes of authentic discourse occur.)

The point is that the analyst is now a facilitator enforcing the four rules of discourse and moving away from the empty symbolism and emotional rhetoric of postmodern society. The analyst does so but fully recognizes that "facts" in politics are subjective, that honest opinions will differ. The facilitator provides guidelines that attempt to keep discussions focused, honest, and relevant. In short, there is a difference between lying and subjective interpretation, there is a difference between grand philosophizing and problem solving.

The philosopher Eric Voeglin, writing on the issue of willingness to participate in a rational discussion, also contributes to the sort of understanding a facilitator needs. Voeglin's essay (found in an anthology of Western thought edited by Hunold 1961, 269–84) takes us back to Plato's Protagoras.[3] In this dialogue, Socrates and Protagoras are debating the possibility of teaching virtue. As Voeglin accurately reports, Protagoras makes a "brilliant speech, embellished with the Prometheus fable, richly interwoven with common-sense wisdom, and even a witty reference to one of the theatrical successes of the season...." The speech, read orally, "takes between twenty and thirty minutes to deliver." Socrates is not pleased with this prolixity, because he recognizes that Protagoras seeks to avoid rational discussion. He is violating the rules of debate to avoid the serious scrutiny of his ideas. Voeglin claims, insightfully, that "in our modern society ... preventing rational discussion has been reduced to such a fine art that it would require a really comprehensive monograph to exhaust the subject." However, he limits himself to cataloging a few of the major variations. Voeglin identifies five methods.

The first method is a group of tricks that goes back to the Sophists. They are "simple, but effective. Their fundamental principle is that they must exhaust the time ... by means of verbosity, appeals to authorities and so on." The second method, also a group of tricks dating back to the time of Plato, Voeglin calls "back-stair psychology." The key here is to skirt around the issue, and he provides the example of attacking the opponent's line of argument as being based on a faulty political ideology or on the opponent's economic interests. Classification is the third method identified. Here, rather than addressing the opponent's argument, one demolishes it by classifying them and their position. (Voeglin tells how he had been classified and dismissed at various times as a Catholic, a Protestant, an anti-Semitic, a typical Jew, a liberal, a conservative, and a fascist.) Voeglin's fourth method involves a systematic dogmatism, namely, making the statement that values absolutely do not belong in rational discussions. One example he gives is brushing aside discussions of values as being unscientific. The fifth and final method he lists is connected to what Voeglin calls "the neo-positivist method of social sciences." While value is not an appropriate topic for debate, the method is. Thus the debate gets stuck arguing about the method used rather than the fundamental questions.

Voeglin's contribution is the recognition not only of more violations to watch for (although a great contribution), but also the recognition that rational discussion cannot occur if participants wish to stop it. Thus, issues we will soon broach, such as ground rules for meetings, help from participants in enforcing the rules, setting the tone, grounding, and selling the process are all key matters. Box 7-5 provides an explanation of one of the problems of our current public discourse.

---

[3]We are indebted to Dr. Michael Federici for introducing us to Voeglin's philosophy and sharing his expertise on its interpretation.

7-5. Monologic Communication

Monologic communication is an oxymoron, a contradiction in terms. The term "monologic" is used to denote one-way communication. In other words, monologic refers to the dissemination of information. The receiver of the information has no means to confront the speaker on meaning. The speaker does not have to justify what is spoken. In contrast, communication refers to "evoking understanding between two or more people." In a conversation, the speaker and receiver go back and forth, testing meaning and searching for common understanding.

Much of what passes as our public conversation in contemporary times is really monologic information dissemination. Look at these examples taken from a week of political news from a local newspaper:

- "Most of the kids who shoot other kids come from single-parent families." (Letter to the editor)
- "Environmentalists are working with the United Nations to take over our public lands." (From a story on road closings in a national forest)
- "The city is trying to take my property over. It is already a crime that I must pay taxes for a school that I don't use but now they want my property also. (From a story on a city's plan to create an area of impact outside the city's boundaries—the statement was made at a public hearing)

In each of these instances, the speaker is not challenged. In the first example, the newspaper failed to include a parenthetical quote that revealed that nearly all the kids involved in the school shootings came from two-parent families. In the second comment, the journalist did not ask the speaker to provide specific evidence of the environmental and United Nations conspiracy. Contemporary journalism is more interested in sensationalism and a good quote than they are in fact finding. Outrageous quotes like the ones provided here often go unchallenged in newspaper, television, and radio outlets across the country. The third example, from a public hearing, likewise went unchallenged, not only in the newspaper but in the public hearing itself. City planners had tried to explain to this individual earlier that if an "area of impact" is created, the city can annex this person's farm property only if he sells it to a subdivision developer. One person on the city council tried to explain this to the speaker but he was barked down by the angry resident.

In all of these examples, individuals were allowed to make statements of "facts," when in all three cases their remarks were purely declarations of opinion, bias, stereotype, anger, or frustration. But these uninformed sources of information quickly feed the policy "dialogue" and most often contribute to conflict, incorrect problem definition, and hostility toward government rather than partial consensus and democratic problem solving.

Tool #2: Futuring

Background   During the Clinton administration, the U.S. Department of Housing and Urban Development (HUD) adopted a new approach in their efforts to deal with homelessness. This approach, known as the Continuum of Care, sought to "encourage" communities to develop a coordinated and community-based process of identifying needs and building a system to respond to those needs. All projects seeking funding were forced to be part of a consolidated or associated approach. HUD's nationally competitive grant process awarded points for several different factors. Scoring on a 100-point basis, only 40 points were based on needs per se. The process and strategy used to develop the proposals was worth 30 points (inclusivity and collaboration being key), and carefully tethering the proposed projects to the priority of needs established through the Continuum of Care process as well as the extent to which those projects are consistent with that priority, can score you another 20 points. The final 10 points depended on leveraging your proposal with other dollars from private and state and local government sources. Struggles over turf, agency competition rather than cooperation, glaring gaps instead of a seamless system, and failure to see the big picture were problems this approach sought to overcome.

Evidence gathered by the Mercyhurst College Institute for Child and Family Policy as part of assisting with the grant application suggested that on any given night there were approximately four hundred homeless people sleeping in emergency shelters and transitional living facilities in Erie County, and approximately six hundred more requests (from individuals and families) that were not being served. Erie County, comprising the city of Erie (third largest in Pennsylvania) and thirty-eight other municipalities, had failed to overcome its fragmented system, and its 1996 HUD application was not funded. Spurred by this failure, Erie County and the city government created a new process designed to meet HUD's requirements.

Beginning in March 1997, a series of meetings were held that included fifty-two service providers and advocacy groups. As a result, a broad-based permanent coordinating committee was established, a mission statement was drafted and approved, and a process was established to annually allow service providers to collaboratively respond to the needs of the homeless through a fair, open, and inclusive competition for inclusion into the community's Consolidated Application to HUD. Along with surveys and other research being done, the permanent committee decided that it was important to have an open forum where the concerns, ideas, and beliefs of homeless service providers, homeless advocates, and homeless and formerly homeless persons could be shared. At the direction of one of your authors, this was advertised as a futuring session. Over a hundred professionals and homeless/formerly homeless were invited to participate.

In May 1997, the futuring session began at 9:00 A.M. at a neutral site, with an exercise that led to a discussion of dominance, cooperation, compromise, negotiation, and nonverbal communication relative to having a successful dialogue, overcoming obstacles, and succeeding through trust and having a common goal.

The participants were then introduced to the idea that "futuring" is not just about facts, but is also a social interaction process that recognizes that people have feelings, that values fairness and inclusivity, that honestly seeks (rather than provides) input, and that is sensitive to the issues we had just discussed as part of the exercise. A set of ground rules drawn up by the facilitator were then reviewed and accepted by the participants, who agreed to be the "enforcers" of any violations by anyone—including the facilitator. These rules were as follows:

1. Personal attacks will not be tolerated.
2. The integrity, motivations, and values of participants will not be questioned.
3. The facilitator will not impose his personal views.
4. Disagreements will be regarded as valuable discoveries.
5. The session will not be used as a "gripe session"—the focus of the session will be on the future.
6. It is the joint responsibility of the facilitator and all participants to make sure the ground rules are observed.
7. It is the responsibility of the participants to come to a consensus as to what was said, even if unable to reach consensus on the issues.
8. Under no circumstances will the meeting continue past noon.

Futuring was explained to the participants as the name of a simple process that could be described technically as: (1) having a community list input on cards that are collected; (2) using that input to identify and discuss issues and goals—and all input received will be kept; (3) further using the discussion to combine this information into a broader and smaller set of issues and goals deemed critical by and for the community. It was explained that we would look for cross-themes, for ideas at odds, and try to narrow—without losing anything—the list of issues and goals.

Participants were told that the assumptions, philosophical premises, and aspirations behind futuring were as follows:

• To provide adequate and equal opportunities to express preferences
• To create commitment to, and a sense of community ownership and control over, the goals, priorities, and processes of the community through participation
• To gather data, to strive for consensus, and to honestly seek direction from the community (i.e., it is not to be an opportunity to direct your choices)

The facilitator told participants that input from them was desired, required, and hopefully would be acquired. The role of the leader (one of your authors), an outsider to the service provider community with no real stake in the outcome other than concern for the community and the individuals of the community, was explained as being not to educate but to facilitate and to help the participants successfully complete their roles. The participants' role was explained as being the primary initiators in clarifying, prioritizing, planning, and then perhaps directing this community's effort to better address this serious need (i.e., to be both leaders and listeners).

The session then began by providing the participants with a list of eight high-priority needs identified by the community through the Gaps Analysis Survey, the Client Survey, a spring 1995 group forum, and the HUD Grant needs criteria. The participants were asked to prioritize this list in a way that allowed it to be scored using three different voting systems.

First, they ranked all eight priorities from most to least important. It was explained to them that this allowed for two separate scoring systems. The total points would be summed to identify importance using the "Borda Count" method, where the lowest point total is best. It would also be scored using the simple "plurality" system where each "number one" vote represented their most important priority.

Second, they identified all of the priorities they felt to be of "first tier" importance through an asterisk in an example of "approval voting." With approval voting, a vote is cast for all of the "options" approved of. The participants were told that the results from this part of the session would be presented to them at their next meeting.

The participants were then asked to write down on one side of a note card one or two things that are positive things that this community is doing well to address the problems of the homeless, and on another card to record one or two things that are negatives, or issues of concern, in terms of how the community is responding to the problems of the homeless. On a third card, the participants were asked to briefly identify what the Erie County Continuum of Care would look like in five, seven, or ten years if it was a success.

The bulk of the rest of the session was used to have the participants discuss, explain, explicate, and, where appropriate, consolidate the positives and negatives identified. The facilitator, with the help of a skilled assistant, listed the results on a large flip chart. Twelve participants listed as positive the process and cooperation now being developed, four listed the inclusion of consumers, and eight mentioned the high level of commitment among providers that produced a willingness to forego turf battles. All of these comments were linked by a theme identified by the participants as "process."

Finally, before ending the session on time, participant responses to the question of envisioning success were read back to them. As throughout the session, participants could identify themselves as authors or not. One advantage of using the cards is that it allows participants to remain anonymous. Of course there are trade-offs to this approach, but a recent study (Morrell 1999, 293–322) suggested that small groups, mirroring, and other techniques sometimes used during discussions can lower collective decision acceptance because the participants get tied too closely to their views.

At a follow-up meeting, the results of their three votes were revealed and discussed. They were presented as well with the detailed results from the listing and discussion of the positives and negatives, and a summary (and the raw comments) from the envisioning success question. The facilitator once again provided the participants with the chance to discuss, clarify, and correct the information gathered from them.

It was then explained that these results would be used to complement the other data in generating the local Request For Proposal (RFP), and indeed it was. Appropriately, it was then used to design a Goeller Scorecard used by a seven-member selection committee to grade proposals for the Consolidated Application to HUD. With the new process in place, money from HUD once again started flowing into the community.

Story: Good and Bad Facilitation   Sometimes the best way to learn how to be a good facilitator is to watch a bad facilitator in practice. A state government regulatory agency had started a program that would allow communities greater input into the regulatory process and wanted to conduct a series of community input sessions to begin the program. Communities, under this new program, could prioritize their environmental problems. Then communities would work with state and federal agencies to fix these problems and use timetables and financial arrangements that met the community's needs.

An outside facilitator was asked to facilitate two of the meetings. This person traveled over 140 miles to the first meeting. The meeting's goal was simply to seek initial community input on regulatory matters. The facilitator had planned to pass out 3 x 5 index cards, record responses on a flip chart, and allow the citizens to articulate their concerns about environmental regulation. The facilitator arrived and met the state agency personnel. The meeting began at around 7:00 P.M. with about ten citizens in attendance. The originator of the agency program decided that he wanted to kick off the evening's session by introducing the program. He went into a long speech telling the audience how this program already "had made national headlines" and how the "program was going to be a model for the rest of the country to follow." Like a good politician, and unlike a good facilitator, the agency person talked and talked and talked about this great "community-based" program and how local citizens and elected officials could have input into regulatory matters. Unfortunately and ironically, the citizens and elected officials who had attended this session were never given any chance to articulate their views. Soon it was 8:30 P.M. and the tired citizens began to leave, as they had other commitments. The outside facilitator who had been asked by the agency to come to this meeting (traveling 140 miles) was never given a chance to say a word or to facilitate a real public input session. Instead, all in attendance were forced to listen to the words of a self-aggrandizing politician.

The facilitator was asked to facilitate another meeting for the agency some two months later. This time the facilitator traveled about 160 miles through a mid-January snowstorm. This second meeting was held at a local high school gym. Again the facilitator had flip-charts and index cards ready and wanted to allow the citizens and elected officials in attendance to speak. The meeting started and once again everyone present was treated to a ninety-minute speech that informed the audience of the "importance of the project," "the national scope of the project," and how truly "innovative this really is." Finally, after 90 minutes the speech was over. The outside facilitator handed out some index cards, collected them, and went home.

His two trips were not wasted however. He learned a great deal about facilitation and about the strengths of his own style. He arrived at these conclusions:

- A good facilitator is a good listener. A bad facilitator is more interested in listening to himself or herself.
- A good facilitator "disappears in a room." That is, a good facilitator simply sets up and enforces ground rules and moves the process in a certain direction. A bad facilitator is the "show" and wants to be the center of attention.
- A good facilitator is not afraid of receiving information that might be critical of the facilitator or the program. A bad facilitator carefully arranges questions and situations so criticism is avoided. A bad facilitator is a manipulator of views.
- A good facilitator asks questions. A bad facilitator answers questions.
- A good facilitator is humble. A bad facilitator is arrogant.

As you begin your policy analysis career, be sure to watch the facilitation skills of others. Most likely, you will meet skilled individuals who can gather citizen input easily and gracefully. In fact, facilitation is most easily learned from watching others do it successfully. Both of your authors have had the opportunity to watch skilled and talented facilitators. Don't, however, discount watching bad facilitators, for in their incompetence you can often identify the exact components which make a good or bad facilitation style.

Tool # 3: Conflict Resolution and Consensus Building Techniques

There are several techniques available for resolving conflicts among groups of individuals and for achieving consensus. The following technique is one that has been used extensively in rural development issues and should be of use to analysts promoting participatory democratic approaches.

Phase I: Establish a Grounding and Ground Rules for the Issue   **Grounding** is an important activity with which to start any meeting. Participants arrive at meetings with some level of apprehension or uncertainty about what will occur. The process of grounding allows the apprehension of the participant to be recognized. To understand this conflict resolution approach, we must first understand the problems and limitations of traditional public hearing methods. Typically, public meetings are set up in a hierarchical style, with decision makers sitting at a podium or table that is typically higher than the rest of the audience. Speakers then walk up to a microphone and are given a set period of time to make their arguments. There is no interplay between the speaker and the rest of the audience and the interplay between the speaker and the elected officials is limited. Typically, one of the elected officials, normally the mayor, will tell the speaker when time is up and might answer specific questions posed by the speaker. Speakers cannot engage elected officials in any discourse and elected officials do not attempt to engage the speaker. In addition, there is no attempt to build consensus among the different speakers. The citizen and interest group speakers simply make their points and then the elected body votes on the issue at hand. This type of public meeting represents a very thin version of democracy. Participants who come to conflict resolution sessions are likely to expect this type of hearing. They will come to the meeting with a prepared five-to-ten minute presentation that represents their agenda.

Conflict resolution techniques get drastically away from traditional public hearing approaches. First, the facilitator arranges the room in a circle. All participants, including elected officials or any other influentials, sit in the circle. The circle approach is explained to the participants, emphasizing that there is no hierarchy in the circle and that everyone in the circle is considered equal.

One of your authors once facilitated a conflict resolution session in a small town. The issue involved annexation. The session was held at the city council meeting room. The mayor of the community wanted to sit at his normal chair, which was placed on a platform some three feet higher than the rest of the room. As the meeting began, the mayor refused to sit in the circle of participants, instead, sitting mightily above the proceedings. After some thirty minutes, the facilitator had to stop the meeting and again ask the mayor to sit in the circle. His comments, directed down to the circle, were destroying any chance of finding consensus. The mayor again refused and the facilitator called for an early break. The facilitator asked the help of some community elites who then negotiated with the mayor to sit in the circle. After some fifteen minutes, he agreed to come down and sit with the participants and the meeting became very constructive. The facilitator should not have even started the meeting with the mayor on his perch, for the sight of the mayor sitting above the circle violated a major ground rule of the session.

In addition, it is important that the facilitator assigns seats within the circle. Otherwise, allies will sit together and enemies will sit apart. The facilitator must also explain that the circle allows the participants to occupy the room with the sound of their voice and thus helps them establish verbal territory. Once a person's voice is in a room, it becomes easier for them to speak, especially if others listen to them. The facilitator then sets the ground rules for the session. The exact ground rules depend on the nature of the conflict, structure of the meeting, participants, and time frame. The ground rules would be tailored from the four Fox and Miller discourse rules, Voeglin's insights, and the following:

- All participants will listen with respect.
- There will be no personal attacks.
- Each participant will be given ample time to present their views.

At the beginning of the session, the facilitator may want the participants to introduce themselves to each other (with smaller groups, a team-building exercise may be useful). In addition, participants should be given the full opportunity to voice their apprehensions about the meeting and to "get anything off their chest." Typically, participants will note that they "doubt much will be accomplished" or that they are "very tense about this whole situation."

The circle is an intense process. It forces individuals who might not like each other very much into an environment where they must deal with each other as human beings rather than as the abstract enemy. It is very important that the facilitator enforce the ground rules from the beginning. Once a model of listening with respect has been established and enforced, respondents are likely to follow the lead of the facilitator in their behavior.

Phase II: Establish a Two-to-Four-Person Panel to Talk about the Issue The facilitator should have prior knowledge of the composition of the participants in order to assure that the panel is made up of individuals on both sides of the issue. The rest of the group is told to listen carefully and take notes.

Phase III: Question Answering and Listening These sessions typically revolve around controversy that was generated from either an already implemented policy or a suggested policy. With this in mind, the following two questions need to be asked:

1. What is your view of the situation?
2. How do you feel about it?

Begin with an individual who represents the current policy (or proposed policy) discussing her view of the situation and how she feels about it. For example, in the Yellowstone bison case, a representative from the State of Montana would present their views of the Interim Bison Management Plan. A person from the other party would respond by answering the same two questions. This is repeated by the other panel members, in turn. Establishing the panel provides order to begin the discussion. The party with the issue begins by describing it in both intellectual and emotional terms. The other party gets to provide their group's view and this brings balance. The panel members are expected to represent their group views, clearly define issues as they see them, and speak for only three-to-five minutes per panel member.

Phase IV: Listeners Respond to the Panelists   The rest of the group then responds to what they heard from the panelists. Three questions are posed to the listeners:

- What did you hear or learn from the panelists?
- What is your view of the situation?
- How do you feel about the situation?

The listening members are first asked to report what they heard. The facilitator or an assistant uses a flip-chart to quickly summarize the listener's points, thus beginning a record of the event. This response allows the panelists to hear how clearly they were listened to and how clearly they presented the issue. In stating their view of the situation and how they feel about it, the listeners add to the common information base.

Phase V: Panelists Respond to the Listeners   In the reverse order in which they spoke, the panelists are given the opportunity to respond to the listener's report. This allows the panelists to clear up any misunderstandings and add any additional clarifying data. Again, this information is written quickly on flip-charts and added to the common knowledge base.

Phase VI: Key Issues   Each participant is then provided a three-by-five index card and asked to write down the key issues they have heard so far. This information is recorded on the flip chart and posted on a wall or bulletin board, along with any earlier flip-chart pages. The entire group must be comfortable with what has been written on the flip-charts. Typically, the facilitator and assistant will try to summarize and combine information so that a coherent elaboration of the participants' views are included. It is important that no views are excluded.

Phase VII: Declaration of Worst Outcomes   The facilitator then directs the participants toward the collective statement and asks them, "Based on this information, what are the outcomes that you do not want?" Responses of the participants are then recorded on a flip-chart. This phase is important because most individuals organize to prevent something from happening and this approach allows the participants to constructively lay their agendas out on the table.

Phase VIII: Break At this point, the session has probably taken at least one and one-half hours.

Phase IX: Declaration of Best Outcomes Upon reconvening, the facilitator asks the participants to return their attention to the collective statement of the group and asks them, "Based on this information, what is the best possible outcome that you want?" This question is rarely asked in policy debates, instead, energies are most likely focused on avoiding worst outcomes. This question attempts to move the participants toward positive energy. Once again, answers are recorded on a flip-chart.

Phase X: Develop a Collective Statement of the Worst and Best Outcomes The collective statement puts all the views together in one group statement. This will take some time to put together and will be posted on a flip-chart once again.

Phase XI: Best Outcome Policies The participants are then asked to brainstorm for policies, strategies, and actions that would result in the best outcomes being realized. All input is recorded and none is judged at this point. This allows the group to explore options or action items that might solve the issues.

Phase XII: Solution or Solutions The facilitator asks, based on Phase XI, "What is the solution we seek that would make the best outcome happen?" The facilitator should discuss this question with the group and see if any common answer arises. The facilitator should never force an answer on the group or ask the group to force an answer. If no common solution arises, the facilitator moves to another step and waits until another day for consensus.

Phase XIII: Closure The facilitator asks the participants the following questions:

- How do you feel about what we did?
- What did you learn that will help us?
- How do you feel about the progress made at this session?
- What must we do to continue to be successful?

The participants' answers should help you design the next session.

Ethics as Democracy

Postmodernism originates from a political view that sets forth normative claims. These claims urge the adoption of an ethical code that seeks a fuller democracy. Postmodernism worries about the lack of citizen's stories in the policy process. In essence, the key ethical charge of postmodernism is the promotion of a broad, participatory dialogue. A postmodern analyst would listen for the narratives of, and advocate for, the weak; tear down walls that oppress and obscure; and work toward the sort of democracy where the stories of everyday people are as valued as the stories of experts and other powerful players. But hold on; aren't these ideas bizarre, extreme, and utopian? Is democracy really the key ethical issue for public policy analysis? Are these positions shared by other viewpoints or somehow unique to postmodernists? Consider three voices outside the postmodernist camp: H. George Frederickson, John Rawls, and a recent report on citizenship.

The place was Syracuse University's Minnowbrook conference site; the year was 1968; and the world was in turmoil. Dwight Waldo, noted public administration scholar, was the editor-in-chief of the leading journal in the field, *Public Administration Review (PAR)*. Waldo believed that turmoil, perhaps even revolution, was also affecting public administration, so he invited a number of younger academics to what became known as the "Minnowbrook Conference." H. George Frederickson's paper *Toward a New Public Administration* was clearly one of the most significant papers to come out of the conference. The essence of this paper was that, to the old values of public administration (particularly efficiency), *New Public Administration* added the value of "social equity." Social equity meant enhancing the political power and economic well-being of minorities for whom pluralistic government was a losing proposition because they lacked the resources to compete (money, votes, and presence in positions of power).

This was a dramatic paradigm shift that called for maximalist ethics (one is obligated to use power for the good; it is too dangerous to disconnect one's behavior from moral standards of right and wrong; ethics as beyond the law) to replace minimalist ethics (administering without sympathy or enthusiasm; it is unethical to use one's position in service of personal values; ethics as whatever the law says). In short, public administrators, contrary to Max Weber's ideal of neutral competence and the politics/administration dichotomy, should not be neutral, and public organizations should make sure their results distribute the "goods" to the have nots.

Frederickson also detailed how to make this happen, including making the organizational structure of the public organizations less hierarchical and less authoritative; teaching public sector workers to tolerate conflict and ambiguity; and breaking down boundaries between the organization and its clients. *New Public Administration* was significant because it had a powerful impact on practitioners.

Postmodernism also calls for advocacy for the disadvantaged, for social equity, and for inclusion of the disadvantaged, in terms of both consideration and actual input, in the decision-making process. This leads us to Rawls. John Rawls is the most famous name in the area of distributive justice. His central focus was the idea of justice as fairness. When trying to make a moral choice, Rawls suggested that what was fair, was just.

His key suggestion for achieving fair decisions was adopting a "veil of ignorance." The idea of this veil is that you should make decisions as if you were the one on the end of those decisions. Remember Stone's story of dividing up the cake? Rawl's point is that if one group gets to cut the pieces (e.g., the nine males in the class), and another group gets to decide how to distribute the pieces (let's say the nine females), the males will divide the cake into eighteen equal-sized pieces. They will do so, hoping that the women will distribute it "fairly." Moreover, Rawls says that this is how we should always make decisions, as if we are on the receiving end of the decision and are looking out for our own best interests.

In an introductory public administration class taught by one of your authors, the students read Jonathan Kozol's (1995) powerful nonfiction story (*Amazing Grace*) of poverty in the South Bronx and the inspiring, and yes, amazing grace with which the impoverished people conduct their lives in the face of racism, indifference, violence, poverty, and bureaucratic failure. One common reaction of students is a sense that they would not like to be treated as these citizens were by the government and public workers.

Our discussion turned to Rawls' veil of ignorance, fairness, and a recognition by the students that, in contrast to the stereotypes of disadvantaged neighborhoods, the people Kozol introduced them to were not that different from themselves—and that many of them, against all odds, were leading heroic and inspiring lives. Indignation aimed toward failed and flawed policymaking ran strong, as did the idea that those in charge should follow Rawls' decision-making advice and his definition of justice as fairness. Postmodernism differs not with the idea of fairness as justice, but argues for replacing the "veil of ignorance" with "knowledge revealed." What we mean is that, rather than guessing what people would want, one could actually ask them. (Don't you think it's possible that people who have been through the welfare system might have valuable insight into how to reform it?)

Finally, the National Commission on Civic Renewal released a report in the late 1990s that, like many other organizations and experts, criticized the state of citizenry in the United States. Their study's conclusion about the state of democracy was revealed in the title: *A Nation of Spectators: How Civic Disengagement Weakens America and What We Can Do About It* <http://www.puaf.umd.edu/civicrenewal>. There emerged in the late '90s a general consensus that the lack of civic participation reflected in but certainly not limited to voting was a serious problem. The various calls for greater citizen involvement share with postmodernism a belief that public discourse is central to democracy.

Thus, the ideas of postmodernism are not bizarre or extreme. They may not be utopian, but there are no easy answers, and few—if any—suggested directly by postmodernists. Are their positions shared by other viewpoints or somehow unique to postmodernists? The postmodern normative position is not totally unique, but the emphasis and the insights on language and stories are very valuable. Is democracy really the key ethical issue for policy analysis? Well, that is a subjective judgment call, but perhaps democracy is the key ethical issue for public policy analysis if the following apply:

- If you assume that a fuller democracy is central to fairness and justice
- If you believe that everyone has stories to tell and that those normally excluded should have more say in the decisions that affect their lives
- If you believe that increased and enhanced participation is central to strengthening democracy

Concluding Thoughts

Remember that major issues cannot be solved in quick three-hour meetings. Instead, the process that we introduced provides you, a policy analyst, with a method of participatory policy analysis, that if, given time and the right amount of skill, might well provide some consensual solutions to major policy issues. Moreover, the process itself is important. You will also be doing democracy, and increasing civic literacy. This is the fifth step. The mini-case that follows provides you with an opportunity to reconceptualize the entire five-step model.

Southern-Fried Analyst

The city you work for is the largest in the South. Yesterday, during lunch, you found an interesting site <http://www.cpn.org> that described an organization called the Civic Practices Network. You remembered having read about it before, so last night you dug out your all-time favorite text from your classes at the university, and stayed up late into the evening rereading the seventh chapter and its advice regarding "doing democracy." Wow, are you ever glad you didn't sell it to one of those used-book companies for about an eighth of what you paid for it. Even if you use it only once every two years, it would be worth the pittance they offered you for this classic. Shoot, for the amount of money they wanted to pay, you couldn't even eat lunch at the food court.

Anyway, today it is aggressively hot and humid, your boss Juanita calls you in and tells you that Mayor Ahmed Kieron wants the city policy shop where you work to prepare a report on where the city should be in 2025. What the mayor wants is a Blueprint 2025 that will serve as a sort of strategic plan for the community in the decades to come. He wants the final report in no more than fourteen months, ideally sooner.

Juanita respects your skills as an analyst, but this is ridiculous. You are to have a three-page executive summary on her desk tomorrow morning (for goodness sakes), that lays out how you would go about developing such a report.

Explain, in a paragraph or two, the philosophy that would drive your design, and then provide as many specifics as you can, as specifically as you can, without exceeding the three-page limit (normal size font, normal margins, double-spaced). Be prepared to discuss this orally, and to defend it from the budget-conscious office cynic known as "the professor."

Key Concepts

communitarianism and democracy (p. 246)
conflict resolution and consensus building techniques (p. 262)
defining democracy (p. 236)
democracy as an ambiguous symbol (p. 236)
discourse rules for achieving "some talk" (p. 253)
doing democracy: a postpositivist approach (p. 253)

futuring (p. 258)
postmodern critique of positivism and democracy (p. 240)
Step V: Civic Engagement (p. 251)
structuring democracy (p. 244)
democratizing steps I–IV (p. 250)

Glossary Terms

grounding (p. 262)
Smith's Invisible Hand (p. 248)

References

American Society of Public Administration (ASPA). *Code of Ethics.* <http://www.aspanet.org.>

Barber, Benjamin R. 1984. *Strong Democracy: Participatory Politics for a New Age.* Berkeley, CA: University of California Press.

Biddle, William W., and Loureide J. Biddle. 1965. *The Community Development Process: The Rediscovery of Local Initiative.* New York: Holt, Rinehart and Winston, Inc.

Carnevale, David G. 1995. *Trustworthy Government: Leadership and Management Strategies for Building Trust and High Performance.* San Francisco, CA: Jossey-Bass Publishers.

Chambers, Robert, Randall Clemons, and Richard H. Foster. 1990. "Leadership and Community Revitalization." *Economic Development Review* 8, no. 3:29–34.

Dahl, Robert A. 1982. *Dilemmas of Pluralist Democracy: Autonomy vs. Control.* New Haven, CT: Yale University Press.

Danziger, Marie. 1995. "Policy Analysis Postmodernized: Some Political and Pedagogical Ramifications." *Policy Studies Journal* 23, no. 3:435–50.

deLeon, Peter. 1997. *Democracy and the Policy Sciences.* Albany, NY: State University of New York.

Etzioni, Amitai. 1996. *The New Golden Rule: Community and Morality in a Democratic Society.* New York: Basic Books.

Fox, Charles J., and Hugh T. Miller. 1996. *Postmodern Public Administration: Toward Discourse.* Thousand Oaks, CA: Sage Publications.

Held, David. 1987. *Models of Democracy.* Stanford, CT: Stanford University Press.

Frederickson, George H. 1971. *Toward a New Public Administration: The Minnowbrook Perspective.* Edited by Frank E. Marini. Chandler Publishing Co.

Hunold, Albert, ed. 1961. *Freedom and Serfdom: An Anthology of Western Thought.* Dordrecht, Holland: D. Reidel Publishing Company. Pp. 269–84.

Kemmis, Daniel. 1990. *Community and the Politics of Place.* Norman, OK: University of Oklahoma Press.

Kozol, Jonathon. 1995. *Amazing Grace: The Lives of Children and the Conscience of a Nation.* New York: Crown Publishers, Inc.

Lasch, Christopher. 1995. *The Revolt of the Elites and the Betrayal of Democracy.* New York: W. W. Norton and Company.

Lasswell, Harold D. 1966. *The Analysis of Political Behavior: An Empirical Approach.* Hamden, CT: Archon Books.

Lawler, Edward E. 1996. *From the Ground Up: Six Principles for Building the New Logic Corporation.* San Francisco, CA: Jossey-Bass Publishers.

Morrell, Michael E. 1999. "Citizens' Evaluations of Participatory Democratic Procedures: Normative Theory Meets Empirical Science." *Political Research Quarterly* 52, no. 2 (June): 293–322.

Osborne, David, and Ted Gaebler. 1992. *Reinventing Government*. Reading, MA: Addison-Wesley Publishing Co.

Peirce, Neal. 1998. "A County Budget that Is for and by the People." *Erie Daily Times*, 5A-6A.

Peters, B. Guy. 1996. *Governing: Four Emerging Models*. Lawrence, KS: University Press of Kansas.

Public Administration Review. 1998. May/June.

Public Administration Review. 1998. July/August.

Rawls, John. 1971. *A Theory of Justice*. Cambridge, MA: Belknap Press of Harvard University Press.

Schachter, Hindy Lauer. 1997. *Reinventing Government or Reinventing Ourselves*. Albany, NY: State University of New York.

Simon, Herbert. 1998. "Why Public Administration?" *Public Administration Review* 58, no. 1:ii.

Stone, Deborah. 1997. *Policy Paradox: The Art of Political Decision Making*. New York: W. W. Norton.

Study Circles Resource Center. 1998. *Focus on Study Circles* (Pomfret, CT) 9, no. 4 (fall).

Watson, Douglas J. 1997. *Innovative Governments: Creative Approaches to Local Problems*. New York: Praeger.

Zanetti, Lisa A., and Adrian Carr. 1999. "Exaggerating the Dialectic: Postmodernism's 'New Individualism' and the Detrimental Effects on Citizenship." *Administrative Theory & Praxis* 21, no. 2:205–17.

CHAPTER 8

THE POSITIVIST TOOLBOX

Integrated Case
"Sheila the Policy Analyst"

Okay, so you are probably tired by now. After all, we have challenged your mind by providing you with a theoretical understanding of policy analysis. You understand how public problems are politically created. You have a basis to evaluate theoretical models and know the strengths, limitations, and uses of the rational model and the political model. You have spent time in Allegheny County and Yellowstone National Park. You have seen the failings of American policy in Vietnam and debated the causes of school shootings. In short, you should start to feel that you are becoming familiar with the role of the policy analyst. You have knowledge and skills. These skills—stakeholder mapping, narrative analysis, content analysis, focus group facilitation—are going to be useful for any future policy analyst. We would like to conclude and send you on your way now. That is, have you go out into the world and practice the policy analysis taught in this book. But unfortunately, there are a large number of skills that you still need to learn.

This chapter includes what we call "positivist tools" of analysis and we present them to you in the form of a toolbox. Think about the metaphor of a toolbox for a minute. Let's suppose that you were repairing a fence in your backyard. We decide that you need some tools to help you build the fence and we want to teach you how to use the tools necessary to build a fence. We are skilled but practical carpenters who don't lift weights, so our toolbox only has tools in it that we use a lot. We have removed tools that we rarely, if ever, use. To build a fence, you only need a few tools (a hammer, a drill, a tape measure, a level, a power saw, a handsaw). When we show up at your door, we don't have to teach you how to use all of the tools in the toolbox. Instead, you need only learn how to use those tools necessary to build a fence. But in the future when you decide to build a new deck in your backyard you will know that you have a toolbox nearby with all the major tools necessary to build the deck.

This metaphor explains how we see this chapter. It is not a chapter that is easily read from page to page. However, as we explain later, we believe that we would be failing the reader if we did not include these basic positivist tools of analysis. But just like building a fence, you don't always have to use all the tools in the toolbox. Instead, your professor should determine which tools in the box are most important for the goals of the class. While you may skip the discussion of some tools, you may also come back to them later as you begin or continue your careers as policy analysts. For each tool, our goal was to provide a clear, albeit basic, understanding of how and when to use it, and the limitations of that tool. Both of us have our favorite textbooks from our college days and we often go back to them for specific information. We hope that this chapter can play that role for you and that as you actually do policy analysis this chapter, along with the others, will be referred to often.

Finally, some of these tools might even be described more as research methods tools rather than traditional policy analysis tools. However, it is our belief that they are all necessary tools that a practicing analyst must use. When we were students, we were frustrated when textbooks only made casual references to certain methods and then informed the reader: "This topic is beyond the scope of the course." The reality is that in many smaller undergraduate programs and master of public administration programs, students will not have the opportunity to take a research methods course that is geared solely toward practicing policy analysts—that is, in most programs, students will take a general research methods course but not one that deals specifically with applied methods in policy analysis. We want to avoid the narrow drawing of lines between fields, and, as always, we are guided by pragmatism instead of idealism. Although these tools are positivist tools, they are particularly important in securing community input. Since our book deals with the need to reinvigorate democracy in policy analysis, we believe that these tools of input and analysis are essential for the practicing analyst. So there you have it—our explanation of the toolbox. Go ahead and dig in, but remember the key trick for many jobs is to possess and select the right tools. Good luck with that fence.

Introduction

In this chapter we examine seven tools of analysis: (1) sampling and mail surveys, (2) extrapolation and forecasting, (3) measures of central tendency, (4) discounting, (5) deflating money, (6) per-capita analysis, and (7) cost-benefit analysis.

Our list is by no means exhaustive. There are literally hundreds of tools in the positivist approach. Many positivist tools, while of theoretical and analytical importance, are simply rarely used by most practicing analysts. Most analysts are going to work in local governments, in nonprofit organizations, and in state agencies. The first lesson, for the beginning analyst, is that time-lines are always too short, resources are too limited, and political priorities almost always outweigh attempts at "scientific" analysis. In fact, many decisions are still made without much or any analysis.

As practicing analysts ourselves we have rarely, if ever, used the indifference curves and computer modeling that we struggled to learn as graduate students. Instead, we have found that there are something like seven basic positivist techniques that we have used in practice in addition to the skills, models, and post-positivist techniques taught in the previous chapters of this book. In addition, our experiences with our students tend to reinforce that these are the seven tools most likely to be used in the average careers of policy analysts. Some of you may end up working in a major federal, state, local, or nonprofit agency and you will require extensive experience in more sophisticated tools. Our goal here is to provide you with the basics. In addition, these tools provide a fuller flavor than we have so far provided of the positivist approach to policy analysis. However, this chapter is not meant as an endorsement of these techniques. Operator manuals for power tools offer cautions and warnings as well as instructions. Similarly, we not only offer instructions but also critique these tools, showing the often immensely subjective underlying assumptions of these "rational" and "scientific" tools of analysis. Most importantly, we want you to consider the appropriateness of these tools for democracy.

A potential problem with several of these tools is that they promote an appearance of objectivity and neutrality on issues that are instead value-laden and political. Furthermore, positivist tools such as cost-benefit analysis often automatically assume that costs, benefits, and other quantitative factors are the major criteria for decision making. They tend to encourage the efficiency fallacy (at the expense of effectiveness) and to discourage democracy by squelching debate. Analysts decide based on pluses and minuses, rather than asking whether it is appropriate to do this or not, rather than asking who estimated the costs and benefits, and rather than asking if benefits must always outweigh costs. Remember, at the heart of policymaking are normative questions. For example, "Should we have bison on public lands with cattle?" and "Should we have sustainable development policies?" These are questions that need to be answered through democratic participation. Yet they are questions that policy analysts often try to answer by themselves using rational techniques that displace democratic decision making with a form of technocracy. In short, these are the seven positivist tools that practicing analysts will use, but these tools should only be used with a deep understanding of their limitations and of the potential for abuse they present.

Sheila the Policy Analyst

To assist our understanding of the positivist method, we are going to examine the application of each of the seven tools through a simple case. The major problem with teaching and learning positivist methods is that often the techniques of analysis seem remote, theoretical, and detached from application. The case helps place the use of the tools in practical situations. The case involves the fictional community of Boondocks (population 50,500) and a policy analyst named Sheila. Boondocks is a small town that has grown substantially in recent years. Ten years ago there was concern that the town was going to become a modern-day "ghost town" since a variety of external forces had led to the closing of several major businesses and industries. Today, Boondocks is a thriving community faced with new problems.

Growth has created much opposition to economic development policies that were implemented ten years ago. Many in the community believe that the community's quality of life is suffering as increased growth has led to subdivision development, increased traffic, and noise pollution. Others are more concerned that the growth is leading to increased tax rates as there are demands for new schools, hospitals, sewer lines, water lines, and recreation facilities. An interest group, "Citizens Against Growth" (CAG), has formed and they have been highly visible in their opposition to policies that will further economic development. CAG is currently opposing the proposed building of a new community swimming pool. The community only has one public pool and it was built in 1935. The City of Boondocks has proposed a new pool be built either in the old pool location (which is in a low-income section of the town) or in a newer location that is more accessible to most of the city's newer population bases. CAG has called for simply repairing the pool or doing nothing. They suggest instead that swimming could be provided by private recreation firms.

Sheila is an analyst for the City of Boondocks. She has just received her Master of Public Administration (MPA) degree from Boondocks University. Luckily, like you, she had some great professors and learned her craft well. In this integrated case study you will see how Sheila uses various techniques to inform policymakers and assist in decision making. In addition, as promised, you will see the subjective and even arbitrary nature of some of the techniques.

Tool #1: Sampling and Mail Surveys

A useful tool for gathering citizen input on an issue is to design and mail a survey. Sampling and mail survey research requires years of practical experience before one can truly be proficient in its application. But a grounding in the basics of the process is useful knowledge for any policy analyst. In this section, we examine how to determine sample size, techniques of random sampling, sample bias and weighting, the politics of surveys, and the technicalities of survey design. Remember, we will move our discussion along by using the Boondocks case to illustrate the major principles of the seven tools.

Sample Size

The determination of sample size is dependent on such things as **confidence levels**, margin of error, and the size of the population you are sampling from. Our purpose is not to go into a detailed explanation of sampling theory but rather to provide some general rules of thumb. Generally, for policy analysis purposes, a confidence interval of 95 percent with a margin of error of +/–5 percent is acceptable. This would mean, for example, that if, after completing the mail survey, you find that 65 percent of citizens support the building of a new pool in a new location, you are 95 percent confident that if surveyed the entire population numbers would fall between 60 percent and 70 percent of support. Sometimes, when there is enough money, analysts will attempt to reach a +/–3 percent margin of error. In Table 8-1, notice the much larger sample requirements for smaller margin of errors.

Remember that the numbers reported in the table are not the number of surveys that you will mail. Instead, these are the number of responses that are needed to achieve the desired level of precision. So analysts must play a guessing game with their response rate. Return rates for public policy issues vary widely depending on such disparate factors as size of the population, political culture, level of controversy surrounding the survey project, time of year, length of survey, and clarity of survey. In smaller communities, it is not uncommon to reach return rates of over 50 percent in a first mailing. In larger communities, return rates average around 25 percent or less for one-time mailings and a rate this low may not guarantee the reliability desired. Only experience can provide the analyst a feel for what type of return rate to expect. Generally, it is always best to oversample. In the case of Sheila

TABLE 8-1   SAMPLE SIZES FOR 95 PERCENT CONFIDENCE INTERVAL

POPULATION	+/–5% SAMPLE SIZE	+/–3% SAMPLE SIZE	+/–1% SAMPLE SIZE
500	222	250	250
1,000	286	500	500
2,000	333	714	1,000
3,000	353	811	1,500
4,000	364	870	2,000
5,000	370	909	2,500
6,000	375	938	3,000
7,000	378	959	3,500
8,000	381	976	4,000
9,000	383	989	4,500
10,000	385	1,000	5,000
15,000	390	1,034	6,000
20,000	392	1,053	6,667
50,000	397	1,087	8,333
100,000+	400	1,111	10,000

Source: These numbers were calculated using a statistical software package.

(assuming she uses the +/–5 percent margin of error), she needs about 397 surveys to hit the desired precision levels. With Boondock's population barely over 50,000, she can probably design a short (one-page) survey and expect a return rate of around 25 percent. Therefore, she needs to mail 1,600 surveys and can expect roughly 400 to return (1,600 x 25 percent = 400). To be safe, Sheila should mail closer to 2,000 surveys. Of course, the number of surveys that can be mailed depends on practical factors like time and money available.

Techniques of Random Sampling

It is very important that analysts conduct random sampling. The term "random" simply means that everyone in the chosen population (that the sample will be generalized to) had an equal chance of being selected as a respondent. There are a host of practical problems that limit the randomness of samples generated, but your goal should always be to produce a sample that is random and that can be replicated by other researchers or citizens. Many communities conduct surveys of citizens on controversial issues. Often these surveys are done in such a manner that many citizens doubt their authenticity (based on experience, they should). One community recently conducted a survey concerning citizen support for curbside recycling. Many citizens were confused about how the sample was drawn and many cynically contended that "the city council just passed out surveys to their buddies who supported the recycling." Unfortunately, on the other hand, most citizens do not understand random sampling and in this example nothing was done by the community to educate citizens on how the sampling was completed.

There are three major random sampling techniques. These techniques should be used by analysts and analysts should be prepared to explain their use and limitations to citizens. Remember, policy analysts must always be educators as well as experts. The chosen sampling strategy must be "transparent" and any limitations to the sample drawn must be honestly noted. The three techniques are "systematic random sampling," "stratified random sampling," and "multistage cluster sampling."

1. Systematic Random Sampling   Here the researcher is given a comprehensive list of names and draws a sample from the list. For example, our policy analyst Sheila wants to randomly select 2,000 names from a list of driver's licenses issued in Boondocks. There are 35,000 names (individuals sixteen years and older) on the list. To randomly sample 2,000 names, Sheila should randomly start somewhere in the list and then select every 18th name (35,000/2,000 = 17.5). Systematic random sampling is the most used sampling strategy among policy analysts. Note, however, that there is a problem in the sampling list. The sample is really a random sample of adults who have a driver's license issued within the city. Excluded are elderly people who no longer drive, new Boondocks citizens who had their driver's license issued elsewhere, and anyone else who for one reason or another does not have a Boondocks driver's license. In practice, you will never find the perfect, all-inclusive sampling list from which to draw your names. Again these limitations should always be acknowledged by the analyst.

TABLE 8-2 BOONDOCKS RESIDENTS BY NEIGHBORHOOD

NEIGHBORHOOD	RESIDENTS	PERCENT
Neighborhood A:	10,000	28.6%
Neighborhood B:	5,000	14.3
Neighborhood C:	5,000	14.3
Neighborhood D:	7,500	21.4
Neighborhood E:	7,500	21.4

2. Stratified Random Sampling   Sometimes it is advisable to stratify your sample. Stratified sampling increases sampling representativeness among subgroups of the population, including age, ethnicity, gender, religion, and urban versus rural. For example, suppose that it is very important that the sample collected by Sheila has proportional representation from the five major neighborhoods of Boondocks. While a well-done systematic random sample would probably produce results that are fairly proportionate, stratified sampling allows the researcher to be more precise. Sheila would have to find a list that could easily divide residents into the five neighborhoods. Most likely there is a list of citizens by census tracts. Sheila collects the names broken out by neighborhood as illustrated in Table 8-2 (above).

Remember that Sheila still wants to mail 2,000 surveys (she is overmailing to be safe). In her attempt to increase the precision of proportional returns, Sheila will mail the 2,000 surveys proportional to their percentage of the population (see Table 8-3). Neighborhood A will receive 572 surveys (28.6 percent of those mailed), Neighborhood B will receive 286 surveys (14.3 percent mailed) and so on. Sheila will use systematic random sampling to sample within each neighborhood.

Sheila's sampling choices as illustrated in Table 8-3 illustrate a "Proportionate Stratified Sample" (PSS). However, in some situations, stratified sampling can be used to create "Disproportionate Stratified Samples (DSS)." For example, Neighborhood A is a low-income neighborhood and Sheila knows through experience that the return rate for this neighborhood is likely to be roughly one-half of what can be expected from the other four neighborhoods. So if Sheila is expecting a 25 percent return rate from the rest of the neighborhoods, she can expect only a 12.5 percent return rate from

TABLE 8-3 SURVEYS MAILED BY NEIGHBORHOOD

NEIGHBORHOOD	FORMULA		SURVEYS MAILED
Neighborhood A:	.286 × 2,000	=	572
Neighborhood B:	.143 × 2,000	=	286
Neighborhood C:	.143 × 2,000	=	286
Neighborhood D:	.214 × 2,000	=	428
Neighborhood E:	.214 × 2,000	=	428
Total			2000 surveys

Neighborhood A. She may then want to double the number of surveys mailed to Neighborhood A. She would mail 1,144 surveys instead of 572. While this would be preferable, in practice the increased costs of mailing the extra 572 surveys would probably mean that this would not be done. Lack of money is almost always a hindrance to policy analysts trying to "scientifically" create appropriate sample sizes. (In this instance the extra cost would also allow a more democratic survey sample).

3. Multistage Cluster Sampling   This approach is more useful for hand-delivered surveys or for interviews than it is for mail research. It can also be used to generate samples for focus groups. In this approach, the researcher randomly samples at multiple stages. For example, Sheila has been charged with conducting citizen interviews as a follow-up to the mail survey. A multistage cluster sampling technique would proceed as follows: First, Sheila would have to divide the cities into segments. It would probably be most useful to use the five voting precincts or neighborhoods as the first stage. From here, Sheila can randomly choose four of the five neighborhoods. Then having randomly chosen four neighborhoods, she would randomly choose blocks in each of the neighborhoods. For example, if each neighborhood had 100 blocks, Sheila could choose to randomly select 25 blocks from each of the four randomly selected neighborhoods. From these 100 blocks, Sheila then could randomly select 2 houses per block. With her list of 200 houses, she could then arrange an interview with one of the home occupants. To avoid gender bias in male-female headed households, Sheila could randomly select the person who had most recently celebrated their birthday. She would then have a random sample of 200 Boondocks citizens.

The biggest problem with multistage cluster sampling is determining how many units to choose at each stage or in each cluster. For instance, why not randomly sample all five neighborhoods? Why not randomly sample 50 blocks instead of 25 blocks, and so on. The answer is that the number of units sampled at each stage and in each cluster is determined by time and resources. You should always try to sample the maximum number at each stage congruent with your agency's resources. The way that Sheila chose to sample produced 200 citizens to interview. Interviewing 200 citizens is a huge task and will take a lot of resources and time. Many smaller governmental agencies are understaffed and trying to get the resources to interview this many citizens is quite difficult.

Sample Bias and Weighting

Even if the analyst hits the targeted sample size, this does not mean that she necessarily has a sample that is representative of the population. Perhaps only those citizens that were very in favor of, or very opposed to, the swimming pool project returned the survey. Or perhaps retired persons disproportionately returned the survey. How does the analyst deal with the potential for sample bias? For example, perhaps the director of the local senior citizen center put out a flyer erroneously claiming the new pool would result in significant increases in property taxes and would therefore be unfair to people on fixed incomes.

First, the analyst asks demographic questions of respondents on the survey. Typical demographic questions to ask include: age, gender, education, and household income. Of course, any survey must have methodological procedures in place that guarantee the anonymity of the respondents.[1] These results from the demographic section are then compared to U.S. Census data for the community, county, or state under study. In Table 8-4, Sheila has prepared a table that compares sample demographic responses with census data.

At this point, the analyst examines the data and decides if there are problems with nonrepresentativeness in the sample. Clearly, there is no problem with gender, income, and education. However, the sample is skewed in the distribution of respondents by age. Age is a particular problem, with 72 percent of the population being forty-nine years or younger in the census data compared to only 46 percent in the sample data. This is a typical problem in community surveys. As a rule, younger persons are less likely to complete surveys even if the topic (in this case swimming pools) is of interest and importance to them. What does Sheila do in this case? Does she throw out the sample and start over? Of course, the city council and mayor would not be very pleased with the wasted money and time if she did.

Instead, there are a variety of steps that the careful policy analyst must undertake. First, Sheila needs to examine whether there is a determining factor regarding citizen's

TABLE 8-4   A COMPARISON OF SAMPLE DATA WITH CENSUS DATA

BOONDOCKS CENSUS DATA	BOONDOCKS SAMPLE
AGE	AGE
18–24 (8%)	18–24 (2%)
25–49 (64%)	25–49 (44%)
50–69 (22%)	50–69 (55%)
70–85 (5%)	70–85 (0%)
GENDER	GENDER
Male (54%)	Male (52%)
Female (46%)	Female (48%)
HOUSEHOLD INCOME	HOUSEHOLD INCOME
Mean = $35,000	Mean = $36,000
EDUCATION	EDUCATION
12.8 years of education	13.1 years of education

[1]Any government or nonprofit agency that receives federal money must create an "Institutional Research Board" (IRB) that reviews all research that involves human subjects. Any agency that receives federal monies and does not have such a board risks severe consequences, most notably the loss of federal funds. IRBs typically have specific procedures for mail surveys that must be followed to insure anonymity.

attitudes toward the pool. Using statistical computer software, she could run a simple **chi-square test** (consult a statistics book for an explanation of chi-square analysis) and determine if age and support for swimming pool options are related. If they are not, then age is not an important predictor of attitudes and Sheila does not have to worry about sample bias in this case. If, however, age and swimming pool attitudes are related, she must undertake corrective steps.

This is done by weighting cases and giving younger respondents' answers more weight. In the population, 25,200 out of 35,000 adult citizens are in the age range of 18–49 (72 percent). This compares to only 184 persons out of 400 (46 percent) in that same age range in the sample. The analyst can then take the 72 percent (of the population) and divide it by the 46 percent (of the sample) to come up with a weighting factor of 1.56 (72 percent/46 percent). Using a statistical software program such as SPSS, the answers of the individuals in the age range of 18–49 in the sample are multiplied by 1.56. Check the math yourself. If you take the 1.56 and multiply it times the 184 you will receive an answer of 287 persons. Now, the sample is counting 287 persons in this age range out of 400 in the sample (roughly 72 percent) and proportionate. As an example, let us suppose that 25 persons in the age range of 18–49 supported the building of the swimming pool in a new location. When we report frequencies (the number of cases with each of the possible values on a single variable) we would take that number and multiply it by 1.56 (25 x 1.56) and get the number 39. The opinions of younger adults are now proportionately represented in the sample. The analyst should, in her formal report and in presentations, inform her audience that certain cases are weighted.

The Technicalities of Surveys

There are a host of good books and methodology chapters on survey design (e.g., Foltz 1996 and Babbie 1996). The design of a survey is a complex issue that involves a certain level of theoretical understanding of research methodology. We cannot go into an in-depth discussion here. Instead, we are going to provide five key general tips for the analyst seeking to design a good survey.

Tip #1: Write Simple and Clear Questions and Statements   Do your survey questions really ask the questions that you want to ask? A problem with self-administered mail surveys is that the respondent does not have an opportunity to ask the survey designer for clarification about questions. Instead, the respondent must interpret the questions themselves. Awkward wording, the use of negatives, and including multiple information in one question are all sources of survey error. Examine the following statements and question[2]:

1. Do you agree or disagree that the United States should not intervene in the affairs of other countries unless national interests are directly at stake?

---

[2]In survey construction, statements are usually used to measure a respondent's level of agreement or disagreement and are usually used with some type of likert scale. Likert scales ask respondents to place their views on a continuum. For example, do they strongly agree, agree somewhat, (are they) unsure, disagree somewhat, or strongly disagree? A question, on the other hand, typically looks for a *yes* or *no* answer or some other multiple choice type answer.

2. Do you agree or disagree that local taxes are too high and that the city summer recreation program should be discontinued?

3. What is your income?

Statement A is difficult to understand because it is negative. If the respondent agrees with the statement they are agreeing that the United States should not intervene. Thus, they are giving a positive affirmation to a negative statement. A typical respondent would be very confused as to exactly what the survey statement was stating. The statement should be rewritten as follows:

*agree or disagree: The United States should intervene in the affairs of other countries only when national interests are at stake.

Conversely, if using a likert scale, the statement could be written as follows:

*I believe that the United States should intervene in the affairs of other countries only when national interests are at stake.

Statement B is "double-barreled." A respondent may agree that taxes are too high but disagree that the summer recreation program be discontinued. The survey writer assumes that higher taxes and the summer recreation program are somehow unavoidably linked. But this is not necessarily true. Higher taxes could be the result of too much money being spent on golf courses, city council member salaries, an overly generous travel budget for the mayor, or a host of other problems. Sometimes these double-barreled statements are just survey writer errors and at other times they are deliberately misleading and politically inspired. The statement should be rewritten into two separate parts as follows:

*Agree or disagree: The summer recreation program should be discontinued. (If you agree with the statement, please tell us the reason why it should be discontinued).

Once again, it could also be written with a likert scale that would provide a clearer sense of how strongly the respondents agree or disagree and that provides the opportunity to be neutral.

Question C seems okay. It asks a simple question but could have a multitude of answers. A respondent could answer it as gross individual weekly income, gross individual monthly income, net individual weekly income, net individual monthly income, gross individual annual income, net individual annual income, gross household monthly income, gross household weekly income, and so on. This is a common mistake made by survey-question writers. The question writer did not carefully consider the answer that they desired. The question should be rewritten as follows:

What is your annual (gross) household income?

or

What is your net (after taxes) annual household income?

Tip #2: Avoid Bias and Vagueness in Wording   Either intentionally or unintentionally, many survey questions are biased. Take the following example: "Do you agree or disagree that the disastrous policies of Bill Clinton helped create our current foreign policy problems?" The term "disastrous policies" leads the respondent. What rational respondent would disagree that "disastrous policies" helped create our current foreign policy problems? In addition, the phrase, "current foreign policy problems" is both vague and leading. It assumes that the problems are a given and implies that the respondent should know about them. A better question would be: "Do you agree or disagree that Bill Clinton did a good job in handling American foreign policy?"

In addition, another form of biased wording is found in what survey writers term "motherhood and apple pie questions." These are questions that almost exclusively elicit socially desirable responses. For example, "Agree or disagree: Water pollution is bad." or "Agree or disagree: Education is important for our children." These questions are vague and symbolic. Elected officials often like to keep democratic "discourse" at this vague level. Few respondents will disagree about the ill effects of water pollution or disagree about the importance of education. Writing survey questions in this manner is useless unless the questions are used to support an elected official's personal agenda. Instead, the conflict in the answering of these questions occurs when the survey writer crafts a question in a more specific manner. For instance, "Agree or disagree: This community should stop all commercial uses of the river in order to stop water pollution" or "Agree or disagree: "We must incorporate a private voucher system to improve public education." These latter questions will provoke considerable conflict and disagreement and will provide far greater insight into the political conflict surrounding the issues.

Tip #3: Do Not Ask Questions That Will Produce Uninformed Responses   A problem with surveys is that they often ask questions that respondents have little if any information about. For example, asking common citizens to answer questions about "transuranic waste transportation" is not very helpful for the policy analyst. The respondent most likely does not know what "transuranic" is in the first place.[3] Furthermore, they are even less likely to know much about policy issues and very rarely will know the details of specific legislative proposals. One city analyst recently sent out a survey concerning the city sewer system. The survey included the following question:

Is the city sewer system big enough to handle more population growth?

Nearly all respondents answered the question but it is highly doubtful whether any of the respondents had enough information to make an informed response. The purpose of the survey was to determine whether citizens are prepared to handle increased sewer fees in order to expand existing sewer facilities. Instead of asking questions that require such specific and technical knowledge, the survey writer could have written a more general question such as: "Would you support the city expanding its sewer system to accommodate increased population growth even if it meant a one dollar per month increase in sewer fees for all households?

Tip #4: Think of the Statistics That You Want to Produce with Your Questions   A common problem for novice survey question writers is that they ask questions that do

---

[3]*Transuranic* refers to "low-level" radioactive waste. Typically, this waste is the by-product of work done at nuclear facilities. It could include contaminated gloves, clothing, and other disposable items.

not produce the data that they need to run the statistics that they want to produce. Later in this chapter we will discuss different levels of measurement (see Table 8-6). Importantly, certain statistics are calculated for certain levels of measurement. When questions are designed, survey writers must carefully consider what type of data their questions will produce. For example, a beginning analyst was once given the task of creating a survey. The analyst's supervisor wanted to use regression analysis to analyze several questions. Unfortunately, the analyst wrote questions that generated only nominal level data measurements and therefore only chi-square statistics could be produced.

Tip #5: Design the Survey with Consideration of Coding and Reporting of Results Closely related to Tip #4 is the problem of how to code and report data. Coding is simply how numbers are transferred from the survey questionnaire to a data processing program. Often question writers craft questions that produce almost meaningless information or information that is very difficult to analyze and report. Consider the following question:

Please indicate the reasons that you shop in Wilsonville. Check all that apply:

price____   convenience____

quantity of goods____   service____

quality of goods____   location____

Most respondents will check all six reasons. What does this mean and how does the analyst code this data and report it? The answer is that the analyst would have to create a variable for each reason and then "place code" each as 0 = yes (it was checked and 1 = no (it was not checked). But in the final report, little useful information will be provided. A better question would be as follows:

Below are several different reasons why citizens may shop in Wilsonville. Please rank the reasons using a 1 for the most important, a 2 for the second most important, and so on. Rank all items.

This question forces the respondent to critically examine their own preferences and provide a ranking. The analyst can provide much stronger information with this question.

The Politics of Survey Construction

In addition to possessing a technical understanding of survey design, the analyst requires an understanding and appreciation of survey design and administration in a political environment. First, remember that many citizens literally "hate" surveys. To some citizens mail surveys are just another form of junk mail that are quickly tossed in the garbage. Other citizens will return the surveys and chastise the survey sponsors for "wasting tax dollars by mailing this useless piece of crap." Others will use the survey to vent their anger about a wide variety of issues not directly related to the survey itself. So our first piece of advice is to be prepared to take heat and have a thick political skin.

Second, do not overuse surveys. Many analysts and elected officials use surveys as a surrogate for democratic participation. Somehow there is the belief that by sending out 1,000 surveys, receiving 200 back, and writing a 50-page report from the 200 surveys, the analyst and elected officials have broadly achieved community input.

Therefore, many communities conduct survey after survey and write report after report. Unfortunately, the reports are quickly forgotten and normally filed away without being used for any tangible purpose. So our first tip is to use surveys only when the desired information cannot be secured in other ways.

In the Boondocks case, a survey on citizen views toward the swimming pools seems appropriate. It provides a concrete set of choices and the survey design could be short. However, if Boondocks' residents have been bombarded in recent years by a variety of other community surveys, some of which may have been poorly designed and written, the survey is more likely to irritate citizens than to provide a vehicle for democracy.

Third, analysts must carefully seek input from many stakeholders in the design of the survey. Surveys are often political tools rather than tools of democracy. The wording of a question severely impacts results. Examine the following statements. In each, the respondent is to tell the researcher whether they agree or disagree with the statement.

1. "The City of Boondocks should not waste taxpayer dollars on building a new pool in a new location."
2. "I don't have much information about the new pool and need more information before I can decide how I feel about the construction of a new one."
3. "A new pool will make a positive contribution to our community and will bring in tourist dollars; therefore I support the construction of a new pool in the new site."

The first statement is obviously biased against building a new pool. It presumes that building a new pool is equated with wasting taxpayer dollars. Respondents would most likely agree with this statement since few citizens would want to "waste taxpayer dollars." Perhaps the first statement was written by the local businesses that are located near the existing pool. Their goal was to write a question that makes it look like citizens do not want the new pool in a new location. They may support the building of a new pool but only in the existing location.

The second statement is a common ploy by opponents of projects. Citizens typically do not have a lot of knowledge about the intricacies of policies. Instead, citizens tend to make general decisions and value judgments. They either support something or they do not. Approximately 75 percent to 85 percent of the respondents would agree with this statement. Opponents would then use these numbers to argue that the vast majority of the citizens are uninformed and the city council and mayor cannot proceed on the issue. The problem is that at least this percentage of citizens tend to be uninformed on all issues but the city council and mayor still must make decisions and pass ordinances. This second statement may be used as a delay tactic and to increase citizen distrust of city government. Most likely opponents would use these numbers in a newspaper article and state something like, "The city council and mayor are about ready to vote on an issue that 75 percent of the population knows little about. Where is democracy? Why don't they try to inform citizens about the true costs and benefits? Are the elected officials afraid to show the citizens the truth?"[4]

---

[4]This very tactic was used by opponents of planned tax increment financing (TIF) in an intermountain west community. The tactic worked to a degree as some elected officials tempered their support of a plan that would have funded several inner-city infrastructure projects and recreation facilities.

The third statement is leading and again biased but this time in favor of the pool construction. It is also double- or even triple-barreled in that it contains two or three separate pieces of information. For example, it is possible that respondents may agree that the pool will make a positive contribution to the community but they may not believe that it will bring in tourist dollars and they may not support the pool because they see it as unfair competition with private recreation facilities. Conversely, another respondent may agree that the pool will make a positive contribution and bring in tourist dollars but the respondent may not support the new pool.

It is very important that the analyst attempts to create questions that are neutral and fair to all parties. The analyst should create a committee of stakeholders who all individually have veto power over questions. Sheila would want to include the stakeholders from the "CAG" group, citizens from the old pool neighborhood, businesses who would be impacted by any pool decision, swimming groups, and any other identified stakeholders. In creating a survey design committee, the analyst must fully realize that the stakeholders will try to craft questions that favor their interests and that survey design by committee is a long and frustrating process.

One of the authors of this book once spent a month working with a statewide coalition of tax experts to design a statewide survey that was to measure citizen attitudes toward state taxation. Input was sought from academics, elected officials, elected officials' staff, administrative experts, antitaxation groups, and other citizen groups. The survey went through some sixty changes in the course of the month, as stakeholders fought over question construction. Importantly, taxation is an issue that promotes a high level of controversy. There is little agreement over what taxes are most equitable, and suggested changes could have major impacts on individual citizens. The governor of the state even wrote several questions for the survey and vetoed several others. The result was a long survey that, despite the cross-sectional input, still created political controversy in the state.

It would have been easier for a single analyst to design the survey and, in fact, a more effective survey may have been designed this way. However, the analyst, in undertaking the survey by himself, also would have taken a lot of "political heat." Instead, with the wide range of stakeholders, the analyst was able to state that a wide range of input was sought and that all stakeholders had signed off on the final product. This at least gave the survey some legitimacy and deterred some political attacks from interest groups and others. The lesson from all of this is that survey construction is a political process. It is very difficult to objectively and neutrally measure citizen attitudes.

On a more positive note, the other author recently helped redesign a survey of foster parents, their caseworkers, and the nondirect staff (mostly management) who work with them. A broadly representative committee designed the survey. Unlike the tax survey, this project saw stakeholders with much agreement over basic problems and an honest concern for designing a useful survey. They accepted most of the suggestions from their hired analyst, but appropriately kept control of the final form. There were a few questions that were technically flawed but it was their survey. More important, their goal was not to elicit certain responses that they could use to justify changes they wanted to make, but to honestly discover the values/beliefs and current practices, and then later to continue the inclusive dialogue.

8-1. Political Survey Construction in Practice

One of the most famous contemporary uses of surveys to promote political agendas was used by perennial presidential candidate and billionaire Ross Perot. In 1993, Perot, hoping to influence national policy directions, purchased thirty minutes of television time and used it to promote a national survey that was distributed in *TV Guide*, newspapers, and magazines. The first problem is that Perot's sampling technique was not representative of a national electorate. Instead, respondents were likely Perot supporters who watched the television program. Respondents tended to be middle class, white, and older. In addition, the seventeen-question survey was full of poorly constructed and politically inspired questions. The answers provided to these questions are almost purely symbolic and tap into, and build, anger in the public. Consider the following:

- "Should we eliminate foreign lobbyists completely—no loopholes—and make it a criminal offense?"
- "Should Congress and officials in the White House set the example for sacrifice by eliminating all perks and special privileges currently paid by taxpayers?"

In addition, Perot asked the respondents to include their name, addresses, telephone numbers, and congressional districts. This, of course, did not guarantee anonymity of respondent but did provide an excellent mailing list for Perot's then fledgling and unnamed political party (Morin 1993).

At the end of the 1990s, a political party called the "New Party" tried to use tactics similar to Perot's to create a national agenda. The following survey was created by the New Party in 1999. Evaluate these four New Party questions:

1. "While CEO salaries are skyrocketing and stock traders are getting rich, millions of Americans work full-time but still fall below the poverty line. Inequality is bad for people and bad for the economy. The New Party is dedicated to fighting for living wage jobs and increasing the minimum wage so that working people can support their families." ___Agree ___Disagree

2. "The current corruption of our electoral system is a disgrace. We must end the dominance of big money in our political campaigns by strictly limiting campaign contributions and providing full public financing of elections." ___Agree ___Disagree

3. "All Americans should have the opportunity to get an excellent education. The New Party is dedicated to revitalizing our school system and providing equal and adequate funding for all public schools. We oppose giving away public funds for private and religious education." ___Agree ___Disagree

4. "Health care and retirement benefits should be governed by what's best for the people's health and security, not corporate profits. The New Party believes Social Security and Medicare must be saved as universal programs, and opposes privatization schemes which will enrich Wall Street while risking our future security." ___Agree ___Disagree

Sources: Richard Morin. 1993. "The Pollsters' Preemptive Strike Against Perot." *The Washington Post National Weekly Edition*, March 29–April 4; and a 1999 mailing from the New Party.

Tool #2: Extrapolation and Forecasting

Extrapolation is a method of predicting the value of something in the future. The underlying assumption of extrapolation is that what happened in the past will repeat itself in the future. Extrapolation is calculated mathematically by using Formula 8-1:

Formula 8-1: Extrapolation

$P_f = P_0 + AGI(n)$

Where:

P_f = the estimated population (or any other value that needs to be estimated) in the future

P_0 = a chosen base year

AGI = the average growth increment between time periods

n = selected time periods

The best way to understand extrapolation is by seeing its application in a case example. Extrapolation can be used for a variety of policy issues. Below we examine its use in estimating the future population of Boondocks.

Population Extrapolation Case: The City of Boondocks

One outcome of the swimming pool debate is a desire on the part of the decision makers for more information. Sheila has been asked to present a report to the Boondocks City Council on the city's long-term development. In particular, she needs to provide the council with population estimates for the next twenty years. She decides to use extrapolation techniques. She first collects census data going back to 1960. The data is presented in Table 8-5.

Sheila needs to forecast population numbers in 2010 and 2020. She needs to use Formula 8-1 to project population for a future period: 1960 serves as time period zero (P_0), 1970 = P_1, 1980 is P_2, 1990 is P_3, 2000 is P_4.

Using Formula 8-1, the population forecast for 2010 would be as follows:

$P2010 = P_0 + AGI(n)$

Where P_0 = the base year (1960)

AGI = the average growth increment between decades (15,000 + 2,000 + 0 + 8,500/4 decades = 6,375)

n = the number of decades since 1960 (in our case 5 then 6 for calculation of 2020).

TABLE 8-5   POPULATION TRENDS OF BOONDOCKS

1960	25,000
1970	40,000
1980	42,000
1990	42,000
2000	50,500

Thus we are left with the following:

P2010 = 25,000 + (6,375 x 5)
P2010 = 25,000 + 31,875
P2010 = 56,875

To estimate the population for the year 2020, Sheila would simply do the following:

P2020 = 25,000 + (6,375 x 6)
P2020 = 25,000 + 38,250
P2020 = 63,250

Of course there are problems with the extrapolation technique. Most notably, it again assumes that the future will resemble the past. In addition, analysts must choose how far they want to go back in time in order to choose their base year. In the Boondocks example, the large growth rate between 1960 and 1970 was the result of Boondocks annexing another community. Therefore, the 15,000 population increase was not created "naturally" in population ecology terms. Population ecology asserts that human populations can change in three ways: (1) through human births, (2) through human deaths, and (3) through human migration.

Population ecology ignores the fact that population, like all social numbers, is socially created. Population can increase "artificially" through annexation. In addition, the U.S. Census is an imperfect method of determining a community's population. Census numbers are really more an "educated estimate" of a population and one of the most politically contentious issues because it has a huge impact on legislative power distribution and the amount of funding states and communities receive. For example, a western USA community recently "found" four hundred homes that were missing from the U.S. Census Bureau's address catalog. The community development and research department, using a public administration intern from the local university, undertook a comparison of the Census master file with an engineering department list of addresses it granted approval to since 1994. In that time, 400 new homes had failed to make the U.S. Census master list. This means that the community's population will automatically be between 1,200 to 1,500 larger than what it would have been without finding the additional homes. In a newspaper article, the community's development director Robert Chambers was quoted as saying, "That's a significant number of homes and people who should not be left out of the census count. When census data drives funding formulas for government programs, that's important" (Charlambous 1999). In 1995, this same community development research department used a similar review and found enough homes to push the community's population over 50,000, allowing the city to be entitled to over $600,000 in annual community development block grants. Through an aggressive comparison of the U.S. Census list with the city's lists, the community development department has literally brought millions in federal monies into the community.

In our example, because of the annexation between 1960 and 1970, Sheila may believe it would be better to use 1970 as the base year. In doing so, her numbers change quite dramatically as we can see at the top of page 289:

New Base Year (1970):

1970:	40,000
1980:	42,000
1990:	42,000
2000:	50,500

New Calculations for 2010:

P2010 = 40,000 + (3,500 x 4)
P2010 = 40,000 + 14,000
P2010 = 54,000

New Calculations for 2020:

P2020 = 40,000 + (3,500 x 5)
P2020 = 40,000 + 17,500
P2020 = 57,500

Notice the dramatic differences particularly in predicting the year 2020. If the City Council wanted to promote Boondocks as a growing and prosperous city, or wanted to demonstrate the need for a new pool, they would most likely prefer Sheila's first estimation of a Boondocks population of 63,250 in 2020. Conversely, if the City Council wanted to demonstrate the idea that growth was going to be steady but not tremendous, or wanted to downplay the need for a new pool, they would most likely choose Sheila's second estimate of a population of 57,500 in 2020. In either case, many or perhaps most citizens would be dazzled by the impressive number calculations and the appearance of technical precision that it provides. Most citizens do not have an appreciation of how extrapolation numbers are calculated and therefore are very unlikely to understand the problem created by the 1960 base year and instead accept the numbers as unquestionable scientific calculations. "You can't argue with the numbers," someone might even state.

Good analysts get around this problem by supplying several different estimates, using several different base years, and explaining problems like those created by annexation. In addition, the analyst must explain that extrapolation does not account for changes in culture, changes outside of the area, changes in the economy, or other changes that might dramatically affect population growth. The future rarely looks like the past. As always, honesty is the best policy. Unfortunately, in politics, "strategic representation" and "meaning capture" often are more salient than honesty. Analysts should resist the manipulative impulses of elected officials, interest groups, elites, and themselves and present data to citizens that is open to scrutiny and understanding.

8-2. OOPS: Extrapolation in Practice

Often population forecasts are quickly filed away and forgotten. When we do find forecasts that were made twenty to twenty-five years ago, we most often see the severe lack of precision of forecasting techniques. Consider the two actual communities described on page 290.

Community A

In 1975, this community was booming due to the siting of an enormous mining equipment company that had just located in the city. The population in the community grew from roughly 40,000 in 1970 to nearly 45,000 by 1975. This trend was expected to continue for several years and, in fact, it was expected to escalate. There is a rule in economic development circles that states that every 1,000 new manufacturing jobs creates around 1,500 service and retail sector jobs. That is, the manufacturing jobs bring new money into the community and this money is spent on groceries, clothes, homes, and recreation. This creates a larger service sector as grocery stores, restaurants, clothing stores and other service sector employees fill the increased market. The forecasters, using techniques far more complicated than the one we just taught you, estimated that the population of Community A would be 100,000 by the year 2000. City elected officials quickly implemented antigrowth measures, such as large sewer hook-up fees, in the hope of slowing the growth.

But the forecasters could not foresee changes in the mining market that would occur in the late 1970s. Neither could they see that major government deregulation would gut the community of much of its transportation industry. The population of Community A in the year 2000 is around 52,000 instead of 100,000.

Community B

In 1975, Community B was a stable community dominated economically by government. Its population in 1975 was around 60,000. Forecasters believed that, without a major growth industry in the private sector, this community would grow steadily to near 70,000 by the year 2000. Forecasters could not foresee that a booming personal computer industry would locate three major manufacturers in Community B and that outmigration from urban areas would pull thousands to Community B's beautiful river valley. The population of Community B in the year 2000 is over 130,000 instead of 70,000.

Tool #3: Measures of Central Tendency

According to Foltz (1996, 144), "Measures of central tendency are efficient ways to describe and summarize a distribution." There are three measures of central tendency: means, modes, and medians. A *mean* is simply the arithmetic average of a distribution of numbers and is calculated by adding the values of the numbers in a distribution and then dividing by the number of cases in the distribution.[5] Means are used when data collected is "interval ratio," meaning that the data has a true zero point (age in years, weight, number of fires in a city in a given year—see Table 8-6). With

---

[5] One example would be calculating the mean, or average, height of a men's basketball team. Consider a team of ten players. The two centers are both seven footers (7.0, 7.0). The three power forwards are 6'11", 6'10", and 6'10". The two "small" forwards are both 6'8". The two shooting guards are both 6'6". Their great point guard Michael Thomas moved to Australia so they are stuck with Professor Clemons (6'1"). To figure the team's mean height we convert it to inches (lowest common denominator). So: 84 + 84 + 83 + 82 + 82 + 80 + 78 + 78 + 73 = 804 inches. 804 inches divided by 10 (the number of players) = 80.4 inches per person. 80.4 inches = 6' 7½". Of course, old "Doc" would still be 6' 1" and still not be able to dunk.

interval ratio data, the researcher can measure the precise distance between cases. For example, if one person is sixty years old and another person is thirty years old, we can say that the former is twice as old as the latter. Of course the meaning of the phrase "twice as old" only accurately refers to chronological age, but it carries with it individual and social biases and beliefs.

Modes are simply the value of a frequency distribution that occurs the most. Modes are the exclusive choice for a central tendency measure for nominal data. Nominal data is data that has only the characteristic of being exhaustive and mutually exclusive (see Table 8-6). Examples of nominal data include gender and yes and no answers to questions. Modes can also be used with ordinal data (data that has a rank (see Table 8-6) and interval ratio data. Medians are the middle point of a distribution of numbers. If there is a even number of values, the median is the mean of the two middle numbers. Medians are calculated with ordinal or interval ratio data.

TABLE 8-6   THREE TYPES OF DATA

TYPE	DESCRIPTION	EXAMPLES OF QUESTIONS
Nominal	Data that can be considered only mutually exclusive or exhaustive.	1. What is your gender? Male or Female 2. Did you vote in the last general election? Yes or No
Ordinal	Data that is ranked.	3. Please indicate your agreement or disagreement with the following statement: "President Clinton is doing a good job handling the war in Kosovo." A. Strongly Agree B. Agree C. Neutral D. Disagree E. Strongly Disagree 4. Please rank your favorite type of ice cream. (1 = favorite, 2 = second favorite, 3 = least favorite) ____ Chocolate ____ Vanilla ____ Strawberry
Interval-Ratio	Data that has a meaningful zero point.	5. How many times a year, on average, do you call the city police department? ___ times a year 6. How many years have you lived in Boondocks? ___ years

Boondocks and Central Tendency

Perhaps using our analyst Sheila and the City of Boondocks as an example, we can clearly demonstrate the ease of use and usefulness of the three measures of central tendency. In addition, you will find that, as with all numbers, even simple measures of central tendency can be used incorrectly and can be used to mislead or politically manipulate.

Consider the following example from Boondocks. Sheila has been asked to provide data on the average number of crimes reported in Boondocks for the last ten years. (Even in Boondocks there is lots more going on than just a debate about a swimming pool.) The number of crimes committed produces data that is intervalratio, so Sheila can use any or all three of the measures of central tendency. She collects the following data from the Boondocks Police Department as reported in Table 8-7.

TABLE 8-7   REPORTED CRIMES IN BOONDOCKS

YEAR	REPORTED CRIMES
1989	330
1990	380
1991	385
1992	450
1993	600
1994	550
1995	650
1996	600
1997	560
1998	600

Calculating the mean, Sheila comes up with the following:

Sum of crimes reported over the last ten years: 5,105
Number of Years: 10
Mean = Sum of Crimes/Number of years
Mean = 5,105/10
Mean = 510.50 crimes per year

Sheila then uses the same data to calculate the median. Here she must reorder the data into a ranked distribution (from lowest to highest) as shown in Table 8-8 (at the top of page 293).

TABLE 8-8   REPORTED CRIMES IN BOONDOCKS (ORDERED)

YEAR	REPORTED CRIMES
1989	330
1990	380
1991	385
1992	450
1994	550
1997	560
1993	600
1996	600
1998	600
1995	650

We then count down five from the top and five from the bottom to find the midpoint of the distribution between 550 (in 1994) and 560 (in 1997). To find the mid-point, we must add 550 and 560 and divide by two. Thus we find a median of 555.00. Finally, Sheila calculates the mode, which in this case is 600 (occurring three times; in 1993, 1996, and 1998).

Thus, Sheila is left with three differing measures of central tendency. The calculated mean provides the lowest average crimes reported (510.50 per year). The median provides average crimes reported at 555.00 per year. The mode provides the highest measure of central tendency with an average of 600 crimes reported each year. So what measure of central tendency should Sheila report to decision makers?[6]

It should be noted that calculated means are often unreliable because they are the most vulnerable to the distorting effects of **outliers**. In this case, however, there does not seem to be an outlier effect since there is a fairly consistent pattern of increases in reported crime over the past ten years. When there is an outlier problem, the median becomes the statistic of choice because it is less influenced by outliers. In this case, Sheila would do best in reporting all three numbers and explaining the differences between the three. Unfortunately, in politics, numbers are often used for political gain. For example, perhaps the mayor wants to paint the picture of Boondocks as a relatively low-crime area. In this case, Sheila might be pressured to report the mean number. Alternatively, perhaps the Boondocks Chief of Police is arguing to the Boondocks City Council that his department needs more funding because of high crimes reports. The mode of 600 might best fit his political purposes.

There are more problems with the calculation of measures of central tendency. Sheila could, for example, decide to report the average crimes committed based only on the past five years and produce higher averages. For the past five years, the mean is 592, the median is 600, and the mode is 600. These higher numbers might help the

---

[6]It is generally more useful to look at the crime rate trends rather than calculating averages.

Chief of Police secure larger budget allocations but they might also deter Boondocks in its economic development efforts, since companies may not want to relocate to a community with a high crime rate.

In addition, there is a larger problem. The data represents only "crimes reported." So the data is not really a measure of crime in the city but rather just a measure of reported crime. In addition, as an analyst, Sheila would have to be very careful that reporting procedures have been the same in all ten years. Perhaps the community's aggressive "Neighborhood Watch" program that encourages citizens to report "suspicious behavior" is solely responsible for the increases in reported crimes starting in 1993. Successful clearance rates by police also tend to lead to higher reporting of crime because citizens have an increased sense that reporting the crime will make a difference. In other words, citizens may merely be more likely now to report crime compared to earlier years. Perhaps there is no increased crime problem in Boondocks. Instead, changes in police procedures and citizen programs have just increased the number of reported crimes. Moreover, what about comparing the number of crimes to the overall population? Perhaps crime has fallen per capita (you will see how to conduct this analysis later in the chapter). Moreover, our report did not distinguish between more serious crimes and lesser offenses. Maybe murder, rape, armed robbery, and assault is way down but petty theft and forgery is way up. It is also possible that this is due to a significant increase in the percentage of citizens who are males between the ages of 13–19 (since they commit an unusually high percentage of crime). Further, what is a crime? The phrase marital rape used to be an oxymoron—not a crime. Maybe changes in attitudes among police, the courts, and society, have made it easier for victims of rape to report crimes without worrying about being mistreated again by the system.

In addition, the analyst would have to make sure that the police department did not alter their reporting procedures in other ways. For example, perhaps from 1989–92, reports of juvenile activity were not reported since police believed the activity was merely the result of harmless juvenile hijinks. But possibly concern over teenage gang activity led the police department to change its reporting procedures in 1993, which could help explain increases in crime. Always remember, social data is socially constructed.

Tool #4: Deflating Money

The ability to deflate money is a useful technique for policy analysts. It is clear that, due to inflation, $1,000,000 in 1975 is more valuable than $1,000,000 in 2000. Prices for automobiles, clothing, health care, movie and sporting event tickets, and so forth have all increased over time. The deflation of money is not complicated. It involves the use of an "Implicit Price Deflator" (IPD) published by the Bureau of Labor Statistics, U.S. Department of Labor (Table 8-9). An IPD is merely a price index. The price index that most Americans are familiar with is the "Consumer Price Index" (CPI). In government, price indexes allow us to account for the impact of inflation on such things as salaries, budgets, and fees. We have chosen to use the Gross Domestic Product (GDP) index as our IPD. The GDP index provides a wider range of goods and services in its index than the CPI. Box 8-3 provides a clear explanation of how indexes are calculated.

Deflating money is most useful when comparing the costs incurred by a government over time. Because of inflation, comparisons can only be made if the dollar figures are converted to "constant dollars." The formula for deflating money is as follows:

Formula 8-2

Current dollars x base year IPD/current year IPD = current dollar value in base year

For example, in 1997–98, the Boondocks Police Department received $1,000,000 in their annual budget allocation. In 1989–90, the Boondocks Police Department received $650,000. Some critics within the city government and community believe that the Boondocks Police Department budget is out of control. The Boondocks newspaper recently published a newsstory where a local interest group leader proclaimed, "The Boondocks Police Department budget has increased 350,000 dollars in the past eight years. Are we really getting that much better police protection?"

Analyst Sheila is charged with determining the current dollar value of the $1,000,000 in 1989–90 dollars to see how much of an increase there really has been. To calculate this, Sheila finds the index values for Gross Domestic Product (GDP) in Table 8-9. Using this data she calculates the following:

$1,000,000 x 91.50 (base year IPD)/113.7 (current year IPD) = $804,749 (current dollar in base year)

TABLE 8-9   GROSS DOMESTIC PRODUCT INDEX NUMBERS 1980–98

YEAR	INDEX VALUE	PERCENT CHANGE
1980–81	63.3	9.8
1981–82	68.2	7.7
1982–83	71.6	5.0
1983–84	74.5	4.1
1984–85	77.2	3.6
1985–86	79.5	3.0
1986–87	81.7	2.8
1987–88	84.4	3.3
1988–89	88.0	4.3
1989–90	91.5	4.0
1990–91	95.6	4.5
1991–92	98.7	3.2
1992–93	101.3	2.6
1993–94	103.8	2.5
1994–95	106.5	2.6
1995–96	109.0	2.3
1996–97	111.4	2.2
1997–98	113.7	2.1

Source: California Postsecondary Education Commission (1999). This is an interesting internet site for policy analysts. This data is found at <http://www.cpec.ca.gov/fiscal/final97/disply~62.htm>.

Sheila demonstrates that this budget has not increased by $350,000. Instead, in real dollars, it has increased $154,749 ($804,749 – $650,000 = $154,749). Thus, the police department budget has indeed increased but the majority of the increase is due only to inflation.[7]

8-3. Calculation of an Index

An index examines the prices of a basket of goods. For example, suppose a person purchases only three items. To construct a simple index we would survey that person's spending habits on those three items for one year (1996). Let's say that in the base year of 1996, Pete bought his family 50 tacos per month at an average price of $1.00. He also bought one new sweater per month at $30.00 and rented five videos per month at $4.00 per video. We are then left with these base year figures:

ITEM	AVERAGE PRICE	AVG. QUANTITY PER MONTH	AVG. EXPENDITURE (MONTHLY)
Taco	$1.00	50	$50.00
Sweater	$30.00	1	$30.00
Videos	$4.00	5	$20.00
Total			$100.00

Prices, of course, typically increase. Below is what the prices of these items were in 2000:

ITEM	PRICE PERCENTAGE	INCREASE SINCE 1996
Tacos	$1.50	50
Sweater	$37.50	25
Videos	$5.00	20

We can now examine price changes from 1996 to 2000 by buying the same quantity in 2000 as was purchased in 1996:

ITEM	AVERAGE PRICE	AVG. QUANTITY PER MONTH	AVG. EXPENDITURE (MONTHLY)
Tacos	$1.50	50	$75.00
Sweater	$37.50	1	$37.50
Videos	$5.00	5	$25.00
Total			$137.50

---

[7]People are sometimes confused by the phrase "real dollars." It does not refer, as the phrase might seem to imply, to the amount actually spent. Rather, it refers to the real value of the amount spent after accounting for inflation. The amount actually spent is referred to as "constant dollars." This phrase suggests that we ignore inflation and pretend dollars have a constant value.

This analysis shows that what once cost Pete $100 (50 tacos, 1 sweater, 5 videos) now costs him $137.50. We can now calculate a Price Index (PI). A price index is calculated by using this simple formula:

PI = Cost of budget in current year/Cost of budget in base year x 100

We then put in the numbers from our example:

PI = $137.50/$100 x 100

PI = 137.50

So the Price Index (PI) is now 137.50, meaning that the cost of living has increased 37.50 percent. The GDP index simply calculates changes for all goods and services included in the GDP.

Source: Based on a discussion in Baumol and Blinder (1988).

Tool #5: Per Capita Analysis

Per capita analysis is used to determine the value of something per a certain number of population (i.e., cost per person). It is a useful tool to examine changes in numbers by population over time. Continuing with the Boondocks Police Department budget analysis, and as suggested earlier, Sheila may want to determine the per capita spending on police protection when comparing 1989–90 to 1997–98. In 1989–90, Boondocks had a population of 42,000. In 1997–98, the population of Boondocks was 50,000. She could then calculate per capita spending on police protection using the real dollar total she calculated using her deflating money technique discussed earlier. After this analysis, her numbers look like this:

1989–90: $650,000/42,000 residents = $15.48 per resident
1997–98: $800, 865/50,000 residents = $16.01 per resident

With this analysis, Sheila concludes that spending on police protection in Boondocks has increased but it by no means has increased as much as it initially appeared. In real dollars, Boondocks spends only $0.53 more per capita on police protection in 1997–98 than it did in 1989–90. She can then calculate the percentage increase in spending per capita in real dollars. The percentage increase is calculated by taking the current year per capita dollar figure, subtracting the base year per capita dollar figure, and then dividing by the per capita figure of the base year and multiplying this number by 100. It is represented in Formula 8-3.

Formula 8-3
Percentage Increase = Per Capita Figure^{cy} – Per Capita Figure^{by}/Per Capita Figure^{by} x 100
Where: ^{cy} = current year
^{by} = base year

Thus, the percentage increase in per capita spending is calculated as:

Percentage Increase = $16.01 – $15.48/$15.48 x 100 = 3.42 percent increase in spending per capita.

Of course, reported crimes (referring back to Table 8-2) have increased from 330 in 1990 to 600 in 1998. She could create a per capita crime rating as well. In 1990, per capita crime was:

330 crimes/42,000 residents = .0079 crimes per resident.

In 1998, per capita crime equaled:

600/50,000 = .012 crimes per resident.

We can then calculate a percentage increase in per capita crime. Using Formula 8-3, we calculate:

.012 – .0079/.0079 x 100 = 51.9 percent increase in per capita crime.

So while spending has increased only 3.42 percent per capita, the crime rate has increased 51.9 percent per capita. What does it all mean? Perhaps the budget of the Boondocks Police Department needs to be increased since spending has not kept up with increases in crime. Or perhaps, the Police Department is not doing a good job since it has had a real increase in per capita spending but crime has increased at a faster pace than the increase in spending. In fact, did you notice we stopped referring to increases in reported crime and started discussing an increase in per capita crime. Maybe these numbers show that the increased spending per capita has led to greater citizen awareness and confidence. Perhaps it was even spent helping to organize neighborhood watch groups that have resulted in both an increase in reported crime and an increase in arrests and convictions. Or perhaps there are many factors contributing to an increase in crime that are beyond the control of the Police Department, and it is unfair and impossible to conclude anything. In politics, after all, the truth is what we are persuaded of … and numbers are used to tell stories that persuade.

Tool #6: Discounting

Discounting is a method for estimating the present value of costs and benefits in the future. For example, your best friend owes you $10.00. If she pays you today, you will receive $10.00. But if she pays you one year from now, the $10.00 that you receive then will not really be worth $10.00 because you will have lost the interest that you would have earned on the money as well as a slight loss due to inflation. At a five percent interest rate, $10.00 earns 50 cents over a one-year period. Thus, if your friend pays you back in one year, she is really only giving back $9.50. ($10.00 minus the .50 in interest that you lost). In short, future costs and benefits have less value than present ones. This is crucial because many policies have costs and benefits that are not immediately realized but rather have costs and benefits that flow forward into time.

Boondocks and Discounting

In discounting, an analyst chooses an interest rate that estimates what a government or citizen could earn on an investment over the period of time in question. While there is a discount rate set by the Federal Reserve, these rates change over time. So there is subjectivity in the choice of an interest rate number. It is difficult to estimate discount rates three, four, or five years in the future. Remember that Boondocks wants to construct a new swimming pool and that it would cost one million dollars. The work will not be completed for a year, thus costs would not be incurred for one year. In the meantime you can earn one year of interest so the costs decrease. Sheila would have to determine the present value of the one-million dollar expenditure that will be spent next year. Formula 8-4 provides the method for calculating present value:

Formula 8-4

$$PV = \frac{Sn}{(1 + r)^n}$$

Where: Sn = a sum of money spent or received in the future

r = the discount rate

n = the number of years until the money is received

In our example, we plug the $1,000,000 into Formula 8-4 and assume an eight percent discount rate.

$$PV = \frac{1,000,000}{(1 + .08)^1}$$

$$PV = \$925,925$$

Suppose that since this money was not currently in the budget, a wealthy donor agreed to pay for construction if the city would pay him back the million dollars in two, three, four, or even five years. Note how each year the cost of the million-dollar pool would drop dramatically. If the money did not have to be paid back for five years, the present value would be around $680,600 (assuming an 8 percent rate).

Discounting and present value is useful in determining two measures of efficiency: net present value and benefit cost ratio. Later we will provide you with help in understanding how benefits and costs are determined in public projects. But for now, let's just realize that benefits and costs are not all realized in the same year. Instead, costs tend to occur up front on a project and benefits are spread out over several years. Consider the swimming pool example given earlier. After one year the costs are $1,000,000, with only minimal annual maintenance and operation costs thereafter. Benefits do not begin to accrue for one year but will then continue in a steady fashion for several years. Sheila developed her cost and benefit numbers using narrow definitions of both costs and benefits. Costs were meant to include only the actual costs of building the pools. These costs include mainly construction costs. The benefits were defined narrowly as revenues that would be generated by the pool. Let's take a five-year period and consider the Net Present Value (NPV) and Benefit Cost Ratio (BCR) of the swimming pool project as presented in Table 8-10 (at the top of page 300). Year one's benefits will be slightly lower because the pool will be operational for less than a full swimming season.

Net Present Value (NPV) is calculated by subtracting the discounted benefits from the discounted costs. You could use Formula 8-4 to calculate the present value for each year's cost and benefit. However, to make things easier we have included the discount factor from Table 8-11 (at the bottom of page 301).

TABLE 8-10   SWIMMING POOL BENEFITS AND COSTS

			YEAR			
	0	1	2	3	4	5
Benefits	0	$10,000	$15,000	$15,000	$15,000	$15,000
Costs	0	$1,003,400	$5,000	$5,000	$5,000	$5,000
Discount Rate	7%	7%	7%	7%	7%	7%
Discount Factor	0	.9346	.8734	.8163	.7629	.7130

The calculation of the discount factor allows you to calculate present value. The formula below demonstrates how the numbers in Table 8-11 (on page 301) are calculated.

Formula 8-5

Discount Factor (DF) = $\dfrac{1}{(1 + r)^n}$

Where: r = the discount rate

n = the number of years

Thus with a discount rate of 7 percent and at year #2, the discount factor (DF) is:

$$DF = \frac{1}{(1 + .07)^2}$$

DF = 0. 8734

In each year, we can take the benefits and the costs and separately multiply them by the discount factor (Table 8-11) to get a present value. Please note that you could use the discounting formula that we discussed earlier and calculate the same answers (try it for yourself). However, Table 8-11 provides you a sample of calculated discount factor numbers. NPV is now calculated merely by taking the discount factor, and multiplying it by the annual dollar benefit or cost.

Below we have taken the numbers from Table 8-10 and calculated discounted costs and benefits.

Discounted Benefits (DB) = $0 (0) + $10,000 (.9346) + $15,000 (.8734) + $15,000 (.8163) + $15,000 (.7629) + $15,000 (.7130) = $56,830

Discounted Costs (DC) = $0 (0) + $1,003,400 (.9346) + $5,000 (.8734) + $5,000 (.8163) + $5,000 (.7629) + $5,000 (.7130) = $953,605

Thus the NPV for the project is:

DB – DC or $56,830 – $953,605

NPV = –$896,775

The Net Present Value of the swimming pool project is a negative $896,775. Using the number calculated above you can now determine the Benefit Cost Ratio (BCR). It is a quick and easy calculation and is represented by Formula 8-6.

Formula 8-6

$$BCR = \frac{DB}{DC}$$

In our example the BCR would be:

$$\frac{\$56,830}{\$953,605} = .0595$$

TABLE 8-11   DISCOUNT FACTORS FOR SELECTED DISCOUNT RATES (UP TO TWENTY YEARS)

	DISCOUNT RATE			
YEAR	5%	6%	7%	8%
1	.9524	.9434	.9346	.9259
2	.9070	.8900	.8734	.8573
3	.8638	.8396	.8163	.7938
4	.8227	.7921	.7629	.7350
5	.7835	.7473	.7130	.6806
6	.7462	.7050	.6663	.6302
7	.7107	.6551	.6227	.5835
8	.6768	.6274	.5820	.5403
9	.6446	.5919	.5439	.5002
10	.6139	.5584	.5083	.4632
11	.5847	.5268	.4751	.4289
12	.5568	.4970	.4440	.3971
13	.5303	.4688	.4150	.3677
14	.5051	.4423	.3878	.3405
15	.4810	.4173	.3624	.3152
16	.4581	.3936	.3387	.2919
17	.4363	.3714	.3166	.2703
18	.4155	.3503	.2959	.2502
19	.3957	.3305	.2765	.2317
20	.3769	.3118	.2584	.2145

The BCR is .0595. Based on this data, the swimming pool project is not an efficient project. If a government wants an efficient use of citizen's money then the BCR should be at least 1.00 or preferably over 1.00. Of course, this begs the question of whether public goods such as swimming pools can be evaluated in terms of their economic efficiency. **Public goods**, by definition, provide benefits that are not divisible to individuals. Swimming pools provide many benefits that are not necessarily tangible or easily quantifiable.

Swimming pools provide opportunities for children to play instead of getting into various forms of mischief. Swim lessons taught there can help protect citizens from drowning in nearby lakes, rivers, creeks, and private pools. Swimming pools help provide a sense of community as children and parents gather in a common place and enjoy recreational activities. Swimming pools might also create external benefits. Swimming pools attract individuals into a central place and local businesses may benefit from swimming pools by selling sun screen, soft-drinks, hot dogs, and candy to children and adults. They are also an asset that might help attract new businesses, concerned with what they can offer employees in terms of quality of life.

Then again, there might be external costs associated with the swimming pool. The pool may take business away from a local health spa that has a pool. Perhaps the community is building the new pool in a new location. Moving the pool from an old neighborhood to a more suburban neighborhood might place tremendous costs on the old neighborhood as this decision would deny poor children of yet another opportunity. To a large degree, those decisions belong to the public and to elected officials. The larger question for an analyst like Sheila is how to calculate "costs" and "benefits" on public projects in order to inform your and others' decisions. There is a methodology that attempts to account for both external costs and intangible costs as well as internal and tangible ones. This method is known as "cost-benefit analysis" (CBA).

Tool #7: Cost Benefit Analysis

Cost-benefit analysis (sometimes called benefit-cost analysis) is a central feature of the positivist school of policy analysis. According to Dunn (1981, 244), "Cost-benefit analysis is an approach to policy recommendation that permits analysts to compare and advocate policies by quantifying their total monetary costs and total monetary benefits." Stokey and Zeckhauser (1978, 134) add, "Benefit-cost analysis is the principal analytical framework used to evaluate public expenditure decisions. This approach requires systematic enumeration of all benefits and all costs tangible and intangible, whether readily quantifiable or difficult to measure, that will accrue to all members of society if a particular project is adopted." Stone (1997, 235) writes of CBA, "You have probably used this method in your own decisions, if not in a formal quantitative way, at least by listing the 'pluses' and 'minuses' of an action you were considering. The only difference between your list of pluses and minuses and the formal cost-benefit analysis done by policy analysts is that the analysts have added numbers to theirs. For every plus and minus listed, they think of a way to measure it. And while you might be satisfied with an intuitive feel from your list as to whether the action is 'worth it,' formal analysts force themselves to measure all the consequences in the same terms so that the measures can be added up."

According to Dunn (1981, 244), CBA has the following characteristics:

1. CBA attempts to measure all costs and benefits to society that may result from a public policy. This includes intangibles that cannot be easily measured in terms of monetary costs and benefits.

2. A policy or program is said to be efficient if its net benefits are greater than zero and higher than those net benefits that would have resulted from an alternative public or private investment.

3. Cost-benefit analysis uses the private marketplace to compare alternative uses of public money. Opportunity costs of a public investment are determined by examining what benefits might have been gained by investing in the private sector instead of the public sector.

Dunn (1981, 245) adds that the strength of CBA is that both costs and benefits are measured in dollars as a common unit of value that allows for easy comparison and thereby allows analysts to subtract costs from benefits. In addition, both benefits and costs are linked to the income of a society. Finally, CBA allows analysts to compare programs in widely differing policy areas since efficiency is measured in the common unit of dollars. Dunn (1981, 245) also recognizes the limitations of CBA.

If you have read Chapters 2, 3, and 4 you can probably already foresee some of the problems with this approach. According to Dunn there are three major problems with CBA. First, efficiency may override equity as a value. Dunn recognizes that public goods are not supposed to be efficient and that CBA ignores ethical or moral dimensions. Second, intangible benefits and costs are difficult to estimate and the estimates that are used might be "arbitrary expressions of the values of analysts" (Dunn 1981, 245). Third, because of the problem of "limited interpersonal comparisons," Dunn (1981, 245) argues that "income is an inappropriate measure of individual satisfaction and social welfare." This latter point means that income is relative to individuals and that a $100 cost to one person may be a great burden, whereas to another wealthier person it is not a burden at all.

Costs and benefits in CBA are defined broadly. We feel that four of these costs and benefits are essential to understand: (1) "inside" costs and benefits, (2) "outside" costs and benefits, (3) "tangible" costs and benefits, and (4) "intangible" costs and benefits. An "inside" cost or benefit is linked directly to the government undertaking the public project. In the Boondocks swimming pool example, the inside cost is simply the cost to the local government that must finance the swimming pool construction. An "outside" cost or benefit (referred to as "externalities) occurs outside of a direct transaction. For example, the local sandwich shop that benefits from the building of the swimming pool receives an external benefit. Externalities are typically viewed more negatively in the form of external costs. The increased traffic around the swimming pool is a cost for people in that neighborhood.

Tangible costs and benefits are easy to determine. An intangible cost or benefit is not directly measurable and is much more difficult to identify and difficult especially to quantify. A "tangible" cost or benefit is something that we can put a real dollar on. The costs of concrete and other materials in the building of the swimming pool are tangible costs. Examples of intangible costs would include increases in crime from the increased traffic in the neighborhood with the swimming pool. An intangible benefit from the pool might be an increase in community spirit. Intangible costs also include "opportunity costs" defined as "the next best alternative foregone." For example, if you decide to spend $1,000,000 on a swimming pool then perhaps roads will not be repaired, baseball programs not expanded, or fire protection not enhanced.

Typically, in public projects, tangible costs are easy to identify and quantify whereas intangible costs are much more difficult. There is one final difficulty to CBA; Stokey and Zeckhauser (1978, 134) argue that whereas profit and loss statements are "ex ante" or after the fact, benefit-cost tries to determine the costs and benefits of a project before it is undertaken. Thus, CBA involves prediction and not simply the accounting of costs and benefits already accrued.

There is a methodology for CBA and the approach attempts to account for all the various costs that we have just discussed. Dunn (1981, 248–49) specifies the tasks of CBA. In essence, he recommends the rational model:

- Specification of Objectives
- Identification of Alternatives
- Collection, Analysis, and Interpretation of Information
- Specification of Target Groups
- Identification of Types of Costs and Benefits
- Discounting of Costs and Benefits
- Estimation of Risk and Uncertainty
- Specification of Criteria for Recommendation
- Recommendation

Boondocks, CBA, and Swimming Pools

We now return to our example of the Boondocks swimming pool (discussed in the section on discounting) and you can see if your new-found knowledge of CBA changes the costs and benefits of the project. Let's see how Sheila analyzed the project in a simple manner using each of the nine steps of CBA.

Step 1: Specification of Objectives   The city's recreation department had created the following objectives: (a) to provide water recreation for 5,000 citizen visits per year and (b) to achieve 90 percent or better evaluation ratings on quality of service provided to customers.

Step 2: Identification of Alternatives   Sheila identified four alternatives: (1) do nothing (which would lead to no public-owned swimming facility in the community; (2) repair the existing pool that is not ADA accessible, which will cost more to maintain than a new pool, and which has several health code problems (without repair it must be closed immediately); (3) build a new pool at the current location at an initial cost of $1,000,000; (4) build a new pool at a new site at an initial cost of $1,000,000 (the costs are the same here as they are at the old site because the city already owns the new site land).

Step 3: Collection, Analysis, and Interpretation of Information   Sheila is trying to be both fair and thorough in completing the chart on page 305. (Note that both benefits and costs are more inclusive than those listed in Table 8-10.)

ALTERNATIVE	COSTS	BENEFITS
Do Nothing	–loss of public sponsored swimming (difficult to quantify costs —maybe $50,000 in increased crime) –loss of swimming to lower income families ($50,000) –loss of regional swim meets ($100,000 in gasoline, motel, restaurants, retail purchases) –loss of business in swim area (approximately $50,000 of lost revenue to local businesses over a four-month summer period.	–money from swimming pool can be reallocated to other programs or returned to taxpayers. ($1,000,000)
Repair	–bids for repair range from $1.025 million to $1.5 million. –Opportunity cost for private swim clubs (loss of $25,000 from expanded public swimming services) –Annual operation and maintenance costs ($7,000).	–retain swimming and retain swimming meets and sales to local businesses ($100,000) –potential for lower delinquency ($50,000) $15,000 in user fees.
Build a new pool (in a new area)	–$1,000,000 for an outdoor pool. –$5,000 annually in operation and maintenance costs. –Existing site is too small for new pool since parking is inadequate. New pool would have larger parking area and could accommodate larger swim meets and more customers. However, the moving of the pool would mean that local businesses in the area would lose money. (loss is estimated at $50,000). –Opportunity cost for private swim clubs (loss of $25,000 from expanded swimming services).	–New pool would keep children off the street and would reduce delinquency (estimated at $100,000 in reduced property crime). –A user fee of $3 would be charged, which would raise $15,000 annually. –New pool at new location could lead to more swim club meets which would attract more outside customers and bring money into local economy (estimated at $250,000 annually)
Build a new pool in the existing site	–$1,000,000 in construction costs. –$5,000 annually in operation and maintenance costs. –Opportunity Cost: loss of an extra $50,000 annually to local economy would occur with new pool/new site (more swim meets).	–5000 customers at $3 per customer for $15,000 –Would retain local business profits of $50,000. –Reduced delinquency ($100,000)

Note: This chart only illustrates how some costs and benefits would be quantified. It is not intended to include all possible costs and benefits.

Step 4: Specification of Target Groups

Stakeholders
- swimmers
- swimming clubs
- service clubs
- private recreation clubs
- local businesses such as restaurants, fast food establishments, candy stores, etc.
- police
- citizens
- childcare providers

Step 5: Identification of Types of Costs and Benefits (to Stakeholders)   As you know, stakeholder mapping is too time consuming and involved to use frequently. Sheila does a quick and dirty, but accurate, analysis:

- swimmers (direct benefit—intangible)
- swimming clubs: (direct benefit—intangible)
- service clubs: (direct benefit—intangible)
- private recreation clubs (indirect, tangible costs—lost business)
- local businesses (in old location): indirect and tangible costs if pool is relocated; direct and tangible benefits if pool is retained in current location
- local businesses (in new location): indirect and tangible benefits if pool is relocated; direct and tangible costs if pool is retained in current location
- police: new pool may lower delinquency and help police

Step 6: Discounting of Costs and Benefits

Alternative	Total Costs	Total Benefits
Do nothing	$250,000 (annually)	$1,000,000 (one time benefit)
Repair existing pool	$1,025,000 (low bid and opportunity costs—one time cost) $25,000 annual cost for loss of potential swim meets $7,000 O & M	$165,000 (annual benefit)
Build new pool in a new site	$1,000,000 (one time costs) $80,000 (annually)	$365,000 (annual benefits)
Build new pool in existing site	$1,000,000 (one time costs) $55,000 (annual costs).	$165,000 (annual benefits)

In Tables 8-12 through 8-15 that follow (starting on page 307 and ending on page 308), Sheila calculates NPV and the Benefit Cost Ratio (BCR) using the principles of Tool #6.

TABLE 8-12   THE DO NOTHING ALTERNATIVE

ALTERNATIVE: DO NOTHING (DISCOUNTED OVER 5 YEARS AT 7% DISCOUNT RATE)

			YEAR			
	0	1	2	3	4	5
Costs	0	$250,000	$250,000	$250,000	$250,000	$250,000
Benefits	0	$1,000,000	0	0	0	0
Discount Rate	—	7%	7%	7%	7%	7%
Discount Factor	—	.9346	.8734	.8163	.7629	.7130

Discounted Benefits = $1,000,000 (.9346) = $934,600
Discounted Costs = $250,000 (.9346) + $250,000 (.8734) + $250,000 (.8163) + $250,000 (.7629) + $250,000 (.7130) = $1,025,050
NPV = $934,600 – $1,025,050 = –$90,450
BCR = $934,600/$1,025,050 = 0.91

TABLE 8-13   THE REPAIR ALTERNATIVE

ALTERNATIVE: REPAIR

			YEAR			
	0	1	2	3	4	5
Costs	0	$1,057,000	$32,000	$32,000	$32,000	$32,000
Benefits	0	$165,000	$165,000	$165,000	$165,000	$165,000
Discount Rate	—	7%	7%	7%	7%	7%
Discount Factor	—	.9346	.8734	.8163	.7629	.7130

Discounted Benefits = $165,000 (.9346) + $165,000 (.8734) + $165,000 (.8163) + $165,000 (.7629) + $165,000 (.7130) = $676,534
Discounted Costs = $1,057,000 (.9346) + $32,000 (.8734) + $32,000 (.8163) + $32,000 (.7629) + $32,000 (.7130) = $1,089,170
NPV = $676,534 – $1,089,170 = –$412,636
BCR = $676,534/$1,089,170 = 0.62

TABLE 8-14   THE NEW SITE ALTERNATIVE

ALTERNATIVE: BUILD AT NEW SITE

			YEAR			
	0	1	2	3	4	5
Costs	0	$1,080,000	$80,000	$80,000	$80,000	$80,000
Benefits	0	$365,000	$365,000	$365,000	$365,000	$365,000
Discount Rate	—	7%	7%	7%	7%	7%
Discount Factor	—	.9346	.8734	.8163	.7629	.7130

Discounted Benefits = $365,000 (.9346) + $365,000 (.8734) + $365,000 (.8163) + $365,000 (.7629) + $365,000 (.7130) = $1,496,572
Discounted Costs = $1,080,000 (.9346) + $80,000 (.8734) + $80,000 (.8163) + $80,000 (.7629) +$80,000 (.7130) = $1,262,616
NPV = $1,496,572 – $1,262,616 = $233,956
BCR = $1,496,572/$1,262,616 = 1.19

TABLE 8-15   THE EXISTING SITE ALTERNATIVE

ALTERNATIVE: BUILD NEW POOL AT EXISTING SITE

				YEAR		
	0	1	2	3	4	5
Costs	0	$1,000,000	$55,000	$55,000	$55,000	$55,000
Benefits	0	$165,000	$165,000	$165,000	$165,000	$165,000
Discount Rate	—	7%	7%	7%	7%	7%
Discount Factor	—	.9346	.8734	.8163	.7629	.7130

Discounted Benefits: $165,000 (.9346) + $165,000 (.8734) + $165,000 (.8163) + $165,000 (.7629) + $165,000 (.7130) = $676,527

Discounted Costs: $1,000,000 (.9346) + $55,000 (.8734) + $55,000 (.8163) + $55,000 (.7629) + $55,000 (.7130) = $1,108,708

NPV = $676,527 – $1,108,708 = –$432,253

BCR = $676,527/$1,108,708 = 0.61

Step 7: Estimation of Risk and Uncertainty   There are a variety of methods that can be used in this step. The analyst attempts to give the decision makers some sense of the probabilities of various outcomes. In addition, the analyst can provide data on how price changes of certain key elements of a public project could increase or decrease costs and benefits. One simple method of estimating risk and uncertainty is by drawing a decision tree and providing probabilities of various outcomes. We have included two simple decision trees that Sheila could create for the Boondocks' swimming pool issue. However, first we must briefly provide you with some information about decision trees.

Decision trees are graphic models designed to induce clarity and rationality in regards to the options available and outcome (or expectation) probabilities. The analyst would attempt to weight the probabilities and, if revenues and costs are involved, those estimates can also be built into the decision tree. Decision trees span out sequentially from the initial decision into chance or outcome branches stemming from the uncertainty nodes. The analyst grafts probabilities and estimates onto the tree as well. The quality of the decision tree depends largely on the quality of the analyst and the information used to consider various likelihoods.

Figure 8-1 provides a look at Sheila's options, including probabilities in regard to increasing the number of new swim meets. As you can see from this decision tree, it appears that the highest probability of bringing in new swim meets rests with building a new pool at a new site. Repairing the old pool is not likely to bring in new swim meets. However, there is some political support from the local neighborhoods to repair the old pool. Thus, the choice has been narrowed to either repairing the old pool, or building a new pool at the new site. Sheila could forecast higher usage by the public if a new pool is built, and thus higher user fees. This amount could then be multiplied by the probability of the higher usage outcome. If, for example, Sheila predicts the probability that a repaired pool will have high usage as 0.6 (60 percent likely) and low usage as 0.4 (40 percent likely), and if she estimates annual revenue at high usage as $100,000 and low usage as $50,000, then she can calculate each as possible outcomes of repairing the pool; and add them together to arrive at a revenue estimate of $80,000. See Figure 8-2 for illustration.

$100,000 x 0.6 = $60,000
$50,000 x 0.4 = $20,000
                $80,000

For a new pool Sheila estimated high usage as 0.8 (80 percent likely) and low usage as 0.2 (20 percent likely). Her fiscal estimates regarding revenue remain unchanged. The calculation now looks like this:

$100,000 x .8 = $80,000
$50,000 x .2 = $10,000
               $90,000

FIGURE 8-1   BOONDOCKS SWIMMING POOL DECISION TREE

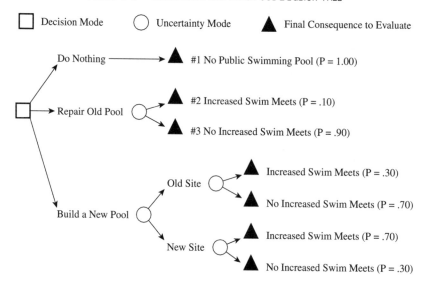

FIGURE 8-2   DECISION TREE FOR SWIMMING POOL USAGE

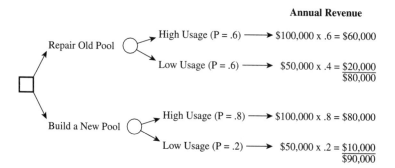

If the annual operating costs will not increase due to higher usage, the net revenue yield from the new pool will exceed the repaired pool, and should obviously be the choice. Remember though, all the numbers (probabilities and revenue estimates) are just guesstimates. And, what issues are left out? For example, this ignores the cost of building versus repairing and the creation of hard feelings in the old neighborhood.

Don't forget that these precise numbers mask the imprecision of the future. Like CBA in general, it is easy to get it right after the fact, but when standing in the "buzzing, blooming confusion" of the now, and looking forward into that ambiguous abyss called the future, it's a whole other ballgame. The potential consequences of each decision are summarized below:

1. Consequence #1: Do Nothing: Leads to no public swimming, which will lead to a political liability as parents will be unhappy that their children no longer have a major summer recreation activity to keep them occupied. Could lead to increases in juvenile delinquency and loss of sense of community. Costs of private swimming may be prohibitive to some families. Loss of regional swimming meets. Loss of business to local businesses in summer months.

2. Consequence #2: Repair: This will keep public swimming in the community and will satisfy parents. However, there is no extra advantage in that there is only 10 percent chance of the newly repaired pool attracting additional regional swim meets. The repair will please the local businesses around the pool because they will retain existing summer business even though there are other factors that could affect summer business, like bad weather.

3. Consequence #3: Repair: The repaired pool will not be big enough to accommodate increased citizen demand as the population of Boondocks increases. In addition, the repaired pool is highly unlikely (90 percent) to attract additional regional swim meets. The pool is located in a section of town with limited parking and limited activities. The current trend is that Boondocks is hosting fewer and fewer swim meets each year. Even with repairs, it is unlikely that the trend will be reversed. This will lead to political unhappiness from the Boondocks Tourism and Visitor Center and the motel industry and among other businesses that benefit from regional swim meets.

4. Consequence #4: Build at Old Site: A new pool (at the old site) is preferable to the alternative of repairing the old pool. The city would continue to provide public swimming and the pool would remain an economic asset to the older section of town. However, public growth in the community is happening in areas of the town that are miles away from the existing pool site. Many of these new neighborhoods complain that the existing pool is located in a dangerous neighborhood and is inconvenient. The new pool at the existing site is unlikely to attract more regional swim meets because of its location.

5. Consequence #5: Build at New Site: Building a new pool at the new location would allow Boondocks to continue the provision of public swimming. The new pool at a new location would likely attract increased numbers of regional swim meets. This would lead to increases in dollars spent by outsiders in the community as a whole. Businesses located near the existing pool site would lose some summer business. The location of the pool is more convenient for citizens in the growing population centers of the city.

Step 8: Specification of Criteria for Recommendation   Based on Steps 1–7, Sheila writes, "From my analysis it is clear that we must be concerned with the overall impact of the swimming pool decision. This is a community project and the community as a whole must benefit. Therefore, I recommend that the major criterion is Net Present Value (NPV). We must carefully promote a policy that will increase benefits to the city as a whole rather than to select groups of individuals."

In short, Sheila had to decide upon the major criteria or criterion for making a decision. There are several criteria to be used. But it is clear from the analysis so far that decision makers in this case have already decided that net efficiency improvement is the major one. That is, the proposal of building a new pool at a new site is the only proposal that had a BCR of more than one. Sheila's second decision tree concerning usage and revenue could also be used to support this value decision with apparently impartial numbers. The key criterion appears to be the possibility of attracting additional regional swim meets to the community. Moving the pool will create losers (the old neighborhood and neighborhood businesses) and winners (the new neighborhood and neighborhood businesses). But the analyst seems content that the overall increased benefit to the community will outweigh the loss to the old neighborhood.

Step 9: Recommendation   Sheila writes the following to the city council:

> Based on the CBA analysis, the best decision is to build a new pool in a new site. No other alternative meets the CBA criteria of net efficiency improvement. The "Do Nothing Alternative" produced a BCR of 0.91, the "Repair Alternative" produced a BCR of 0.62, the "Existing Site Alternative" produced a BCR of 0.61; whereas, the "New Site Alternative" produced a BCR of 1.19. Further this choice is likely to yield more annual revenue than the repair alternative. Based on my analysis, the project that will maximize benefits and minimize costs is, once again, to build a new pool at the new site location.

Note that Sheila avoided all other criteria in her written recommendation, and focused on the criterion the decision makers wanted fleshed out. The story below provides a real-life example of CBA.

Story 8-1: Up to My Elbows and Beyond

Q: How many professors does it take to change a light bulb?
A: None, they have to get help.

The above isn't always true; your professor may actually possess skills and job experiences that amaze you. One of this text's authors actually has a fork-lift driver's license that dates back to years of working in a mill, cleaning various grass seeds (mostly Kentucky Bluegrass, Ryegrass, and various Fescues). One of the machines he ran, known as a debearder, had long metal teeth that spun at a fast rate, beating the beard (sort of a hairy growth) off recently harvested seed.

Sometimes a part off a combine, a hammer, a shovel, a pair of jeans, or some other inexplicable item would show up in the bulk seed and jam the debearder. Other times the seed would just bridge due to the crud picked up and the cottony beard. At this point the solution was to turn off the debearder, open up the doors on the cylinder, reach up into it, and remove the object (not as easy as it sounds). One problem for whoever took on this task was that every time you put your arm into this machine you were worried about a fellow worker accidentally turning it on.

The off-set steel teeth were each about eight inches long, two inches wide, and one inch thick, and the clearance rate between them and the walls was virtually paper thin. They spun at hundreds of revolutions per minute. Sometimes you were up to your elbows and beyond to reach the plug. Usually, to be careful, your author would not only turn it off, he would go to the power room and turn it off there as well. Once, with a different machine he had to climb into and stand in with his feet in an auger that would have smashed his feet off his ankles, he even took the fuses out of the fuse box and hid them.

In 1979 the government had rules ready to go into place to protect workers from this problem. It was known as the lockout rule. The Occupational Safety and Health Administration (OSHA) denied a petition to require lockout devices on electrical switches for such machines, but moved forward with the process to establish such a regulation (i.e., advanced notice of proposed rule-making, an invitation for comments, and hearings).

This regulation would be simple to implement. Switches today often have lockout capability. This is as simple as a guard with a hole on the on-off switch that allows one to place a padlock through it. With the padlock on, you cannot move the guard and turn on the machine. Every decade (including the eighties), a thousand or more workers died in horrible accidents due to this problem, and many more were injured, often very seriously.

So what happened to the government's proposed rule? Why did this policy languish during the eight years of the Reagan administration? The tragic mystery begins during his original campaign for office and his promise to get government off the backs of the people and business. Shortly after his election President Reagan issued an executive order (No. 12291) that revised, complicated, slowed, and discouraged rulemaking by government agencies.

Executive Order No. 12291 placed the Office of Management and Budget (OMB) squarely in the middle of all regulatory decisions. It called for a Regulatory Impact Analysis (RIA) for all major rules, regulations, and standards; and for the OMB to review the RIA and determine if the rule's potential benefits to society outweighed its potential costs to society. It required "to the extent permitted by law" all executive agencies not to issue regulations unless the benefits exceed the costs. (This phrase is important, since Congress did, for example, forbid the use of cost-benefit analysis when OSHA was considering safety standards).

Further, if alternative approaches exist, the one that leads to the least net cost to society must be chosen (and the condition of both the regulated industries and the national economy had to be considered as well). It also froze virtually all rules that had worked their way through the system under the Carter administration, but that had not yet been put into place. It was now the OMB's call to delay or veto proposed regulations. In January 1985 President Reagan issued Executive Order No. 12498 which supplemented No. 12291 and further expanded the role of the OMB.

President Reagan's rhetoric and his election, his appointments, and his executive orders all created an ambiance and a process that discouraged rulemaking and which encouraged cost-benefit analysis. When you were up to your elbows (or beyond) in the debearder, such a rational approach was of little comfort. To the families of those killed and to all those seriously hurt, it might even seem that slowing and stopping government regulation was not an unmitigated good.

By the way, workers are still being killed and maimed. In Robert Reich's memoir (1998, 161) of his service as Secretary of Labor during President Clinton's first term, he tells of four workers who worked for Bridgestone Tire suffering these types of accidents within less than a year's time (three at their Oklahoma City tire plant, the other in Morrison, Tennessee). One "died when his head was crushed in an assembly machine that was supposed to have been shut off before he tried to reset it." Another had his arm "severely mangled and broken" trying "to unjam another machine that was also supposed to have been shut off." The third (April 1994) "was bashed in the head and badly burned." In Tennessee, coworkers rescued a worker whose head was "caught in an assembly machine ... but not before his face was badly mangled." Reich points out that OSHA has tried to "coax" Bridgestone into preventing lockout accidents by installing locking mechanisms on all their machines. He reports that the cost is approximately "six dollars per machine to buy and install" but that Bridgestone would not budge. (Story sources: Executive Order 12291—46 *Federal Register* 13193, 1981; Executive Order 12498—50 *Federal Register* 11036, 1986; Steven Cann. 1995. *Administrative Law*. Thousand Oaks, CA: Sage Publications; Robert Reich. 1998. *Locked in the Cabinet*. New York: Vintage Books.)

Analysis of the Use of CBA

Our view of the use of CBA is quite simple. First, CBA is a major tool used in the field of practice. Therefore, practicing analysts have to understand its application. Second, practicing analysts have to be able to recognize the subjectivity and outright "voodoo" quality of CBA. Analysts should be prepared to give several estimates of costs and benefits and be quite forthright in telling decision makers and the public that there are many policy outcomes that cannot be quantified. Third, we view CBA as an analytical tool. It is only a technique to encourage a serious discussion of the various costs and benefits of a proposed project and how the costs and benefits affect various stakeholders. This stakeholder analysis can be viewed as democratic, as CBA's differentiation of costs into tangible/intangible and direct/indirect is a good method to force decision makers to think about the large-scale impact of a project on various groups.

While it is easy to criticize positivist-oriented textbooks and their advocating of CBA, it is fair to point out that even most positivist policy analysis scholars recognize the limitations of CBA. Stokey and Zeckhauser (1978, 134) argue that this technique (what they call benefit-cost analysis) works best on specific and concrete projects, like choosing between pollution control systems or "deciding whether road repairs in a community should be made with a new, more weather resistant asphalt." They admit that for wider-ranging programs it is more useful as a "paradigm" (Stokey and Zeckhauser 1978, 135). Stokey and Zeckhauser (1978, 135) write of the use of benefit-cost analysis for larger programs: "A detailed quantitative analysis of such programs would be impossible, but thinking about the way such an analysis might be carried out forces policymakers to think hard about categories of benefits and costs, to define their expectations about outputs, and to pay attention to the tradeoffs that are important in their decisions."

Unfortunately, the carefully thought out application of CBA advocated by such positivists as Dunn and Stokey and Zeckhauser often gets lost in the very hectic and political world of practice. As Stokey and Zeckhauser themselves write (1978, 135):

> Our general approach to benefit-cost analysis is positive and enthusiastic. But it would be unfair to praise the merits of project evaluation techniques without identifying their liabilities as well. Benefit-cost analysis is especially vulnerable to misapplication through carelessness, naivete, or outright deception. The techniques are potentially dangerous to the extent that they convey an aura of precision and objectivity. Logically they can be no more precise that the assumptions and valuations that they employ; frequently through the compounding of errors, they may be less so. Deception is quite a different matter, involving submerged assumptions, unfairly chosen valuations, and purposeful misestimates.

We are further troubled by the potential problem of the analyst becoming the single point of the decision. As stated earlier, CBA does have some potentially democratic aspects[8] (e.g., the inclusion of the costs and benefits accruing to various stakeholders). However, as Stone (1997, 242–43) writes in this regard, positivist policy analysis tends to be undemocratic in its execution because:

> In the polis, authority on issues of significance is usually dispersed, shared, negotiated, and constantly contested. Most policy issues involve questions of who has the power to decide. The rational decision model assumes this problem has been resolved or does not exist. The adherents of rational decision models are hardly troubled by the omission, however. Quite the contrary, they tout as one of the virtues of these methods that "true" interests are revealed without the distortions of politics.

What often happens with the use of CBA is that an analyst collects data, makes calculations, and presents a recommendation to an elected official. CBA becomes the ritual that reinforces government accountability and mythical aspects of democracy. Jackson and Maughan (1978, 126–27) write of CBA, "The public has reason to feel anxious that agencies of government and politicians will waste their tax dollars—that the cost of programs to the public will exceed the benefits. We feel that benefit-cost analysis and other formal methods of policy analysis produced by agencies often embody many of the elements of ritual. Often their function is to reassure the public of the myth's validity and that its interest is protected."

The CBA process involves the gathering of extensive data, stakeholder analysis, and risk calculation. The output of the process is impressive and a subjective, value-laden, political question is turned into a rational one. Democracy no longer consists of bargaining, trading, negotiating, power, interests, information, knowledge, and trust. Rather with CBA, "democracy" is often wrongly represented by a CBA report. In place of the complicated and value-laden nature of democracy, we find seemingly complicated numerical calculations of Net Present Value, Benefit to Cost Ratios, and Internal Rates of Return. Once the CBA report is turned over to elected officials, the final decision becomes a "fait accompli" (a thing that has been done). Despite the subjectivity of the number calculations, decision makers accept the mathematics because it

---

[8]Of course this would depend on how "democracy" is defined. CBA is democratic only under a limited "technocratic view of democracy." CBA is most certainly not democratic in a participatory sense.

provides them cover, projects a sense of objectivity, and perhaps even protects them psychologically from worrying about the potential arbitrariness of and irrationality of, and selective harm stemming from, the decision.

"Politics" is a dirty word in American political culture. Even elected officials themselves have difficulty accepting the fact that much of what they do in public life is political and that their decisions are tied to their and their supporters' interests. Policy analysts have an even more difficult time accepting the inevitability of politics. They have been trained, after all, to believe that it is possible to be scientific and value-neutral technicians. They have been trained to believe that ambiguity and subjectivity must be avoided. CBA, used poorly, provides elected officials cover for their political interests and it provides policy analysis an appearance of certainty, or at least probability, in a political world that offers neither.

Our critique of the use of CBA then, is really a larger critique of the rational model. It is helpful in forcing decision makers to gather information and carefully examine the effects of potential policies. But ultimately, all the data, all the statistics, all the number crunching, pushes out the politics, the bargaining, the compromises, and the shared values that encompass democracy. It is a problem that stems from the progressive era in American history when well-meaning citizens, scholars, and elected officials tried to take the "politics out of politics."

Public administration was in the forefront of the effort to rationalize and professionalize American government. Public policy analysis, and the larger field of public administration, is dedicated to rationalizing and professionalizing policymaking. Because of politics, policymaking is messy, full of conflicting demands, and subjective interpretations. CBA, as part of the rational policy analysis tradition, makes policy development look efficient, rational, tidy, and decisive. It does so by making the analyst the central focus of the decision. It is the analyst who, despite all the possible input gathering, gets to decide final costs and benefits. It is the analyst who decides that one set of criteria is more important than another. It is the analyst who decides that one set of stakeholders is more important than another set. Again, CBA and the larger rational model in which it exists seemingly takes the "politics out of politics." Stone (1997, 242) writes, "The advocates of rational decision models come close to promising that politics will eventually become unnecessary."

But CBA does not take the politics out of politics. Politics is not removed but hidden. We pretend it isn't there, demean it and try to hide it. Politics is not vanquished, but transformed into an unhealthier version of itself. Instead, CBA shifts politics from a multitude of groups and individuals to a single decision maker. What is the answer then? If a practicing analyst needs to know how to use CBA, then how should it be used? We recommend the following:

1. When conducting a CBA, try to gather as much original data as possible. That is, do not make subjective interpretations of how various stakeholders view the costs and benefits of a project. Instead, talk to the stakeholders, conduct focus groups and surveys. Allow the stakeholders to see your conclusions well before the final report is submitted. Talk to them openly about your conclusions and their views.

2. Do not try to hide the subjectivity of "shadow pricing" (your attempt to quantify intangible and indirect costs and benefits). It is impossible to quantify most of

what government does. How do we really put a dollar amount on clean air, clean water, safe streets, worker safety, and city recreation programs? Advocates of CBA contend that these examples do have "implied prices" and that we can determine costs. But to tie cost or price numbers to an example like public education is to destroy the very definition of a public good. Public choice theory that assumes that we can attach costs and benefits to everything eventually destroys the role of government. Government exists because in the long run we all benefit from providing public schools, public bus systems, and recreation programs. The benefits, however, cannot be tied directly back to individuals. So when you are asked to create a "shadow price" for the benefits of recreation, fully admit that the numbers you provide are simply estimates, and perhaps provide a wide variety of different scenarios using different ranges of numbers. Tell your audience that the shadow price is often just a political argument for or against a certain project. Demonstrate in your CBA how various shadow prices can change the final outcome. Do not be afraid to show your audience the subjective and value-laden aspect of such benefit and cost determination. After all, politics and policymaking is subjective and value-laden. However, take this advice with the full warning that your bosses (elected officials and fellow analysts) may not like you exposing the often quasi-scientific number-crunching of the profession. Elected officials might well believe that you are destroying attempts at providing citizens with data that will make them comfortable with governmental choices. Fellow analysts might well think that you are hurting the profession by "lifting the curtain" that has veiled the subjectivity of the profession for years. Our advice here is to be politically subtle and incorporate this suggestion incrementally. Gain the trust of your elected officials and fellow analysts. Quietly point out the subjectivity of your number calculations and subtly move policy analysis in your department toward a more democratic approach.

3. Wherever possible, conduct the CBA as part of a team. This will help bring in additional viewpoints and lessen the problem of a single decision maker. In a similar vein, allow stakeholders and others to bargain for various definitions of costs and benefits, seek diversity for the CBA team, and be inclusive when considering stakeholders.

4. Stress to decision makers the real value of CBA. Tell them that the numbers can be almost meaningless and that its only value is in rationally looking at how various groups are potentially affected by various policy options and in deriving very rough estimates of benefit/cost ratios.

5. The CBA should never be used as a sole criterion for a final decision. Instead, it should be only one tool used among many. CBAs are essentially just a form of political argument for or against a certain policy proposal.

6. CBAs should be simple. Numerical calculations and subjective determinations should be readily understood by elected officials, interest groups, and citizens. Note that, throughout the toolbox, we have not asked you to perform more than a very basic level of high school math. Alternative calculations and interpretations should be stressed.

Unfortunately, these suggestions would make CBA less efficient and the final decision less predictable. Politics, human nature, and the positivist orientation make this difficult to obtain. Bureaucratic government demands efficiency, neutrality, and predictability. A more democratic CBA process would undermine many of these values, for it would be less efficient, it would reveal subjectivity, and it would provide a final solution that would not be definitive. But, at least, it would be an effort at honesty.

Concluding Thoughts

Throughout this book, and this chapter, we have argued that pragmatism demands that policy analysis be political and that in the field it is largely political. Moreover, our chapters have provided an alternative to the traditional positivist methodology. We have encouraged you to think politically and to understand that public problems are socially constructed. We have also advocated a more democratic approach to policy analysis. Public policy analysis based on our approach is much more than the technical manipulation of models, numbers, and statistics.

With that said, however, these seven key positivist tools are ones that any practicing analyst should understand and be able to apply (fully cognizant of their limitations and the way in which—intentionally or not—they have often been used to limit democracy). The chapter closes with eight problems based on the chapter's tools. The answers to the questions are provided after the problems.

Key Concepts

analysis of CBA (p. 313)

cost benefit analysis (p. 302)

deflating money (p. 294)

decision trees (p. 308)

discounting (p. 298)

extrapolation and forecasting (p. 287)

measures of central tendency (p. 290)

per capita analysis (p. 297)

politics of survey construction (p. 283)

sampling and mail surveys (p. 274)

sample bias and weighting (p. 278)

sample size (p. 275)

technicalities of surveys (p. 280)

techniques of random sampling (p. 276)

Glossary Terms

Chi-square test (p. 280)

confidence level (p.275)

outliers (p. 293)

public goods (p. 302)

References

Babbie, Earl. 1996. *The Practice of Social Research*. Belmont, CA: Wadsworth Publishing.

Baumol, William J., and Alan S. Blinder. 1988. *Economics: Principles and Policy: Macroeconomics*. San Diego, CA: Harcourt Brace Jovanovich Publishers.

California Postsecondary Education Commission. 1999. <http://www.cpec.ca.gov/home.htm>

Cann, Steven. 1995. *Administrative Law*. Thousand Oaks, CA: Sage Publications.

Charlambous, Nicholaus. 1999. "City Finds 400 Homes Uncounted." *Idaho State Journal* (July 7): A-1.

Dunn, William N. 1981. *Public Policy Analysis*. Englewood Cliffs, NJ: Prentice Hall.

Executive Order 12291—46 *Federal Register* 13193 (1981).

Executive Order 12498—50 *Federal Register* 11036 (1986).

Foltz, David H. 1996. *Survey Research for Public Administration*. Thousand Oaks, CA: Sage Publications.

Jackson, Donald W., and Ralph B. Maughan. 1978. *An Introduction to Political Analysis: The Theory and Practice of Allocation*. Santa Monica, CA: Goodyear Publishing.

Morin, Richard. 1993. "The Pollsters' Preemptive Strike Against Perot." *Washington Post National Weekly Edition*.

Reich, Robert B. 1998. *Locked in the Cabinet*. New York: Vintage Books.

Stokey, Edith, and Richard Zeckhauser. 1978. *A Primer for Policy Analysis*. New York: W. W. Norton and Company.

Stone, Deborah. 1997. *Policy Paradox: The Art of Political Decision Making*. New York: W. W. Norton and Company.

The New Party. 1999. Survey received in the mail by author. The website for the group is <http://www.newparty.org>

Problems

Sampling Applications

1. Test your ability to conduct a random sample by completing the following assignment:

   You want to mail surveys to only those 18 or older (this is your population).

COUNTY	POPULATION (18 YRS.+)	PERCENT
Payment	16,434	3.3%
Jim	11,844	2.4
Boze	3,509	0.7
Gibbons	90,076	18.2
San Bueno	205,775	41.7
Moreland	8,392	1.7
Nomore	21,205	4.3
Kemmis	727	0.2
Goodland	11,633	2.4
Arid Falls	53,580	10.8
Seinfield	15,138	3.1
Richland	13,552	2.7
Abe	3,308	0.7
Minico	19,361	3.9
Kammina	19,532	3.9
Total	494,066	100%

   Using these counties, prepare sampling strategies to send mail surveys. Your sample size should have a confidence interval of 95 percent with an accuracy of +/–3 percent. Remember: Sample size is *not the amount of surveys you mail*. Based on research, expect a 40 percent return rate for this survey. *After completing these questions make a recommendation on what sampling method to use.*

   a. Prepare a strategy to prepare a systematic random sample. What is the process and how many surveys do you mail?

   b. Prepare a strategy to create a proportionate stratified sample (stratify rural versus urban: Arid Fall, San Bueno, and Gibbons are all urban; the rest are rural). What is the process and how many surveys do you mail to each stratum?

c. Prepare a disproportionate stratified sample. You know from literature and experience that we can expect a 33 percent response rate in rural areas compared to a 50 percent in urban areas. What is the process and how many surveys do you mail to each stratum?

Extrapolation

2. The following data has been collected by the city of Hamptonville.

YEAR	POPULATION
1950	56,800
1960	61,000
1970	65,000
1980	67,000
1990	69,500
2000	72,350

a. Project the population in years 2010 and 2020, using extrapolation techniques.
b. Discuss the benefits and limitations of extrapolation in this case.

Net Present Value and Benefit Cost-Ratio

3. Find the Net Present Value (NPV) and Benefit Cost Ratio (BCR) of the following with a discount rate of 8 percent:

			YEARS		
	0	1	2	3	4
Benefits	0	$8,000	$6,000	$6,000	$6,000
Costs	$0	$25,000	$2,000	$2,000	$2,000

a. What is the NPV?
b. What is the BCR?

4. Re-do question number three, assuming a discount rate of 6 percent. Does it change your analysis? If so, how and why?

Survey Design

5. Design a survey for the Boondocks swimming pool policy project. Try to keep it simple, short, technically correct, and politically sensitive. Ask citizens their views of the swimming pool controversy.

Measures of Central Tendency

6. An analyst has collected the data on page 320 on the number of complaints about garbage collection made over the past ten years. Calculate a mean, median, and mode. Which measure of central tendency are you must likely to use and why?

YEAR	NUMBER OF COMPLAINTS
1990	34
1991	42
1992	24
1993	43
1994	20
1995	45
1996	28
1997	42
1998	38
1999	40

Cost-Benefit Analysis

7. You work as a policy analyst for the city of Acequia. The mayor has asked you to write a one-page memo to her about the use of cost-benefit analysis. Write that one-page memo.

Deflating Money

8. The city of Acequia is concerned that their budget for fire protection has increased "too dramatically" in the last twenty years. In 1980, the city spent $650,000 for fire protection. In 1998, the city spent $800,000. Using your knowledge of deflating money, provide a real-dollar amount to the city's elected officials.

Answers to Problems

1. a. Mail 2,778 surveys based on a 40 percent expected return (you need 1,111 surveys returned). Randomly choose from driver's license lists or other convenient sampling lists.

   b. There are 394,431 (71 percent) residents from urban counties. There are 144,635 residents from rural counties (29 percent). Mail 1,972 surveys to urban counties and 806 surveys to rural counties. Be sure that sampling is random.

   c. Mail 1,578 surveys to urban counties and 968 surveys to rural counties.

2. The average growth increment is 3,110 per decade (1950 base year). Therefore, we would predict 75,460 residents in 2010 and 78,570 residents in 2020.

3. a. Discounted Benefits = $21,724, Discounted Costs = $27,921

   NPV = –$6,197

   b. BCR = 0.778

4. Discounted Benefits = $22,677, Discounted Costs = $28,628

   NPV = $–5,951, BCR = 0.792

5. Answers may vary. Be sure you follow the survey tips and practical considerations given in the chapter (Tool #1).

6. Mean = 35.60, Median = 39, Mode = 42. (Students often fail to rank order the data before calculating the median.)

7. Answers may vary. Make sure that you understand the major strengths and limitations of CBA. Your answer should also attempt to incorporate democracy into CBA.

8. The real dollar increase is $445,383.

CHAPTER 9

THE CONCLUSION: PRAXIS

Mini-Case
"Drug Abuse and Waterville"

We will keep this last chapter very brief. This book began by throwing you into the political firestorm of doing public policy analysis in the mini-case "Drug Abuse and Waterville." When you were done you were asked the following questions:

- How would you describe the process you used to respond to your task?
- Did you try to be objective? Did you recognize your values coming into play? Do you believe that it is appropriate for an analyst's personal values to affect policy recommendations?
- Who in Waterville would you be trying to please? Who do you work for?

The Waterville case and the discussion questions sought to make you think about issues you might not normally have thought about. The case is typical of cases administered during competitions for public management jobs and internships, which are designed to evaluate how much prospective public managers know about public policy analysis.

After you completed the case we explained our belief that public policy analysis is complex and requires a method, tools, and political knowledge. We also claimed that it is affected by the analyst's values—especially her or his understanding of democracy and view of the appropriate role of government. We then told you that throughout this book you would be learning and applying lessons, skills, and a public policy analysis methodology, all of which would help you tremendously with this task. Then we promised (or threatened, depending on your subjective perspective) that at the end of the book you would be offered the opportunity to redo this case. Well, we certainly hope you are better prepared now to tackle this case. It is time to deliver on our promise, time for you to show off how much you have learned, and then time for us to offer seven final discussion questions, and a very, very brief conclusion.

Drug Abuse and Waterville

Directions

1. Read the information carefully.
2. Respond to the one-page case study in any format you feel is appropriate.
3. All necessary information to analyze this situation is provided in the background section.
4. Your response should be no more than three pages long.
5. Please note that calculations and research are not necessary for your response.

Background

The community of Waterville, Pennsylvania (population 6,543), once mostly known for its historic hotel where both George Washington and the French General Lafayette slept, has recently taken note of what many community residents term "a major teenage drug problem." The recent busts by the state police of five "meth houses" in the space of one month and the arrests of several well-known Waterville High School athletes who are allegedly involved in the community drug trade have led to calls from community leaders to combat the drug problem.

Waterville is a community with a per capita personal income of $23,500. This compares to a state average of $28,000. The story of local businesses closing has been a frequent one in recent years and the one major industry in Waterville left town last summer when the corporate bosses in Houston, Texas, decided to relocate the plant to Mexico. This left slightly over four hundred people, who had been earning above-average wages, unemployed. It will also cost Waterville a significant portion of city and school tax monies.

Divorces and births to unmarried teens have been steadily increasing in the past decade and have soared beyond the state and national averages. There is also a great deal of racial tension in the town, where 25 percent of the population is Hispanic. There have been significant conflicts between city officials and leaders within the Hispanic community. Conflict has centered on issues such as use of the city parks; zoning; dances; and police practices, hiring policies, and priorities.

Several members of the city council are concerned that the drug problem is an "epidemic" and are calling for a "war on drugs." Mayor Joyce Allen told the local paper that without some type of action from the city government this problem will destroy the community and drive out more businesses. A local priest told his congregation that the very soul of the town and its children were on the line.

The city manager has asked you to conduct a public policy analysis to identify the potential problems, issues, and policy alternatives, and to prepare and present a recommendation to the city council. What do you do?

Discussion Questions

1. According to Danziger, we are all "embedded practitioners" (i.e., we are biased by our professional community, our life experiences, etc.). Based upon your efforts with the cases in this book, think about the biases or prejudices you brought to your role as analyst (in general). Did these biases affect how you interpreted cases—especially the Waterville Drug Abuse case—and your proposed process and solutions?

2. Postmodernism believes that "public problems are ultimately artificial" (i.e., they are socially constructed—they have no existence outside of human values and consciousness). Using the cases in this book as your examples, reflect upon this postmodern claim, and then respond to it in terms of the Waterville case.

3. The Sophists of ancient Greece argued that ultimately the "truth is what we are persuaded of." This conclusion, of course, is unsettling since we want public policy to be based on hard, scientific facts—not just rhetorical persuasion. Based on your experiences in completing the cases in this book, do you believe that there is a "truth" in policymaking? What was the hard scientific truth in this Waterville case?

4. A central question that any public policy analysis student must answer is: "What is the role of the policy analyst in a democracy?" The answer to this is, of course, dependent on how one defines democracy. Based upon your values, and the readings and case assignments, what do you think is the role of the expert analyst in democratic government? How did this belief affect your handling of the Waterville case?

5. It may have been surprising to you that as political science, public administration, and policy students we had to spend time making decisions about technical and scientific issues outside our area of expertise. We talked about such topics as drug abuse, economics in rural communities, brucellosis transmission, juvenile violence, and swimming pool construction. It is not unusual for policy analysts to have to attempt to understand information and interpret data outside of their area of expertise. How much of a problem is this? Can you think of ways to minimize problems with this? What technical or scientific issues might have arisen in the Waterville case?

6. Were the policy analyses you completed while responding to the book's assignments rational-scientific documents, subjective narratives of political persuasion, or a combination of both? Explain how that is relevant to the Waterville case.

7. We have talked about the connections between theory and practice (Section I) and between practice and theory (Section II). This section of the book draws you back to our point that what is needed is synthesis/praxis not only between theory and pragmatism but also between competing theories that each offer us part of the puzzle. In what way did your answer to the Waterville case reflect upon the idea of praxis?

Concluding Thoughts

As postpositivism asserts, public policy analysis needs to be more democratic; but it happens in bureaucracies that value rationality, neutrality, and efficiency. Public policy analysts need to understand the relevance of theory; but in the end analysts need practical advice more than they need insightful critiques and clever rhetoric. Policy analysis requires knowledge (particularly about politics), skills (both positivist and postpositivist), and a methodology. Public policy analysis requires synthesis and praxis.

Rather than positing rational decision making and makers, policy analysts need to recognize limitations, subjectivity, ambiguity, and public interests. Rather than playing the role of the expert, analysts need to be educators and facilitators. Rather than trying to take the politics out of policy and letting power hide in fancy words and carefully scripted numbers, let's bring politics out into the open. Aldo Leopold's writings make the point that you cannot both love game animals and hate predators, because both are part of the harmony of nature. Public policy analysis requires synthesis and praxis (and sunshine).

We wrote this book for you, the student analyst. Ultimately, it is your values and beliefs that matter. It matters that you believe in democracy, in yourself and in the possibility of making a difference. Public policy analysis requires synthesis and praxis and you.

Appendix

Researching on the Net

This book could not have been written as rapidly as it was without the internet. E-mail alone has altered work patterns and possibilities (and at the end of this appendix we offer you the chance to alter future editions of this book). Students and professors alike, across the disciplines, have come to rely on the internet when doing research. We recognize that as you work on the various cases in this text, you are likely to want to use internet sites. Further, practicing analysts also increasingly rely on the internet. However, as professors in the daily classroom trenches, we also recognize that many of our students need some assistance. This appendix cannot serve as a full-fledged guide to internet research, but we try to quickly accomplish three things. First, we offer some general comments and advice. Second, we proffer specific tips on how to be an informed internet researcher. Third, we present fifty sites we believe may be of particular value to you.

Use of the Internet for Research

It has become increasingly clear that countries, corporations, communities, and individuals who are more attuned and connected to the internet have an advantage over those who eschew this wave of the future. Information is power, and there is an almost embarrassing wealth of information available today. However, remember four crucial things: (1) Knowledge and information are two different things, and knowledge is much more important than information; (2) information off the web, like information from any print source, must be evaluated; (3) your task will rarely be merely to gather and reproduce the sort of information one finds in an atlas, almanac, or encyclopedia—instead your task is to analyze, evaluate, and argue; (4) you must, of course, properly cite all web sites. Of these four items, the one we will focus on is the need to evaluate information retrieved from the web. How do you evaluate it?

Before we get specific, allow us to tell two little stories. First, one of our students was doing research on a country in Africa. He went to that country's web pages and based his report largely on the information he found there. Having failed to utilize enough sources, he fell victim to the fact that there is no filtering mechanism on the web. The costs of creating a web site are minimal and today the technology makes technical know-how relatively unimportant. And, unlike your campus library, there are no professors or librarians deciding which books by which authors are worthy of inclusion. This democratizes information significantly, but means that the risks of its being reliable and accurate go down dramatically. Had the student simply done enough research, found enough sources, and balanced his internet research with other sources, he would not have reported that this country's human rights-violating, corrupt, tin-horn dictator was one of the world's most respected leaders whom other world leaders frequently turn to for advice. It was silly and earned him a poor grade. The country's web pages were pure propaganda that was even worse than a travel brochure.

The second story had one of your authors jumping on the internet shortly before class one day, trying to quickly find out, before heading up to teach an American Foreign Policy class, if that day was the anniversary of the liberation of the concentration camp at Auschwitz. He couldn't remember with certainty how to spell it, so after grabbing a search engine, he typed in the word Holocaust. Much to the professor's disgust, six of the first nine sites identified claimed that the Holocaust never happened.

There is no reason to fear the internet. It is a valuable tool. However, you need to be a skeptic. You need to remember that the filtering devices you are used to with other forms of research are not there. You need to carefully evaluate the information you find. In short, you need to learn the tricks necessary to become a literate internet researcher. It is to those specifics we now turn.

Evaluating Internet Sites

We have organized these tricks of the trade into a sort of checklist, but don't assume that there are any shortcuts that will guarantee the credibility of what you find. As suggested above, balanced and extensive research is the only way to truly protect yourself. Moreover, the credibility of the site is no guarantee that it is of value to you in terms of the assignment you are working on. Nonetheless, these questions and the issues they raise must be considered by anyone doing research on the web.

Type of Internet Source

- Is the retrieved information from a World Wide Web site, or some other site?
- Do you need to rely on this source? Is the same, or perhaps better, information available elsewhere?

When searching for information the first question to ask is about the source of the information. Different sources need to be evaluated—and cited—differently. A personal e-mail document is different from information retrieved from a listserv, which is different from a newsgroup message. It is your job to evaluate quality and credibility, even when search engines discriminate for you in terms of quality (often based merely on the number of hits).

Purpose of the Site

- Is the purpose of the site stated? Can you discern it from the tone and language used?
- Is the information designed to inform, persuade, anger, entertain, spark creative thinking, challenge conventional wisdom?
- Who is the target audience (particularly in terms of age and education level)?

The intentions of the site creator are an important factor as you evaluate. A company or country that maintains its own site is unlikely to provide you with information particularly critical of the current CEO or prime minister.

Author/Creator of the Site

- Who is this and what makes them an authority?
- Is there an organization associated with the site? What is the relationship? What is that organization's reputation, political orientation, etc.?
- Does the site provide an e-mail address, phone number, etc., that you can use to contact the author/creator (and to check them out)?
- What is the (.gov, .org, .edu, .com) domain name/URL extension?

Professor Hasimota, the (fictional) occupant of the (fictional) Mother Teresa Endowed Chair of Ethics at Harvard could be wrong in terms of information about cloning—but she would begin with more credibility than Frank Benekos (noted amiable liar, Steeler fan, sailor, and bar owner).

Documentation

- Does the site make clear the source of the information?
- If there are statistics presented, are they presented fairly? Who gathered and analyzed them? Are the dates of the research, the number of people interviewed, the methods, etc., presented clearly?
- Are references provided?
- Does the site steer you to other quality sources that allow you to check its story?
- Does the information provided square with other sources you've found and with previous course work?
- Has the information passed through any filters (like peer review)?
- Is the currency of the information adequate? What is the date posted and the date revised?
- Is the general quality of the work impressive or are there lots of obvious errors, misspellings, etc.?

While type of source, purpose of the source, and author/creator of the source are important clues, ultimately you are evaluating the information retrieved, and these are key issues to consider. For example, old sources frequently lead to embarrassing mistakes. (We have had students talking about leaders now dead or out of office, bills already enacted as possible future legislation, and similar mistakes that make clear the inadequacy of the research done.) Peer review, one of the best aspects of the scientific method, does not prevent individual mistakes or even prevent faulty paradigms from limiting new insights and breakthroughs, but it does provide a crucial filter. Information radically different from conventional wisdom and what all the experts agree to could be correct, but you need to approach it with the caution akin to what you would use when trying to capture an alligator. Transparency and openness in terms of data is a crucial check.

Key Sites

Before presenting our nifty fifty (perhaps to be more current we should say they are the phat fifty and go with the alliteration instead of the rhyme), we want to mention a site that provides information similar to what we just provided and interesting examples/case studies to clearly demonstrate the problems we alluded to. This site is

<http://libweb.sonoma.edu/Resources/eval.html>.

Another helpful site is

<http://www.library.cornell.edu/okuref/research/webeval.html>.

The fifty sites are organized solely by source (.edu; .gov; .org; or .com) and include only the briefest possible functional descriptions.

Twenty-One DotOrgs

<http://www.greateryellowstone.org>   The Greater Yellowstone Coalition's site.

<http://www.sharetrails.org>   The Blue Ribbon Coalition's site.

<http://www.epn.org>   The Electronic Policy Network is a wonderful link to reports by institutes, foundations, commissions, and journals.

<http://www.aclu.org/>   The American Civil Liberties site is kept very current and covers a broad range of issues.

<http://www.nra.org/>   The National Rifle Association's site.

<http://www.ipl.org/ref/POTUS/>   Information on Presidents of the United States (POTUS).

<http://www.apsanet.org>   The site of the American Political Science Association is a great link to other politically oriented sites as well.

<http://www.ncsl.org/>   The National Conference of State Legislatures' site.

<http://www.nga.org/>   The National Governors' Association's site.

<http://www.rff.org>   Information on environmental and natural resources from the Resources for the Future.

<http://www.c-span.org/>   The C-Span organization's site.

<http://www.vote-smart.org/>   This bipartisan organization provides information on candidates for elections, campaign finance, voting records, etc.

<http://www.un.org/>   The United Nations.

<http://www.wwf.org/>   The World Wildlife Foundation's site.

<http://www.worldwatch.org/>   The Worldwatch Institute's site.

<http://www.commoncause.org/>   The Common Cause site.

<http://www.main.org/leaguewv/home.html>   The League of Women Voters' site.

<http://www.npr.org/>   National Public Radio's site.

<http://www.nrdc.org/index.html>   The Natural Resources Defense Council's site.

<http://www.edf.org>   The Environmental Defense Fund's site.

<http://www.ncsdnetwork.org>   The National Councils for Sustainable Development's site.

Eleven DotGovs

<http://www.doh.wa.gov/Topics/bruce.htm>   A general site on brucellosis.

<http://www.odci.gov/cia/publications/pubs.html>   World factbook provides geopolitical information on all of the countries of the world.

<http://www.usgs.gov>   The National Mapping program provides important spatial information on ecosystems, natural resources, and economic development.

<http://www.census.gov>   The U.S. Bureau of the Census.

<http://thomas.loc.gov/>   The Thomas site was established to help citizens access government information.

<http://www.access.gpo.gov/su_docs/aces/aces140.html>   The Federal Register.

<http://www.access.gpo.gpo.gov/su_docs/aces/aaces002.html>   GPO Access.

<http://www.house.gov/>   Information specifically on the U.S. House of Representatives (but has links).

<http://www.senate.gov/>   Same story as above, but focused on the U.S. Senate.

<http://www.epa.gov/ecocommunity>   Information on the 1999/2000 Sustainable Development Challenge Grant program.

<http://lcweb.loc.gov/global/state/stategov.html>   Information on state and local governments.

Eight DotComs

<http://www.wyellowstone.com>   A site about West Yellowstone, MT.

<http://www.yellowstone-Natl-park.com/index.html>   The "Total Yellowstone Page" maintained by John Uhler of Orem, Utah, is a comprehensive site with important links and statistics.

<http://www.washingtonpost.com/wp-srv/politics/>   This site is maintained by the Washington Post.

<http://www.publicinterestpolling.com>   This site outlines the Americans Talk Issues Foundation's method.

<http://www.nationaljournal.com>   Inside information on current politics.

<http://nt.excite.com/>   Features a news-tracker function that will follow issues for you.

<http://www.piperinfo.com/state/index.cfm>   Information on state and local government.

<http://www.policy.com>   A gold mine for policy information.

Ten DotEdus

<http://www.nap.edu/catalog/5957.html>   A comprehensive study of the brucellosis problem.

<http://www.library.upenn.edu/resources/websitest.html>   Great source for information on population and hunger.

<http://www.si.umich.edu/UMDL>   University of Michigan's "digital" library.

<http://www.lib.umich.edu/libhome/Documents.center/psthink.html>   The University of Michigan provides information on think tanks.

<http://www.umich.edu/~nes/>   University of Michigan's National Election Studies site.

<http://elib.cs.berkeley.edu/>   The digital library at the University of California at Berkeley.

<http://www.informedia.cs.cmu.edu>   The digital library of Carnegie Mellon University in Pittsburgh.

<http://ksgwww.harvard.edu/>   The John F. Kennedy School of Government's site.

<http://spirit.lib.uconn.edu/PoliSci/polisci.htm>   The Political Science virtual library link.

<http://www.etown.edu/vl>   This section of the virtual library links you to over   1,700 international affairs topic sites.

Concluding Thoughts

This time, rather than offer our concluding thoughts, we are soliciting your concluding thoughts. In general we welcome your suggestions, questions, and other input. Or you can take the time to respond to some specific questions we offer below to facilitate your response:

1. Did your experience working with this text change your initial perspective on public policy analysis? Explain.
2. Comment on what was particularly helpful, what you liked best, and what should be a continued focus and emphasis.
3. Comment on what was too difficult or not useful, what you liked least, and what should be done better or eliminated.
4. Are there any specific changes you would recommend for a future edition; any typos or misspellings you caught?

Either way, we are glad to have had this chance to communicate with you, but we do hope you turn it from a monologue to a dialogue. Our students have always taught us much; we hope that circle widens. We can be reached at

rclemons@mercyhurst.edu

or

mcbemark@isu.edu

GLOSSARY

Black letter law   (Chapter 3) An unsophisticated view that the law is concrete, unambiguous, and easy to interpret and apply. The law reads literally and is as clear as the black letters on the white page. Therefore it is easy for judges to render decisions. Our discussion in Chapter 3 suggests otherwise.

Chi-square test   (Chapter 8) A statistical test that allows researchers to determine within probability levels whether two variables are associated. Chi-square tests are typically used on data that is nominal (having only the qualities of being mutually exclusive and exhaustive).

Confidence level   (Chapter 8) The estimated probability that a population parameter lies within a confidence interval (e.g., a poll finds that "65 percent of respondents support candidate A within a confidence interval of +/–5 percent"). The confidence level explains how confident we are that the real population number falls within the established confidence interval of 60 percent to 70 percent. If the confidence level is 95 percent, then we can conclude in the above example that there is a 95 percent chance that the real population figures fall within the 60 percent to 70 percent interval.

Critical theory   (Chapter 3) A school of sociological thought that attempts to reorient Marxist theory toward a more subjectivist orientation and includes a cultural critique of society rather than the traditional Marxist emphasis on economics. Critical theory is part of a postpositivist movement that pushed the social sciences toward a constructivist approach (the belief that social artifacts are socially created). Similar constructivist approaches include symbolic interactionism (the belief that there is not an objective reality but rather a reality created through human intervention and interpretation) and phenomenology (how actors define situations and then act upon the definitions). The key is that all of these approaches believe that humans actively construct their own worlds.

Deductive theory construction   (Chapter 2) A philosophical view of the sciences and social sciences that asserts that research methodology should proceed from theory construction, hypothesis development, operationalization, measurement, and testing.

In the social sciences, the positivist approach has mainly argued that researchers should follow this deductive method. The opposite approach utilizes induction, which begins with observation followed by the development of hypotheses and theories.

Delphi techniques   (Chapter 5) A research technique by which individuals are first asked to address a research topic anonymously (e.g., by using a mail survey). The results are then tabulated and the participants are asked to comment on the survey results (e.g., in a focus group). The anonymity is important, for the focus group participants do not know whose comments and conclusions they are commenting on. Delphi techniques are often used in organizations attempting to restructure operations. A survey is mailed to all employees (including managerial folks) and survey comments and conclusions are reported. In focus groups, employees are allowed to comment on survey responses without knowing whether a specific comment came from a fellow employee or manager.

Epistemology   (Chapter 6) The theory or source of knowledge. In social science terms, how do we know what we know?

Equity   (Chapter 3) An important criterion for policymaking. It means fairness in terms of general principles of justice. Equity is not a synonym for fair treatment. Due to varying circumstances, opportunities, advantages, etc., fairness may mean treating people or groups differently.

Externalities   (Chapter 2) An externality is the effect from a market transaction on individuals outside the actual transaction. Externalities can be either positive or negative. An example of a positive externality could be the increased sales and profits secured by a local sandwich shop when a bank decides to relocate and build nearby. A negative externality is the increased traffic in the neighborhood where the bank decided to located. Thus one group's positive externality is another group's negative externality. These are often referred to as spillovers or side-effects.

Government by Gentlemen   (Chapter 2) A system of federal hiring practices that predominated from 1787 to the election of Andrew Jackson in 1828. This system was defined by President Washington when he asserted that "fitness of character" should be the major criterion for selecting civil servants. Fitness of character was defined by such things as family background, education, occupation, and personal reputation.

Grounding   (Chapter 7) The creation of a productive culture of shared fundamental assumptions about the group process. (See the discussion of Tool #2, Futuring.)

Groupthink   (Chapter 4) This term was coined by Irving Janis to describe limitations in rational decision making among groups of individuals. The lesson of group think is that group decisions are often not ideal or even rational since a variety of social, political, and psychological factors combine to distort group decision-making processes.

Hegemonic lifeworld   (Chapter 6) A postmodern term that needs to be broken into an understanding of its two words. Hegemonic means "political dominance." A lifeworld is the world of symbols, stories, language, and meaning inhabited by individuals. A lifeworld shapes our understanding of the world. Thus a hegemonic lifeworld is one that has the power to shape an entire society's understanding of varying events.

Hobson's Choice   (Chapter 1) This is a strategy of argument where two alternatives are presented. Both alternatives are defined by the speaker but only one alternative is seen as preferred. The preferred alternative is always the alternative of the speaker.

Thus, the "choice" is really a nonchoice. For example, "What we have here are two choices: First, we can continue economic development strategies and see our community prosper or second, we can discontinue these efforts and turn our community into a modern-day ghost-town."

Hubris   (Chapter 3) A term meaning arrogant pride or presumption. It can be a severe limitation on rational decision making as individuals refuse to examine other possible problem definitions or solutions.

Interest Group   (Chapter 1) A group that shares a common interest, whether it is a single interest like gun control, abortion, or whales, or a broader concern like the interests of teachers, or the spectrum of issues a group like Common Cause champions; an organized group that attempts to affect public policy.

Laissez-faire   (Chapter 2) A view of capitalism and government that asserts that the government should take a "hands off" policy toward regulation of the economy. Government's only role is the protection of property.

Metanarrative   (Chapter 6) The grand story. Postmodern philosophers often criticize the metanarrative since within it are all the ideologies and assumption of those who have the power to write it. Postmoderns reject metanarratives.

Normative   (Chapter 1) Used in the context of the social sciences, it typically refers to values underlying policy choices (e.g., whether an individual sees population growth as positive or negative depends on that person's norms or values). In addition, a normative theory is one where a social scientist *prescribes* how a social system should be, as opposed to when they attempt to *describe* how it is actually (descriptive theory). For example, a social scientist may use elitism or pluralism to describe the American political system. But this same social scientist may propose a more participatory system as her normative theory. Interestingly enough, descriptive theories and normative theories are often confused. A social scientist, describing how the political system is dominated by narrow special interests, may be criticized by another social scientist because the latter believes the former is using the theory in a normative rather than a descriptive sense.

Operationalizing   (Chapter 2) Moving from a theoretical level to a more concrete level. For example, public administration has recently been introduced to some postmodern theoretical influences. From this theory building, the field will try to come to concrete tools of postmodernism public administration. The term can be seen as moving from a theoretical level to a practical level where the concept can be measured.

Outliers   (Chapter 8) A number that falls outside of a normal distribution of numbers. There are many different methods to determine whether a number is an outlier. To determine outliers you can calculate inter-quartile ranges for ordinal data or you can calculate standard deviation for interval-ratio data.

Paternalistic   (Chapter 1) In political terms this refers to limiting freedom and responsibility through well-meant governmental regulation and policy. In the Superpatriot theory of consent, citizens obey government because they believe that government is a well-meaning parent whose actions are always in the best interests of the citizens. Paternalism hinges on the idea that citizens, like children, often do not understand what their best interests really are.

Public goods   (Chapter 8) These are goods that have the features of both joint use and nonexclusion. They are goods provided by government. This means simply that with public goods, my use of the city park (a public good) does not limit your use of the same park. Similarly, even if you don't pay taxes you still cannot be excluded from using the park. Compare this to private goods (provided by businesses). With a private good, my purchase of a 1978 Mercury Bobcat means that you cannot purchase that same car. In addition, if I don't pay for the car, there are methods to exclude me from using it. In recent years, moves to privatize government and the incorporation of user fees has often changed the definition of goods provided by government.

Policy primeval soup   (Chapter 4) The word *primeval* means ancient or primitive. The phrase is used here to describe policymaking as chaotic, messy, and difficult to explain. The metaphor was borrowed by Kingdon from the biological explanation of molecules floating around before life began and suggests that as ideas bump into each other, as they stew over time, and as new ideas enter into the cauldron, new combinations of ideas form (come to life).

Political I.O.U.   (Chapter 4) This is a term that describes the situation in which one political actor owes another political actor a favor or a quid pro quo. The debt is simply implied and assumed. However, failure to live up to political I.O.Us can have negative political consequences.

Scenario writing   (Chapter 5) A traditional policy analysis technique by which the analyst provides several qualitative outcomes to a range of alternatives. The scenarios usually encompass a range of possibilities from optimistic to mid-range to pessimistic. They allow the analyst to look at solutions in a variety of ways and to forecast possible political problems.

Smith's Invisible Hand   (Chapter 7) A view of laissez faire capitalism credited to Adam Smith. It holds that the unregulated workings of the marketplace will produce public interests. For example, a capitalist wants to make money by selling hamburgers. His selling of burgers creates jobs for construction workers who build the burger buildings, jobs for those who work in the burger joints, and provides markets for farmers and ranchers who sell their products to the burger capitalist. All of this helps other individuals. Thus, out of one person's desire to make money by selling hamburger, a public interest is provided. This view, of course, neglects many problems of unregulated capitalism (child labor, unsafe working conditions, and monopoly).

Synedoches   (Chapter 6) Using a part to represent the whole. It is a figure of speech. An example would be a "bureaucratic horror story" where one account of bad service from a bureaucracy is turned into calls for policy reforms.

Triggering Event   (Chapter 1) An event in the political system that focuses attention on an event that may or may not require governmental action. In Chapter 6, we learned that these triggering events are often very ambiguous.

Win-Win   (Chapter 1) A policy by which all sides can claim equal victory. Where, for example, the contesting parties both exceed their expectations—where we grow the pie. This is opposed to a traditional "zero-sum" view of policy by which one side's gains are another side's losses—your piece of pie can only be larger if mine is made smaller. There is great controversy about whether public policymaking is necessarily more zero-sum than it is win-win (i.e., should the goal of the policy analyst be to promote win-win solutions or, in reality, does policymaking necessarily create winners and losers).

INDEX